WRITTEN & REALIZED BY
DAN GOLDMAN

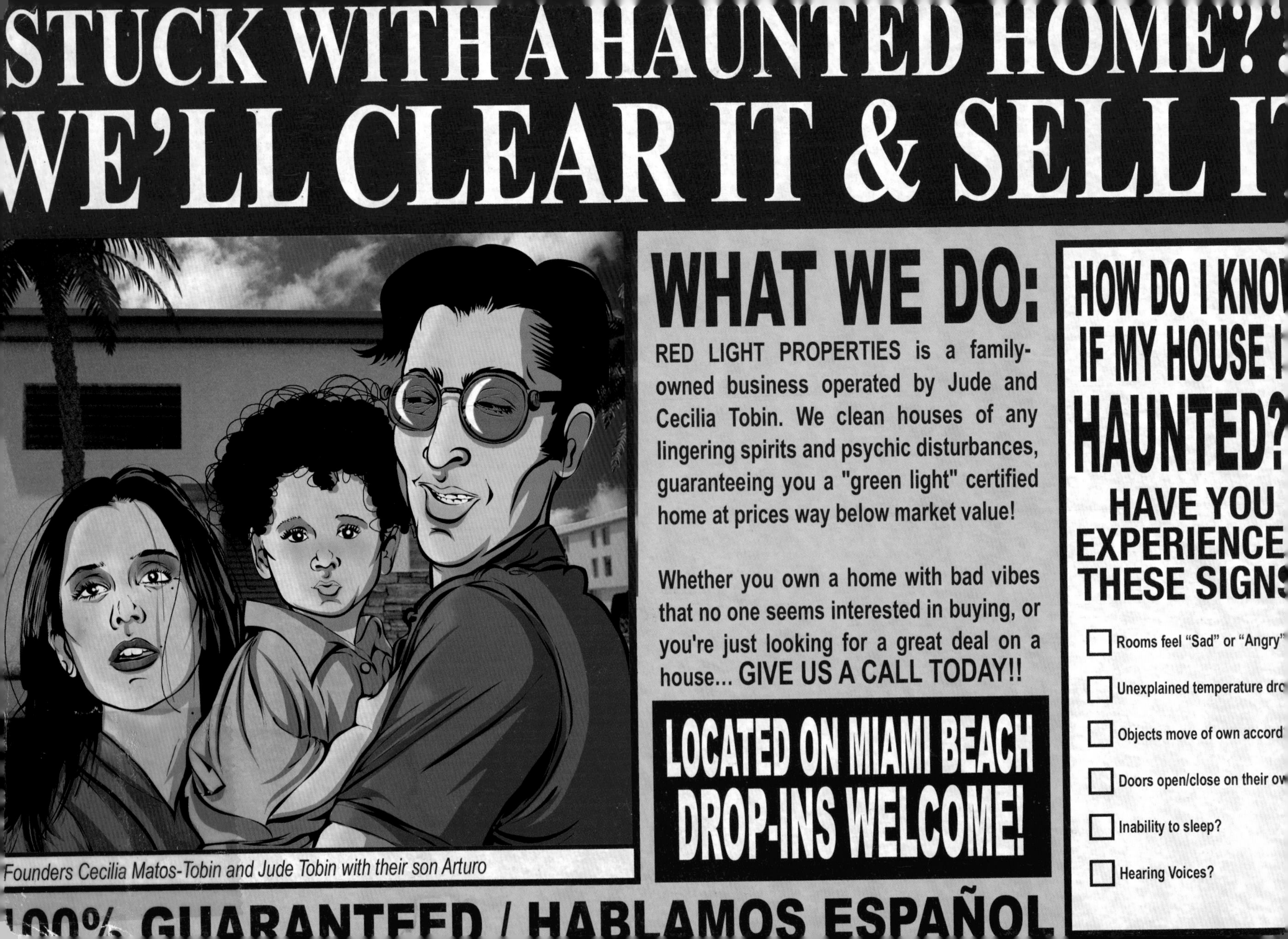
STUCK WITH A HAUNTED HOME?
WE'LL CLEAR IT & SELL I
WHAT WE DO:
RED LIGHT PROPERTIES is a family-owned business operated by Jude and Cecilia Tobin. We clean houses of any lingering spirits and psychic disturbances, guaranteeing you a "green light" certified home at prices way below market value!
Whether you own a home with bad vibes that no one seems interested in buying, or you're just looking for a great deal on a house... GIVE US A CALL TODAY!!
LOCATED ON MIAMI BEACH
DROP-INS WELCOME!
HOW DO I KNO
IF MY HOUSE I
HAUNTED?
HAVE YOU
EXPERIENCE
THESE SIGN
Rooms feel "Sad" or "Angry"
Unexplained temperature dr
Objects move of own accord
Doors open/close on their o
Inability to sleep?
Hearing Voices?
Founders Cecilia Matos-Tobin and Jude Tobin with their son Arturo
GUARANTEED / HABLAMOS ESPAÑOL

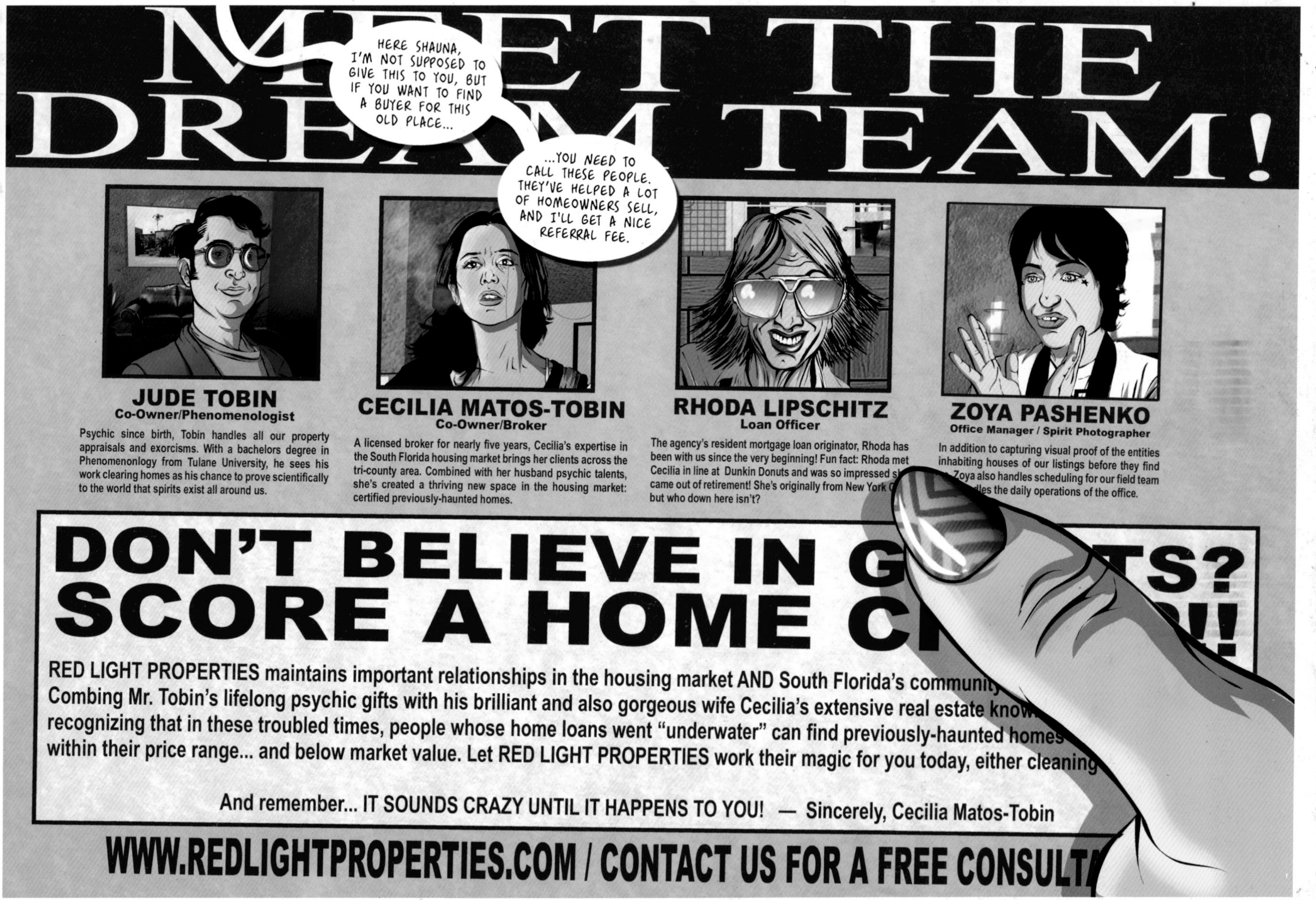
MEET THE DREAM TEAM!
HERE SHAUNA, I'M NOT SUPPOSED TO GIVE THIS TO YOU, BUT IF YOU WANT TO FIND A BUYER FOR THIS OLD PLACE...
...YOU NEED TO CALL THESE PEOPLE. THEY'VE HELPED A LOT OF HOMEOWNERS SELL, AND I'LL GET A NICE REFERRAL FEE.
JUDE TOBIN
Co-Owner/Phenomenologist
Psychic since birth, Tobin handles all our property appraisals and exorcisms. With a bachelors degree in Phenomenonlogy from Tulane University, he sees his work clearing homes as his chance to prove scientifically to the world that spirits exist all around us.
CECILIA MATOS-TOBIN
Co-Owner/Broker
A licensed broker for nearly five years, Cecilia's expertise in the South Florida housing market brings her clients across the tri-county area. Combined with her husband psychic talents, she's created a thriving new space in the housing market: certified previously-haunted homes.
RHODA LIPSCHITZ
Loan Officer
The agency's resident mortgage loan originator, Rhoda has been with us since the very beginning! Fun fact: Rhoda met Cecilia in line at Dunkin Donuts and was so impressed sh
came out of retirement! She's originally from New York C
but who down here isn't?
ZOYA PASHENKO
Office Manager / Spirit Photographer
In addition to capturing visual proof of the entities inhabiting houses of our listings before they find
Zoya also handles scheduling for our field team
dles the daily operations of the office.
DON'T BELIEVE IN G TS?
SCORE A HOME C !!
RED LIGHT PROPERTIES maintains important relationships in the housing market AND South Florida's communit
Combing Mr. Tobin's lifelong psychic gifts with his brilliant and also gorgeous wife Cecilia's extensive real estate know
recognizing that in these troubled times, people whose home loans went "underwater" can find previously-haunted homes
within their price range... and below market value. Let RED LIGHT PROPERTIES work their magic for you today, either cleaning
And remember... IT SOUNDS CRAZY UNTIL IT HAPPENS TO YOU! — Sincerely, Cecilia Matos-Tobin
WWW.REDLIGHTPROPERTIES.COM / CONTACT US FOR A FREE CONSULT

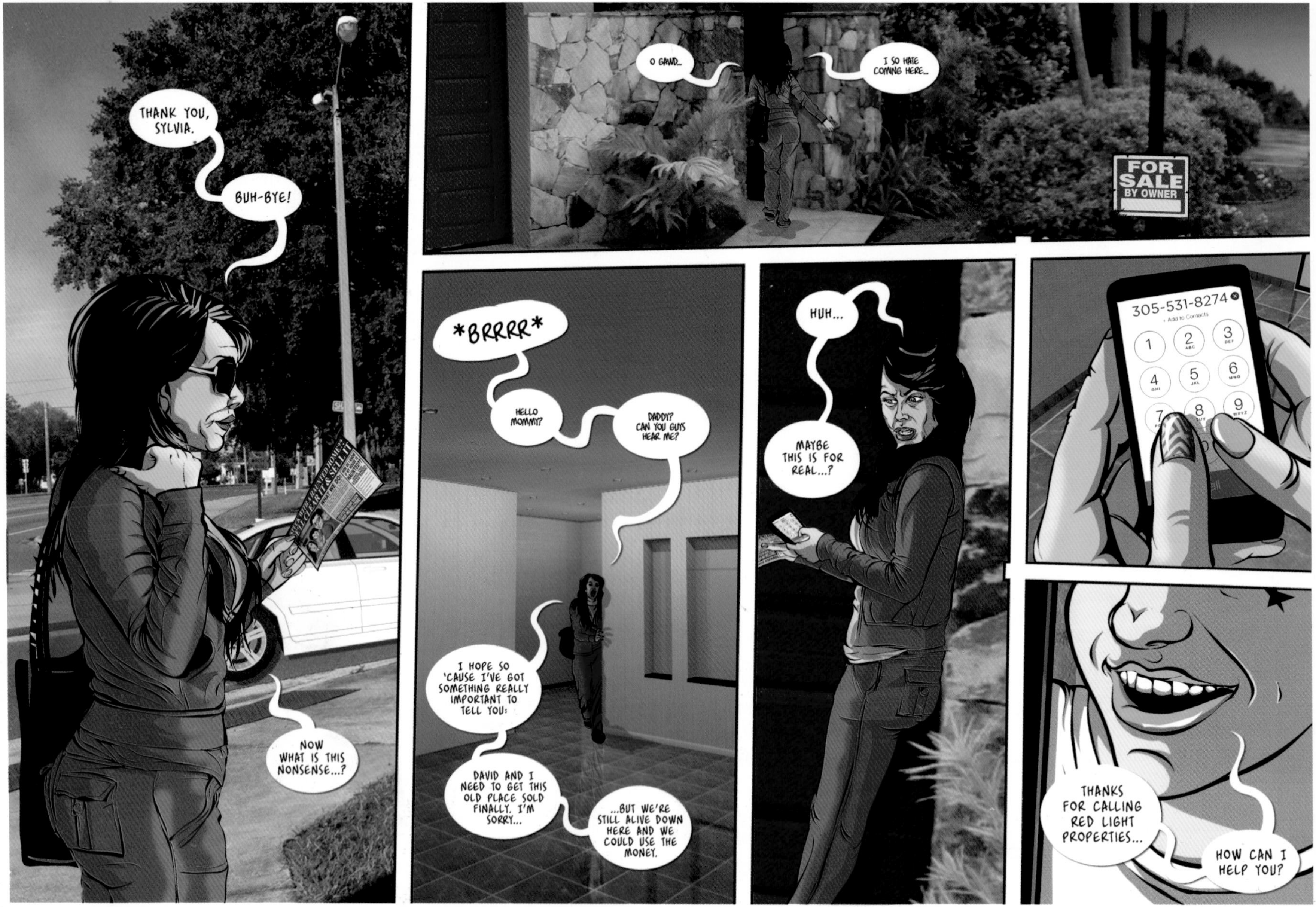
THANK YOU, SYLVIA.
BUH-BYE!
NOW WHAT IS THIS NONSENSE...?
O GAWD...
I SO HATE COMING HERE...
FOR SALE BY OWNER
BRRRR
HELLO MOMMY?
DADDY? CAN YOU GUYS HEAR ME?
I HOPE SO 'CAUSE I'VE GOT SOMETHING REALLY IMPORTANT TO TELL YOU:
DAVID AND I NEED TO GET THIS OLD PLACE SOLD FINALLY. I'M SORRY...
...BUT WE'RE STILL ALIVE DOWN HERE AND WE COULD USE THE MONEY.
HUH...
MAYBE THIS IS FOR REAL...?
305-531-8274
+ Add to Contacts
THANKS FOR CALLING RED LIGHT PROPERTIES...
HOW CAN I HELP YOU?

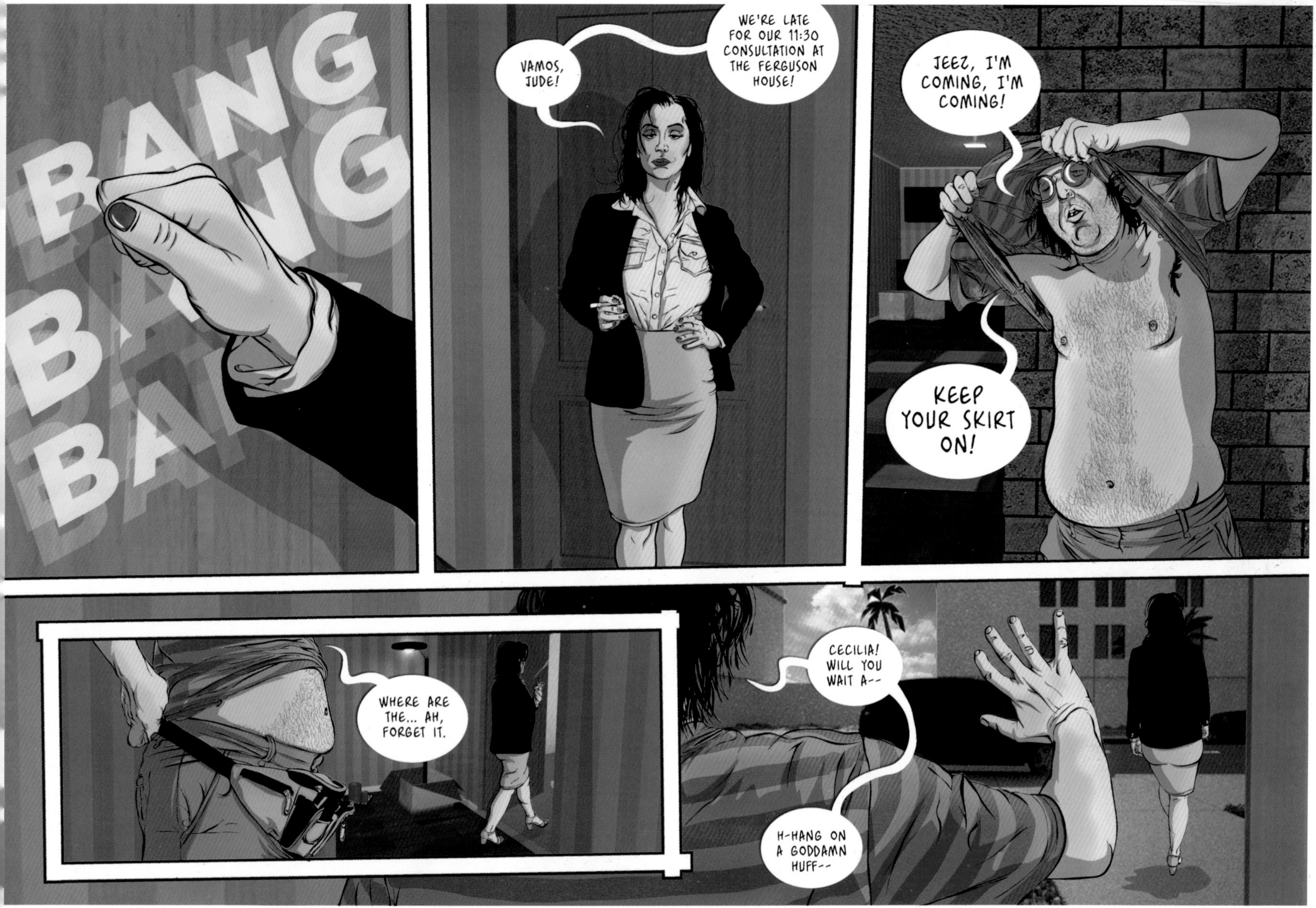
BANG BANG BANG
VAMOS, JUDE!
WE'RE LATE FOR OUR 11:30 CONSULTATION AT THE FERGUSON HOUSE!
JEEZ, I'M COMING, I'M COMING!
KEEP YOUR SKIRT ON!
WHERE ARE THE... AH, FORGET IT.
CECILIA! WILL YOU WAIT A--
H-HANG ON A GODDAMN HUFF--

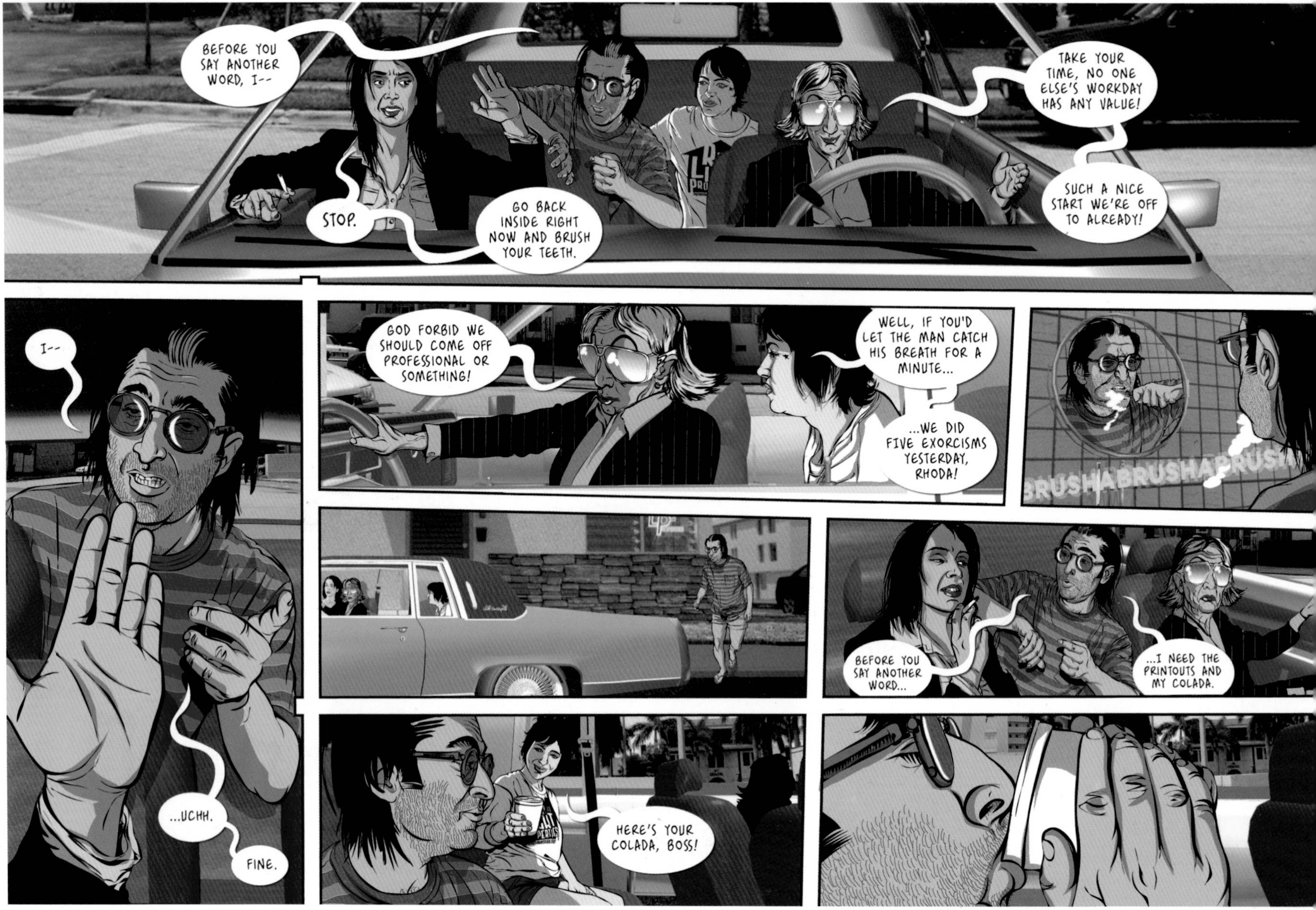
BEFORE YOU SAY ANOTHER WORD, I--
STOP.
GO BACK INSIDE RIGHT NOW AND BRUSH YOUR TEETH.
TAKE YOUR TIME, NO ONE ELSE'S WORKDAY HAS ANY VALUE!
SUCH A NICE START WE'RE OFF TO ALREADY!
I--
...UCHH.
FINE.
GOD FORBID WE SHOULD COME OFF PROFESSIONAL OR SOMETHING!
WELL, IF YOU'D LET THE MAN CATCH HIS BREATH FOR A MINUTE...
...WE DID FIVE EXORCISMS YESTERDAY, RHODA!
BRUSHABRUSHABRUSH
BEFORE YOU SAY ANOTHER WORD...
...I NEED THE PRINTOUTS AND MY COLADA.
HERE'S YOUR COLADA, BOSS!

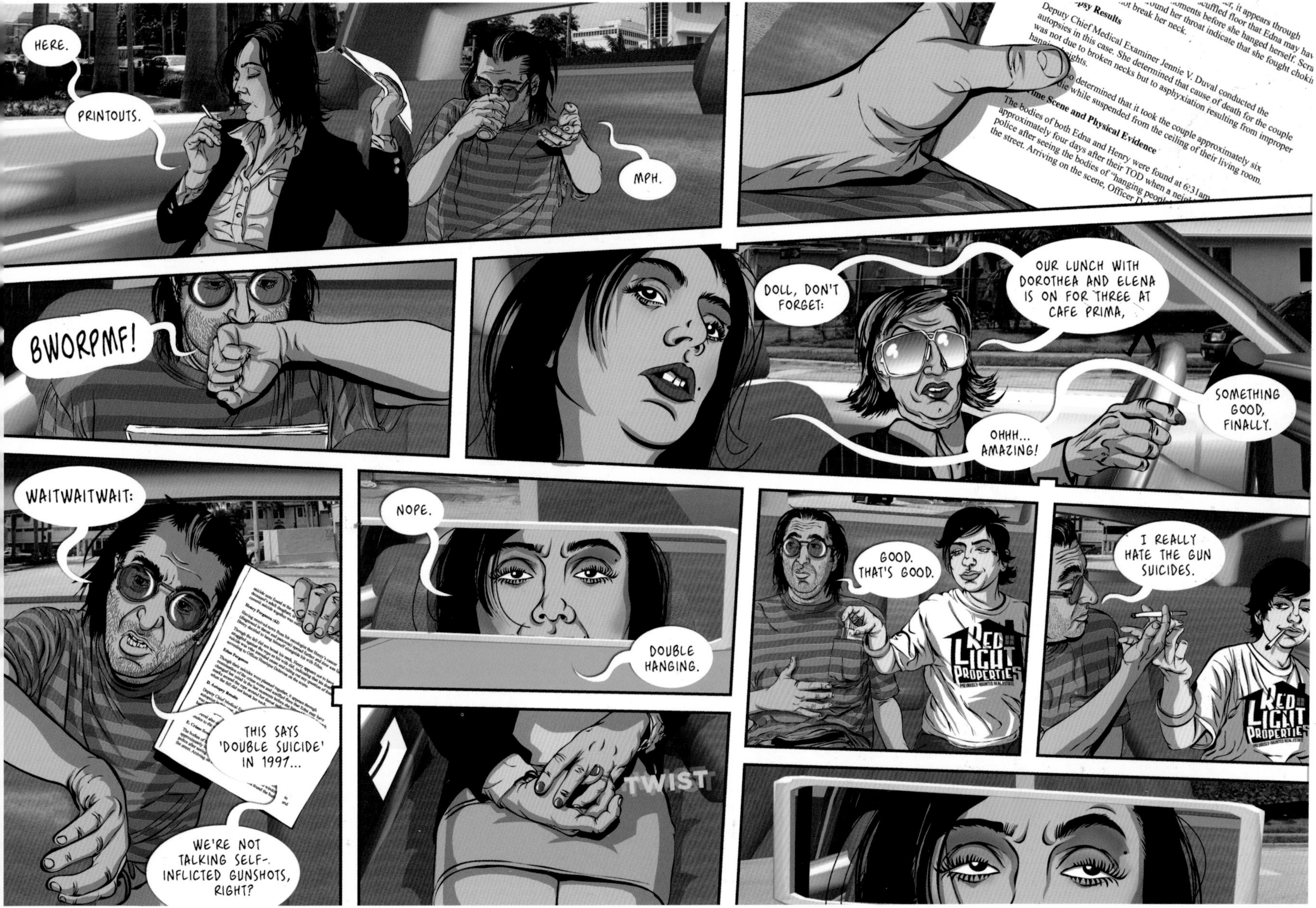
HERE.
PRINTOUTS.
MPH.
Deputy Chief Medical Examiner Jennie V. Duval conducted the autopsies in this case. She determined that cause of death for the couple was not due to broken necks but to asphyxiation resulting from improper
The bodies of both Edna and Henry were found at 6:31am approximately four days after their TOD when a neigh
BWORPMF!
DOLL, DON'T FORGET:
OUR LUNCH WITH DOROTHEA AND ELENA IS ON FOR THREE AT CAFE PRIMA,
SOMETHING GOOD, FINALLY.
OHHH... AMAZING!
WAITWAITWAIT:
THIS SAYS 'DOUBLE SUICIDE' IN 1997...
WE'RE NOT TALKING SELF-INFLICTED GUNSHOTS, RIGHT?
NOPE.
DOUBLE HANGING.
TWIST
GOOD. THAT'S GOOD.
RED LIGHT PROPERTIES
I REALLY HATE THE GUN SUICIDES.

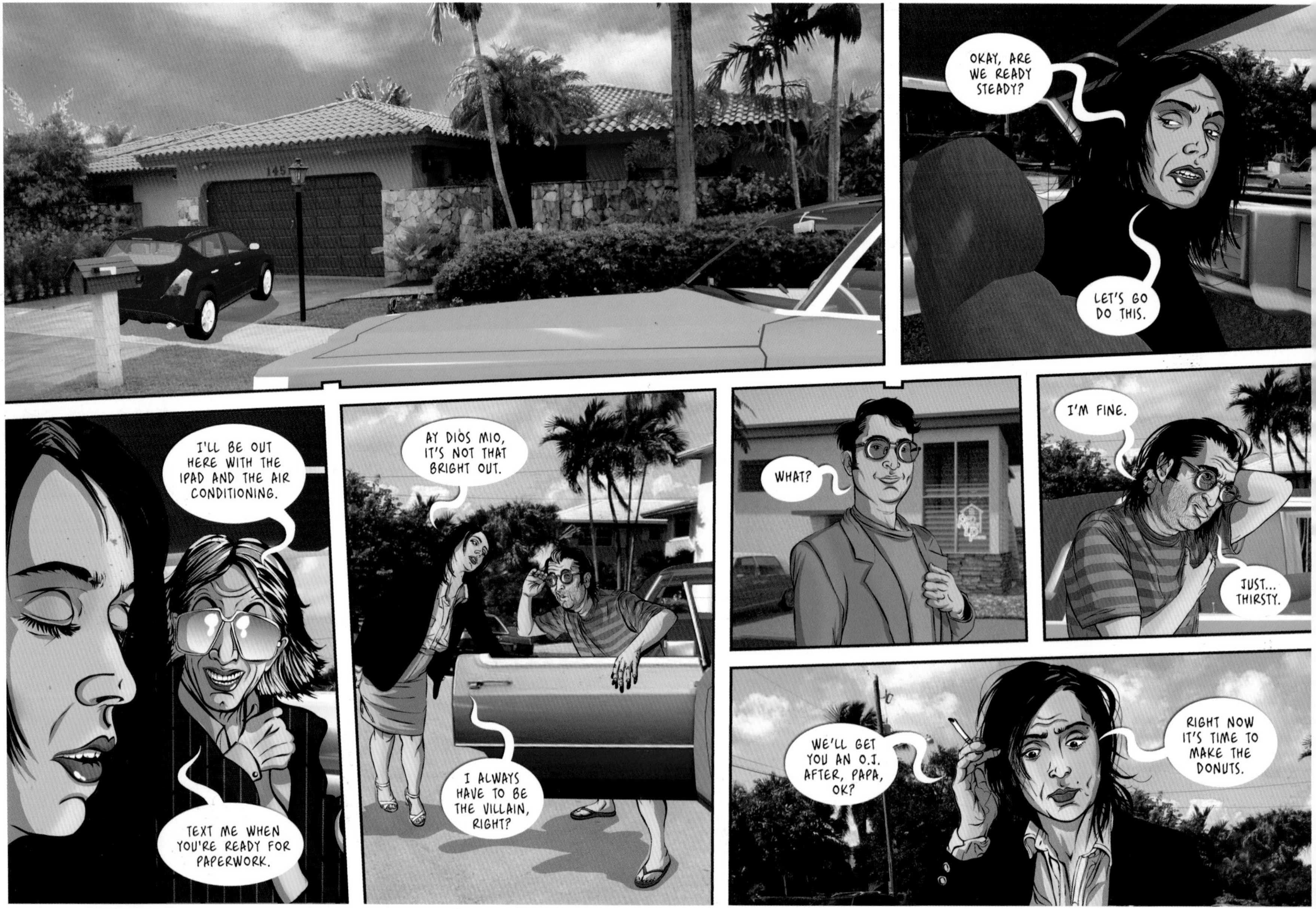
145
OKAY, ARE WE READY STEADY?
LET'S GO DO THIS.
I'LL BE OUT HERE WITH THE IPAD AND THE AIR CONDITIONING.
TEXT ME WHEN YOU'RE READY FOR PAPERWORK.
AY DIOS MIO, IT'S NOT THAT BRIGHT OUT.
I ALWAYS HAVE TO BE THE VILLAIN, RIGHT?
WHAT?
I'M FINE.
JUST... THIRSTY.
WE'LL GET YOU AN O.J. AFTER, PAPA, OK?
RIGHT NOW IT'S TIME TO MAKE THE DONUTS.

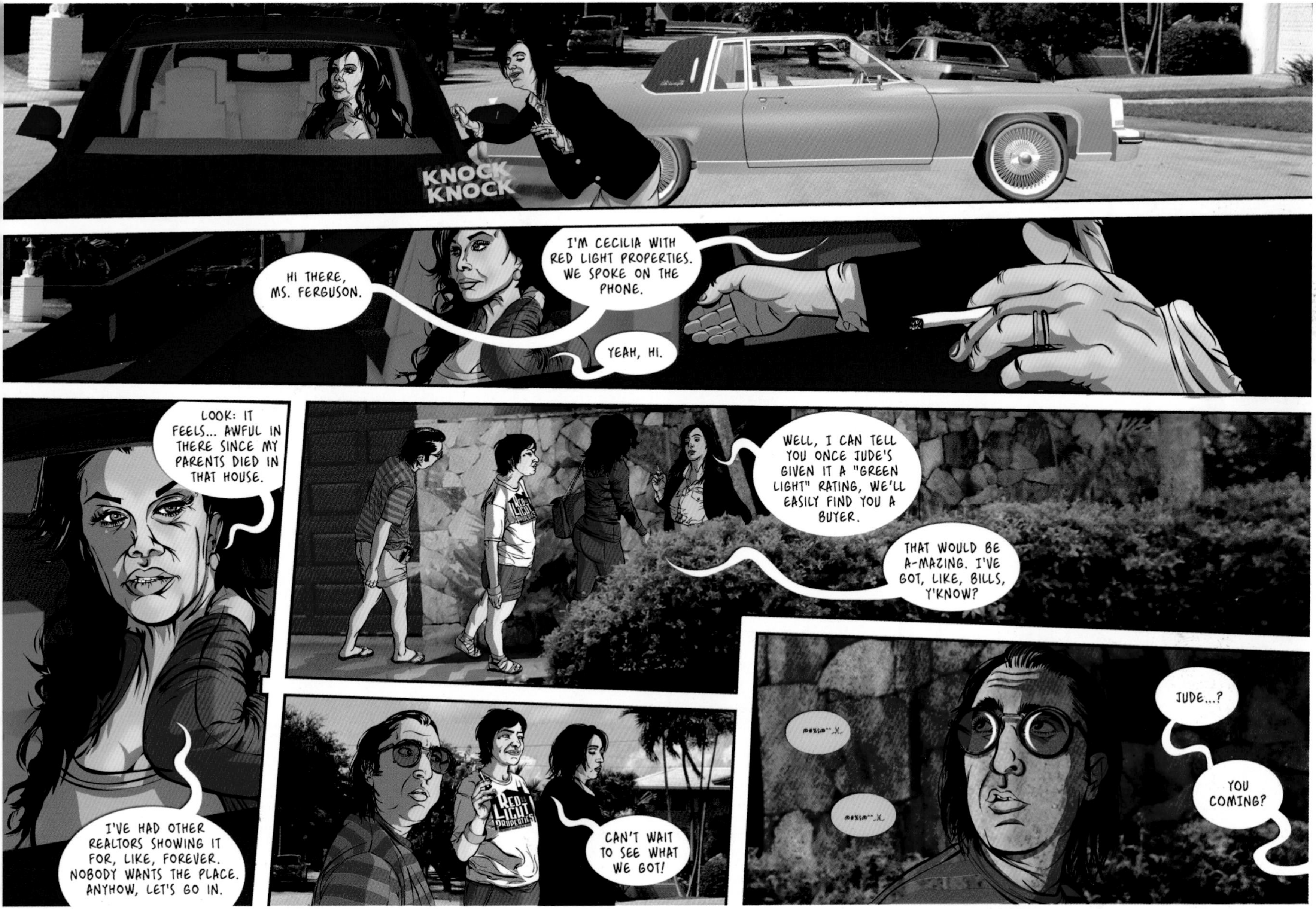
KNOCK KNOCK
HI THERE, MS. FERGUSON.
I'M CECILIA WITH RED LIGHT PROPERTIES. WE SPOKE ON THE PHONE.
YEAH, HI.
LOOK: IT FEELS... AWFUL IN THERE SINCE MY PARENTS DIED IN THAT HOUSE.
WELL, I CAN TELL YOU ONCE JUDE'S GIVEN IT A "GREEN LIGHT" RATING, WE'LL EASILY FIND YOU A BUYER.
THAT WOULD BE A-MAZING. I'VE GOT, LIKE, BILLS, Y'KNOW?
I'VE HAD OTHER REALTORS SHOWING IT FOR, LIKE, FOREVER. NOBODY WANTS THE PLACE. ANYHOW, LET'S GO IN.
CAN'T WAIT TO SEE WHAT WE GOT!
JUDE...?
YOU COMING?

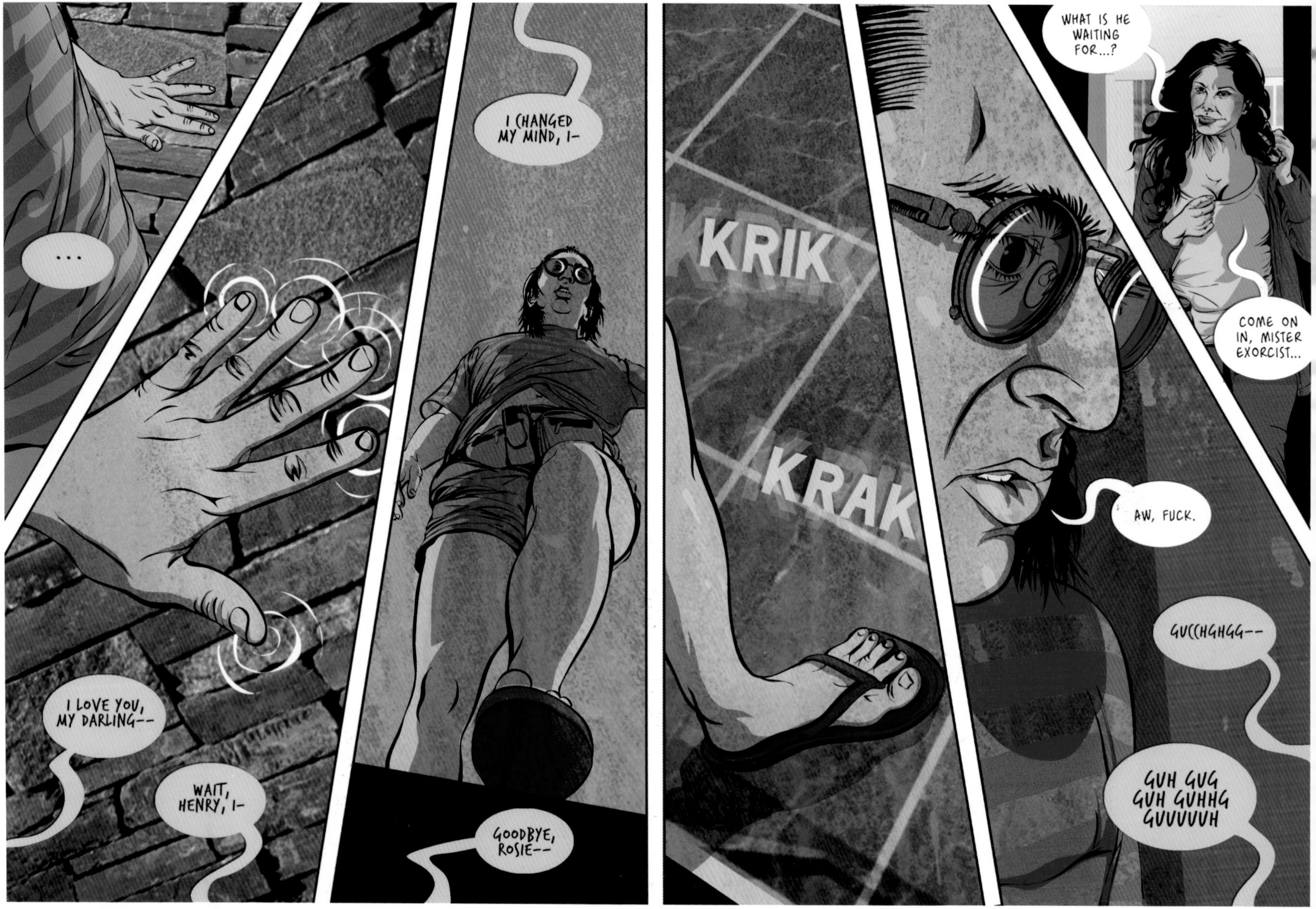
...
I LOVE YOU, MY DARLING--
WAIT, HENRY, I-
I CHANGED MY MIND, I-
GOODBYE, ROSIE--
KRIK
KRAK
WHAT IS HE WAITING FOR...?
COME ON IN, MISTER EXORCIST...
AW, FUCK.
GUCCHGHGG--
GUH GUG GUH GUHHG GUUUUUH

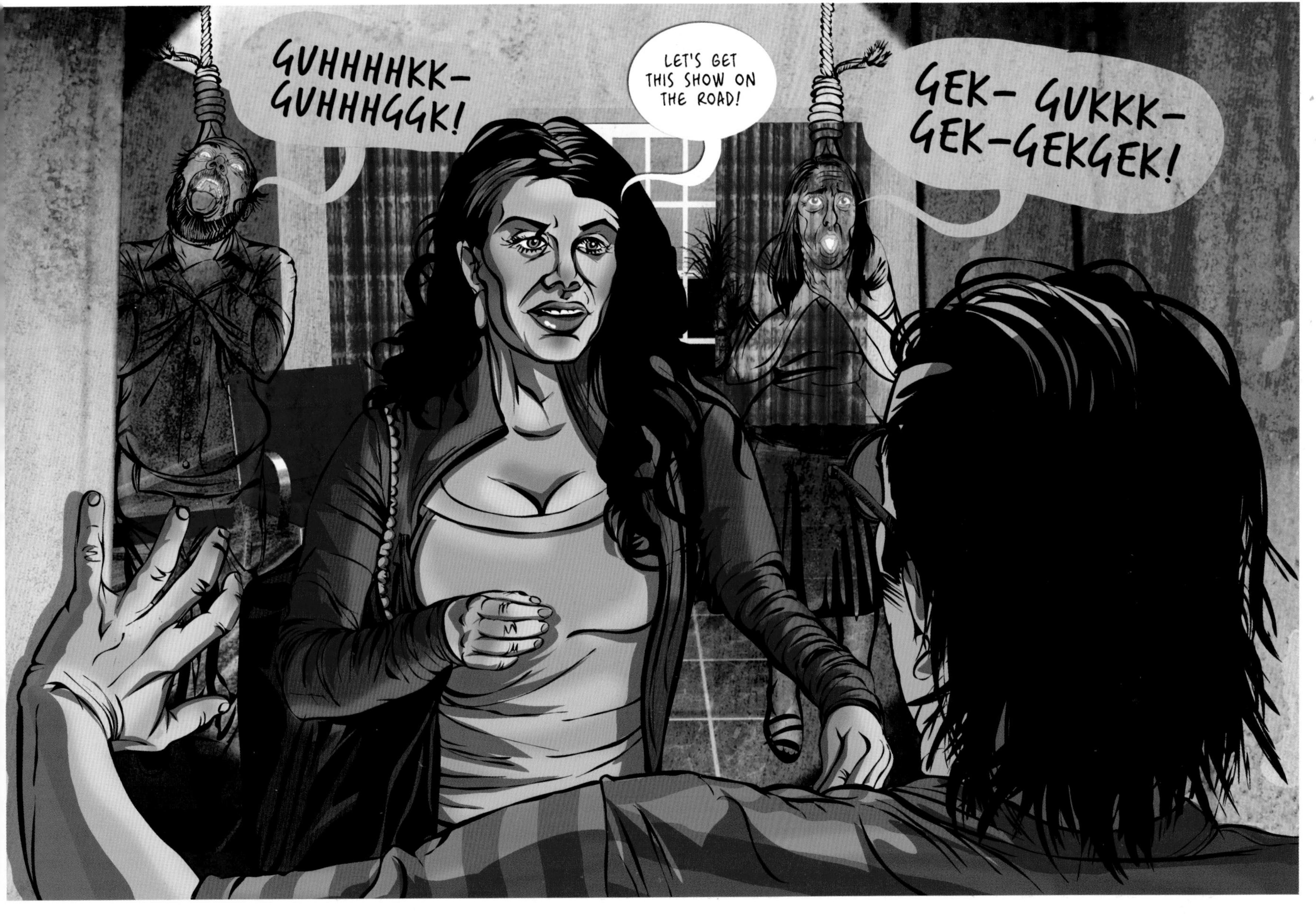
GUHHHHKK-
GUHHHGGK!
LET'S GET THIS SHOW ON THE ROAD!
GEK- GUKKK-
GEK-GEKGEK!

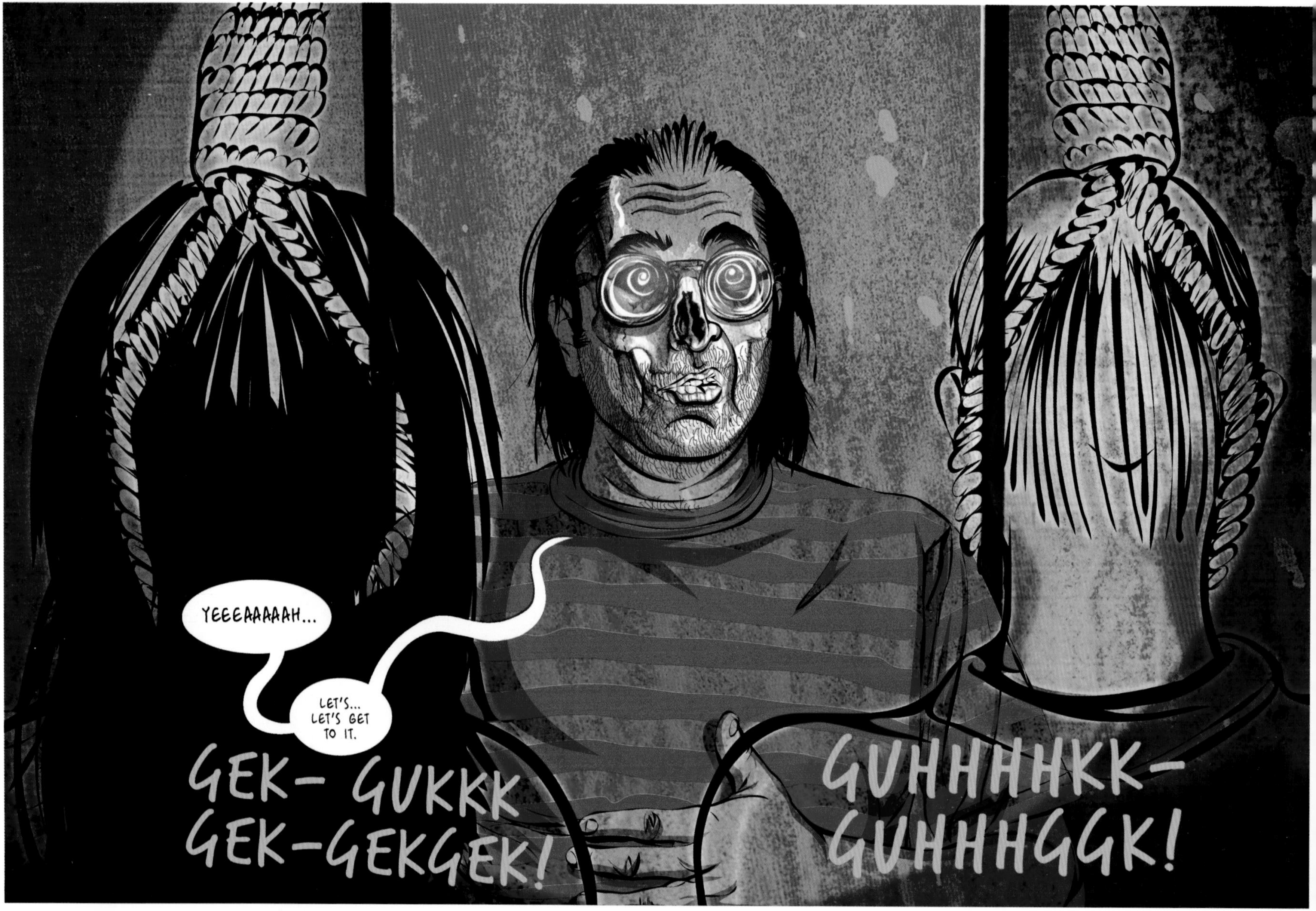
YEEEAAAAAH...
LET'S... LET'S GET TO IT.
GEK- GUKKK GEK-GEKGEK!
GUHHHHKK- GUHHHGGK!

RED LIGHT PROPERTIES

PREVIOUSLY-HAUNTED REAL ESTATE

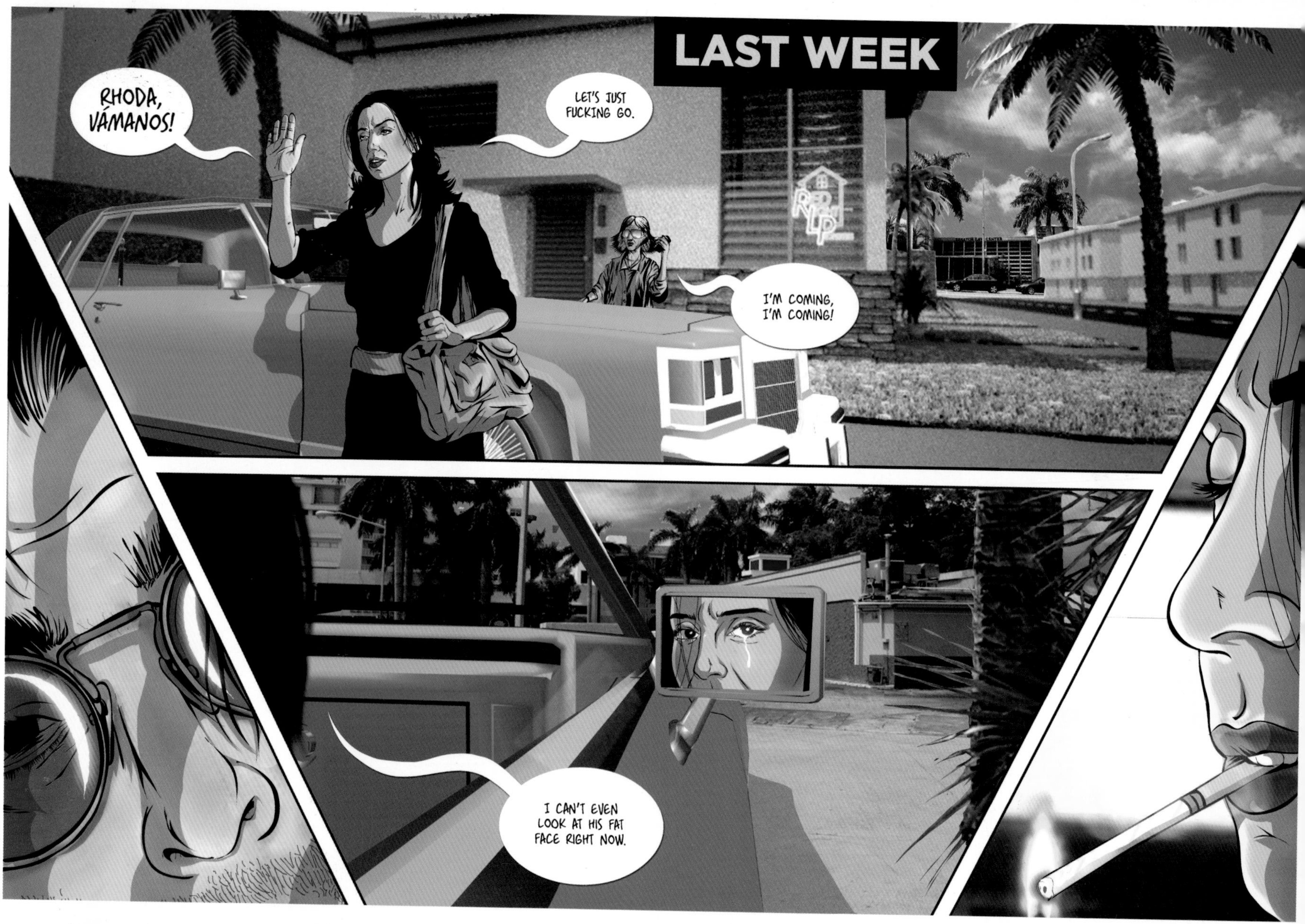
LAST WEEK
RHODA, VÁMANOS!
LET'S JUST FUCKING GO.
I'M COMING, I'M COMING!
I CAN'T EVEN LOOK AT HIS FAT FACE RIGHT NOW.

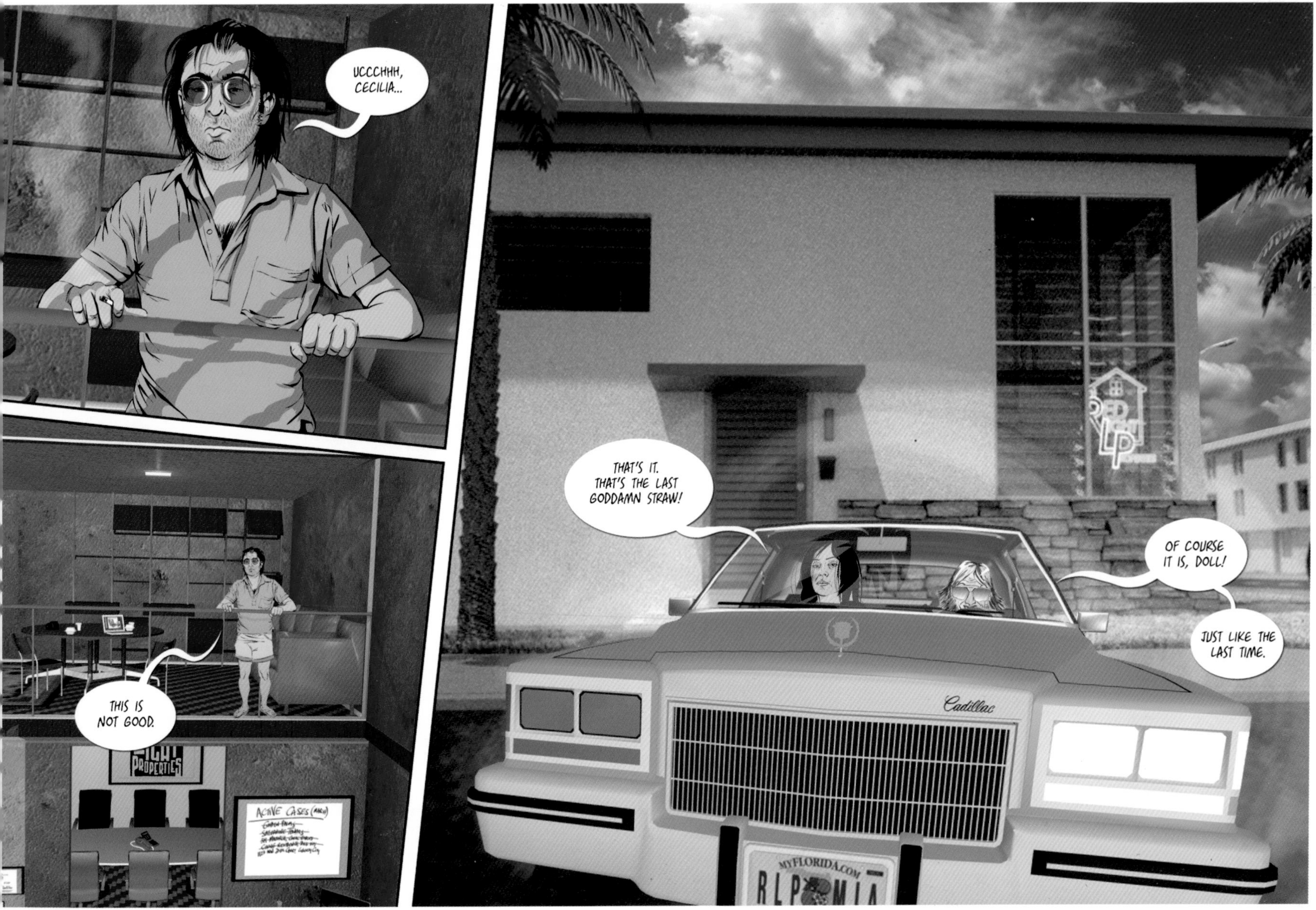
UCCCHHH, CECILIA...
THIS IS NOT GOOD.
THAT'S IT. THAT'S THE LAST GODDAMN STRAW!
OF COURSE IT IS, DOLL!
JUST LIKE THE LAST TIME.
Cadillac
MYFLORIDA.COM

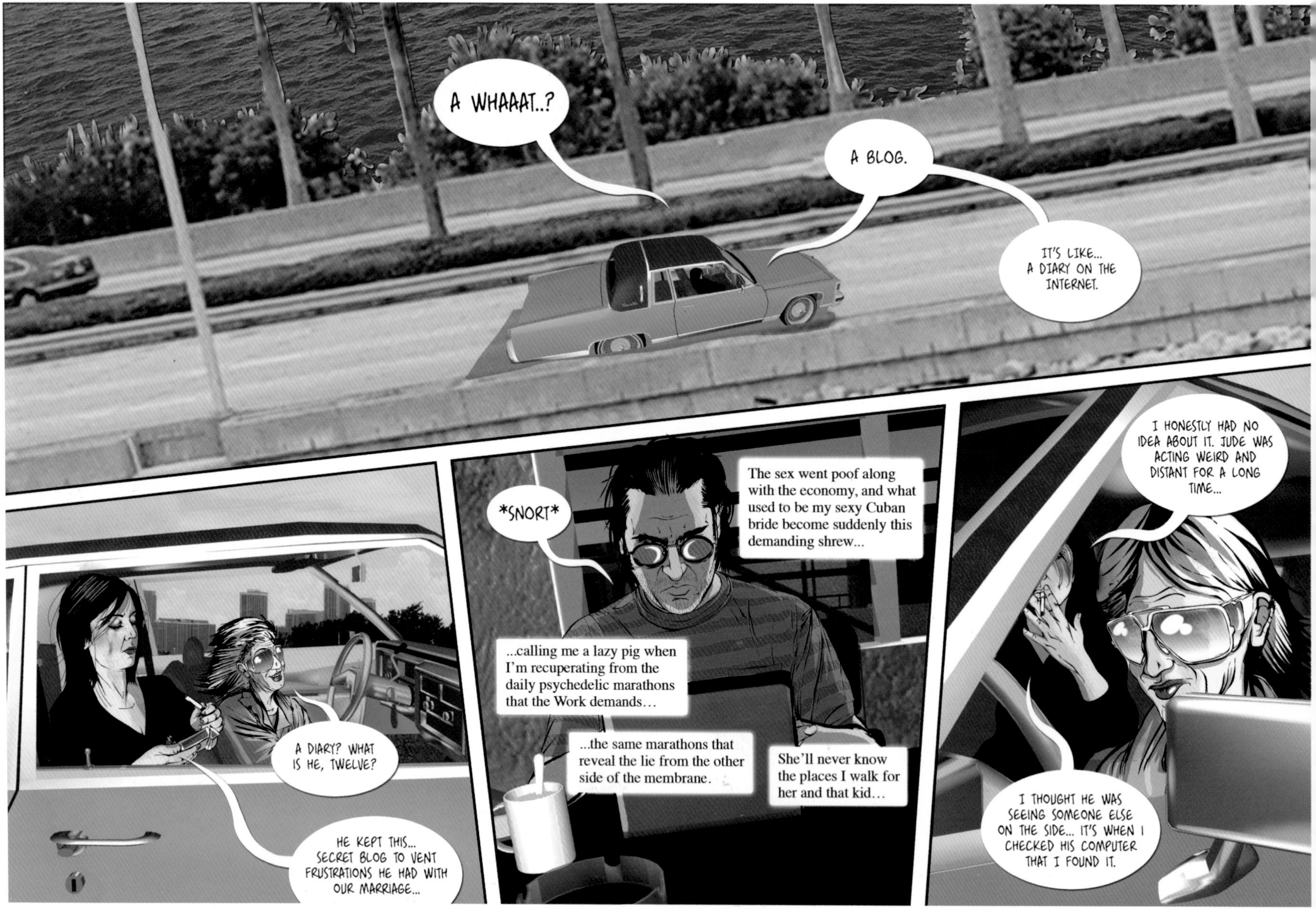
A WHAAAT..?
A BLOG.
IT'S LIKE... A DIARY ON THE INTERNET.
A DIARY? WHAT IS HE, TWELVE?
HE KEPT THIS... SECRET BLOG TO VENT FRUSTRATIONS HE HAD WITH OUR MARRIAGE...
SNORT
The sex went poof along with the economy, and what used to be my sexy Cuban bride become suddenly this demanding shrew...
...calling me a lazy pig when I'm recuperating from the daily psychedelic marathons that the Work demands…
...the same marathons that reveal the lie from the other side of the membrane.
She'll never know the places I walk for her and that kid…
I HONESTLY HAD NO IDEA ABOUT IT. JUDE WAS ACTING WEIRD AND DISTANT FOR A LONG TIME...
I THOUGHT HE WAS SEEING SOMEONE ELSE ON THE SIDE... IT'S WHEN I CHECKED HIS COMPUTER THAT I FOUND IT.

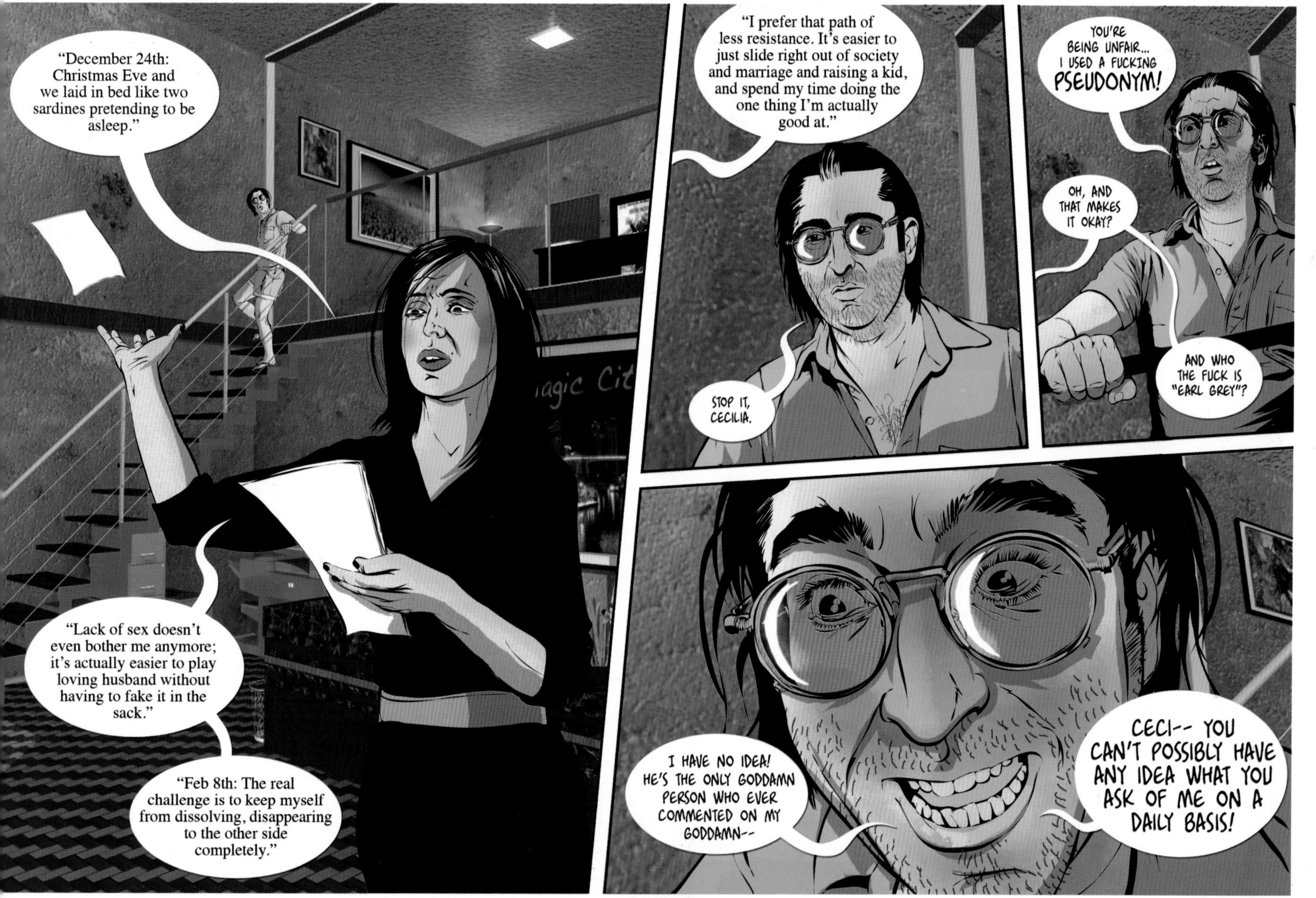
"December 24th: Christmas Eve and we laid in bed like two sardines pretending to be asleep."
"Lack of sex doesn't even bother me anymore; it's actually easier to play loving husband without having to fake it in the sack."
"Feb 8th: The real challenge is to keep myself from dissolving, disappearing to the other side completely."
"I prefer that path of less resistance. It's easier to just slide right out of society and marriage and raising a kid, and spend my time doing the one thing I'm actually good at."
STOP IT, CECILIA.
YOU'RE BEING UNFAIR... I USED A FUCKING PSEUDONYM!
OH, AND THAT MAKES IT OKAY?
AND WHO THE FUCK IS "EARL GREY"?
I HAVE NO IDEA! HE'S THE ONLY GODDAMN PERSON WHO EVER COMMENTED ON MY GODDAMN--
CECI-- YOU CAN'T POSSIBLY HAVE ANY IDEA WHAT YOU ASK OF ME ON A DAILY BASIS!

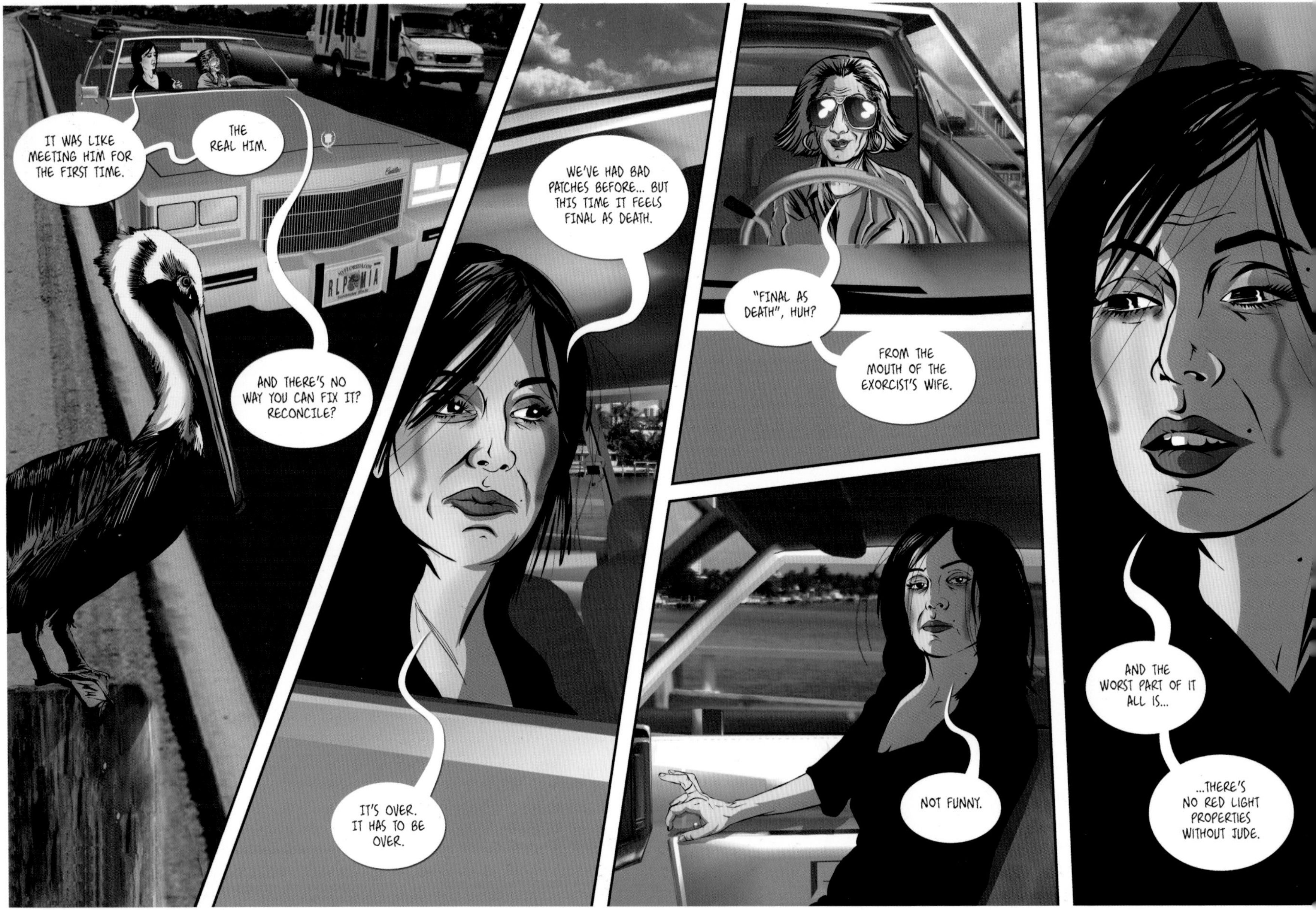
IT WAS LIKE MEETING HIM FOR THE FIRST TIME.
THE REAL HIM.
AND THERE'S NO WAY YOU CAN FIX IT? RECONCILE?
WE'VE HAD BAD PATCHES BEFORE... BUT THIS TIME IT FEELS FINAL AS DEATH.
IT'S OVER. IT HAS TO BE OVER.
"FINAL AS DEATH", HUH?
FROM THE MOUTH OF THE EXORCIST'S WIFE.
NOT FUNNY.
AND THE WORST PART OF IT ALL IS...
...THERE'S NO RED LIGHT PROPERTIES WITHOUT JUDE.

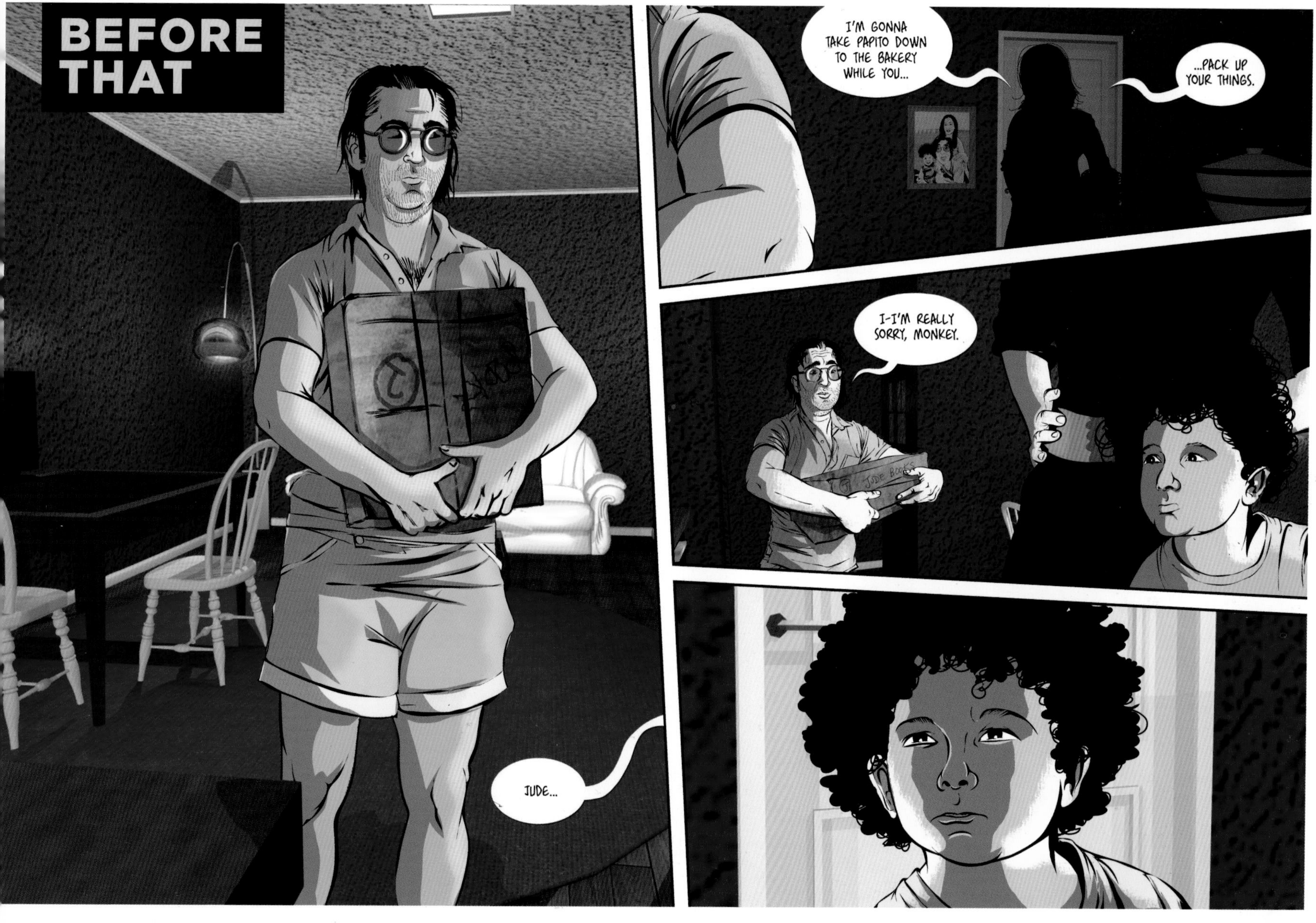
BEFORE THAT
JUDE...
I'M GONNA TAKE PAPITO DOWN TO THE BAKERY WHILE YOU...
...PACK UP YOUR THINGS.
I-I'M REALLY SORRY, MONKEY.
JUDE BOOKS

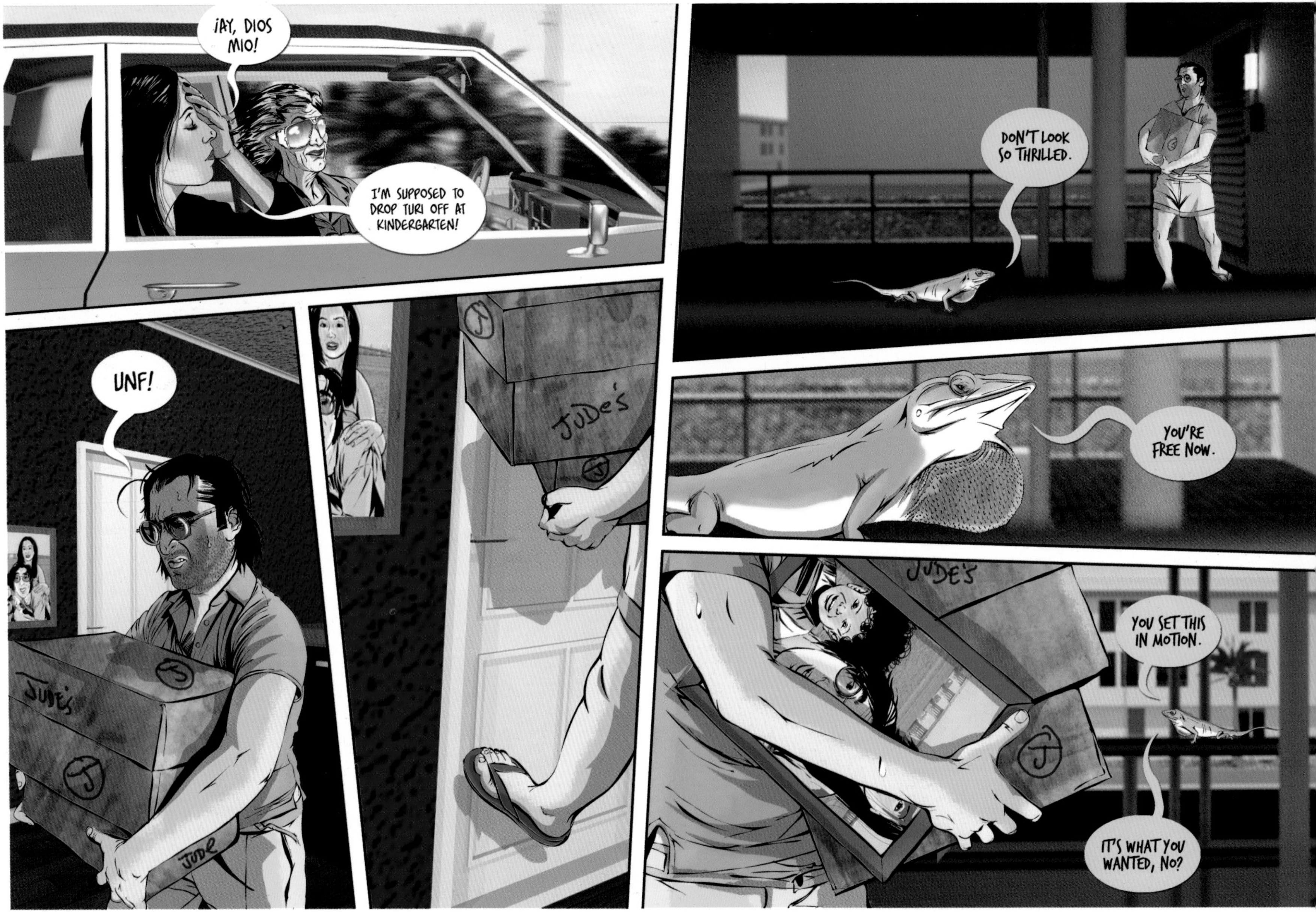
¡AY, DIOS MIO!
I'M SUPPOSED TO DROP TURI OFF AT KINDERGARTEN!
UNF!
JUDE'S
JUDE'S
DON'T LOOK SO THRILLED.
YOU'RE FREE NOW.
JUDE'S
YOU SET THIS IN MOTION.
IT'S WHAT YOU WANTED, NO?

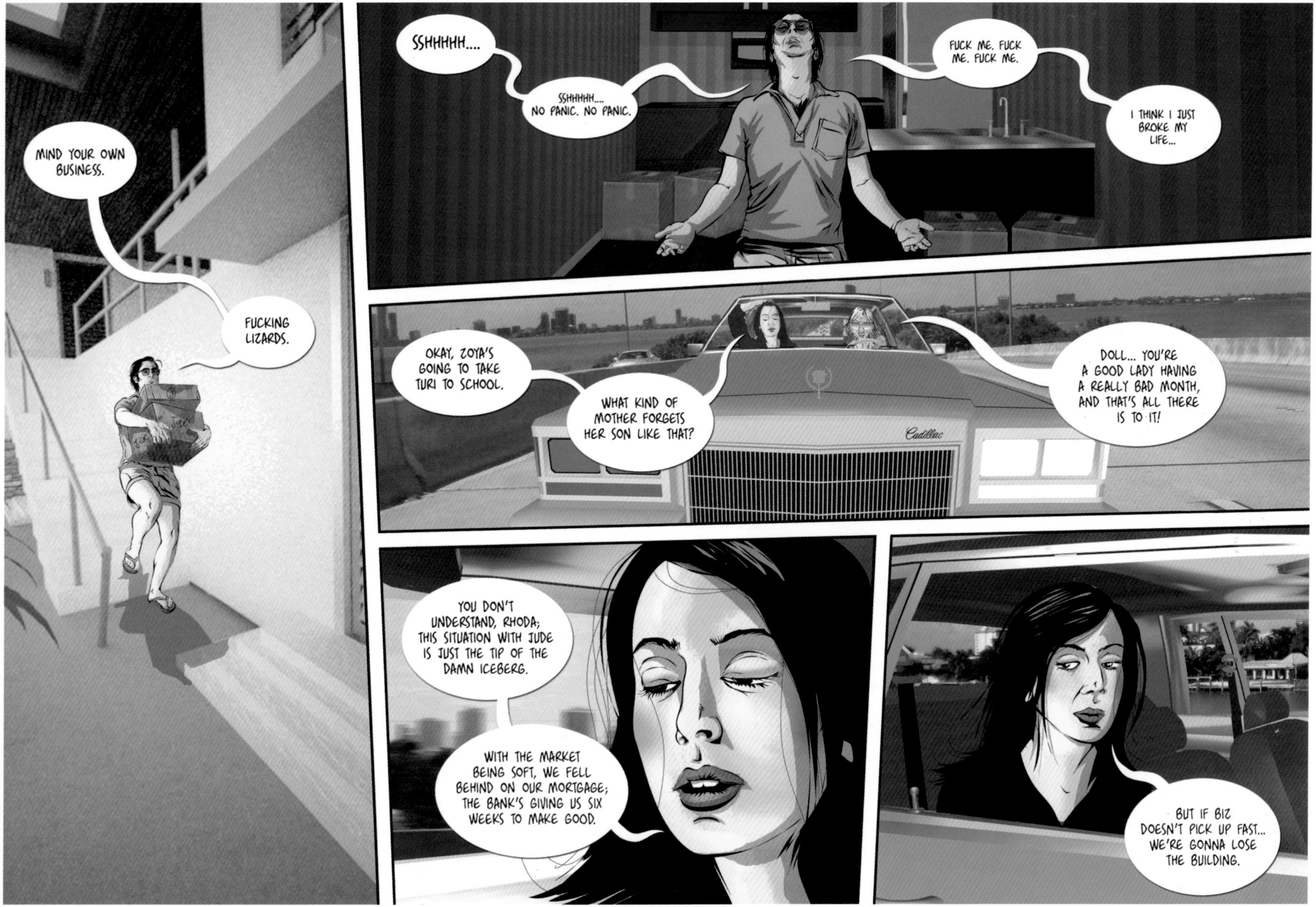
MIND YOUR OWN BUSINESS.
FUCKING LIZARDS.
SSHHHHH....
SSHHHHH.... NO PANIC. NO PANIC.
FUCK ME. FUCK ME. FUCK ME.
I THINK I JUST BROKE MY LIFE...
OKAY, ZOYA'S GOING TO TAKE TURI TO SCHOOL.
WHAT KIND OF MOTHER FORGETS HER SON LIKE THAT?
DOLL... YOU'RE A GOOD LADY HAVING A REALLY BAD MONTH, AND THAT'S ALL THERE IS TO IT!
Cadillac
YOU DON'T UNDERSTAND, RHODA; THIS SITUATION WITH JUDE IS JUST THE TIP OF THE DAMN ICEBERG.
WITH THE MARKET BEING SOFT, WE FELL BEHIND ON OUR MORTGAGE; THE BANK'S GIVING US SIX WEEKS TO MAKE GOOD.
BUT IF BIZ DOESN'T PICK UP FAST... WE'RE GONNA LOSE THE BUILDING.

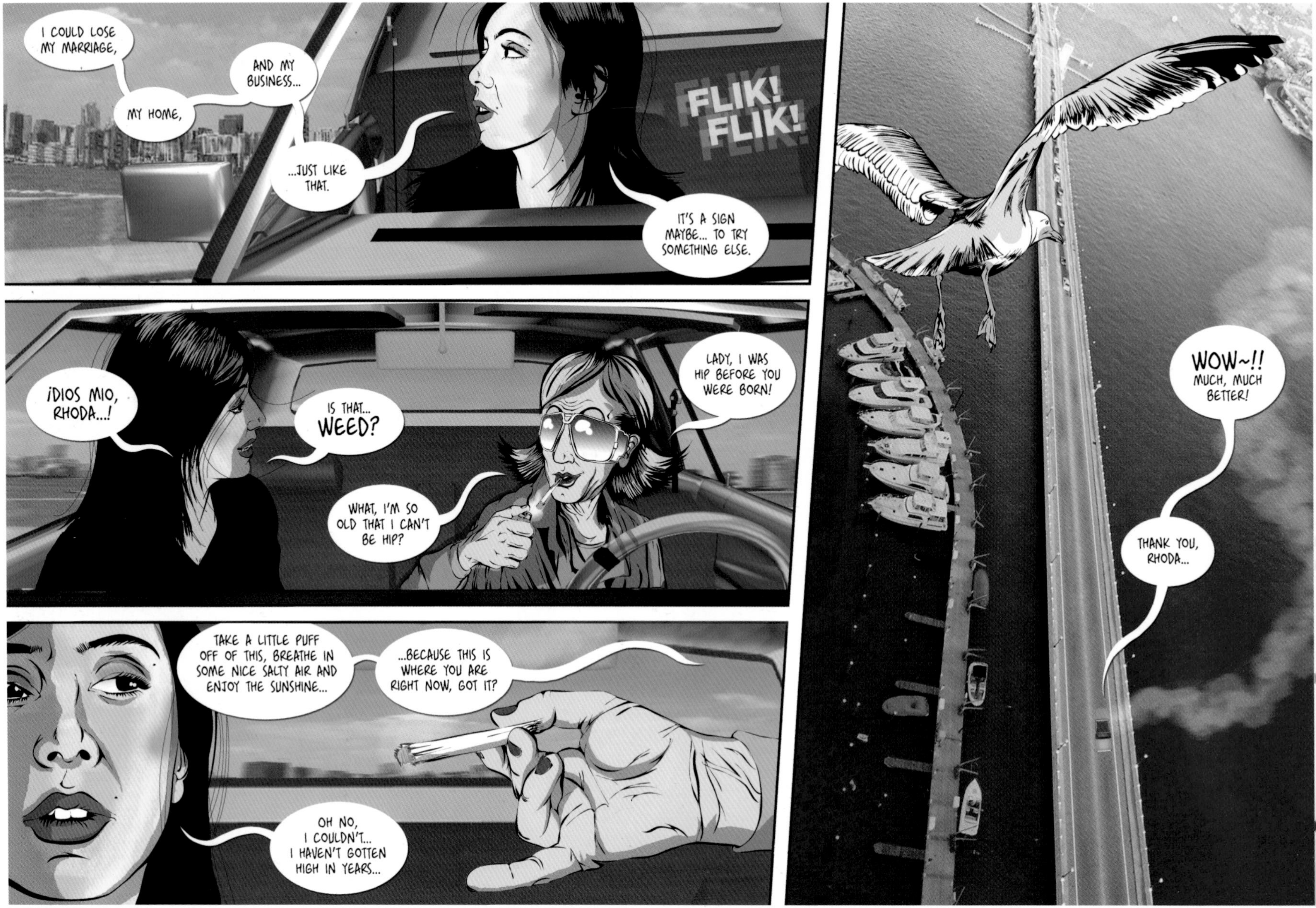
I COULD LOSE MY MARRIAGE,
MY HOME,
AND MY BUSINESS...
...JUST LIKE THAT.
FLIK! FLIK!
IT'S A SIGN MAYBE... TO TRY SOMETHING ELSE.
¡DIOS MIO, RHODA...!
IS THAT... WEED?
LADY, I WAS HIP BEFORE YOU WERE BORN!
WHAT, I'M SO OLD THAT I CAN'T BE HIP?
TAKE A LITTLE PUFF OFF OF THIS, BREATHE IN SOME NICE SALTY AIR AND ENJOY THE SUNSHINE...
...BECAUSE THIS IS WHERE YOU ARE RIGHT NOW, GOT IT?
OH NO, I COULDN'T... I HAVEN'T GOTTEN HIGH IN YEARS...
WOW~!! MUCH, MUCH BETTER!
THANK YOU, RHODA...

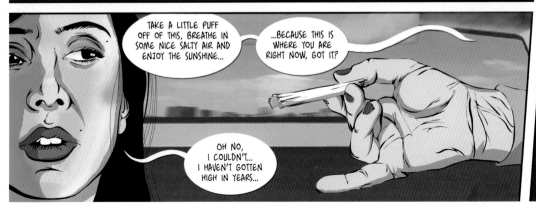

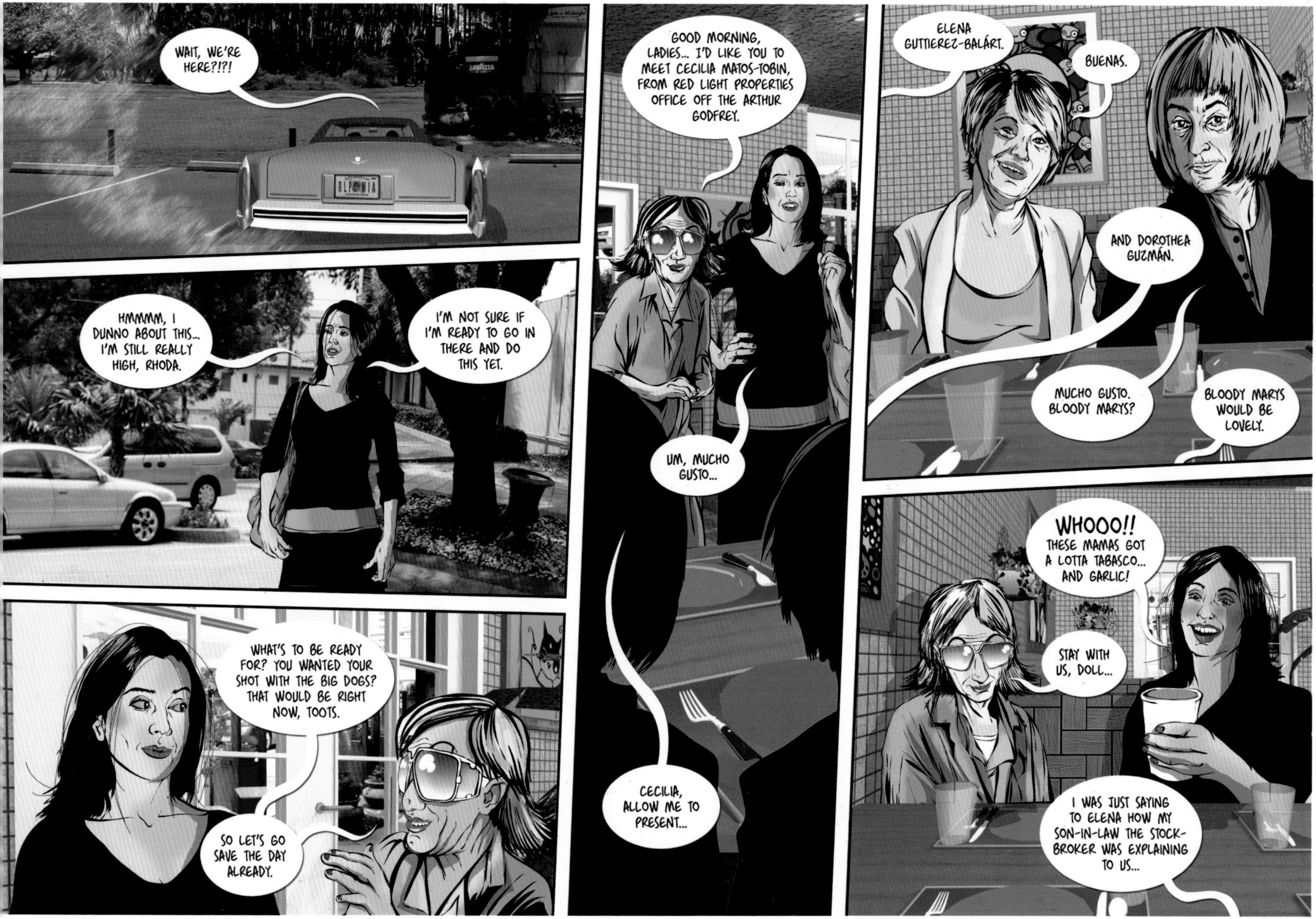
WAIT, WE'RE HERE?!?!
HMMMM, I DUNNO ABOUT THIS... I'M STILL REALLY HIGH, RHODA.
I'M NOT SURE IF I'M READY TO GO IN THERE AND DO THIS YET.
WHAT'S TO BE READY FOR? YOU WANTED YOUR SHOT WITH THE BIG DOGS? THAT WOULD BE RIGHT NOW, TOOTS.
SO LET'S GO SAVE THE DAY ALREADY.
GOOD MORNING, LADIES... I'D LIKE YOU TO MEET CECILIA MATOS-TOBIN, FROM RED LIGHT PROPERTIES OFFICE OFF THE ARTHUR GODFREY.
UM, MUCHO GUSTO...
CECILIA, ALLOW ME TO PRESENT...
ELENA GUTTIEREZ-BALÁRT.
BUENAS.
AND DOROTHEA GUZMÁN.
MUCHO GUSTO. BLOODY MARYS?
BLOODY MARYS WOULD BE LOVELY.
WHOOO!! THESE MAMAS GOT A LOTTA TABASCO... AND GARLIC!
STAY WITH US, DOLL...
I WAS JUST SAYING TO ELENA HOW MY SON-IN-LAW THE STOCK-BROKER WAS EXPLAINING TO US...

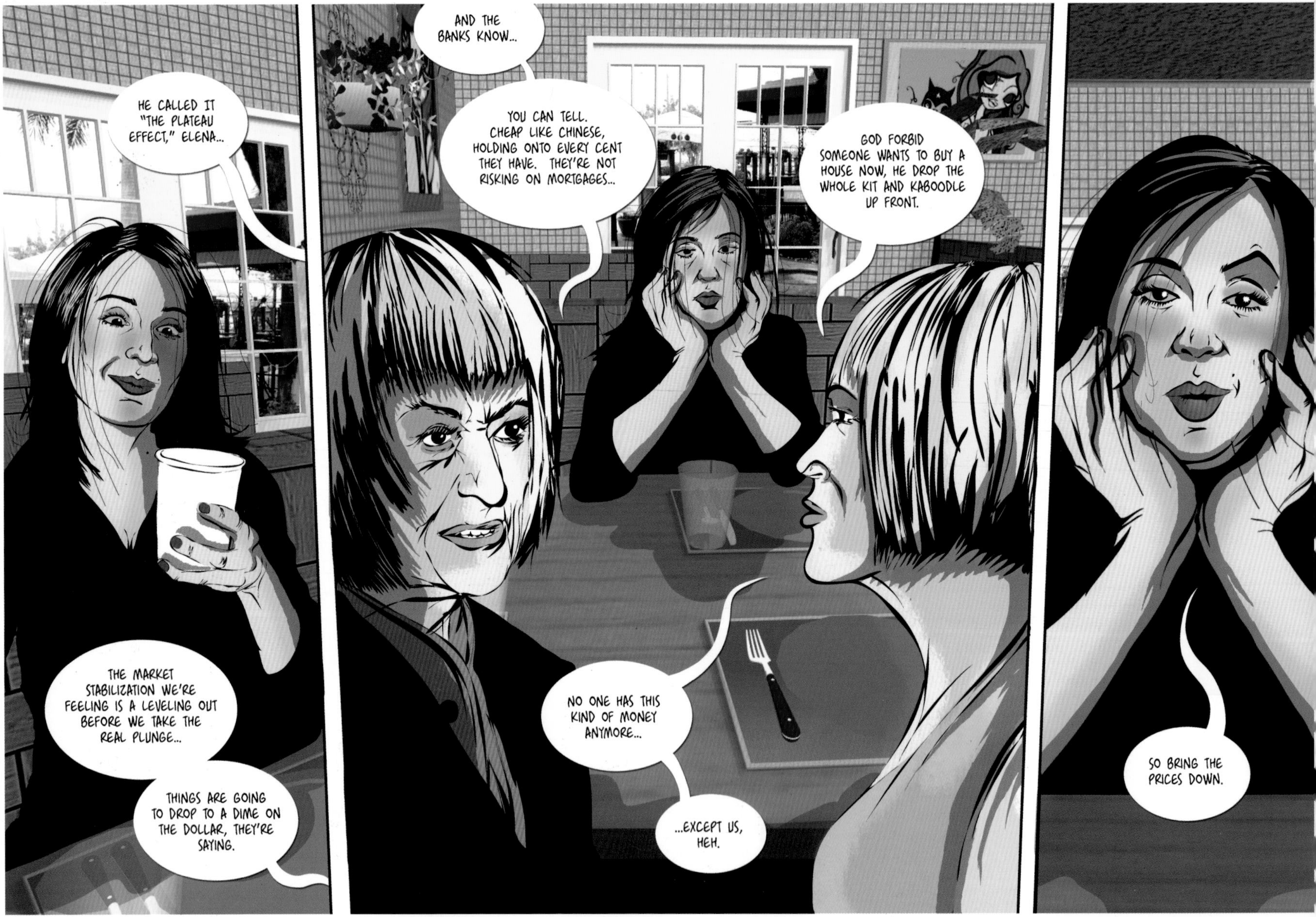
HE CALLED IT "THE PLATEAU EFFECT," ELENA...
THE MARKET STABILIZATION WE'RE FEELING IS A LEVELING OUT BEFORE WE TAKE THE REAL PLUNGE...
THINGS ARE GOING TO DROP TO A DIME ON THE DOLLAR, THEY'RE SAYING.
AND THE BANKS KNOW...
YOU CAN TELL. CHEAP LIKE CHINESE, HOLDING ONTO EVERY CENT THEY HAVE. THEY'RE NOT RISKING ON MORTGAGES...
GOD FORBID SOMEONE WANTS TO BUY A HOUSE NOW, HE DROP THE WHOLE KIT AND KABOODLE UP FRONT.
NO ONE HAS THIS KIND OF MONEY ANYMORE...
...EXCEPT US, HEH.
SO BRING THE PRICES DOWN.

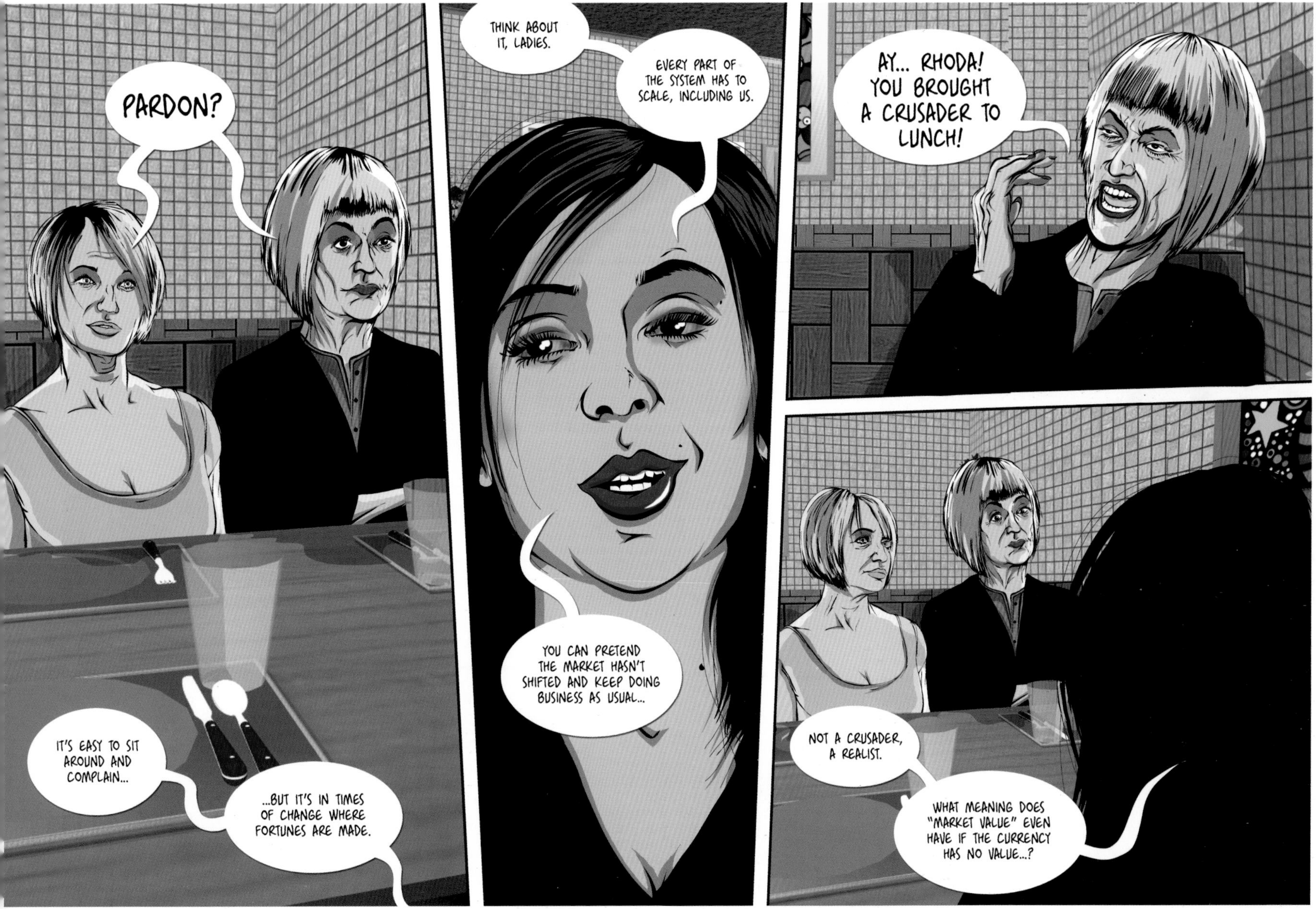
PARDON?
IT'S EASY TO SIT AROUND AND COMPLAIN...
...BUT IT'S IN TIMES OF CHANGE WHERE FORTUNES ARE MADE.
THINK ABOUT IT, LADIES.
EVERY PART OF THE SYSTEM HAS TO SCALE, INCLUDING US.
YOU CAN PRETEND THE MARKET HASN'T SHIFTED AND KEEP DOING BUSINESS AS USUAL...
AY... RHODA! YOU BROUGHT A CRUSADER TO LUNCH!
NOT A CRUSADER, A REALIST.
WHAT MEANING DOES "MARKET VALUE" EVEN HAVE IF THE CURRENCY HAS NO VALUE...?

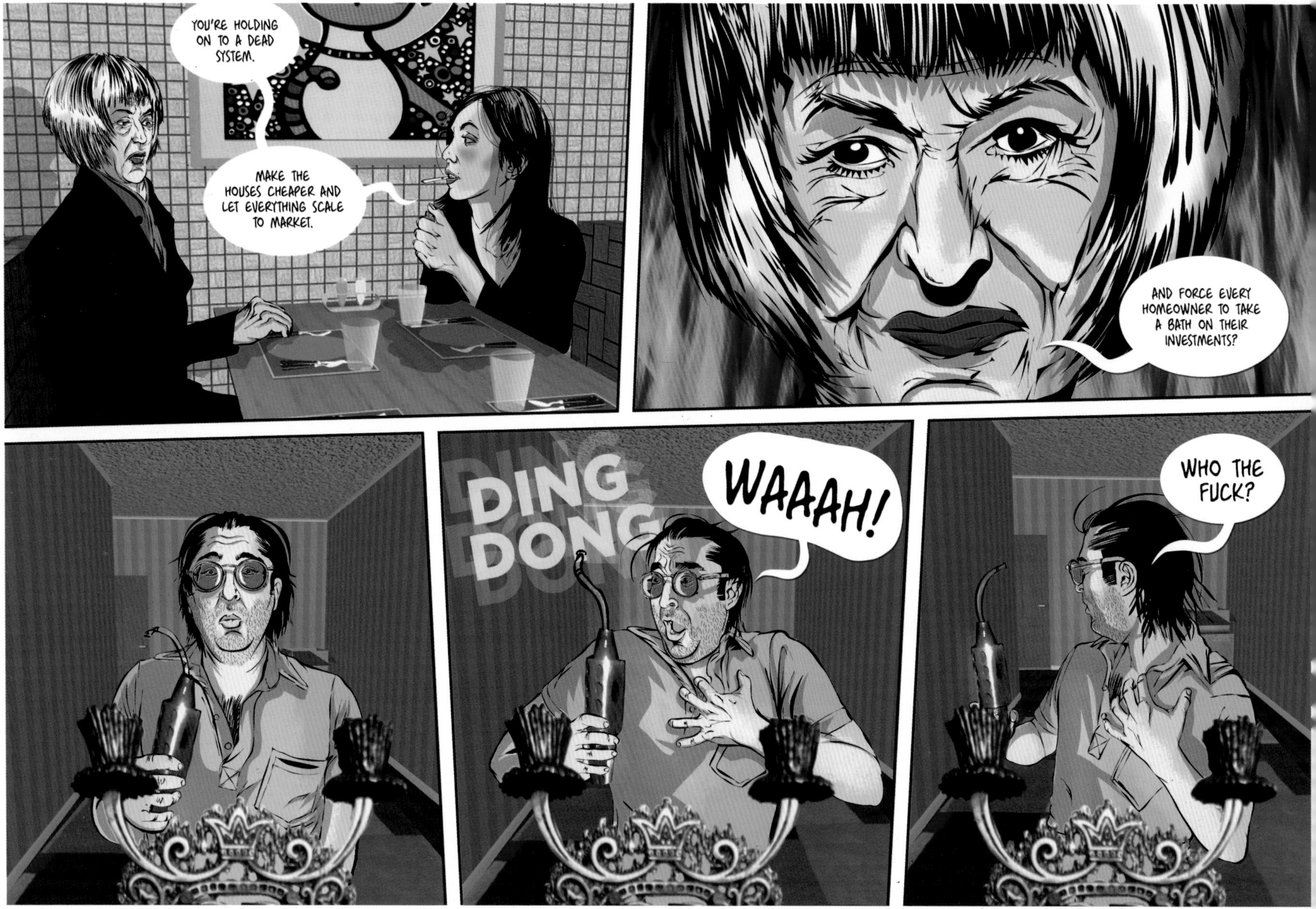
YOU'RE HOLDING ON TO A DEAD SYSTEM.
MAKE THE HOUSES CHEAPER AND LET EVERYTHING SCALE TO MARKET.
AND FORCE EVERY HOMEOWNER TO TAKE A BATH ON THEIR INVESTMENTS?
DING DONG
WAAAH!
WHO THE FUCK?

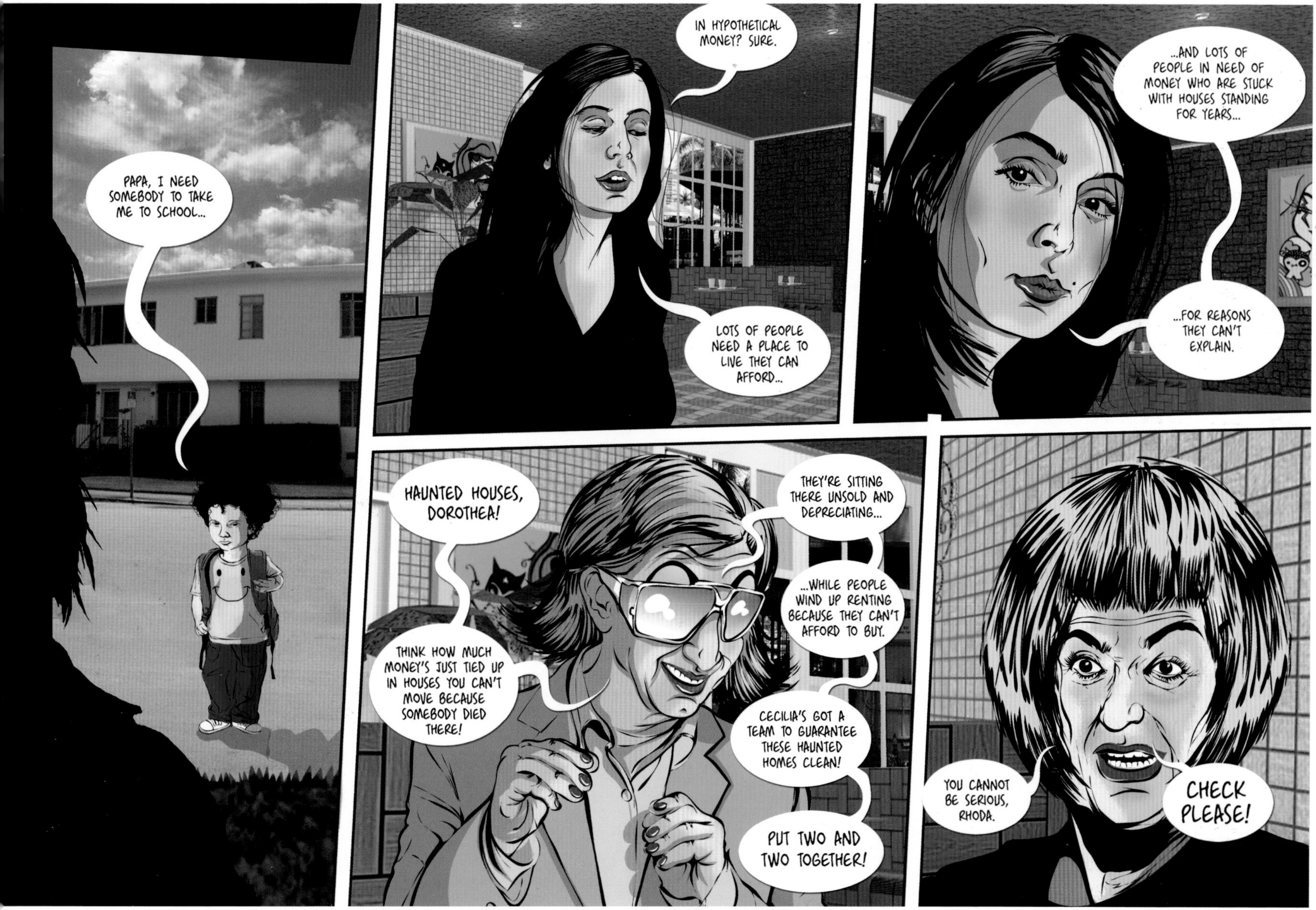
PAPA, I NEED SOMEBODY TO TAKE ME TO SCHOOL...
IN HYPOTHETICAL MONEY? SURE.
LOTS OF PEOPLE NEED A PLACE TO LIVE THEY CAN AFFORD...
...AND LOTS OF PEOPLE IN NEED OF MONEY WHO ARE STUCK WITH HOUSES STANDING FOR YEARS...
...FOR REASONS THEY CAN'T EXPLAIN.
HAUNTED HOUSES, DOROTHEA!
THINK HOW MUCH MONEY'S JUST TIED UP IN HOUSES YOU CAN'T MOVE BECAUSE SOMEBODY DIED THERE!
THEY'RE SITTING THERE UNSOLD AND DEPRECIATING...
...WHILE PEOPLE WIND UP RENTING BECAUSE THEY CAN'T AFFORD TO BUY.
CECILIA'S GOT A TEAM TO GUARANTEE THESE HAUNTED HOMES CLEAN!
PUT TWO AND TWO TOGETHER!
YOU CANNOT BE SERIOUS, RHODA.
CHECK PLEASE!

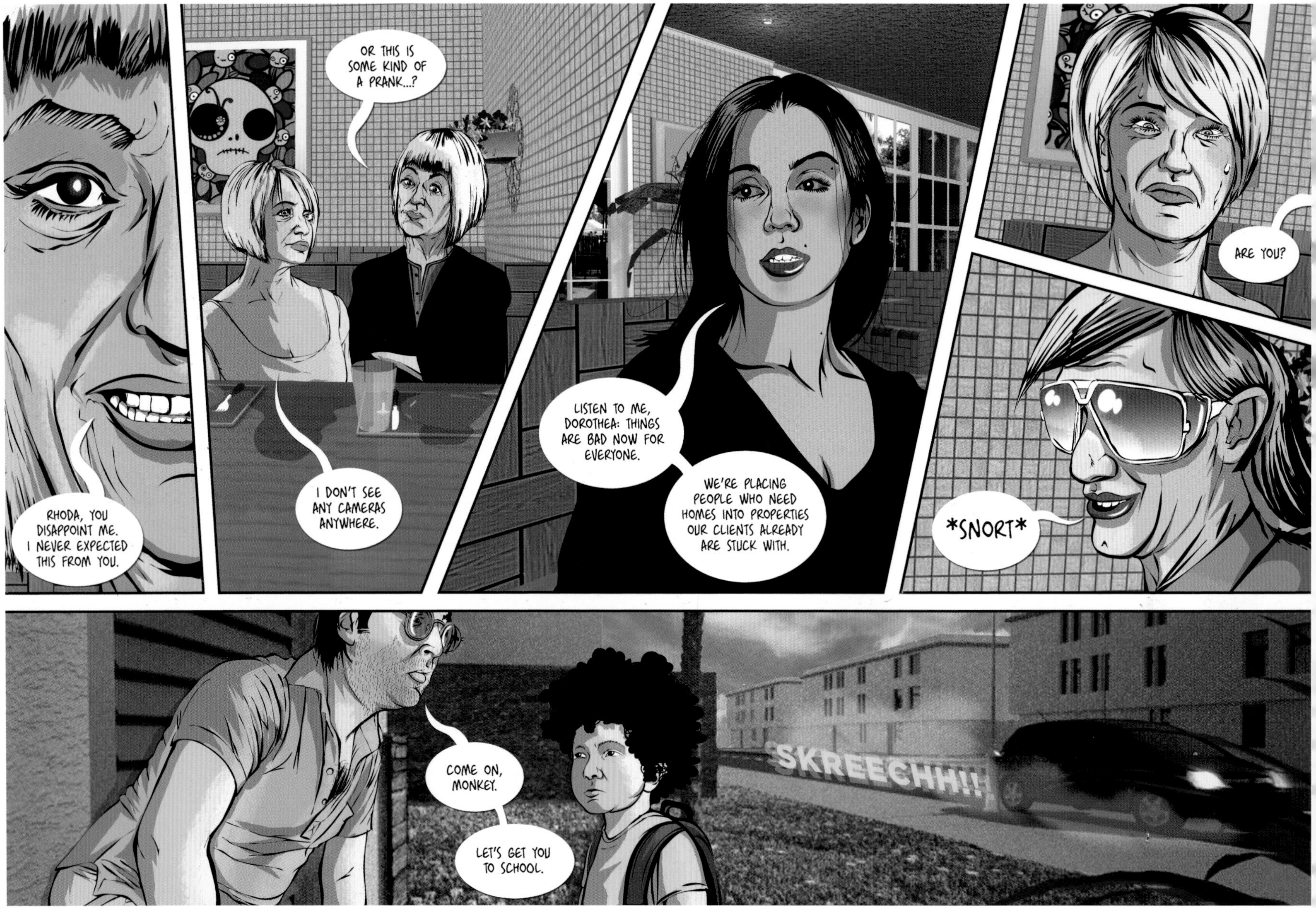
RHODA, YOU DISAPPOINT ME. I NEVER EXPECTED THIS FROM YOU.
OR THIS IS SOME KIND OF A PRANK...?
I DON'T SEE ANY CAMERAS ANYWHERE.
LISTEN TO ME, DOROTHEA: THINGS ARE BAD NOW FOR EVERYONE.
WE'RE PLACING PEOPLE WHO NEED HOMES INTO PROPERTIES OUR CLIENTS ALREADY ARE STUCK WITH.
ARE YOU?
SNORT
COME ON, MONKEY.
LET'S GET YOU TO SCHOOL.
SKREECHH!!

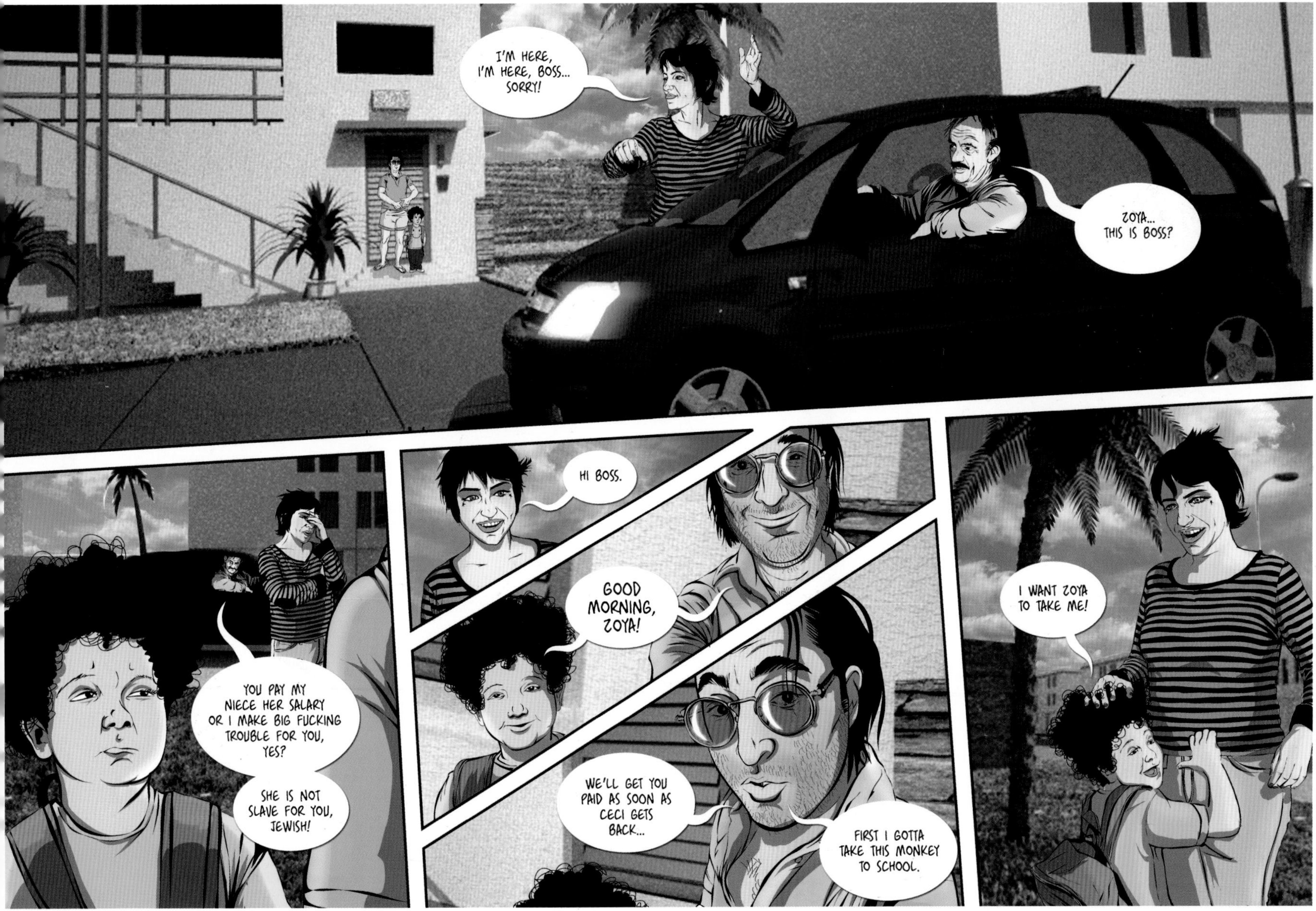
I'M HERE, I'M HERE, BOSS... SORRY!
ZOYA... THIS IS BOSS?
YOU PAY MY NIECE HER SALARY OR I MAKE BIG FUCKING TROUBLE FOR YOU, YES?
SHE IS NOT SLAVE FOR YOU, JEWISH!
HI BOSS.
GOOD MORNING, ZOYA!
WE'LL GET YOU PAID AS SOON AS CECI GETS BACK...
FIRST I GOTTA TAKE THIS MONKEY TO SCHOOL.
I WANT ZOYA TO TAKE ME!

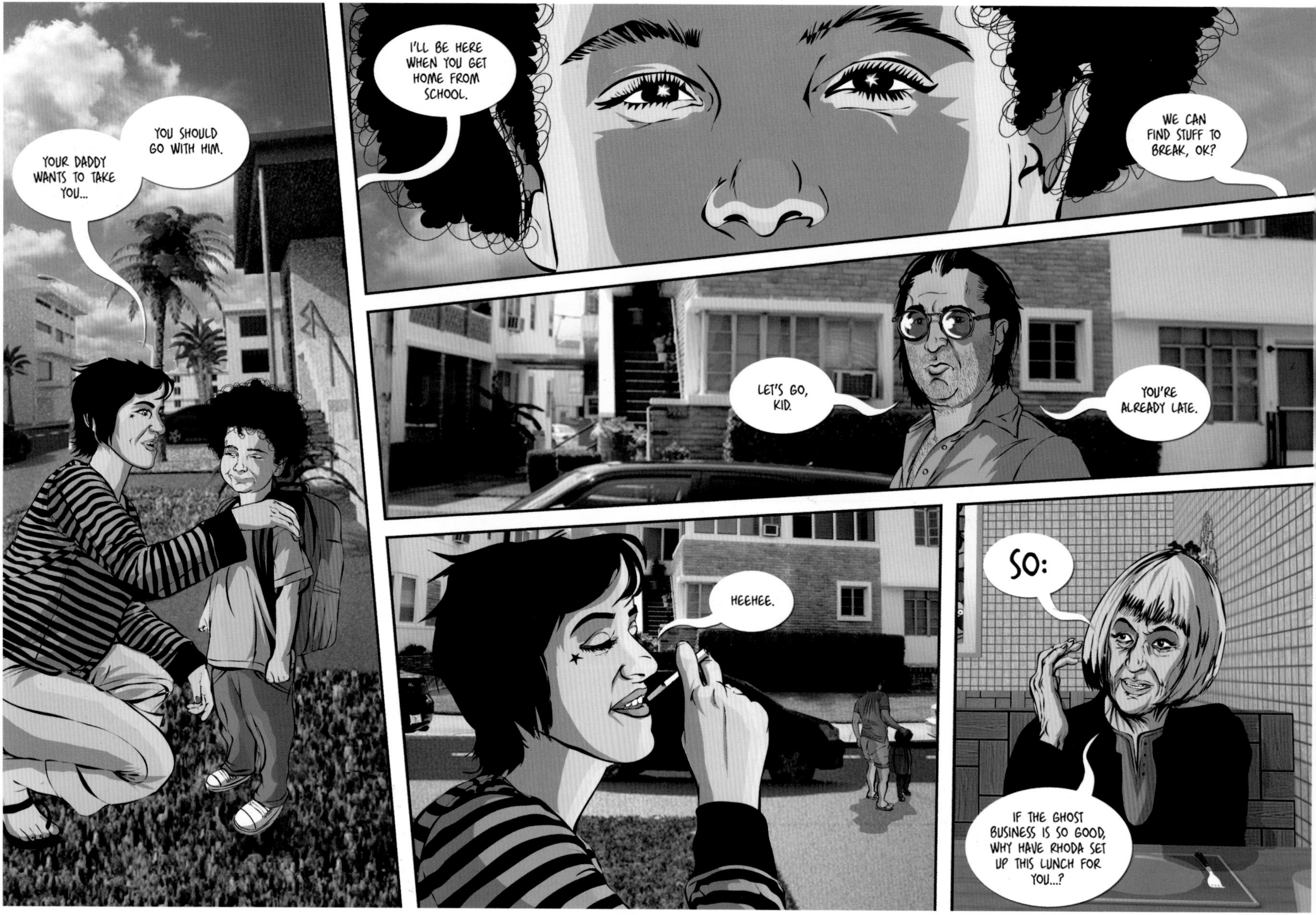
YOUR DADDY WANTS TO TAKE YOU...
YOU SHOULD GO WITH HIM.
I'LL BE HERE WHEN YOU GET HOME FROM SCHOOL.
WE CAN FIND STUFF TO BREAK, OK?
LET'S GO, KID.
YOU'RE ALREADY LATE.
HEEHEE.
SO:
IF THE GHOST BUSINESS IS SO GOOD, WHY HAVE RHODA SET UP THIS LUNCH FOR YOU...?

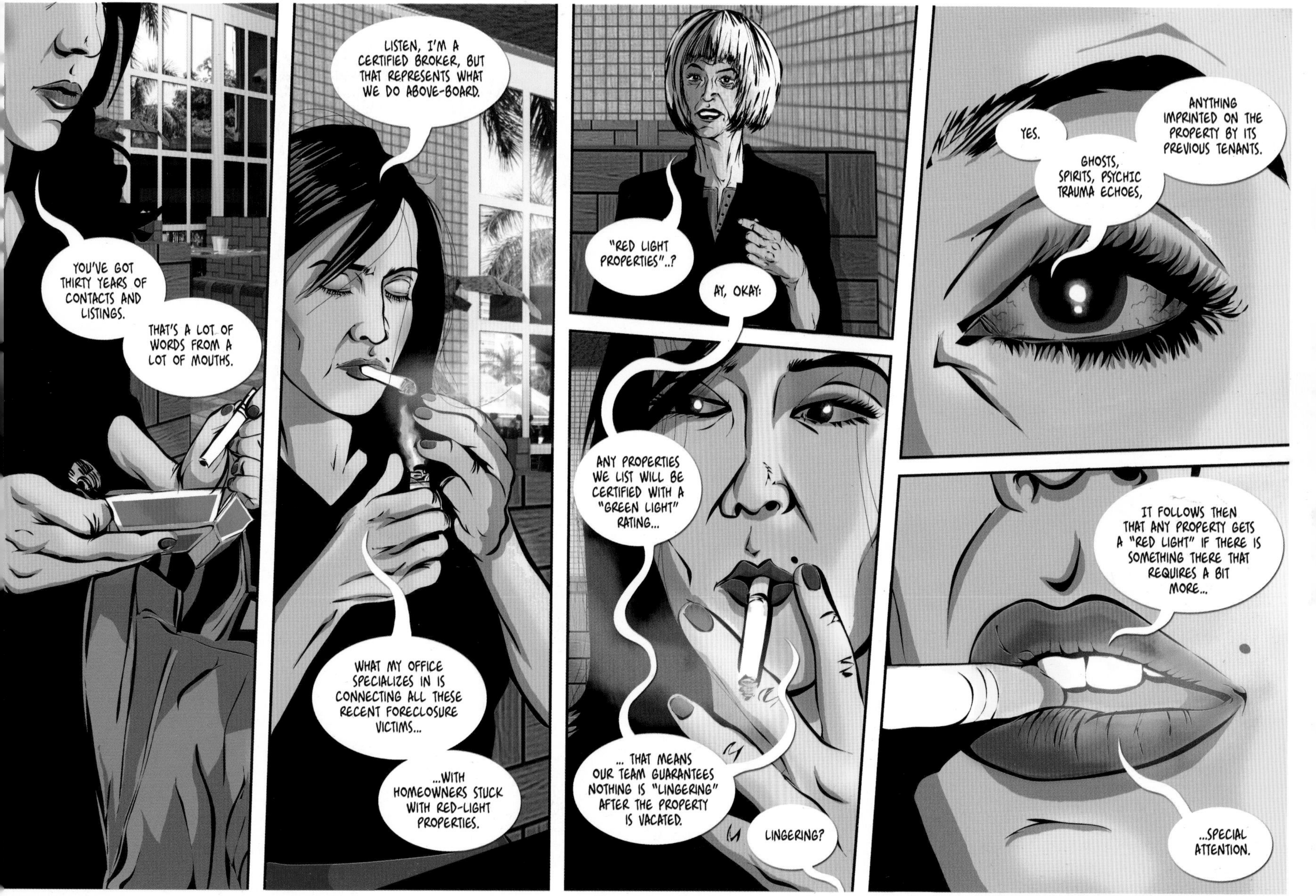
YOU'VE GOT THIRTY YEARS OF CONTACTS AND LISTINGS.
THAT'S A LOT OF WORDS FROM A LOT OF MOUTHS.
LISTEN, I'M A CERTIFIED BROKER, BUT THAT REPRESENTS WHAT WE DO ABOVE-BOARD.
WHAT MY OFFICE SPECIALIZES IN IS CONNECTING ALL THESE RECENT FORECLOSURE VICTIMS...
...WITH HOMEOWNERS STUCK WITH RED-LIGHT PROPERTIES.
"RED LIGHT PROPERTIES"..?
AY, OKAY:
ANY PROPERTIES WE LIST WILL BE CERTIFIED WITH A "GREEN LIGHT" RATING...
... THAT MEANS OUR TEAM GUARANTEES NOTHING IS "LINGERING" AFTER THE PROPERTY IS VACATED.
LINGERING?
YES.
GHOSTS, SPIRITS, PSYCHIC TRAUMA ECHOES,
ANYTHING IMPRINTED ON THE PROPERTY BY ITS PREVIOUS TENANTS.
IT FOLLOWS THEN THAT ANY PROPERTY GETS A "RED LIGHT" IF THERE IS SOMETHING THERE THAT REQUIRES A BIT MORE...
...SPECIAL ATTENTION.

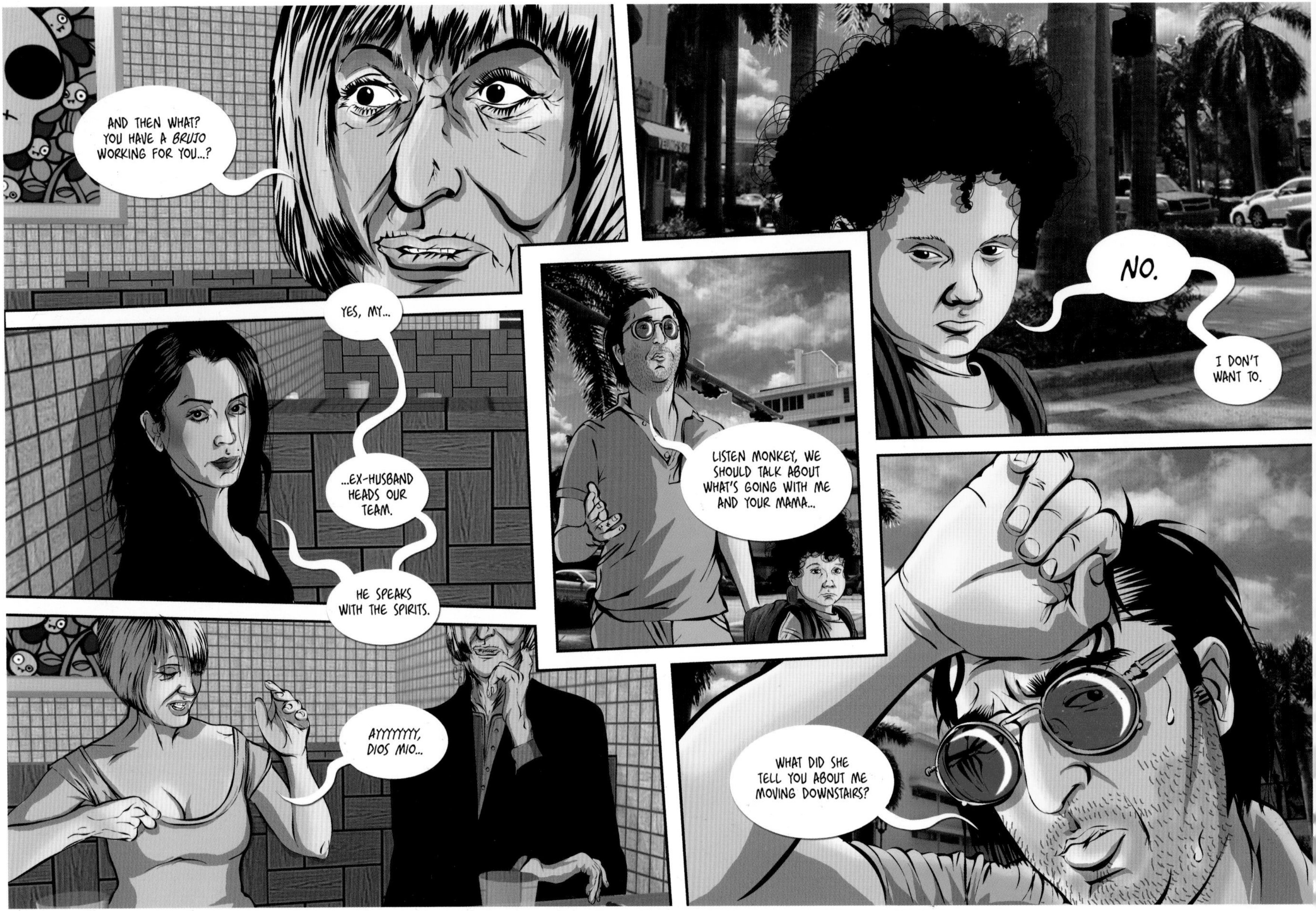

AND THEN WHAT? YOU HAVE A *BRUJO* WORKING FOR YOU...?
YES, MY...
...EX-HUSBAND HEADS OUR TEAM.
HE SPEAKS WITH THE SPIRITS.
AYYYYYYYY, DIOS MIO...
LISTEN MONKEY, WE SHOULD TALK ABOUT WHAT'S GOING WITH ME AND YOUR MAMA...
NO.
I DON'T WANT TO.
WHAT DID SHE TELL YOU ABOUT ME MOVING DOWNSTAIRS?

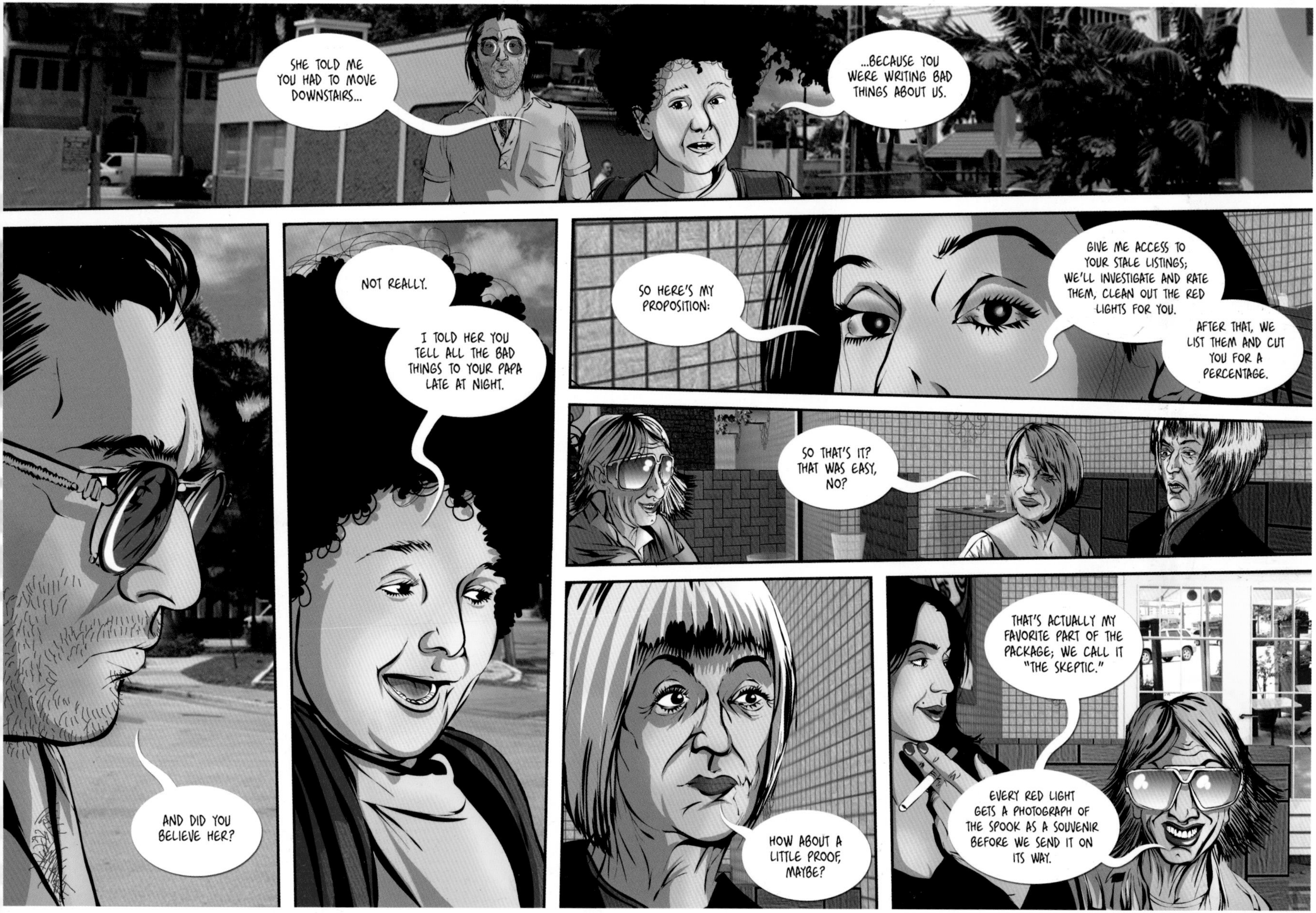
SHE TOLD ME YOU HAD TO MOVE DOWNSTAIRS...
...BECAUSE YOU WERE WRITING BAD THINGS ABOUT US.
AND DID YOU BELIEVE HER?
NOT REALLY.
I TOLD HER YOU TELL ALL THE BAD THINGS TO YOUR PAPA LATE AT NIGHT.
SO HERE'S MY PROPOSITION:
GIVE ME ACCESS TO YOUR STALE LISTINGS; WE'LL INVESTIGATE AND RATE THEM, CLEAN OUT THE RED LIGHTS FOR YOU.
AFTER THAT, WE LIST THEM AND CUT YOU FOR A PERCENTAGE.
SO THAT'S IT? THAT WAS EASY, NO?
HOW ABOUT A LITTLE PROOF, MAYBE?
THAT'S ACTUALLY MY FAVORITE PART OF THE PACKAGE; WE CALL IT "THE SKEPTIC."
EVERY RED LIGHT GETS A PHOTOGRAPH OF THE SPOOK AS A SOUVENIR BEFORE WE SEND IT ON ITS WAY.

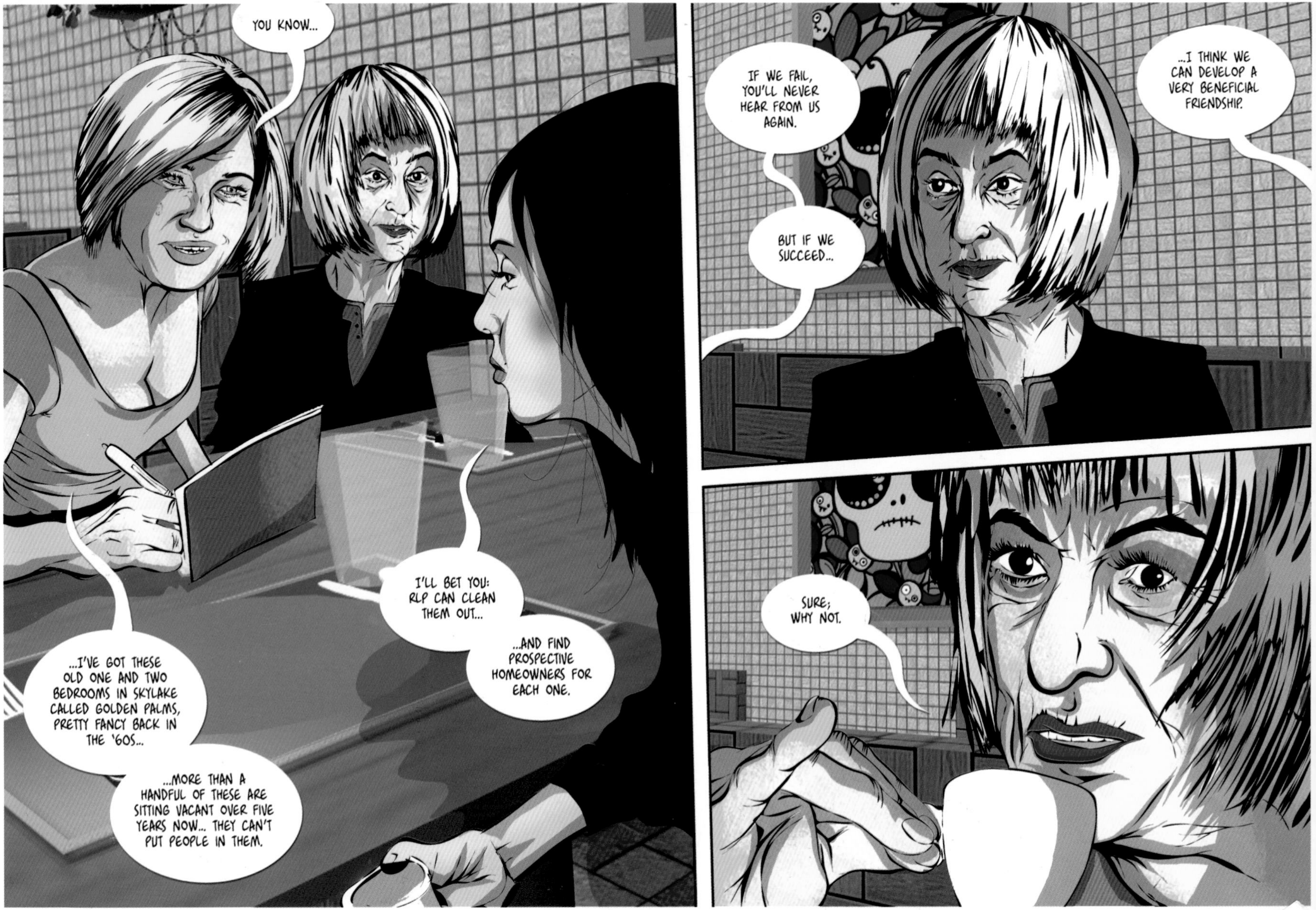
YOU KNOW...
...I'VE GOT THESE OLD ONE AND TWO BEDROOMS IN SKYLAKE CALLED GOLDEN PALMS, PRETTY FANCY BACK IN THE '60S...
...MORE THAN A HANDFUL OF THESE ARE SITTING VACANT OVER FIVE YEARS NOW... THEY CAN'T PUT PEOPLE IN THEM.
I'LL BET YOU: RLP CAN CLEAN THEM OUT...
...AND FIND PROSPECTIVE HOMEOWNERS FOR EACH ONE.
IF WE FAIL, YOU'LL NEVER HEAR FROM US AGAIN.
BUT IF WE SUCCEED...
...I THINK WE CAN DEVELOP A VERY BENEFICIAL FRIENDSHIP.
SURE; WHY NOT.

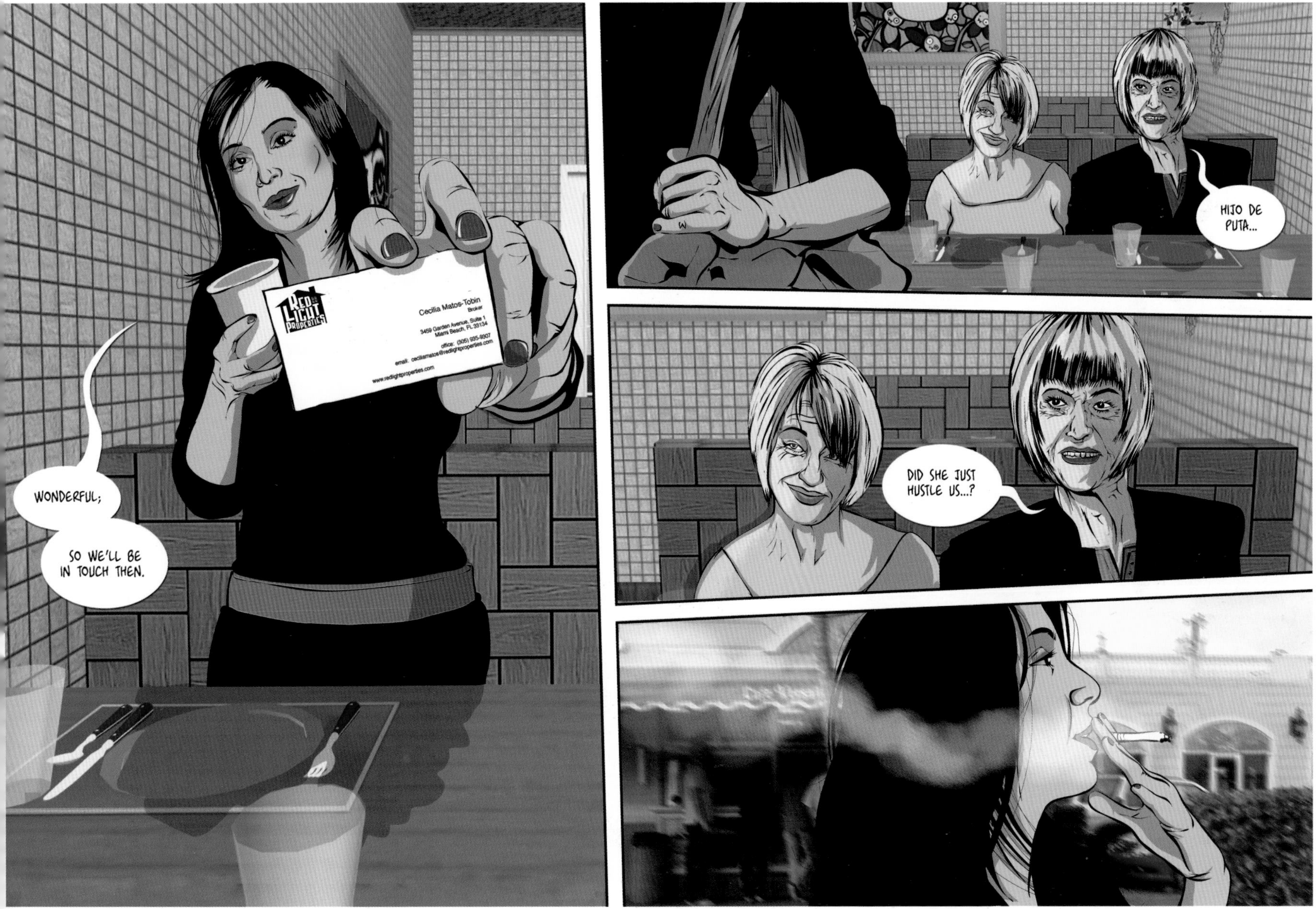
RED LIGHT PROPERTIES
Cecilia Matos-Tobin
Broker
3459 Garden Avenue, Suite 1
Miami Beach, FL 33134
office: (305) 935-9307
email: ceciliamatos@redlightproperties.com
www.redlightproperties.com
WONDERFUL;
SO WE'LL BE IN TOUCH THEN.
HIJO DE PUTA...
DID SHE JUST HUSTLE US...?

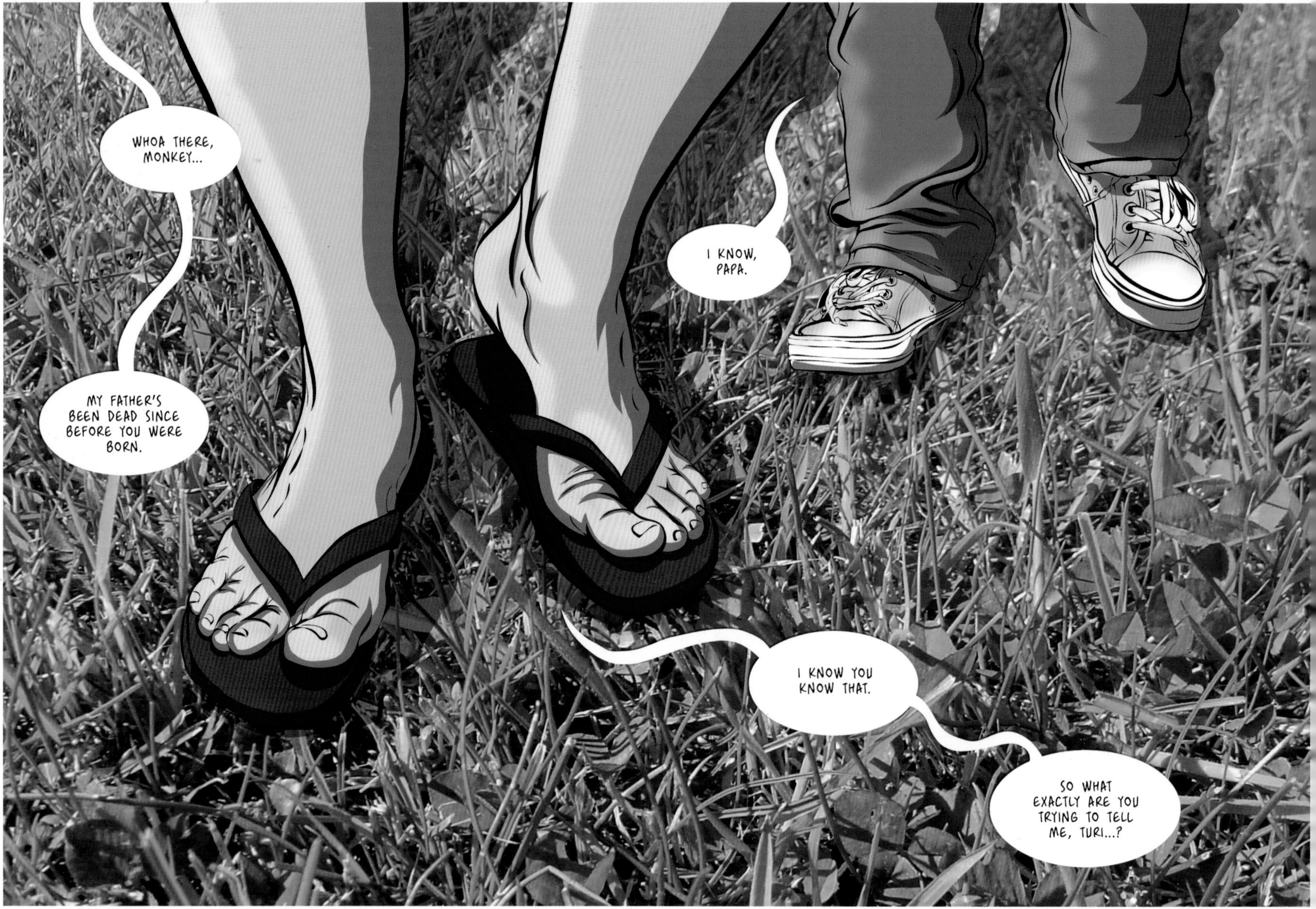
WHOA THERE, MONKEY...
I KNOW, PAPA.
MY FATHER'S BEEN DEAD SINCE BEFORE YOU WERE BORN.
I KNOW YOU KNOW THAT.
SO WHAT EXACTLY ARE YOU TRYING TO TELL ME, TURI...?

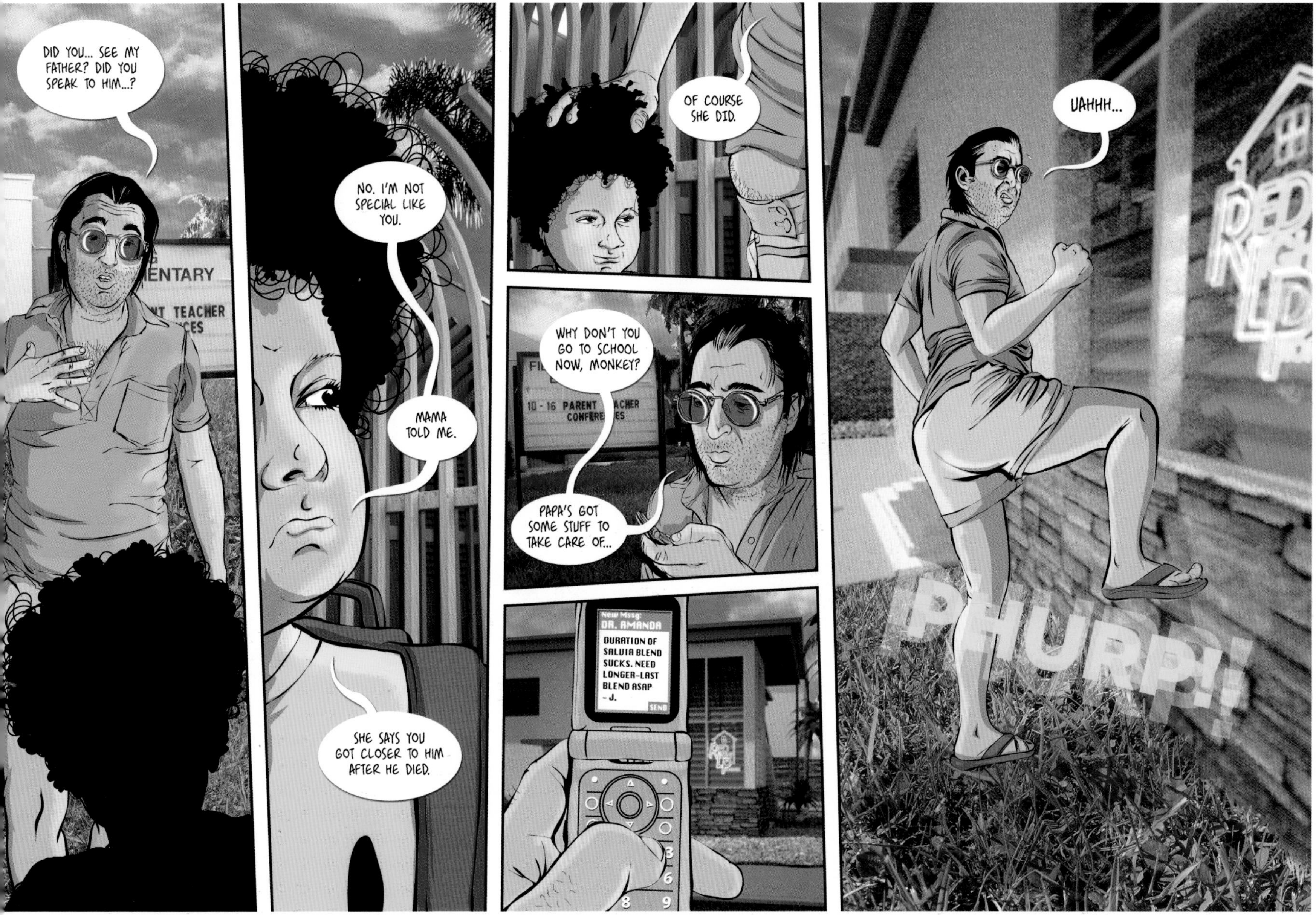
DID YOU... SEE MY FATHER? DID YOU SPEAK TO HIM...?
ENTARY
NT TEACHER
CES
NO. I'M NOT SPECIAL LIKE YOU.
MAMA TOLD ME.
SHE SAYS YOU GOT CLOSER TO HIM AFTER HE DIED.
OF COURSE SHE DID.
WHY DON'T YOU GO TO SCHOOL NOW, MONKEY?
PAPA'S GOT SOME STUFF TO TAKE CARE OF...
10 - 16 PARENT ACHER
CONFERE ES
New Mssg:
DR. AMANDA
DURATION OF SALVIA BLEND SUCKS. NEED LONGER-LAST BLEND ASAP
- J.
SEND
UAHHH...
PHURP!

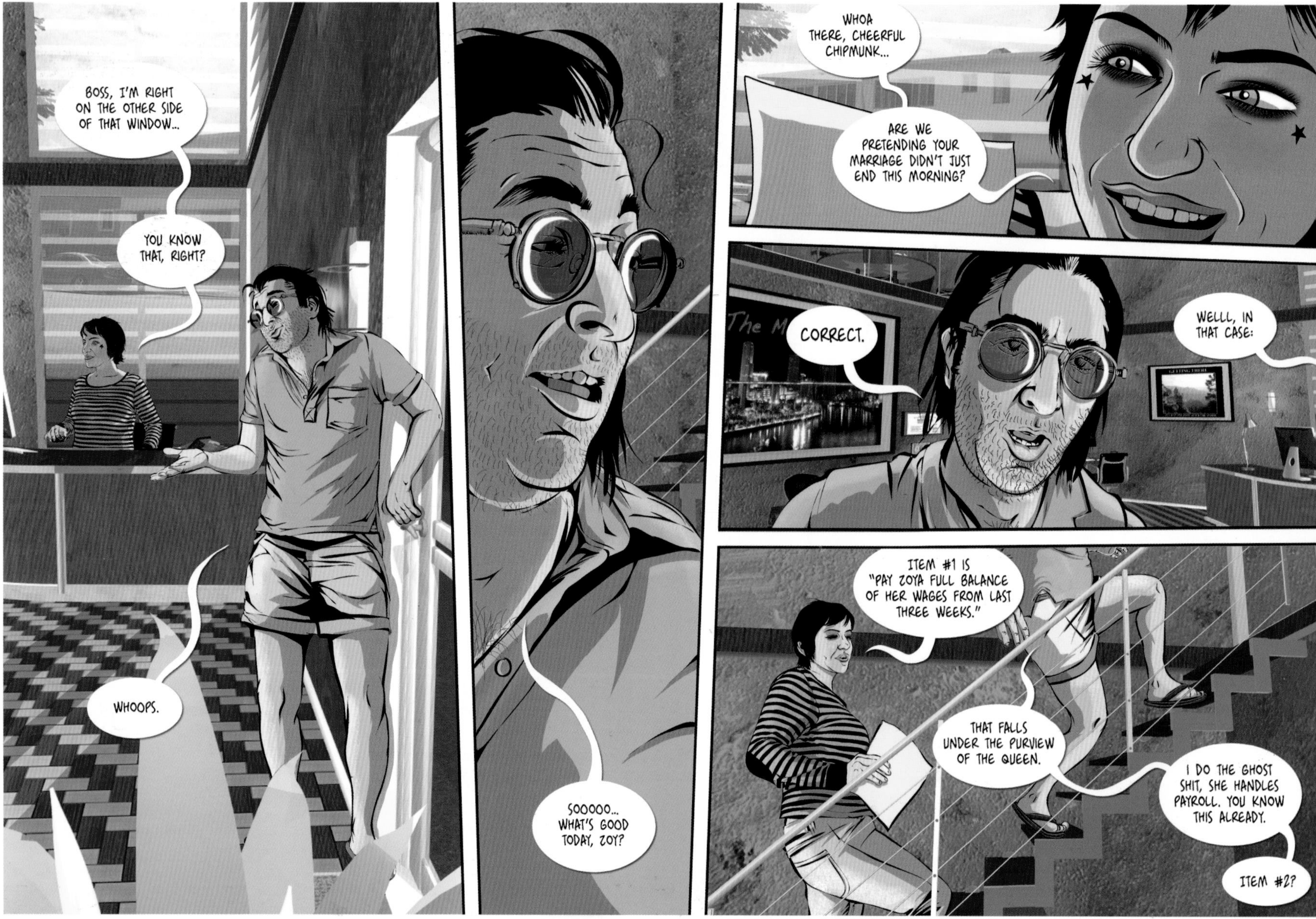
BOSS, I'M RIGHT ON THE OTHER SIDE OF THAT WINDOW...
YOU KNOW THAT, RIGHT?
WHOOPS.
SOOOOO... WHAT'S GOOD TODAY, ZOY?
WHOA THERE, CHEERFUL CHIPMUNK...
ARE WE PRETENDING YOUR MARRIAGE DIDN'T JUST END THIS MORNING?
CORRECT.
WELLL, IN THAT CASE:
ITEM #1 IS "PAY ZOYA FULL BALANCE OF HER WAGES FROM LAST THREE WEEKS."
THAT FALLS UNDER THE PURVIEW OF THE QUEEN.
I DO THE GHOST SHIT, SHE HANDLES PAYROLL. YOU KNOW THIS ALREADY.
ITEM #2?

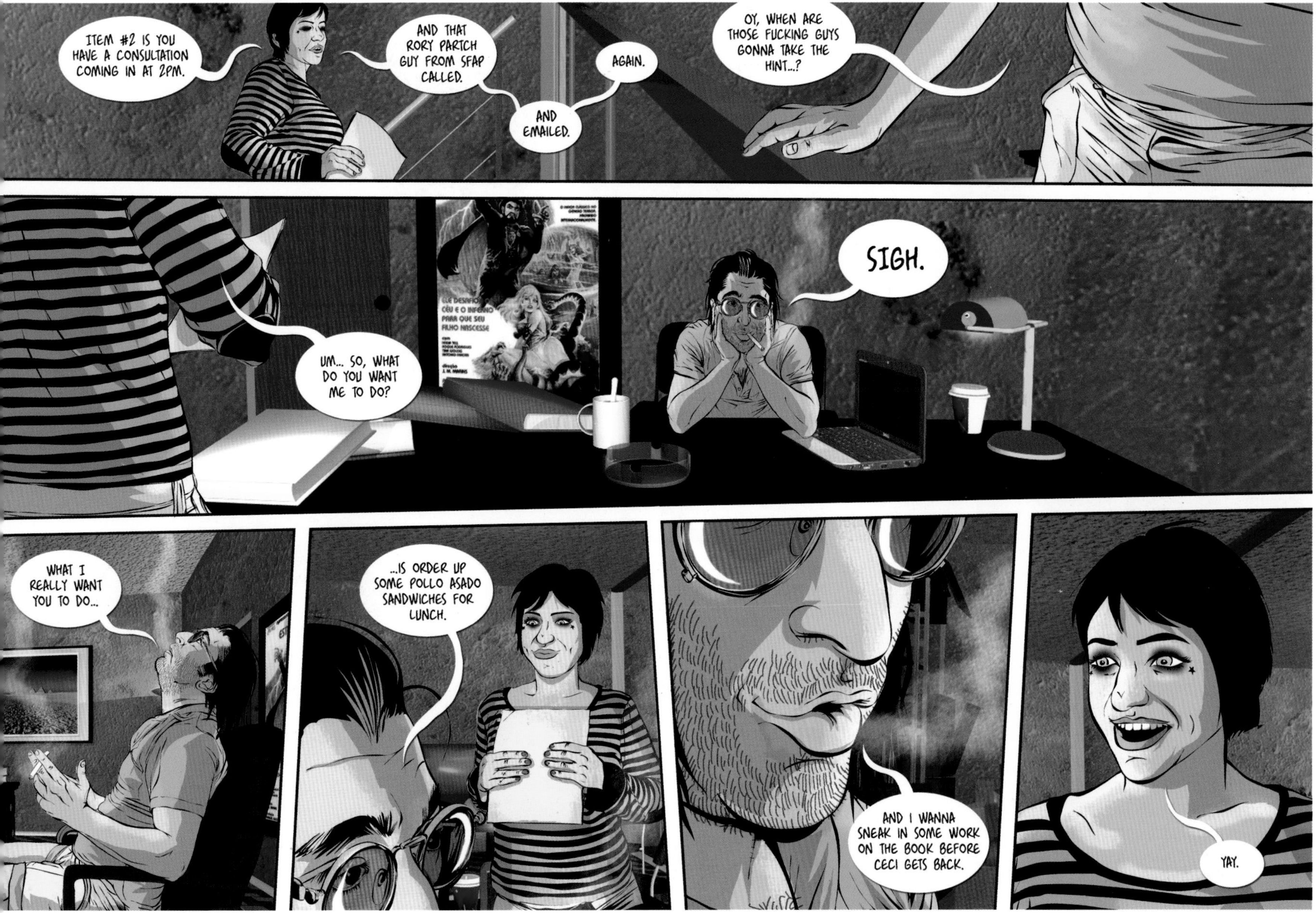
ITEM #2 IS YOU HAVE A CONSULTATION COMING IN AT 2PM.
AND THAT RORY PARTCH GUY FROM SFAP CALLED.
AND EMAILED.
AGAIN.
OY, WHEN ARE THOSE FUCKING GUYS GONNA TAKE THE HINT...?
SIGH.
UM... SO, WHAT DO YOU WANT ME TO DO?
WHAT I REALLY WANT YOU TO DO...
...IS ORDER UP SOME POLLO ASADO SANDWICHES FOR LUNCH.
AND I WANNA SNEAK IN SOME WORK ON THE BOOK BEFORE CECI GETS BACK.
YAY.

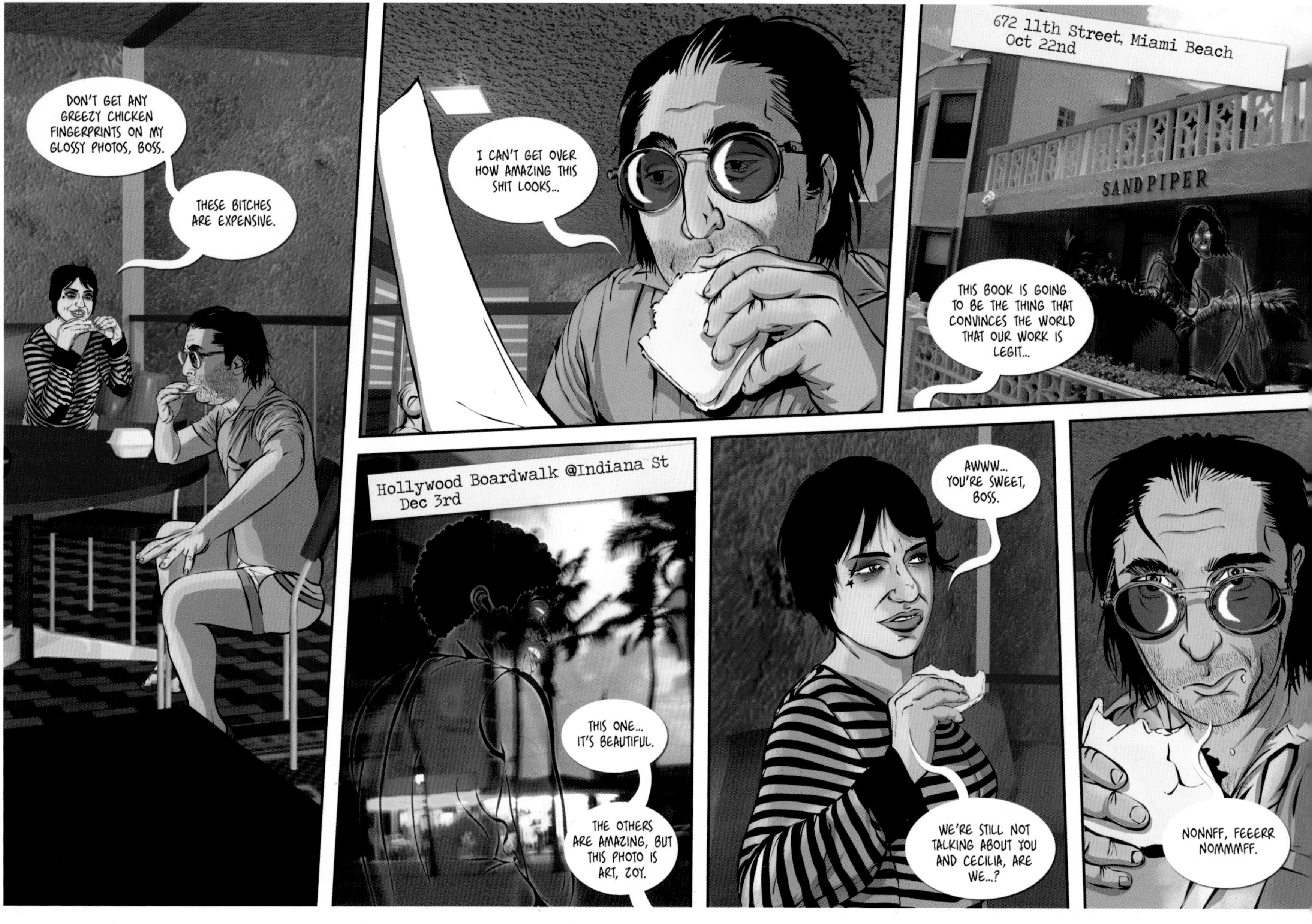
DON'T GET ANY GREEZY CHICKEN FINGERPRINTS ON MY GLOSSY PHOTOS, BOSS.
THESE BITCHES ARE EXPENSIVE.
I CAN'T GET OVER HOW AMAZING THIS SHIT LOOKS...
672 11th Street, Miami Beach
Oct 22nd
SANDPIPER
THIS BOOK IS GOING TO BE THE THING THAT CONVINCES THE WORLD THAT OUR WORK IS LEGIT...
Hollywood Boardwalk @Indiana St
Dec 3rd
THIS ONE... IT'S BEAUTIFUL.
THE OTHERS ARE AMAZING, BUT THIS PHOTO IS ART, ZOY.
AWWW... YOU'RE SWEET, BOSS.
WE'RE STILL NOT TALKING ABOUT YOU AND CECILIA, ARE WE...?
NONNFF, FEEERR NOMMMFF.

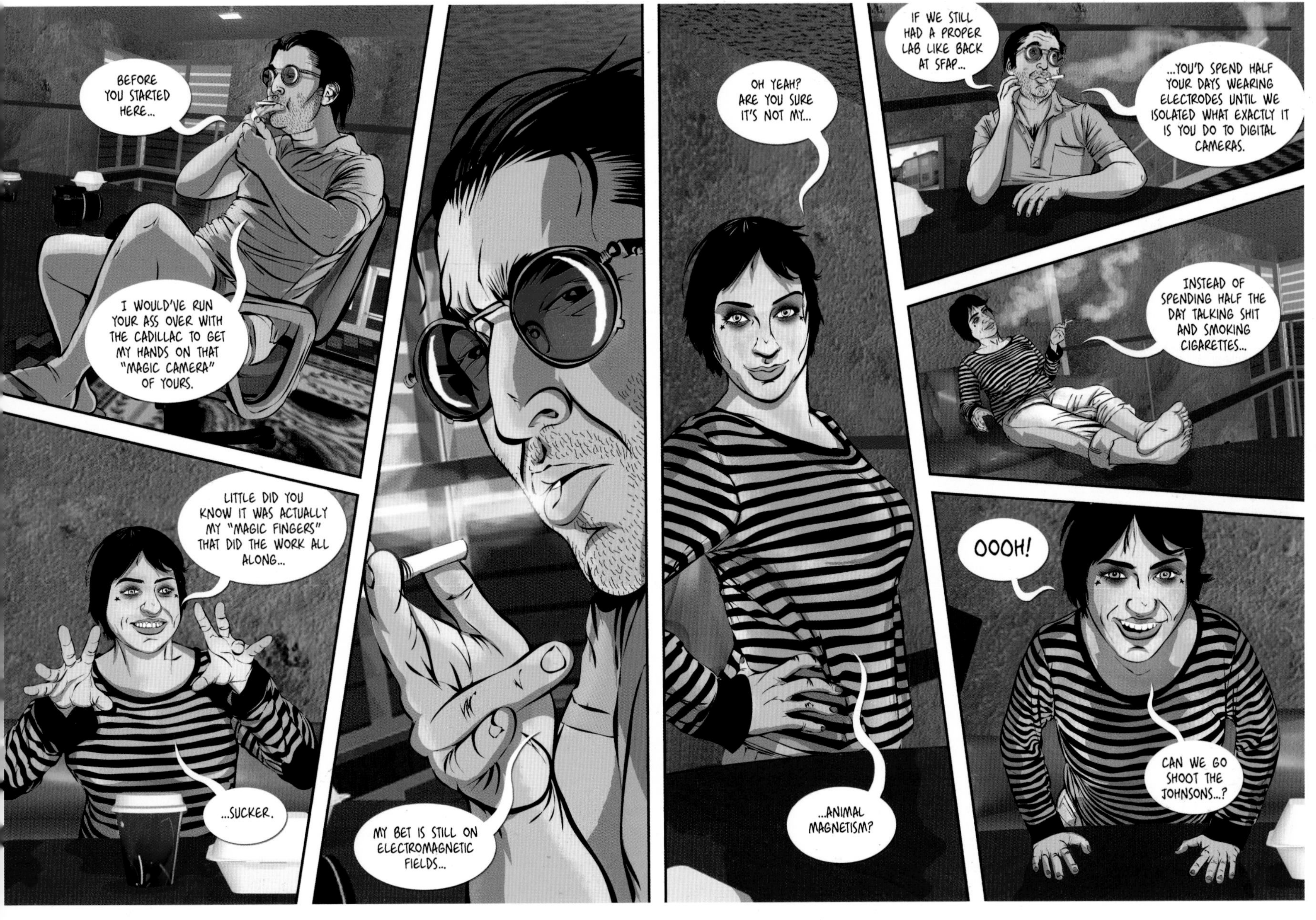
BEFORE YOU STARTED HERE...
I WOULD'VE RUN YOUR ASS OVER WITH THE CADILLAC TO GET MY HANDS ON THAT "MAGIC CAMERA" OF YOURS.
LITTLE DID YOU KNOW IT WAS ACTUALLY MY "MAGIC FINGERS" THAT DID THE WORK ALL ALONG...
...SUCKER.
MY BET IS STILL ON ELECTROMAGNETIC FIELDS...
OH YEAH? ARE YOU SURE IT'S NOT MY...
...ANIMAL MAGNETISM?
IF WE STILL HAD A PROPER LAB LIKE BACK AT SFAP...
...YOU'D SPEND HALF YOUR DAYS WEARING ELECTRODES UNTIL WE ISOLATED WHAT EXACTLY IT IS YOU DO TO DIGITAL CAMERAS.
INSTEAD OF SPENDING HALF THE DAY TALKING SHIT AND SMOKING CIGARETTES...
OOOH!
CAN WE GO SHOOT THE JOHNSONS...?

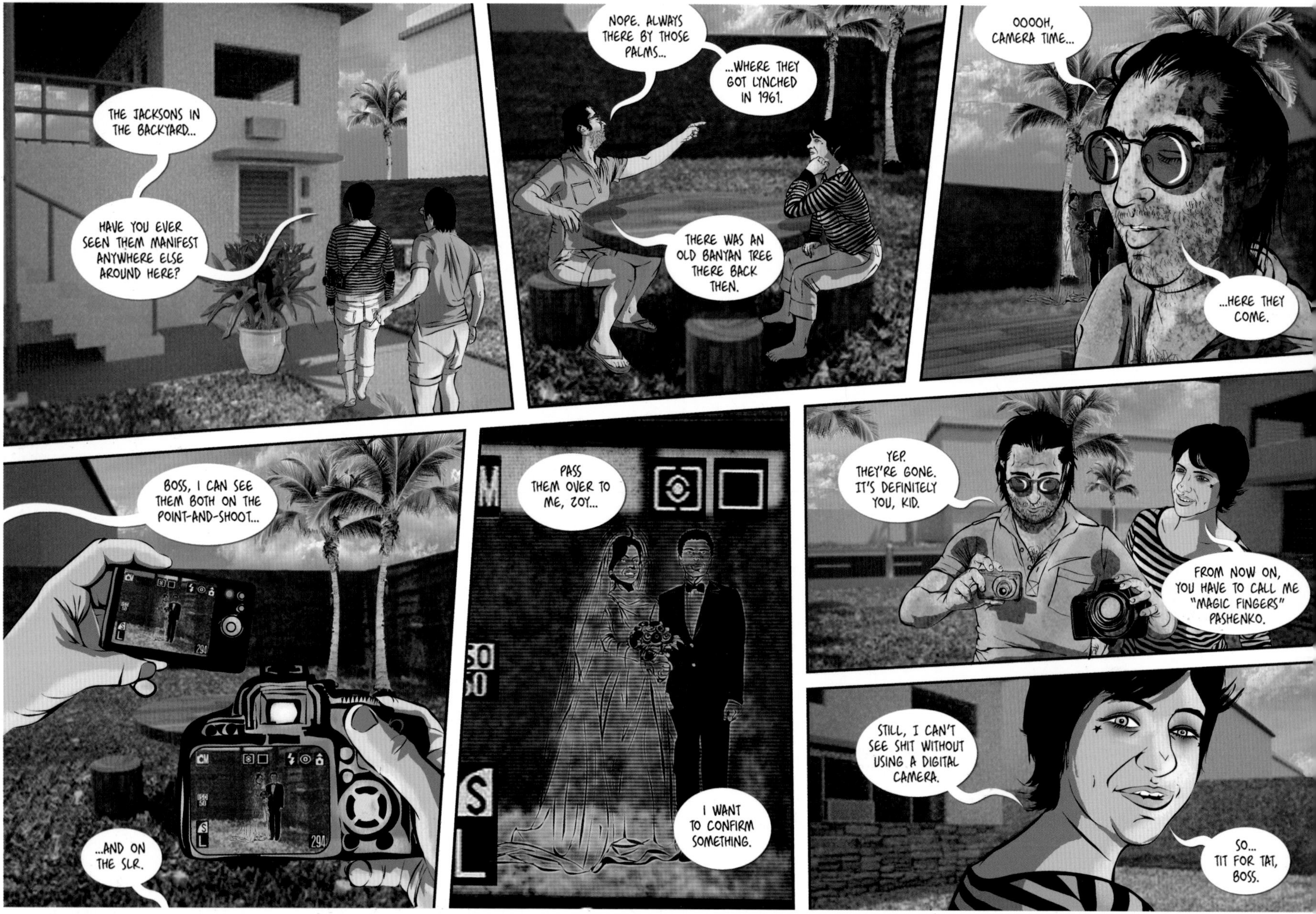
THE JACKSONS IN THE BACKYARD...
HAVE YOU EVER SEEN THEM MANIFEST ANYWHERE ELSE AROUND HERE?
NOPE. ALWAYS THERE BY THOSE PALMS...
...WHERE THEY GOT LYNCHED IN 1961.
THERE WAS AN OLD BANYAN TREE THERE BACK THEN.
OOOOH, CAMERA TIME...
...HERE THEY COME.
BOSS, I CAN SEE THEM BOTH ON THE POINT-AND-SHOOT...
...AND ON THE SLR.
PASS THEM OVER TO ME, ZOY...
I WANT TO CONFIRM SOMETHING.
YEP. THEY'RE GONE. IT'S DEFINITELY YOU, KID.
FROM NOW ON, YOU HAVE TO CALL ME "MAGIC FINGERS" PASHENKO.
STILL, I CAN'T SEE SHIT WITHOUT USING A DIGITAL CAMERA.
SO... TIT FOR TAT, BOSS.

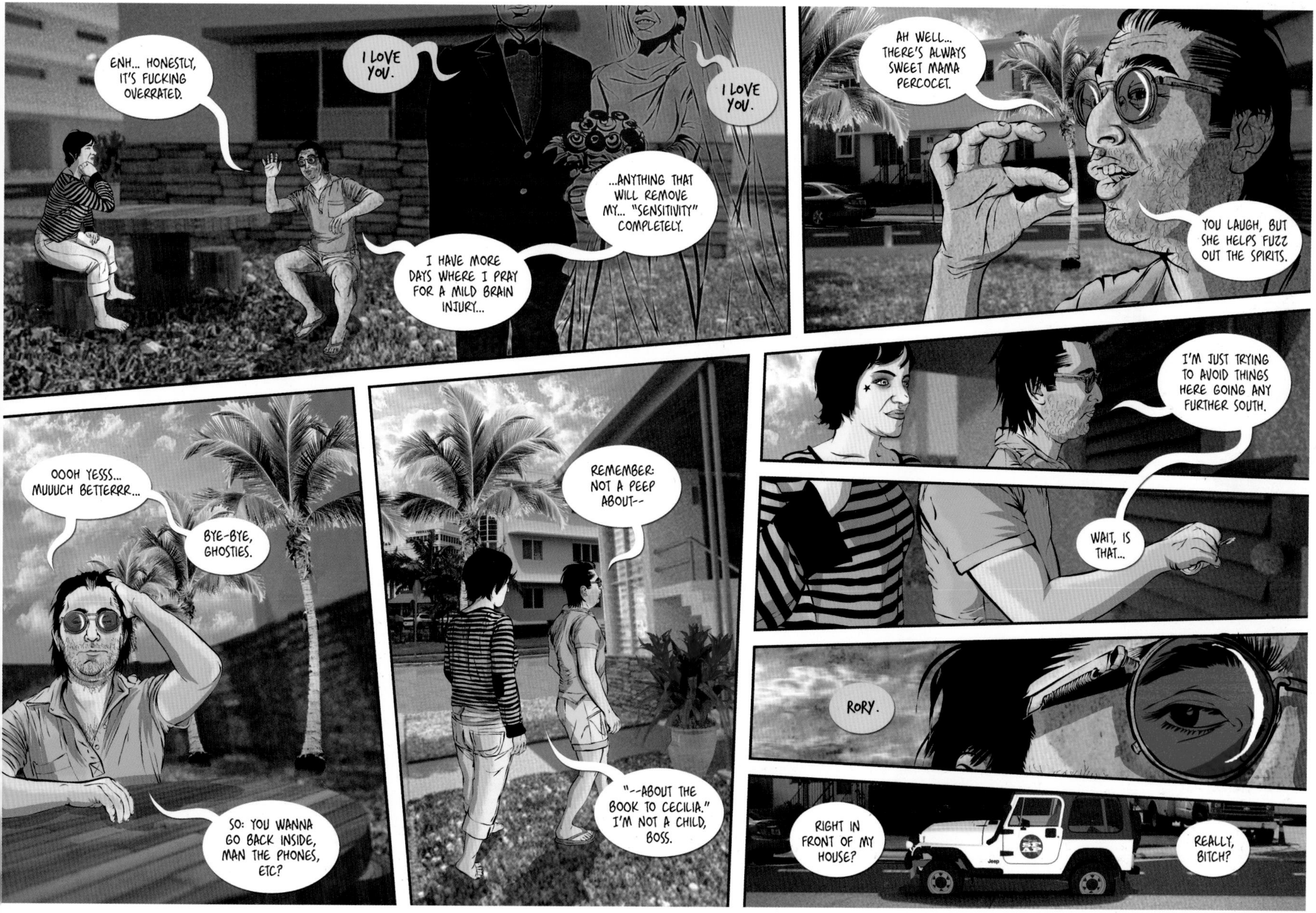
ENH... HONESTLY, IT'S FUCKING OVERRATED.
I LOVE YOU.
I LOVE YOU.
I HAVE MORE DAYS WHERE I PRAY FOR A MILD BRAIN INJURY...
...ANYTHING THAT WILL REMOVE MY... "SENSITIVITY" COMPLETELY.
AH WELL... THERE'S ALWAYS SWEET MAMA PERCOCET.
YOU LAUGH, BUT SHE HELPS FUZZ OUT THE SPIRITS.
OOOH YESSS... MUUUCH BETTERRR...
BYE-BYE, GHOSTIES.
SO: YOU WANNA GO BACK INSIDE, MAN THE PHONES, ETC?
REMEMBER: NOT A PEEP ABOUT--
"--ABOUT THE BOOK TO CECILIA." I'M NOT A CHILD, BOSS.
I'M JUST TRYING TO AVOID THINGS HERE GOING ANY FURTHER SOUTH.
WAIT, IS THAT...
RORY.
RIGHT IN FRONT OF MY HOUSE?
REALLY, BITCH?

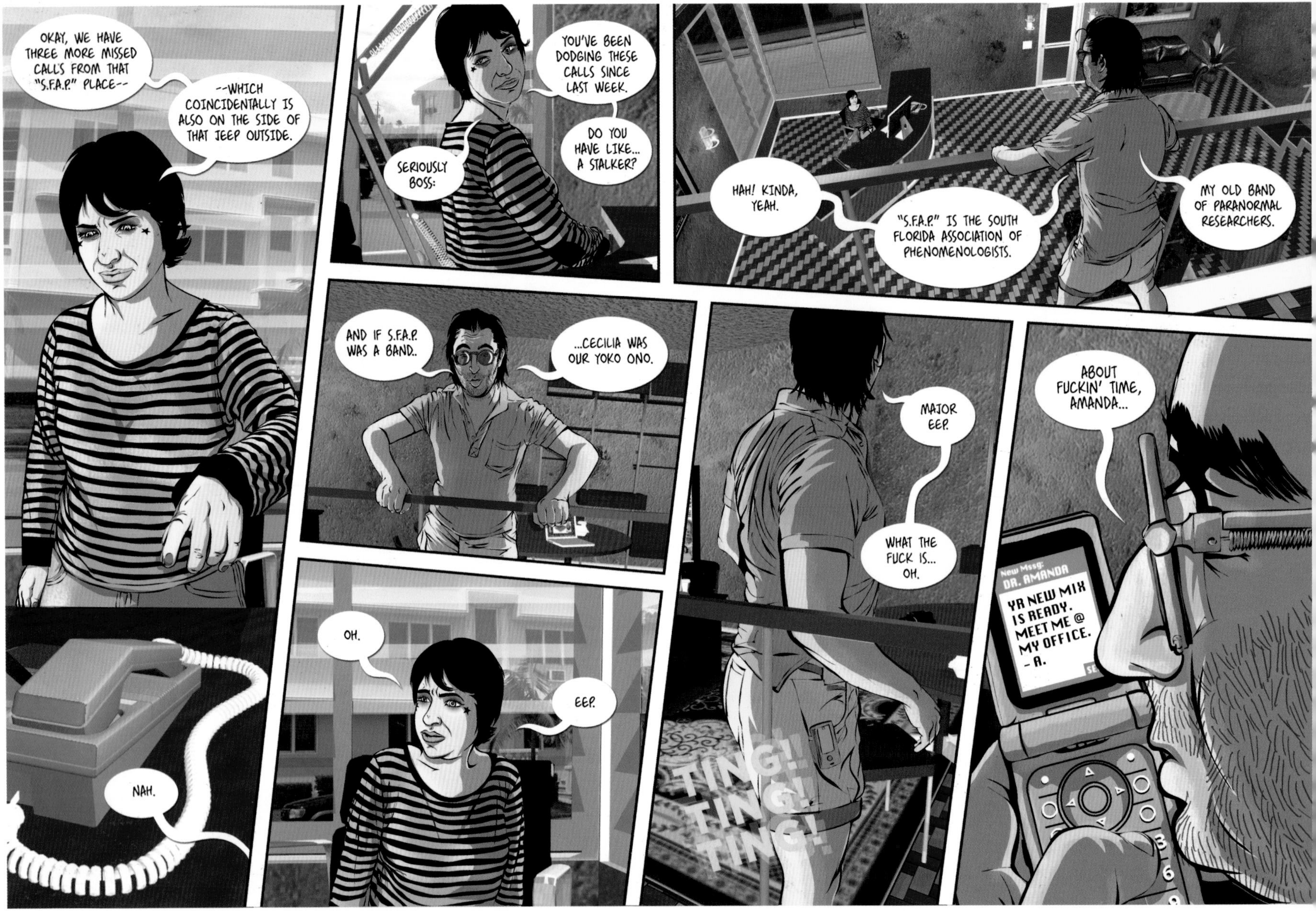
OKAY, WE HAVE THREE MORE MISSED CALLS FROM THAT "S.F.A.P." PLACE--
--WHICH COINCIDENTALLY IS ALSO ON THE SIDE OF THAT JEEP OUTSIDE.
YOU'VE BEEN DODGING THESE CALLS SINCE LAST WEEK.
SERIOUSLY BOSS:
DO YOU HAVE LIKE... A STALKER?
HAH! KINDA, YEAH.
"S.F.A.P." IS THE SOUTH FLORIDA ASSOCIATION OF PHENOMENOLOGISTS.
MY OLD BAND OF PARANORMAL RESEARCHERS.
AND IF S.F.A.P. WAS A BAND..
...CECILIA WAS OUR YOKO ONO.
NAH.
OH.
EEP.
MAJOR EEP.
WHAT THE FUCK IS... OH.
TING! TING! TING!
ABOUT FUCKIN' TIME, AMANDA...
New Mssg: DR. AMANDA
YR NEW MIX IS READY. MEET ME @ MY OFFICE. - A.

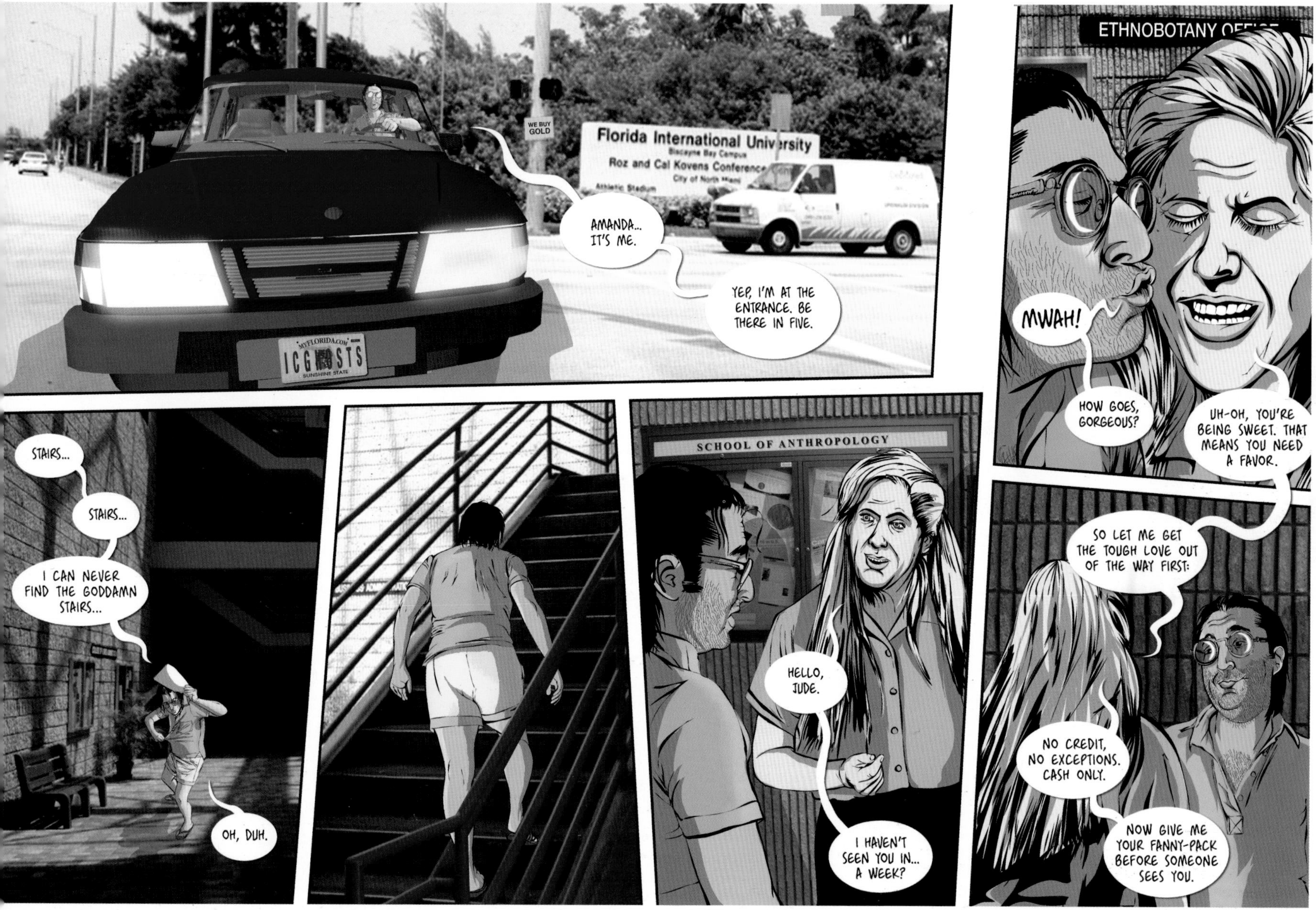

WE BUY GOLD
Florida International University
Biscayne Bay Campus
Roz and Cal Kovens Conference
City of North Miami
Athletic Stadium
AMANDA... IT'S ME.
YEP, I'M AT THE ENTRANCE. BE THERE IN FIVE.
MYFLORIDA.COM
SUNSHINE STATE
ETHNOBOTANY OFFICE
MWAH!
HOW GOES, GORGEOUS?
UH-OH, YOU'RE BEING SWEET. THAT MEANS YOU NEED A FAVOR.
STAIRS...
STAIRS...
I CAN NEVER FIND THE GODDAMN STAIRS...
OH, DUH.
SCHOOL OF ANTHROPOLOGY
HELLO, JUDE.
I HAVEN'T SEEN YOU IN... A WEEK?
SO LET ME GET THE TOUGH LOVE OUT OF THE WAY FIRST:
NO CREDIT, NO EXCEPTIONS. CASH ONLY.
NOW GIVE ME YOUR FANNY-PACK BEFORE SOMEONE SEES YOU.

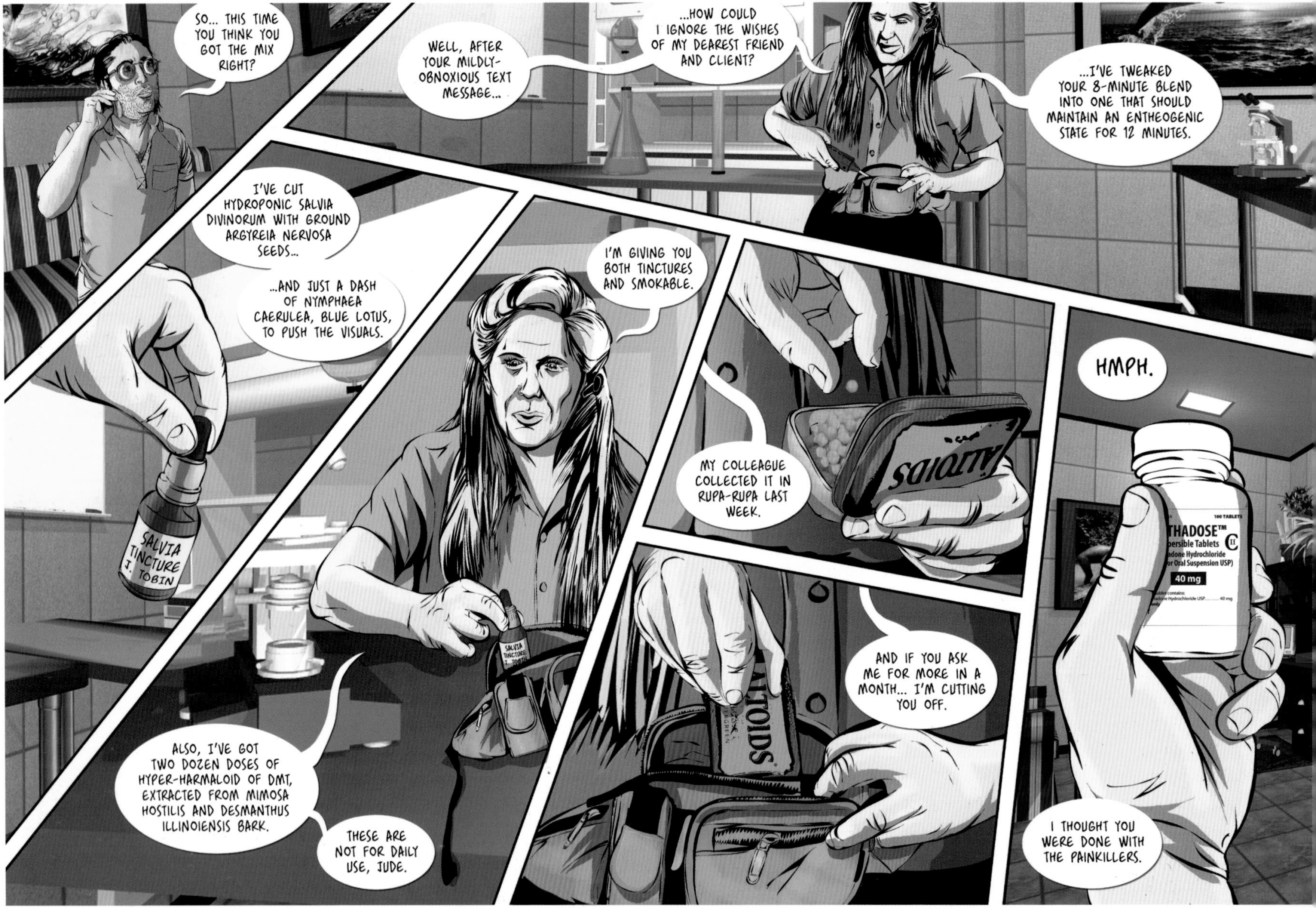
SO... THIS TIME YOU THINK YOU GOT THE MIX RIGHT?
WELL, AFTER YOUR MILDLY-OBNOXIOUS TEXT MESSAGE...
...HOW COULD I IGNORE THE WISHES OF MY DEAREST FRIEND AND CLIENT?
...I'VE TWEAKED YOUR 8-MINUTE BLEND INTO ONE THAT SHOULD MAINTAIN AN ENTHEOGENIC STATE FOR 12 MINUTES.
I'VE CUT HYDROPONIC SALVIA DIVINORUM WITH GROUND ARGYREIA NERVOSA SEEDS...
...AND JUST A DASH OF NYMPHAEA CAERULEA, BLUE LOTUS, TO PUSH THE VISUALS.
SALVIA TINCTURE J. TOBIN
I'M GIVING YOU BOTH TINCTURES AND SMOKABLE.
ALSO, I'VE GOT TWO DOZEN DOSES OF HYPER-HARMALOID OF DMT, EXTRACTED FROM MIMOSA HOSTILIS AND DESMANTHUS ILLINOIENSIS BARK.
THESE ARE NOT FOR DAILY USE, JUDE.
MY COLLEAGUE COLLECTED IT IN RUPA-RUPA LAST WEEK.
AND IF YOU ASK ME FOR MORE IN A MONTH... I'M CUTTING YOU OFF.
HMPH.
40 mg
I THOUGHT YOU WERE DONE WITH THE PAINKILLERS.

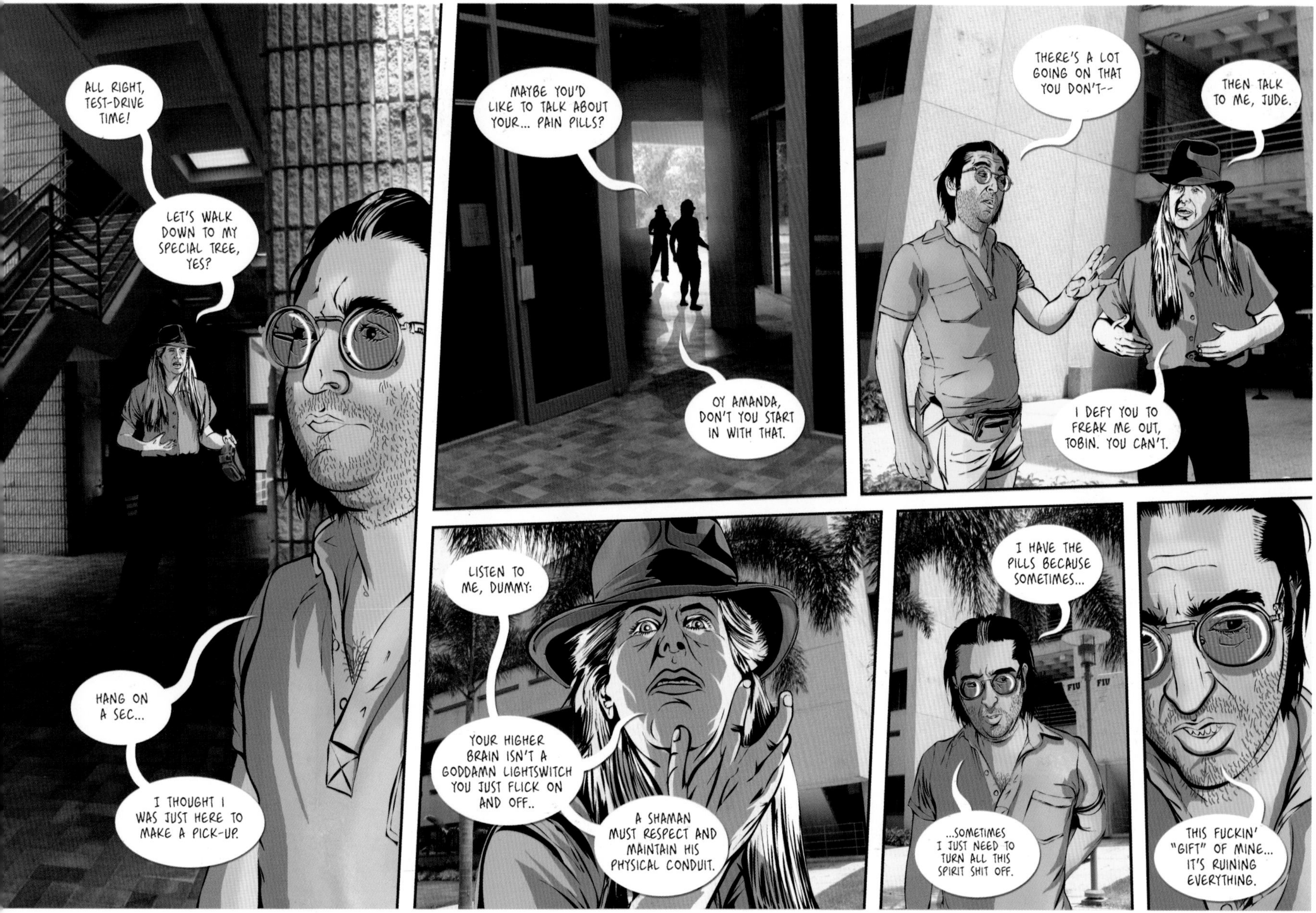
ALL RIGHT, TEST-DRIVE TIME!
LET'S WALK DOWN TO MY SPECIAL TREE, YES?
HANG ON A SEC...
I THOUGHT I WAS JUST HERE TO MAKE A PICK-UP.
MAYBE YOU'D LIKE TO TALK ABOUT YOUR... PAIN PILLS?
OY AMANDA, DON'T YOU START IN WITH THAT.
THERE'S A LOT GOING ON THAT YOU DON'T--
THEN TALK TO ME, JUDE.
I DEFY YOU TO FREAK ME OUT, TOBIN. YOU CAN'T.
LISTEN TO ME, DUMMY:
YOUR HIGHER BRAIN ISN'T A GODDAMN LIGHTSWITCH YOU JUST FLICK ON AND OFF..
A SHAMAN MUST RESPECT AND MAINTAIN HIS PHYSICAL CONDUIT.
I HAVE THE PILLS BECAUSE SOMETIMES...
...SOMETIMES I JUST NEED TO TURN ALL THIS SPIRIT SHIT OFF.
THIS FUCKIN' "GIFT" OF MINE... IT'S RUINING EVERYTHING.

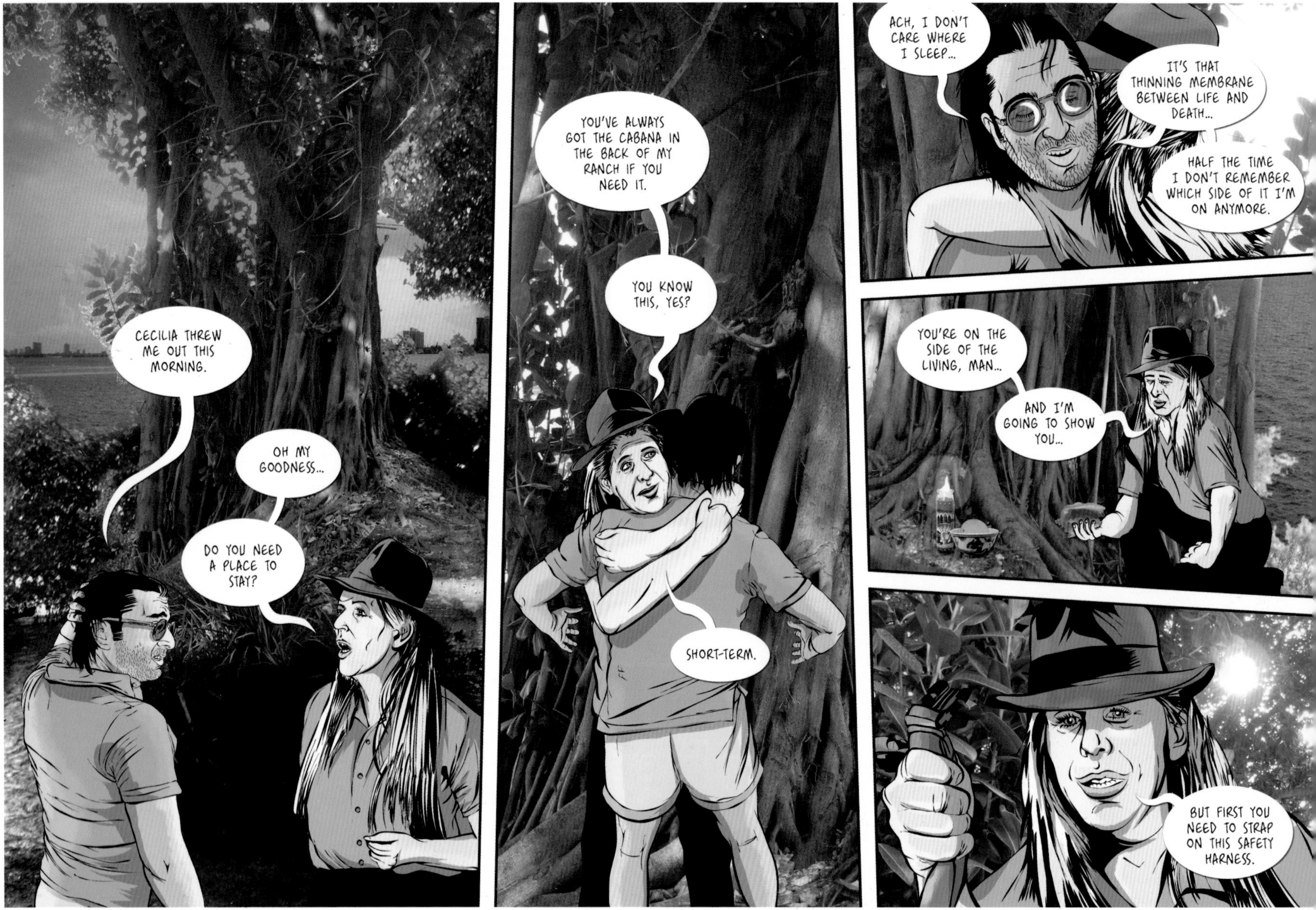
CECILIA THREW ME OUT THIS MORNING.
OH MY GOODNESS...
DO YOU NEED A PLACE TO STAY?
YOU'VE ALWAYS GOT THE CABANA IN THE BACK OF MY RANCH IF YOU NEED IT.
YOU KNOW THIS, YES?
SHORT-TERM.
ACH, I DON'T CARE WHERE I SLEEP...
IT'S THAT THINNING MEMBRANE BETWEEN LIFE AND DEATH...
HALF THE TIME I DON'T REMEMBER WHICH SIDE OF IT I'M ON ANYMORE.
YOU'RE ON THE SIDE OF THE LIVING, MAN...
AND I'M GOING TO SHOW YOU...
BUT FIRST YOU NEED TO STRAP ON THIS SAFETY HARNESS.

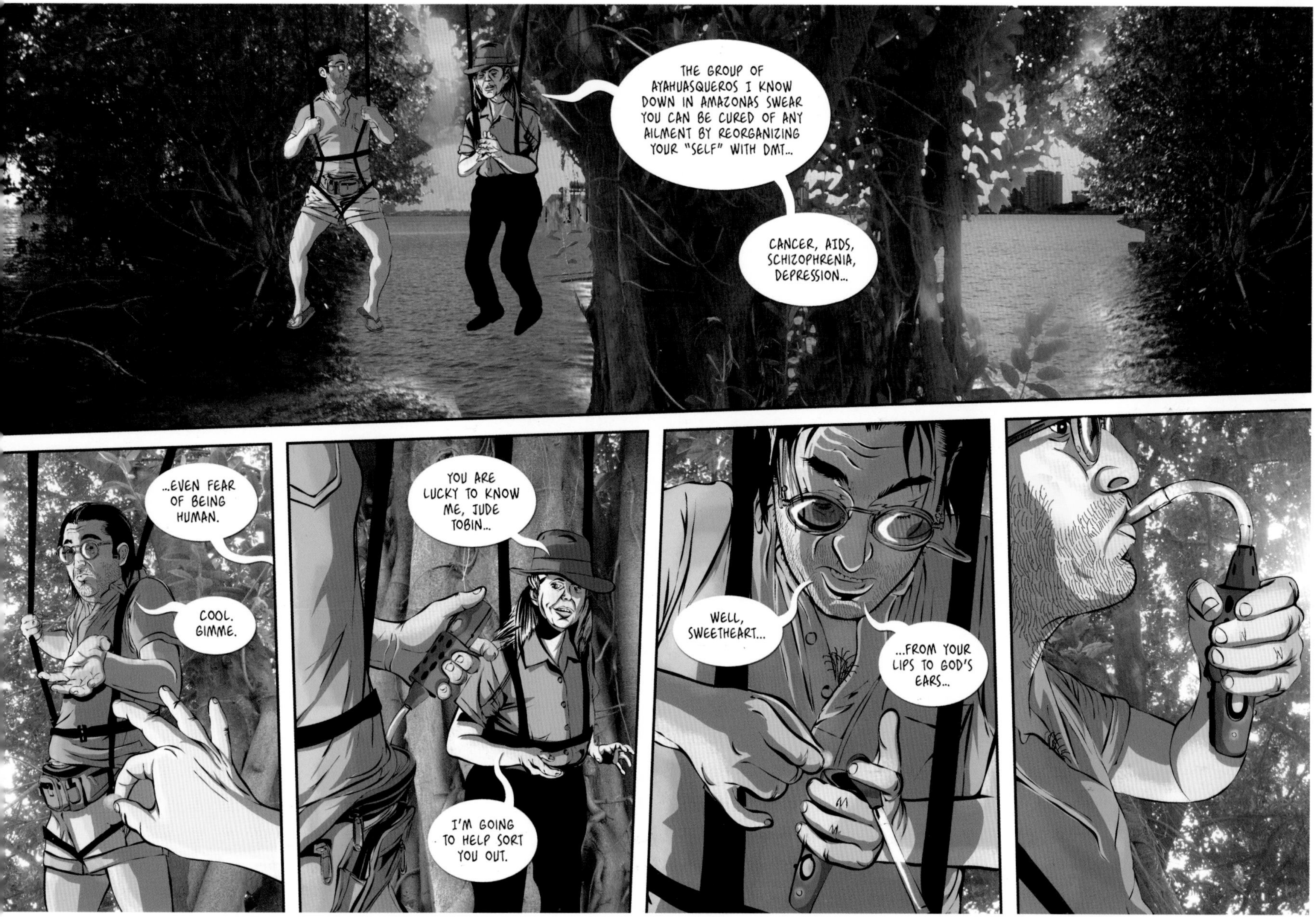
THE GROUP OF AYAHUASQUEROS I KNOW DOWN IN AMAZONAS SWEAR YOU CAN BE CURED OF ANY AILMENT BY REORGANIZING YOUR "SELF" WITH DMT...
CANCER, AIDS, SCHIZOPHRENIA, DEPRESSION...
...EVEN FEAR OF BEING HUMAN.
COOL. GIMME.
YOU ARE LUCKY TO KNOW ME, JUDE TOBIN...
I'M GOING TO HELP SORT YOU OUT.
WELL, SWEETHEART...
...FROM YOUR LIPS TO GOD'S EARS...

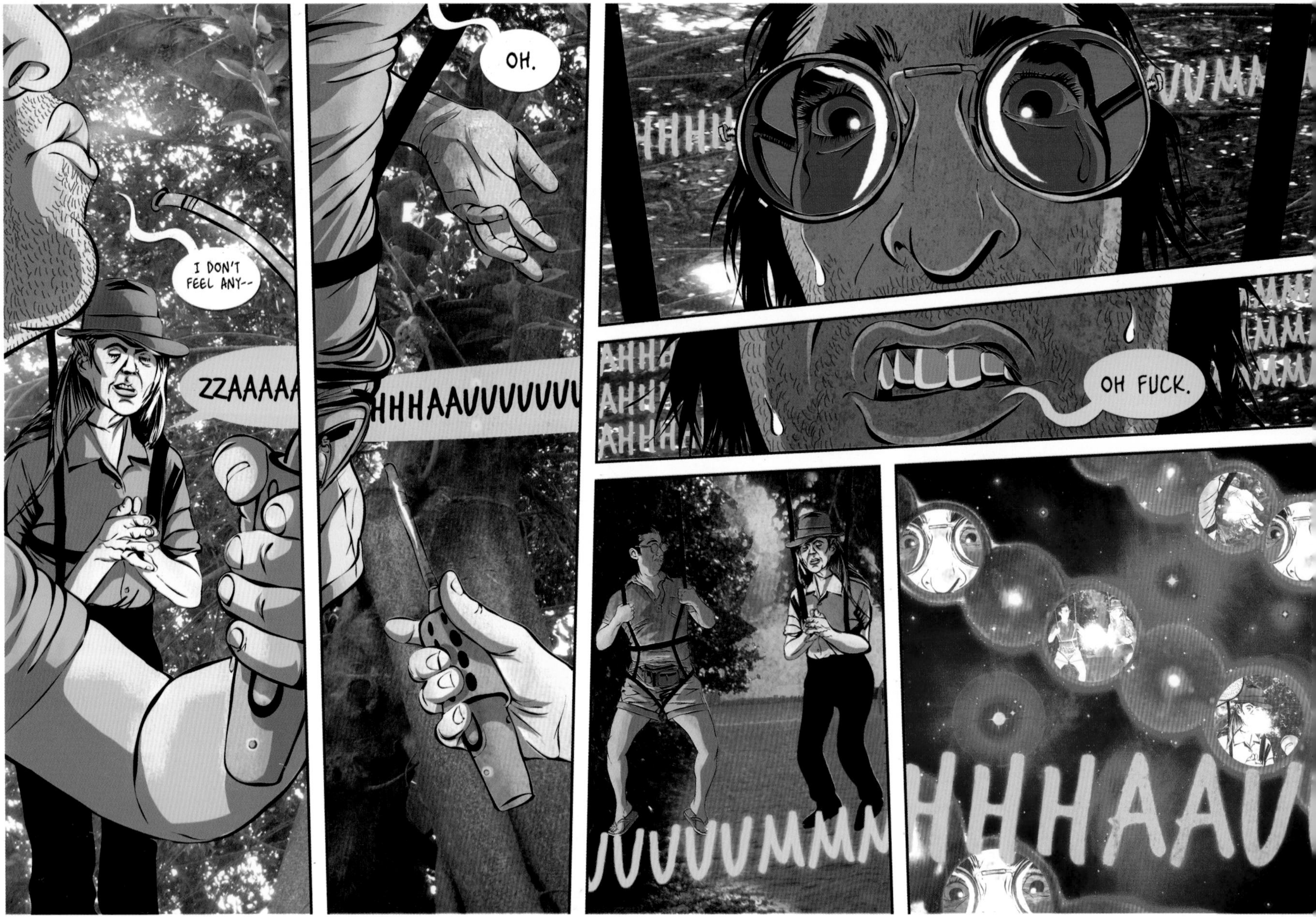

I DON'T FEEL ANY--
ZZAAAAA
OH.
HHHAAUUUUUU
HHHH
UUMM
AHHH
AHHH
AHHH
MMM
MMM
MMM
OH FUCK.
UUUUMMM
HHHAAU

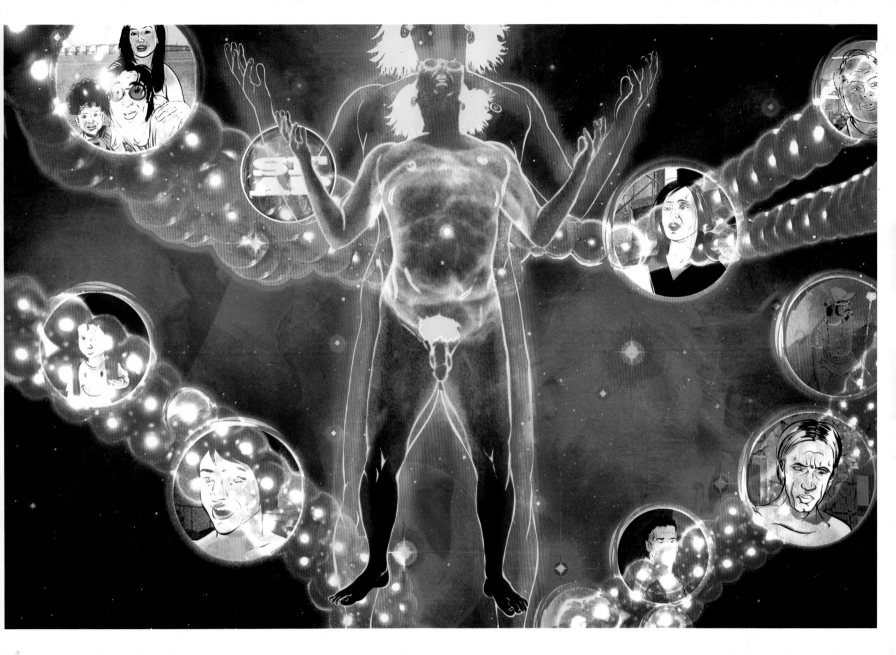

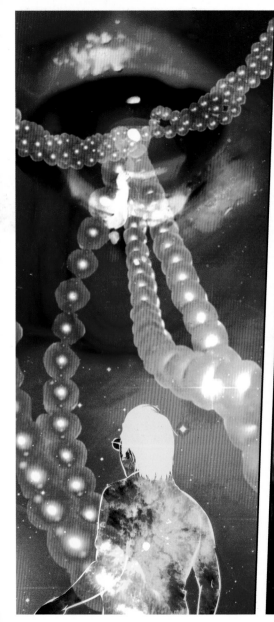

CECILIA...

SURE, HE'S A PART OF ME...

...ONE I WANT SURGICALLY REMOVED.

MUH!

BORT!

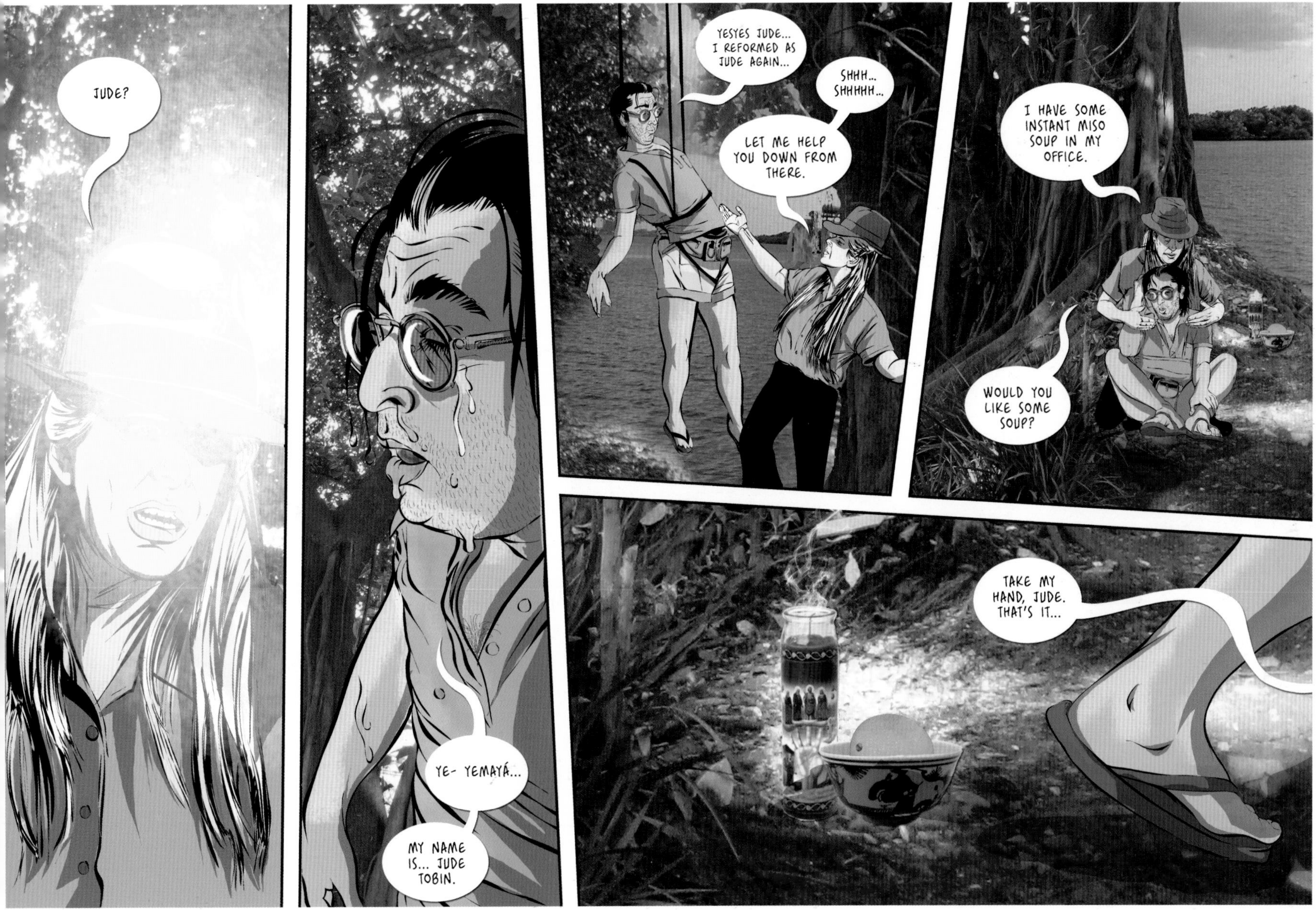
JUDE?
YE- YEMAYÁ...
MY NAME IS... JUDE TOBIN.
YESYES JUDE... I REFORMED AS JUDE AGAIN...
SHHH... SHHHHH...
LET ME HELP YOU DOWN FROM THERE.
I HAVE SOME INSTANT MISO SOUP IN MY OFFICE.
WOULD YOU LIKE SOME SOUP?
TAKE MY HAND, JUDE. THAT'S IT...

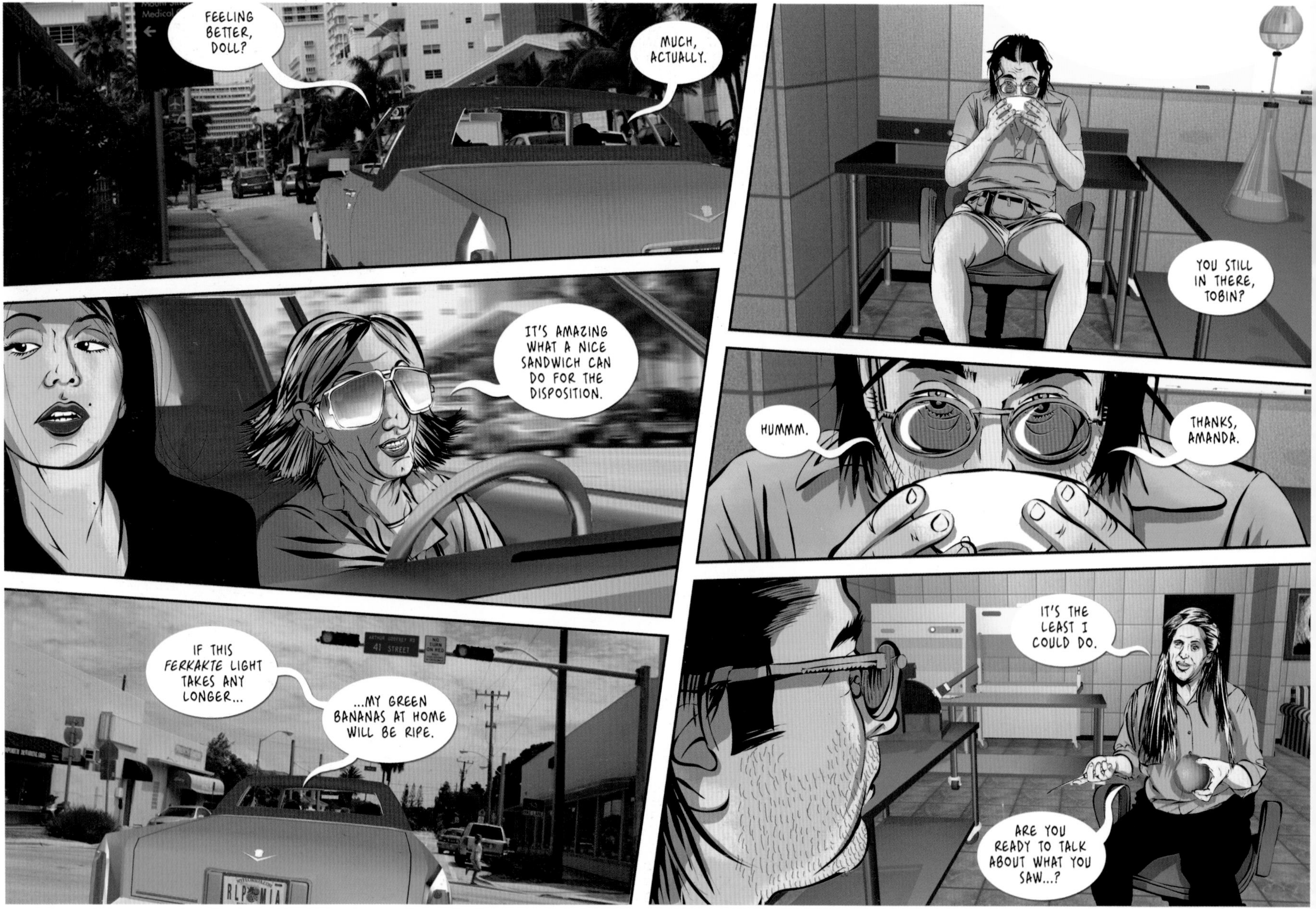
Medical
FEELING BETTER, DOLL?
MUCH, ACTUALLY.
IT'S AMAZING WHAT A NICE SANDWICH CAN DO FOR THE DISPOSITION.
41 STREET
IF THIS FERKAKTE LIGHT TAKES ANY LONGER...
...MY GREEN BANANAS AT HOME WILL BE RIPE.
YOU STILL IN THERE, TOBIN?
HUMMM.
THANKS, AMANDA.
IT'S THE LEAST I COULD DO.
ARE YOU READY TO TALK ABOUT WHAT YOU SAW...?

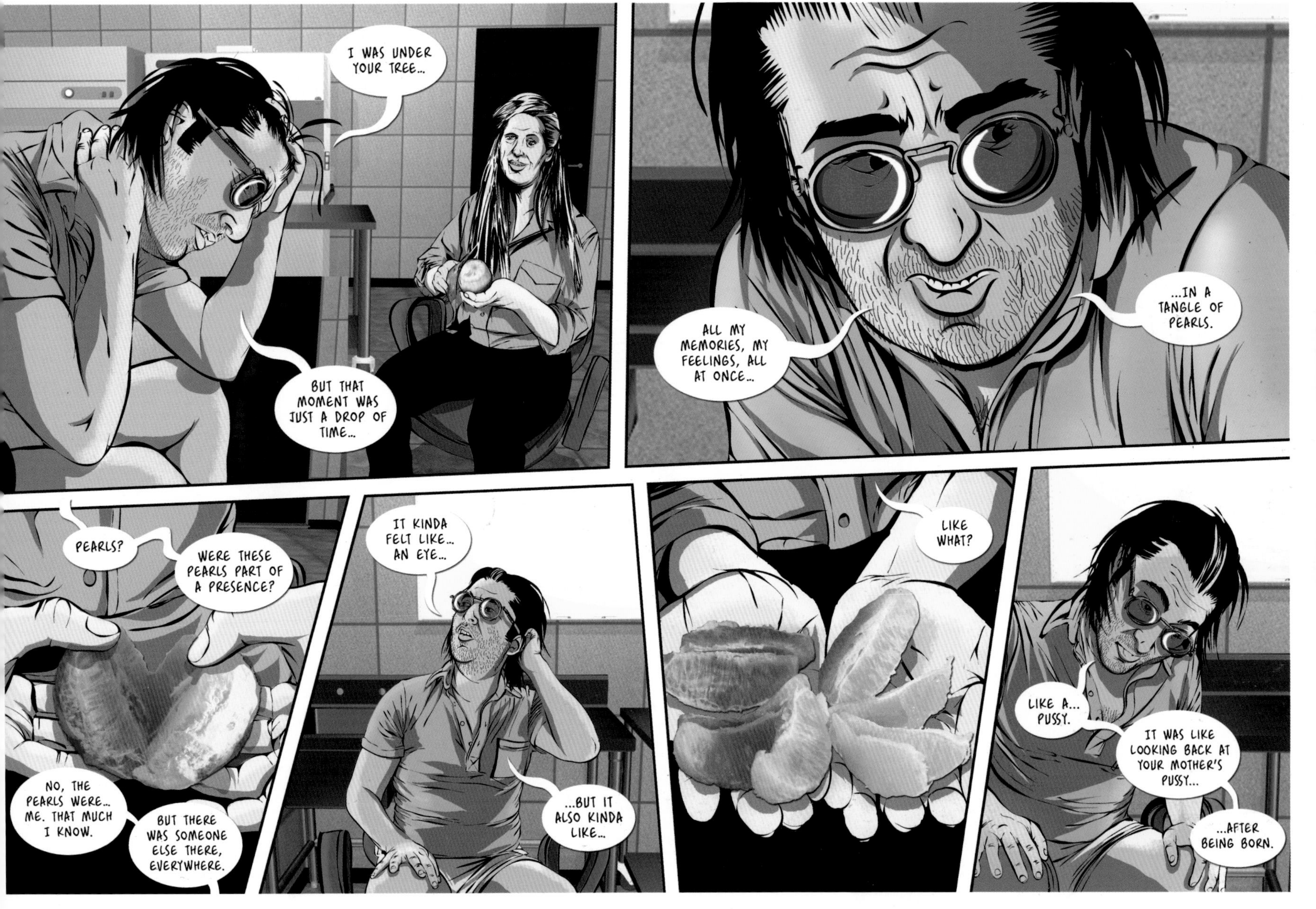
I WAS UNDER YOUR TREE...
BUT THAT MOMENT WAS JUST A DROP OF TIME...
ALL MY MEMORIES, MY FEELINGS, ALL AT ONCE...
...IN A TANGLE OF PEARLS.
PEARLS?
WERE THESE PEARLS PART OF A PRESENCE?
NO, THE PEARLS WERE... ME. THAT MUCH I KNOW.
BUT THERE WAS SOMEONE ELSE THERE, EVERYWHERE.
IT KINDA FELT LIKE... AN EYE...
...BUT IT ALSO KINDA LIKE...
LIKE WHAT?
LIKE A... PUSSY.
IT WAS LIKE LOOKING BACK AT YOUR MOTHER'S PUSSY...
...AFTER BEING BORN.

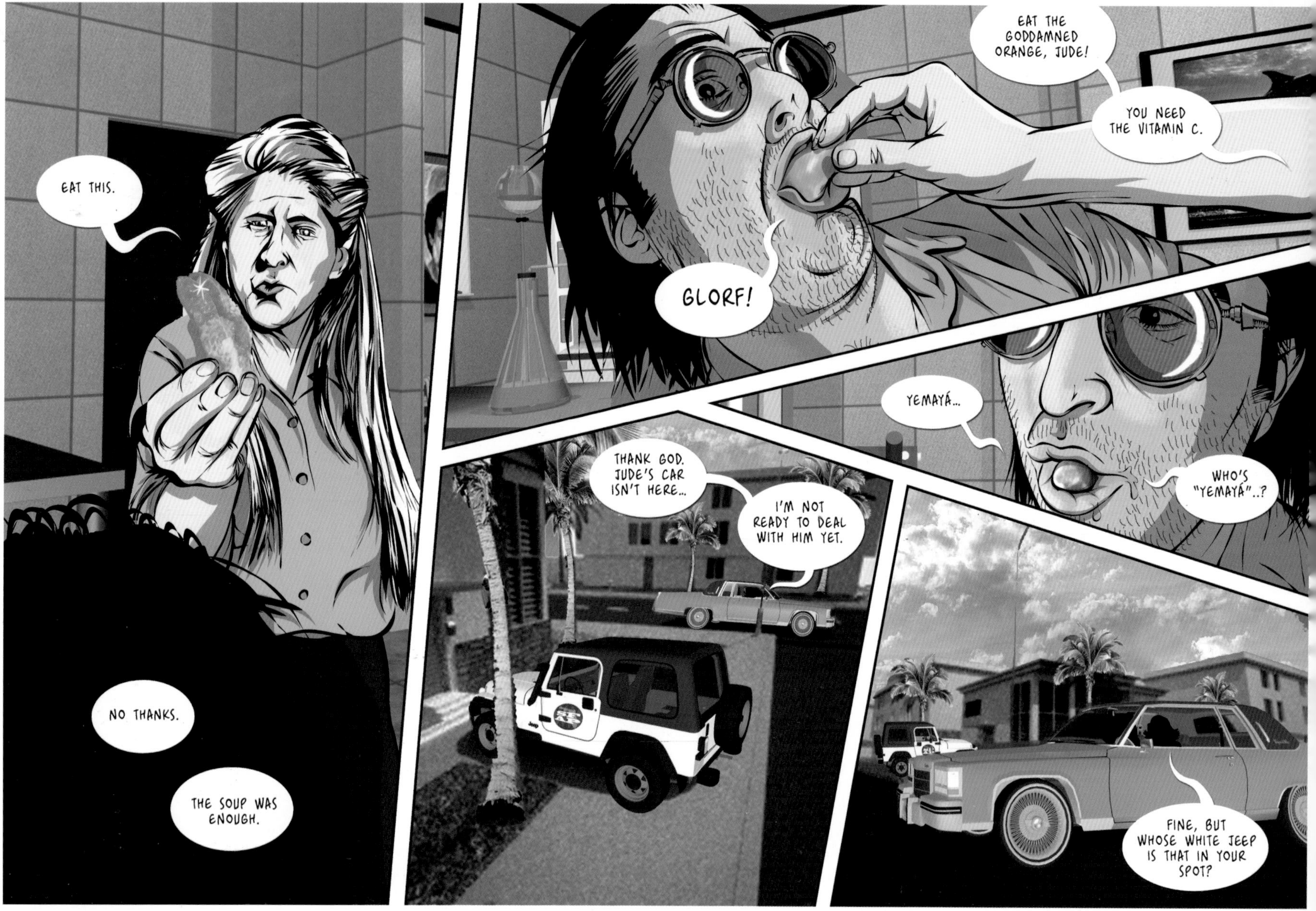
EAT THIS.
NO THANKS.
THE SOUP WAS ENOUGH.
EAT THE GODDAMNED ORANGE, JUDE!
YOU NEED THE VITAMIN C.
GLORF!
YEMAYÁ...
WHO'S "YEMAYÁ"..?
THANK GOD. JUDE'S CAR ISN'T HERE...
I'M NOT READY TO DEAL WITH HIM YET.
FINE, BUT WHOSE WHITE JEEP IS THAT IN YOUR SPOT?

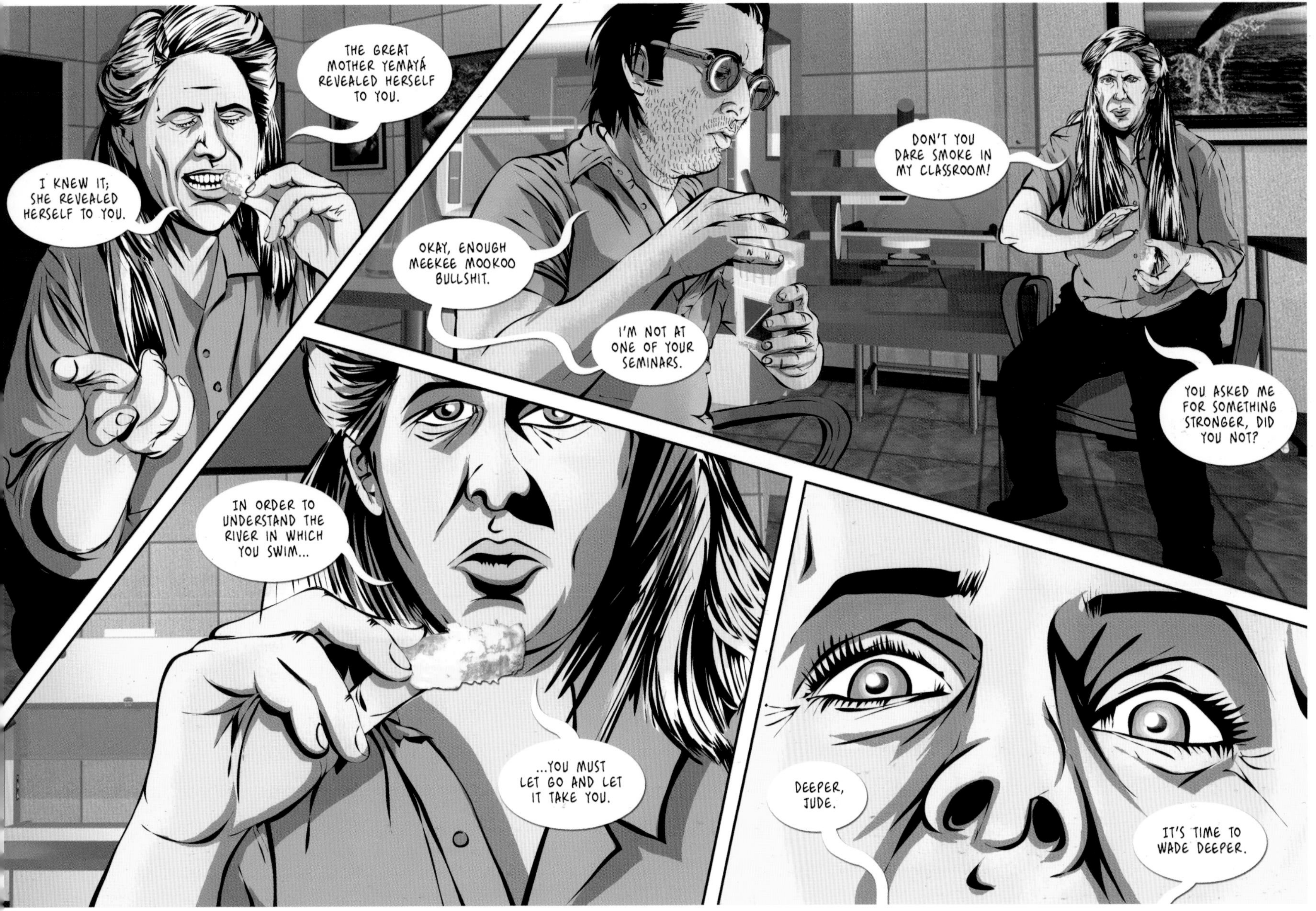
THE GREAT MOTHER YEMAYÁ REVEALED HERSELF TO YOU.
I KNEW IT; SHE REVEALED HERSELF TO YOU.
OKAY, ENOUGH MEEKEE MOOKOO BULLSHIT.
I'M NOT AT ONE OF YOUR SEMINARS.
DON'T YOU DARE SMOKE IN MY CLASSROOM!
YOU ASKED ME FOR SOMETHING STRONGER, DID YOU NOT?
IN ORDER TO UNDERSTAND THE RIVER IN WHICH YOU SWIM...
...YOU MUST LET GO AND LET IT TAKE YOU.
DEEPER, JUDE.
IT'S TIME TO WADE DEEPER.

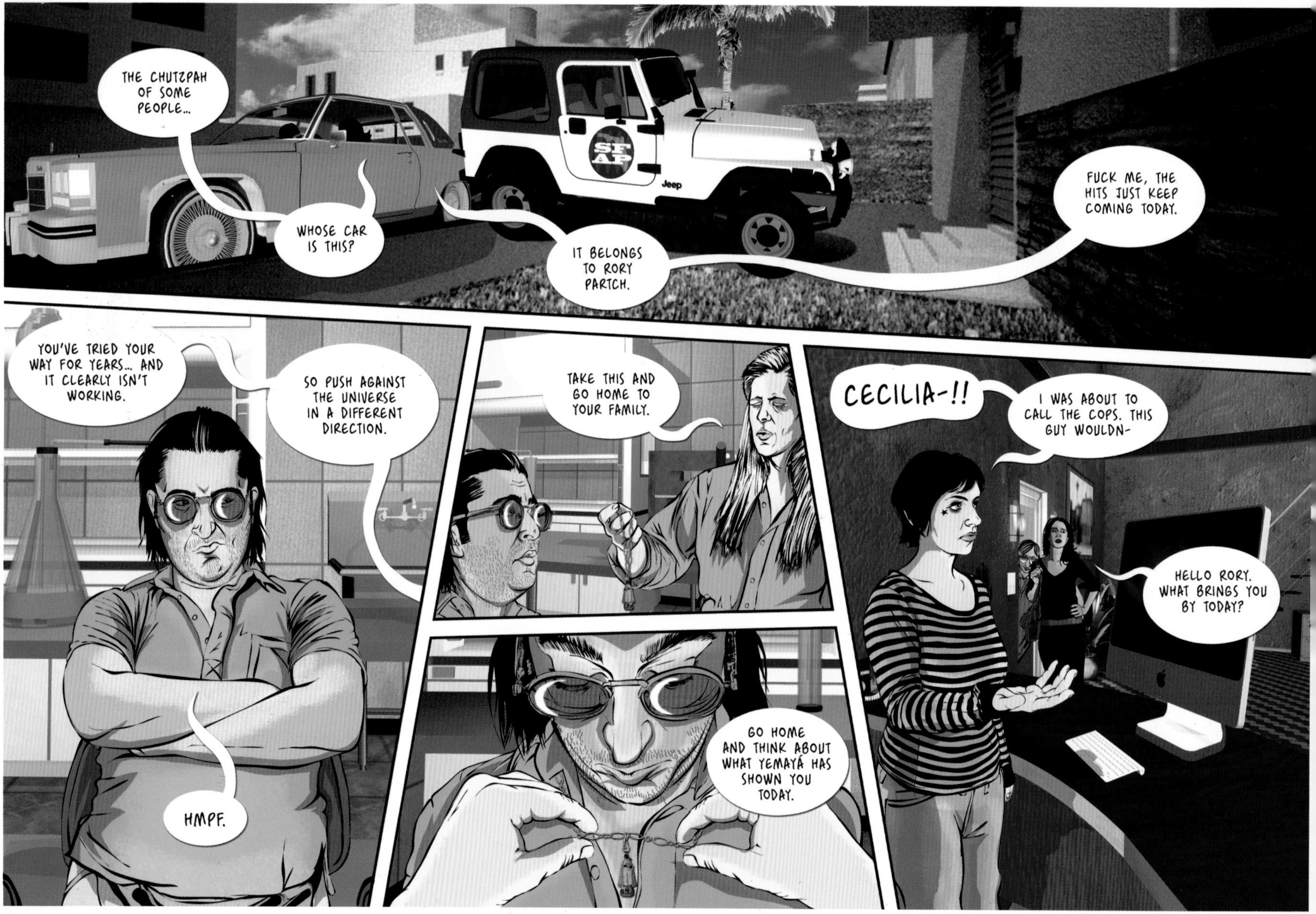

THE CHUTZPAH OF SOME PEOPLE...
WHOSE CAR IS THIS?
IT BELONGS TO RORY PARTCH.
FUCK ME, THE HITS JUST KEEP COMING TODAY.
YOU'VE TRIED YOUR WAY FOR YEARS... AND IT CLEARLY ISN'T WORKING.
SO PUSH AGAINST THE UNIVERSE IN A DIFFERENT DIRECTION.
HMPF.
TAKE THIS AND GO HOME TO YOUR FAMILY.
GO HOME AND THINK ABOUT WHAT YEMAYÁ HAS SHOWN YOU TODAY.
CECILIA-!!
I WAS ABOUT TO CALL THE COPS. THIS GUY WOULDN-
HELLO RORY. WHAT BRINGS YOU BY TODAY?

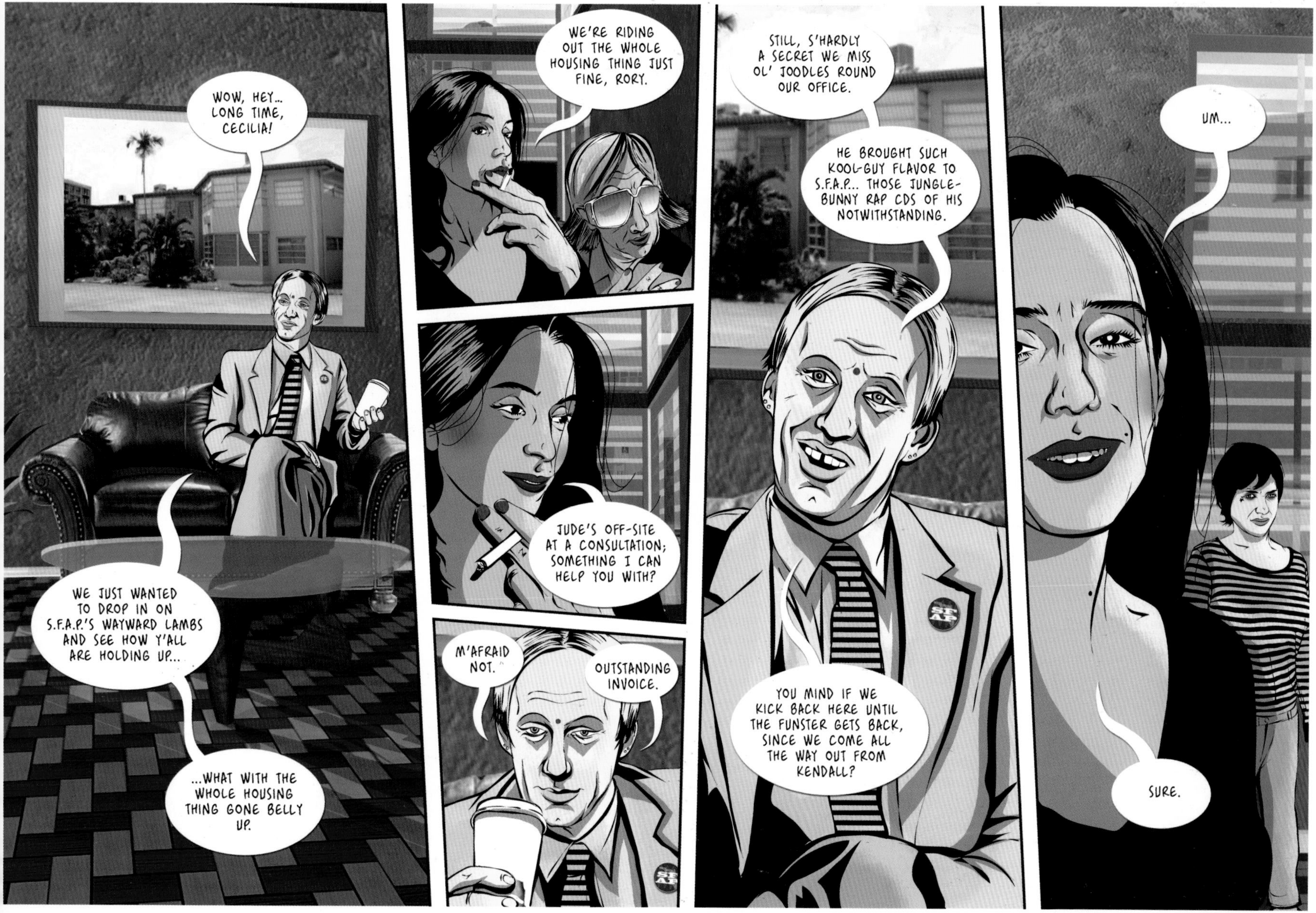
WOW, HEY... LONG TIME, CECILIA!
WE JUST WANTED TO DROP IN ON S.F.A.P.'S WAYWARD LAMBS AND SEE HOW Y'ALL ARE HOLDING UP...
...WHAT WITH THE WHOLE HOUSING THING GONE BELLY UP.
WE'RE RIDING OUT THE WHOLE HOUSING THING JUST FINE, RORY.
JUDE'S OFF-SITE AT A CONSULTATION; SOMETHING I CAN HELP YOU WITH?
M'AFRAID NOT.
OUTSTANDING INVOICE.
STILL, S'HARDLY A SECRET WE MISS OL' JOODLES ROUND OUR OFFICE.
HE BROUGHT SUCH KOOL-GUY FLAVOR TO S.F.A.P... THOSE JUNGLE-BUNNY RAP CDS OF HIS NOTWITHSTANDING.
YOU MIND IF WE KICK BACK HERE UNTIL THE FUNSTER GETS BACK, SINCE WE COME ALL THE WAY OUT FROM KENDALL?
UM...
SURE.

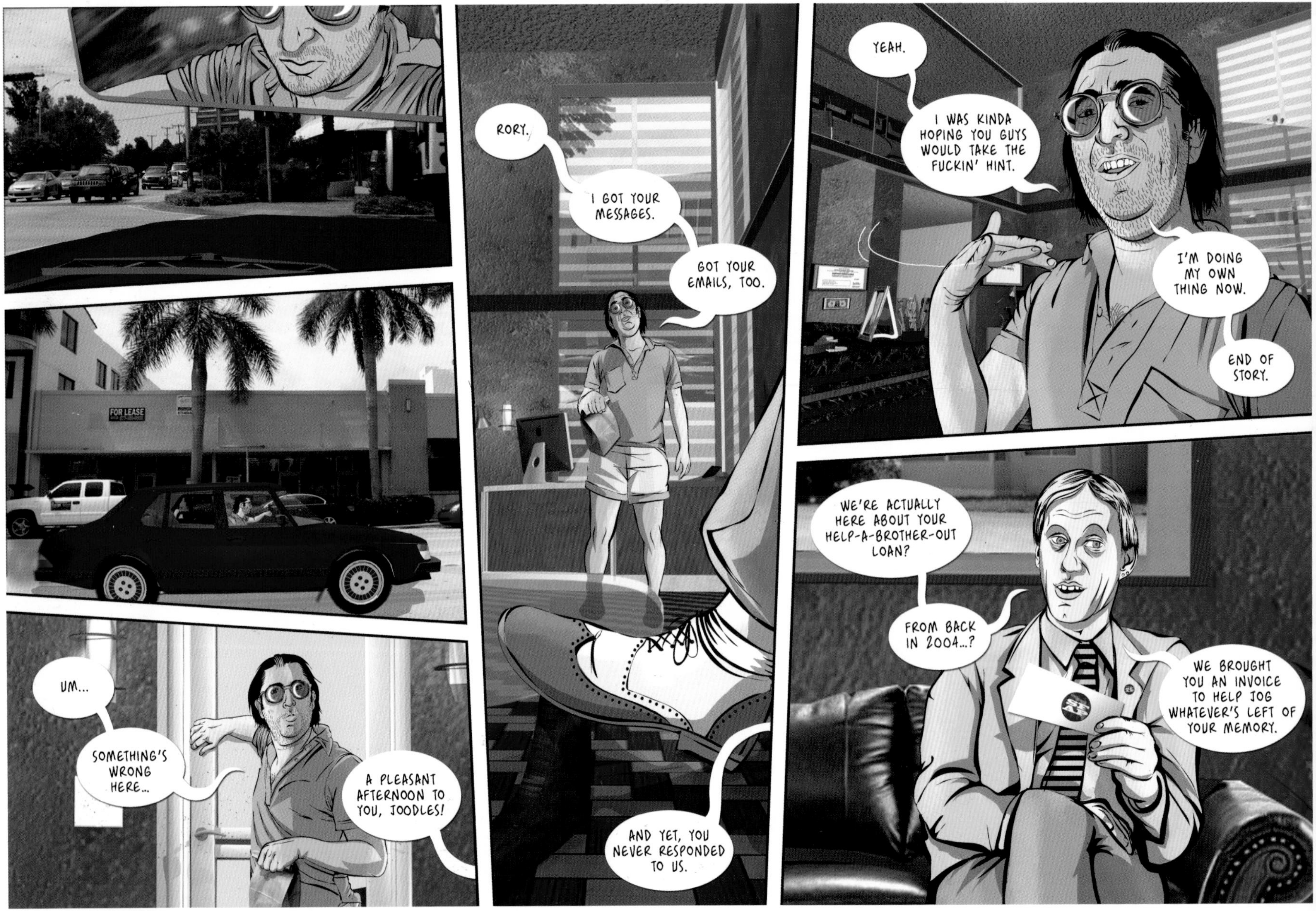
FOR LEASE
UM...
SOMETHING'S WRONG HERE...
A PLEASANT AFTERNOON TO YOU, JOODLES!
RORY.
I GOT YOUR MESSAGES.
GOT YOUR EMAILS, TOO.
AND YET, YOU NEVER RESPONDED TO US.
YEAH.
I WAS KINDA HOPING YOU GUYS WOULD TAKE THE FUCKIN' HINT.
I'M DOING MY OWN THING NOW.
END OF STORY.
WE'RE ACTUALLY HERE ABOUT YOUR HELP-A-BROTHER-OUT LOAN?
FROM BACK IN 2004...?
WE BROUGHT YOU AN INVOICE TO HELP JOG WHATEVER'S LEFT OF YOUR MEMORY.

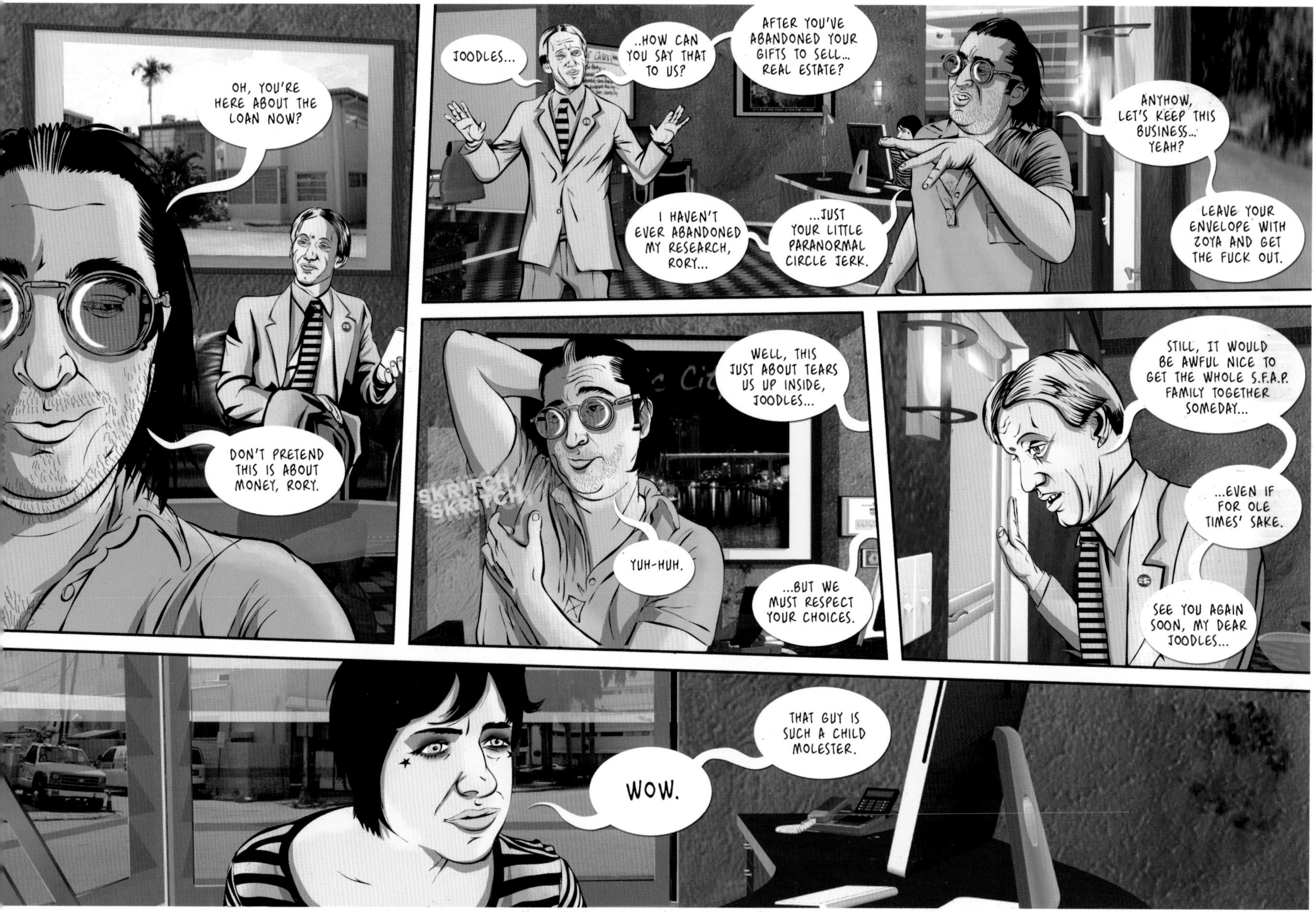

OH, YOU'RE HERE ABOUT THE LOAN NOW?
DON'T PRETEND THIS IS ABOUT MONEY, RORY.
JOODLES...
..HOW CAN YOU SAY THAT TO US?
AFTER YOU'VE ABANDONED YOUR GIFTS TO SELL... REAL ESTATE?
I HAVEN'T EVER ABANDONED MY RESEARCH, RORY...
...JUST YOUR LITTLE PARANORMAL CIRCLE JERK.
ANYHOW, LET'S KEEP THIS BUSINESS... YEAH?
LEAVE YOUR ENVELOPE WITH ZOYA AND GET THE FUCK OUT.
WELL, THIS JUST ABOUT TEARS US UP INSIDE, JOODLES...
SKRITCH SKRITCH
YUH-HUH.
...BUT WE MUST RESPECT YOUR CHOICES.
STILL, IT WOULD BE AWFUL NICE TO GET THE WHOLE S.F.A.P. FAMILY TOGETHER SOMEDAY...
...EVEN IF FOR OLE TIMES' SAKE.
SEE YOU AGAIN SOON, MY DEAR JOODLES...
WOW.
THAT GUY IS SUCH A CHILD MOLESTER.

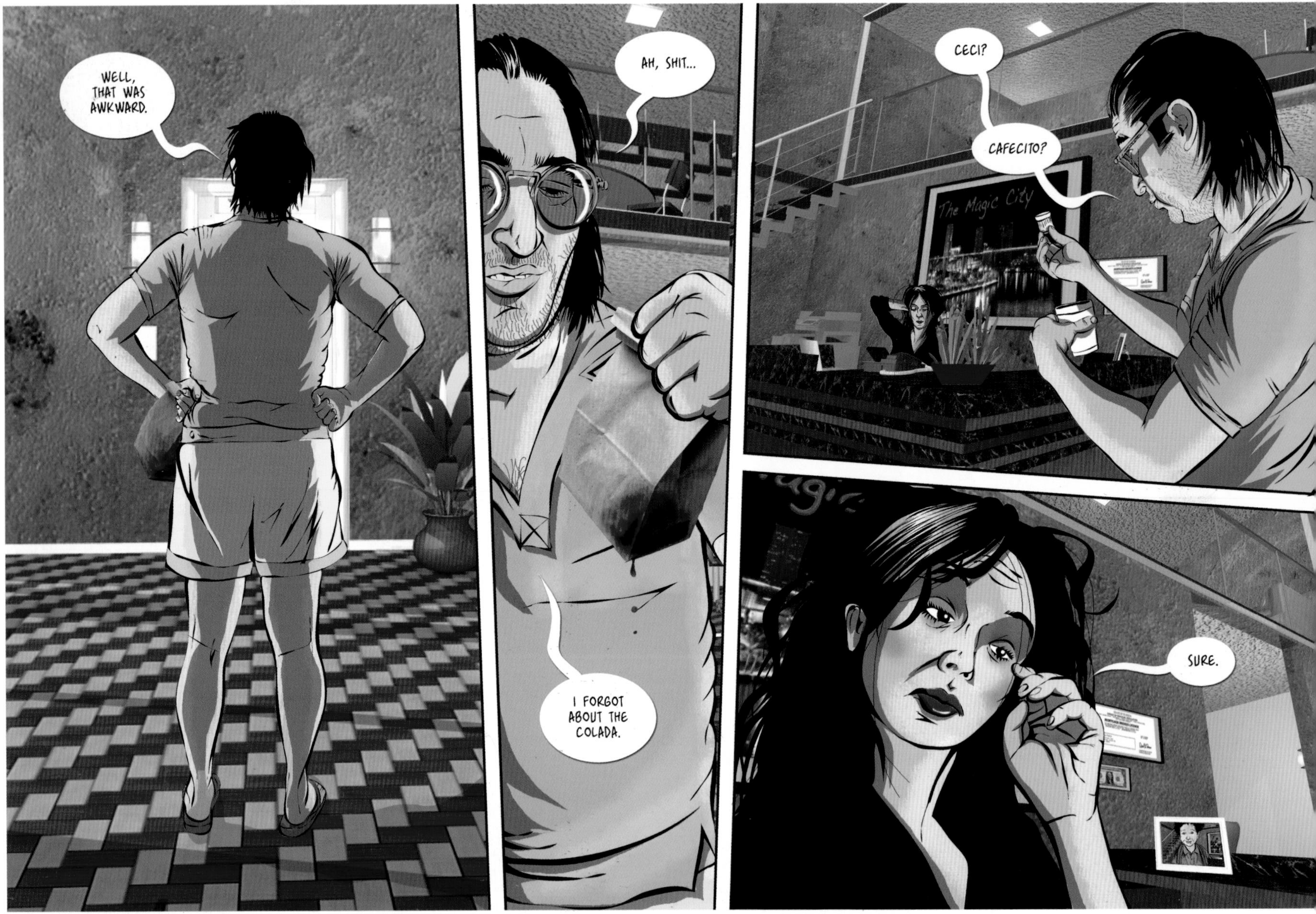
WELL, THAT WAS AWKWARD.
AH, SHIT...
I FORGOT ABOUT THE COLADA.
CECI?
CAFECITO?
The Magic City
SURE.

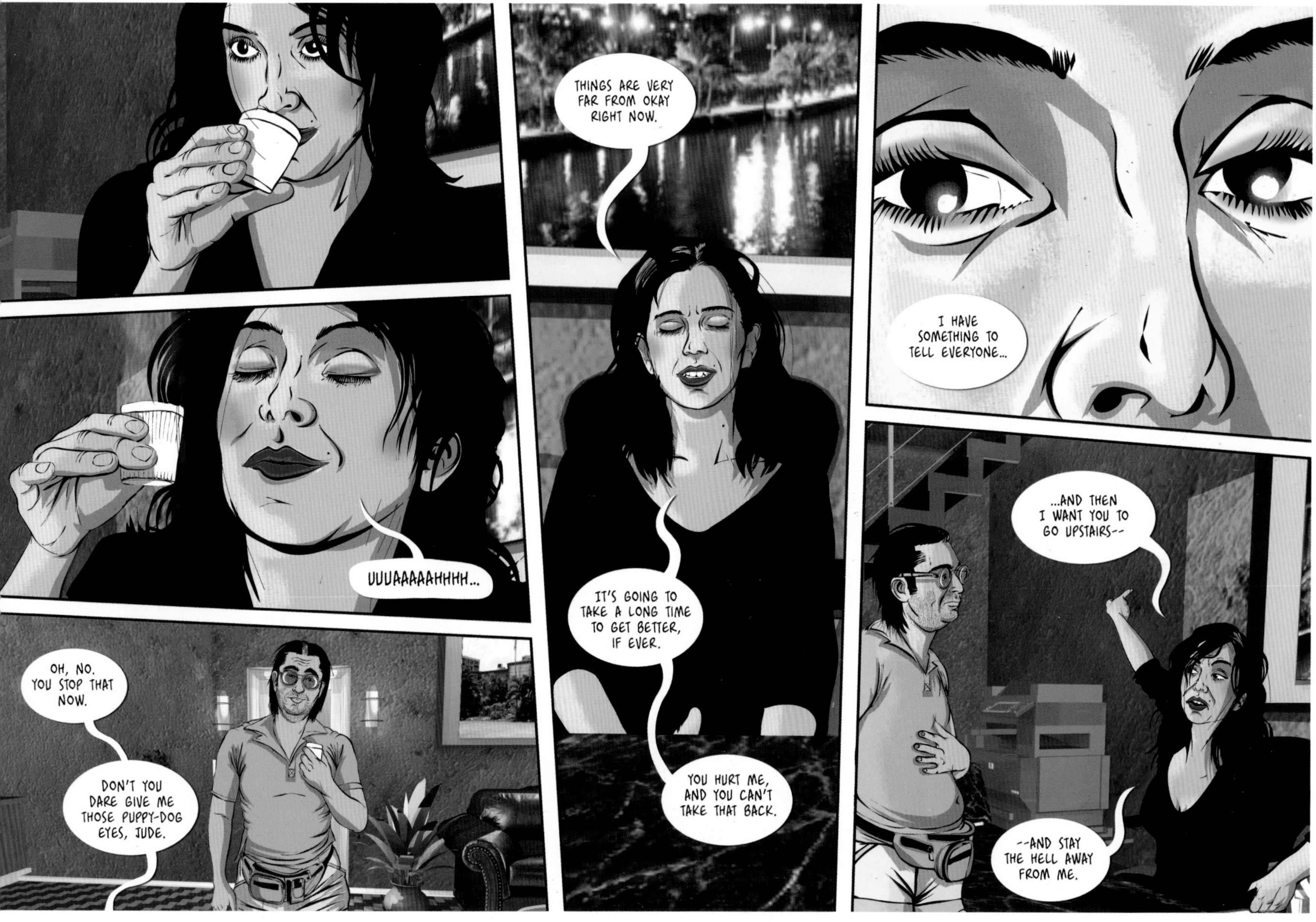
UUUAAAAAHHHH...
OH, NO. YOU STOP THAT NOW.
DON'T YOU DARE GIVE ME THOSE PUPPY-DOG EYES, JUDE.
THINGS ARE VERY FAR FROM OKAY RIGHT NOW.
IT'S GOING TO TAKE A LONG TIME TO GET BETTER, IF EVER.
YOU HURT ME, AND YOU CAN'T TAKE THAT BACK.
I HAVE SOMETHING TO TELL EVERYONE...
...AND THEN I WANT YOU TO GO UPSTAIRS--
--AND STAY THE HELL AWAY FROM ME.

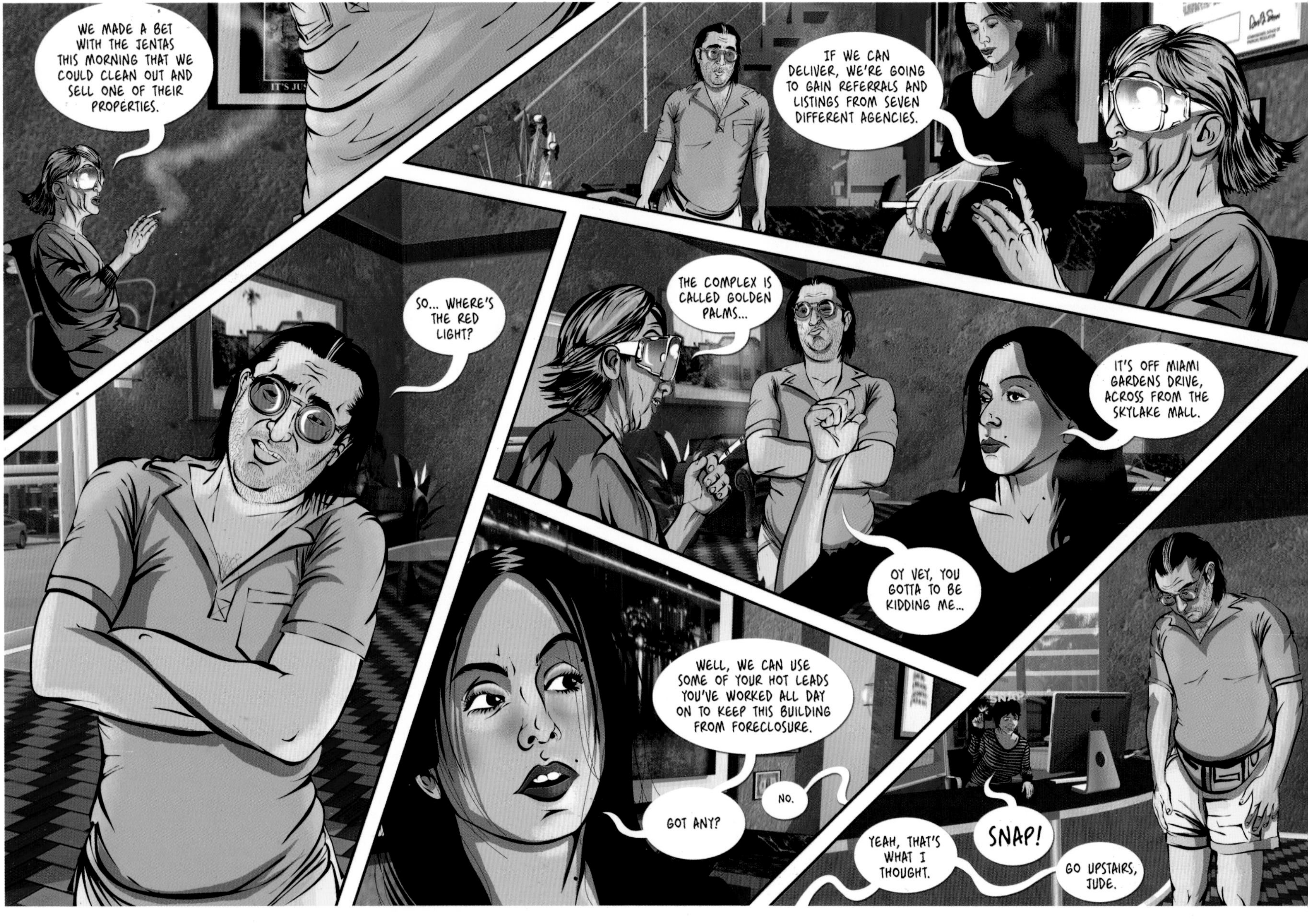
WE MADE A BET WITH THE JENTAS THIS MORNING THAT WE COULD CLEAN OUT AND SELL ONE OF THEIR PROPERTIES.
IF WE CAN DELIVER, WE'RE GOING TO GAIN REFERRALS AND LISTINGS FROM SEVEN DIFFERENT AGENCIES.
SO... WHERE'S THE RED LIGHT?
THE COMPLEX IS CALLED GOLDEN PALMS...
IT'S OFF MIAMI GARDENS DRIVE, ACROSS FROM THE SKYLAKE MALL.
OY VEY, YOU GOTTA TO BE KIDDING ME...
WELL, WE CAN USE SOME OF YOUR HOT LEADS YOU'VE WORKED ALL DAY ON TO KEEP THIS BUILDING FROM FORECLOSURE.
GOT ANY?
NO.
YEAH, THAT'S WHAT I THOUGHT.
SNAP!
GO UPSTAIRS, JUDE.

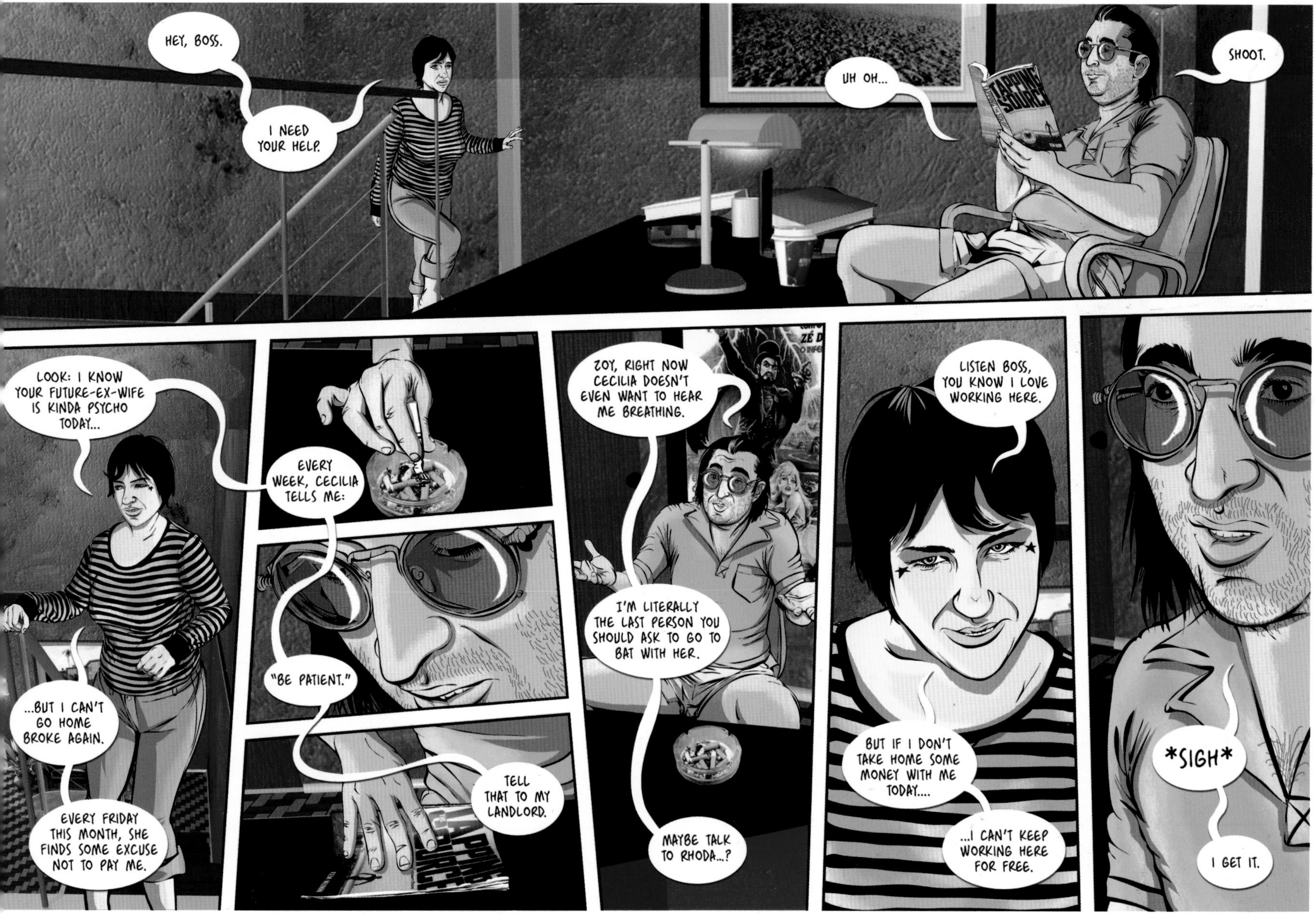
HEY, BOSS.
I NEED YOUR HELP.
UH OH...
SHOOT.
LOOK: I KNOW YOUR FUTURE-EX-WIFE IS KINDA PSYCHO TODAY...
EVERY WEEK, CECILIA TELLS ME:
"BE PATIENT."
TELL THAT TO MY LANDLORD.
...BUT I CAN'T GO HOME BROKE AGAIN.
EVERY FRIDAY THIS MONTH, SHE FINDS SOME EXCUSE NOT TO PAY ME.
ZOY, RIGHT NOW CECILIA DOESN'T EVEN WANT TO HEAR ME BREATHING.
I'M LITERALLY THE LAST PERSON YOU SHOULD ASK TO GO TO BAT WITH HER.
MAYBE TALK TO RHODA...?
LISTEN BOSS, YOU KNOW I LOVE WORKING HERE.
BUT IF I DON'T TAKE HOME SOME MONEY WITH ME TODAY....
...I CAN'T KEEP WORKING HERE FOR FREE.
SIGH
I GET IT.

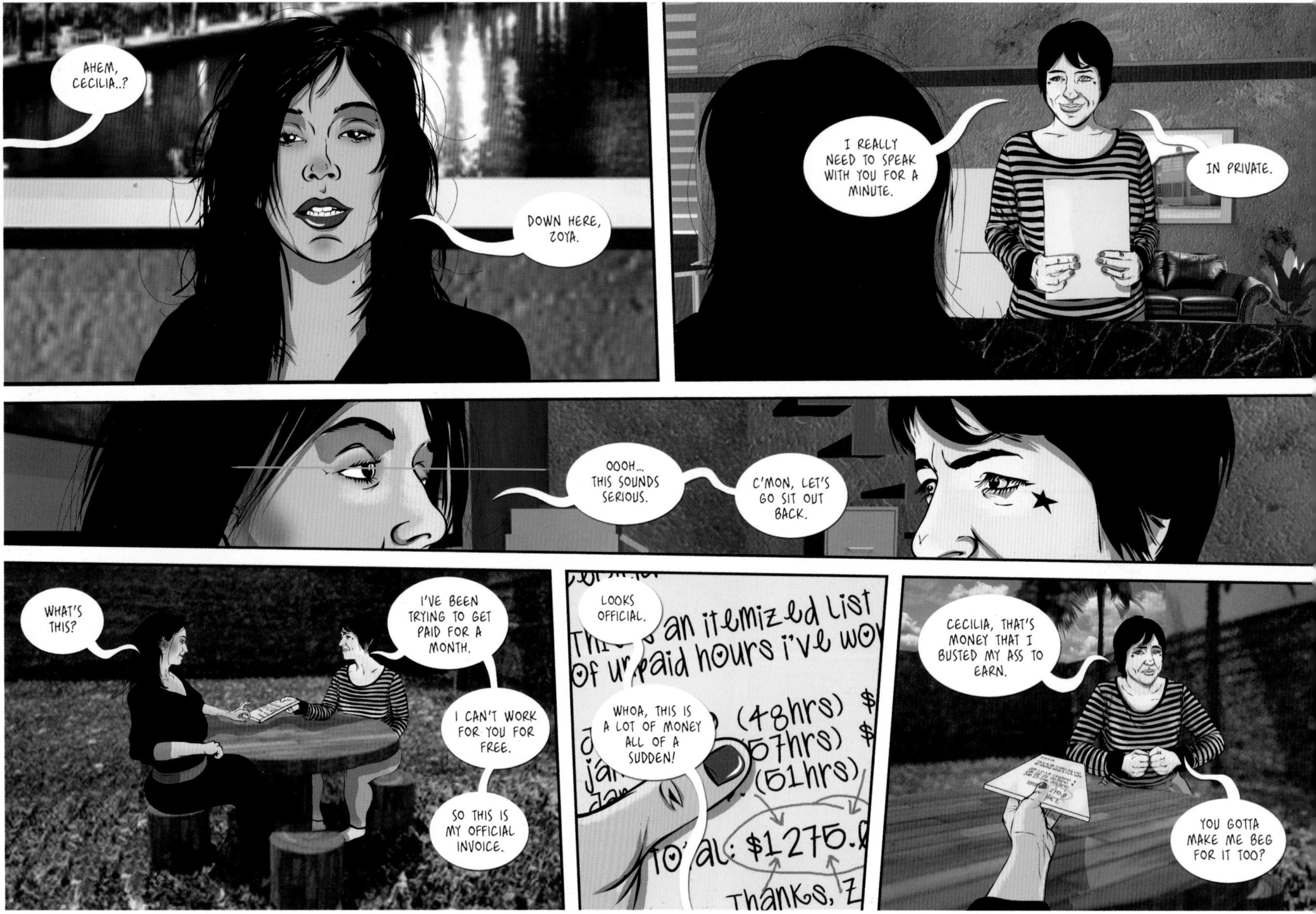
AHEM, CECILIA..?
DOWN HERE, ZOYA.
I REALLY NEED TO SPEAK WITH YOU FOR A MINUTE.
IN PRIVATE.
OOOH... THIS SOUNDS SERIOUS.
C'MON, LET'S GO SIT OUT BACK.
WHAT'S THIS?
I'VE BEEN TRYING TO GET PAID FOR A MONTH.
I CAN'T WORK FOR YOU FOR FREE.
SO THIS IS MY OFFICIAL INVOICE.
LOOKS OFFICIAL.
WHOA, THIS IS A LOT OF MONEY ALL OF A SUDDEN!
an itemized list
of unpaid hours i've wo
(48hrs)
(57hrs)
(51hrs)
$1275.
Thanks, Z
CECILIA, THAT'S MONEY THAT I BUSTED MY ASS TO EARN.
YOU GOTTA MAKE ME BEG FOR IT TOO?

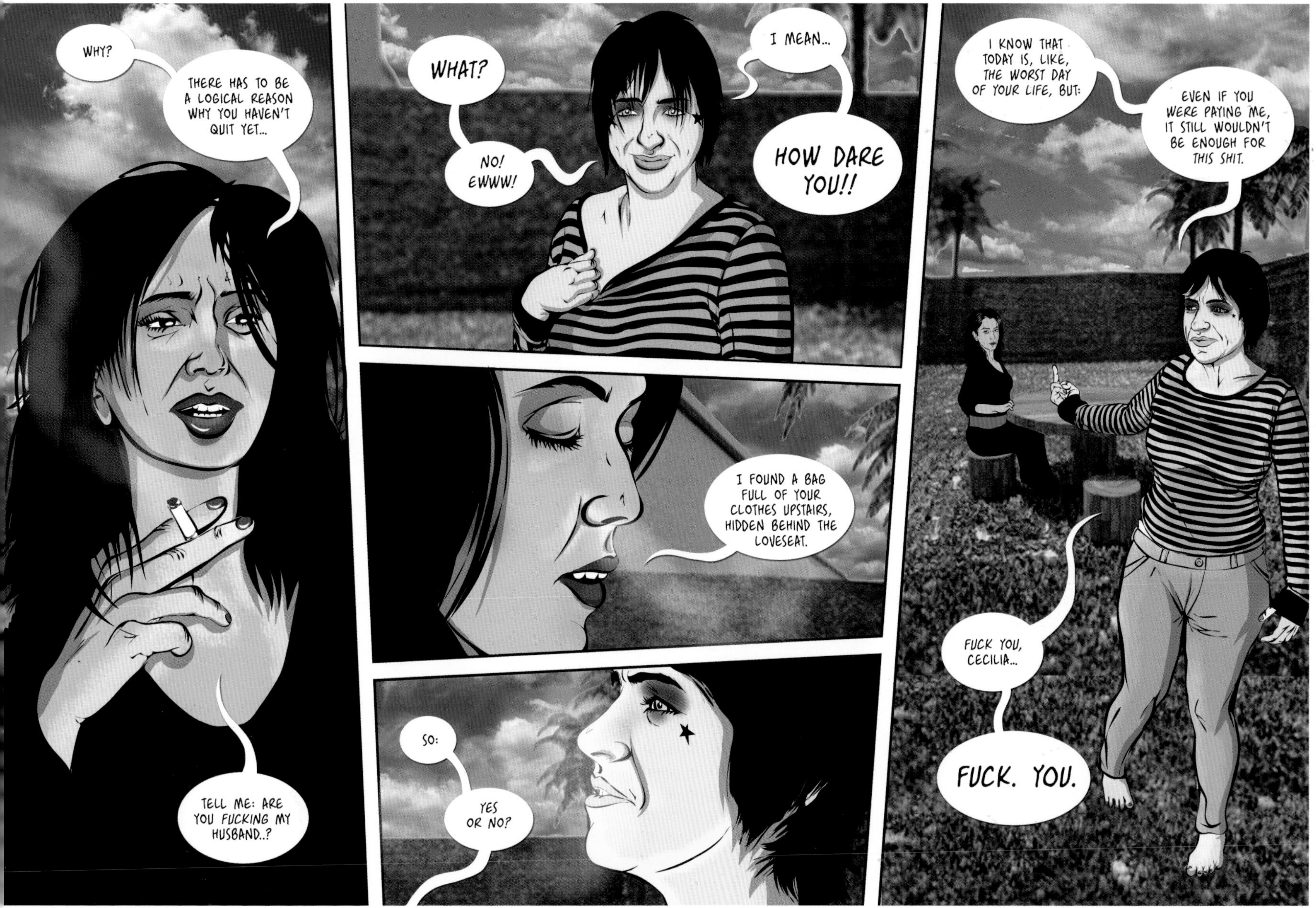
WHY?
THERE HAS TO BE A LOGICAL REASON WHY YOU HAVEN'T QUIT YET...
TELL ME: ARE YOU FUCKING MY HUSBAND..?
WHAT?
NO! EWWW!
I MEAN...
HOW DARE YOU!!
I FOUND A BAG FULL OF YOUR CLOTHES UPSTAIRS, HIDDEN BEHIND THE LOVESEAT.
SO:
YES OR NO?
I KNOW THAT TODAY IS, LIKE, THE WORST DAY OF YOUR LIFE, BUT:
EVEN IF YOU WERE PAYING ME, IT STILL WOULDN'T BE ENOUGH FOR THIS SHIT.
FUCK YOU, CECILIA...
FUCK. YOU.

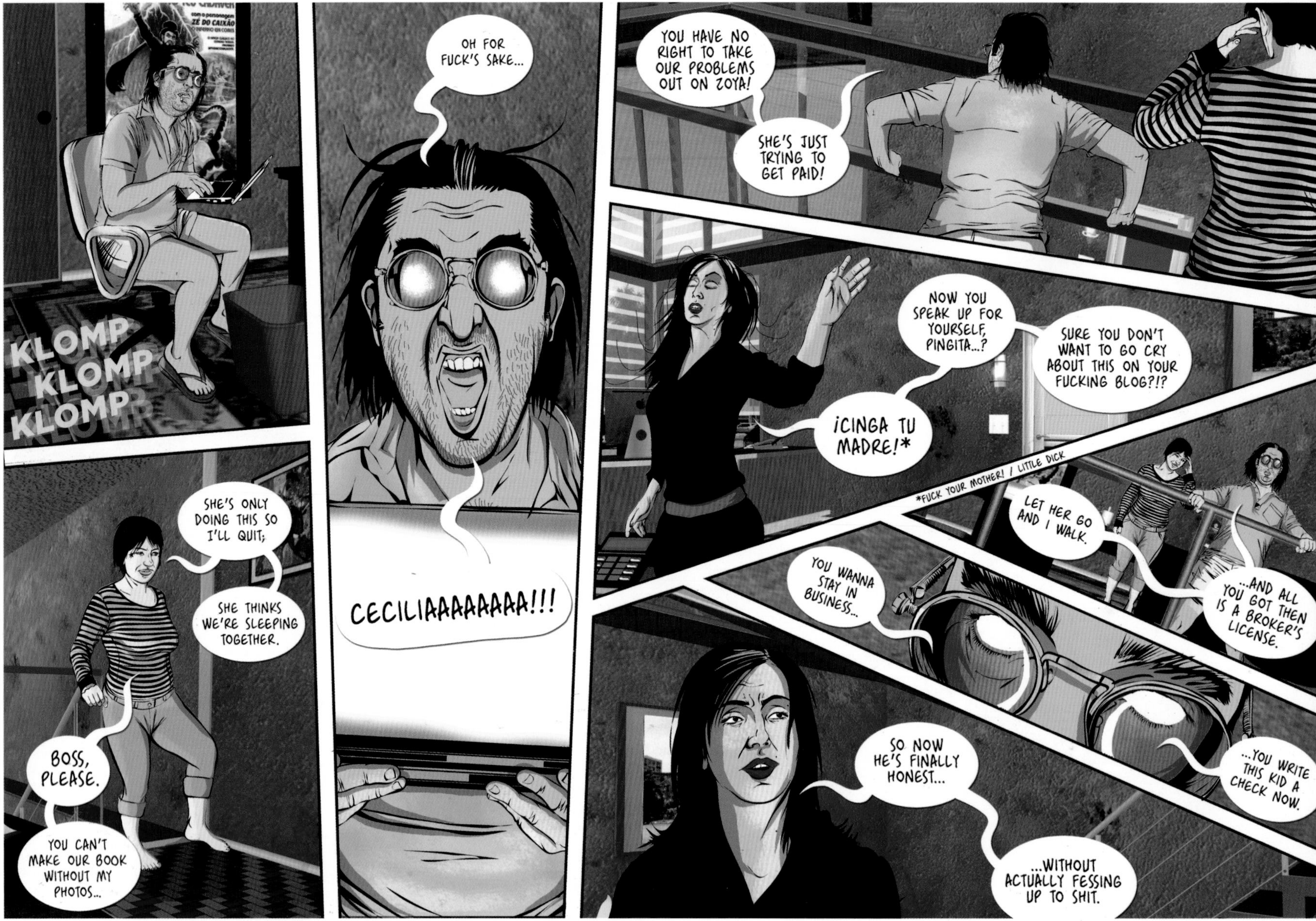
ZÉ DO CAIXÃO
KLOMP KLOMP KLOMP KLOMP
SHE'S ONLY DOING THIS SO I'LL QUIT;
SHE THINKS WE'RE SLEEPING TOGETHER.
BOSS, PLEASE.
YOU CAN'T MAKE OUR BOOK WITHOUT MY PHOTOS...
OH FOR FUCK'S SAKE...
CECILIAAAAAAAA!!!
YOU HAVE NO RIGHT TO TAKE OUR PROBLEMS OUT ON ZOYA!
SHE'S JUST TRYING TO GET PAID!
NOW YOU SPEAK UP FOR YOURSELF, PINGITA...?
SURE YOU DON'T WANT TO GO CRY ABOUT THIS ON YOUR FUCKING BLOG?!?
¡CINGA TU MADRE!*
*FUCK YOUR MOTHER! / LITTLE DICK
LET HER GO AND I WALK.
...AND ALL YOU GOT THEN IS A BROKER'S LICENSE.
YOU WANNA STAY IN BUSINESS...
...YOU WRITE THIS KID A CHECK NOW.
SO NOW HE'S FINALLY HONEST...
...WITHOUT ACTUALLY FESSING UP TO SHIT.

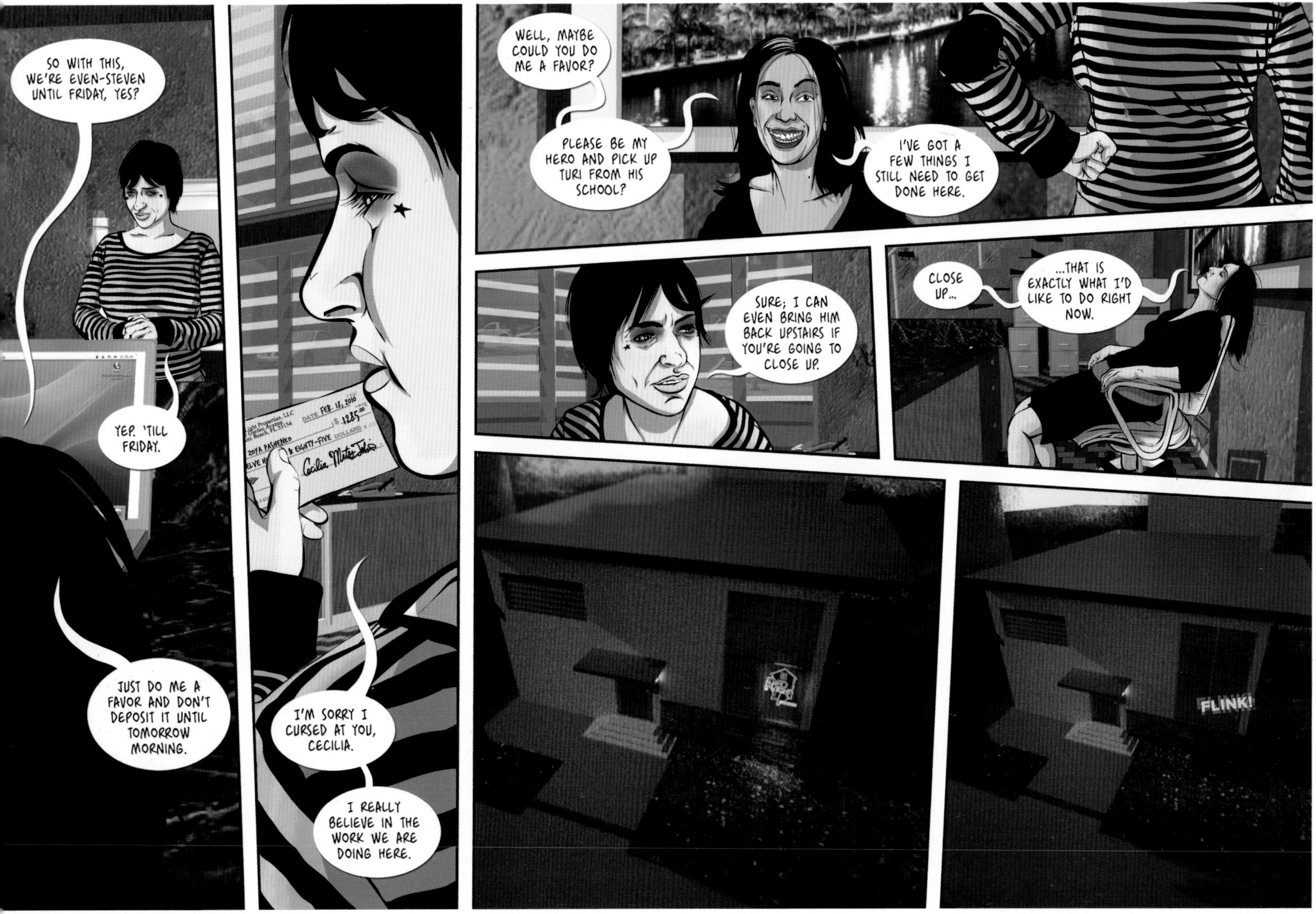
SO WITH THIS, WE'RE EVEN-STEVEN UNTIL FRIDAY, YES?
YEP. 'TILL FRIDAY.
JUST DO ME A FAVOR AND DON'T DEPOSIT IT UNTIL TOMORROW MORNING.
I'M SORRY I CURSED AT YOU, CECILIA.
I REALLY BELIEVE IN THE WORK WE ARE DOING HERE.
WELL, MAYBE COULD YOU DO ME A FAVOR?
PLEASE BE MY HERO AND PICK UP TURI FROM HIS SCHOOL?
I'VE GOT A FEW THINGS I STILL NEED TO GET DONE HERE.
SURE; I CAN EVEN BRING HIM BACK UPSTAIRS IF YOU'RE GOING TO CLOSE UP.
CLOSE UP...
...THAT IS EXACTLY WHAT I'D LIKE TO DO RIGHT NOW.
FLINK!

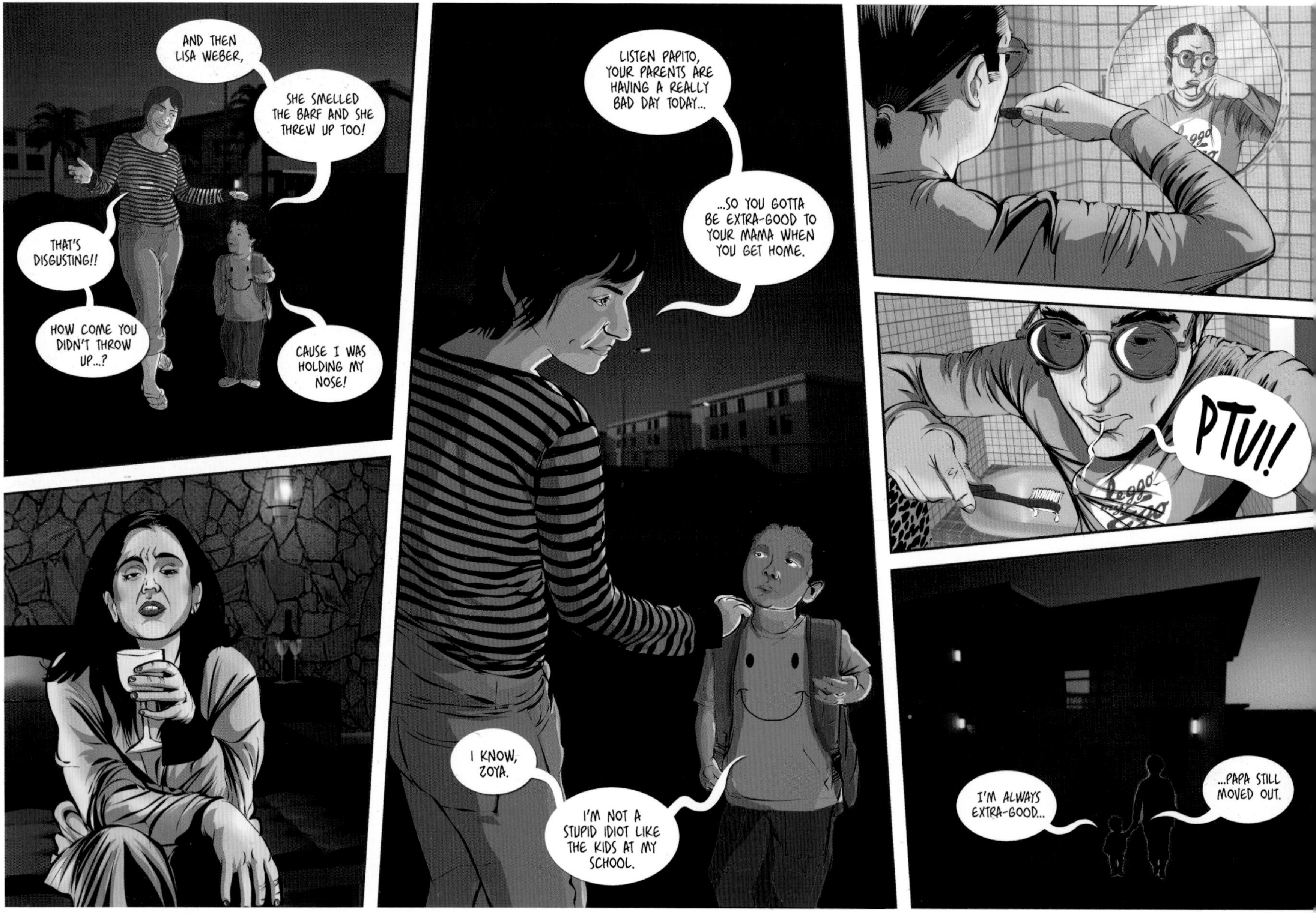
AND THEN LISA WEBER,
SHE SMELLED THE BARF AND SHE THREW UP TOO!
THAT'S DISGUSTING!!
HOW COME YOU DIDN'T THROW UP...?
CAUSE I WAS HOLDING MY NOSE!
LISTEN PAPITO, YOUR PARENTS ARE HAVING A REALLY BAD DAY TODAY...
...SO YOU GOTTA BE EXTRA-GOOD TO YOUR MAMA WHEN YOU GET HOME.
I KNOW, ZOYA.
I'M NOT A STUPID IDIOT LIKE THE KIDS AT MY SCHOOL.
PTUI!
I'M ALWAYS EXTRA-GOOD...
...PAPA STILL MOVED OUT.

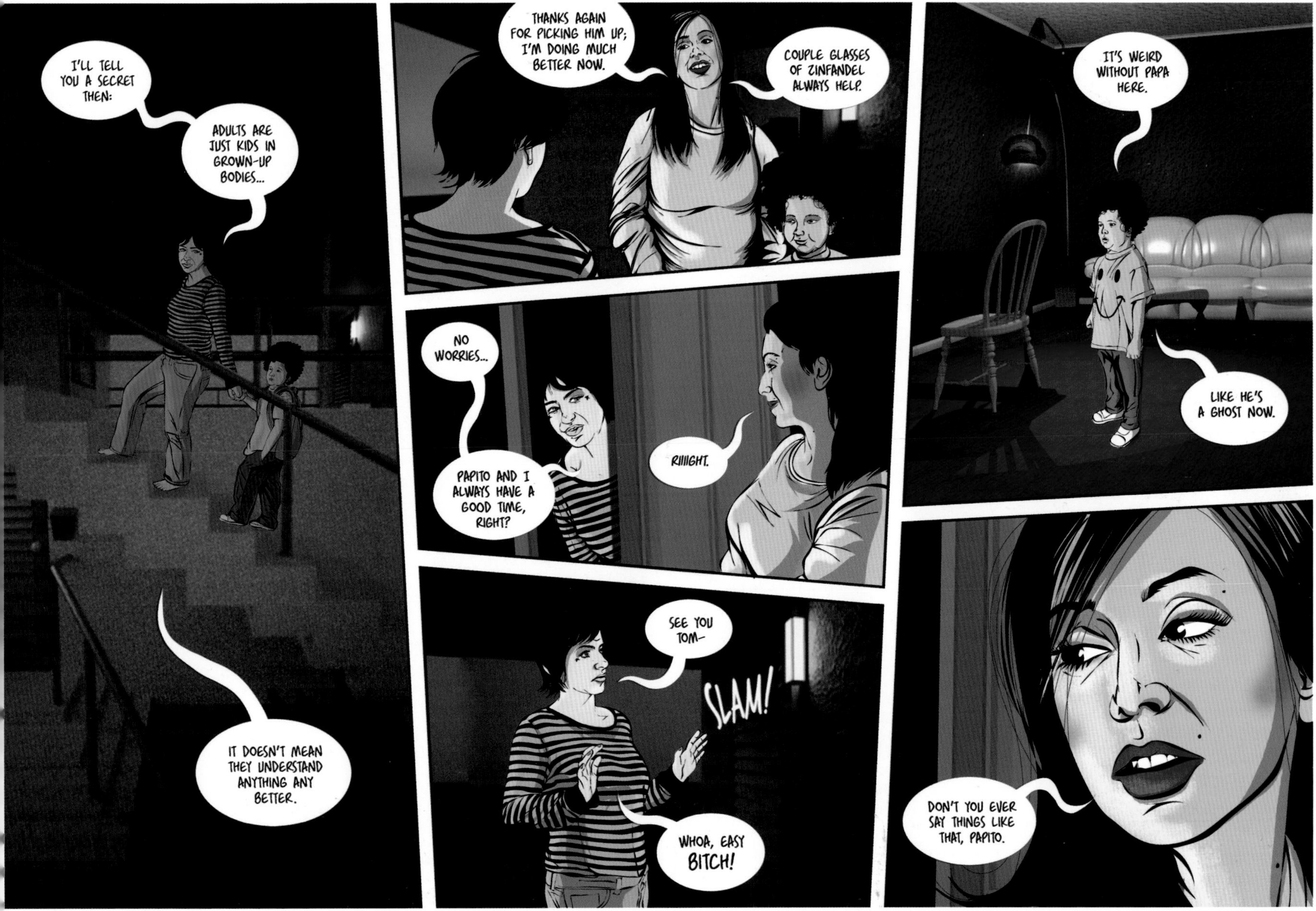
I'LL TELL YOU A SECRET THEN:
ADULTS ARE JUST KIDS IN GROWN-UP BODIES...
IT DOESN'T MEAN THEY UNDERSTAND ANYTHING ANY BETTER.
THANKS AGAIN FOR PICKING HIM UP; I'M DOING MUCH BETTER NOW.
COUPLE GLASSES OF ZINFANDEL ALWAYS HELP.
NO WORRIES...
PAPITO AND I ALWAYS HAVE A GOOD TIME, RIGHT?
RIIIIGHT.
SEE YOU TOM–
SLAM!
WHOA, EASY BITCH!
IT'S WEIRD WITHOUT PAPA HERE.
LIKE HE'S A GHOST NOW.
DON'T YOU EVER SAY THINGS LIKE THAT, PAPITO.

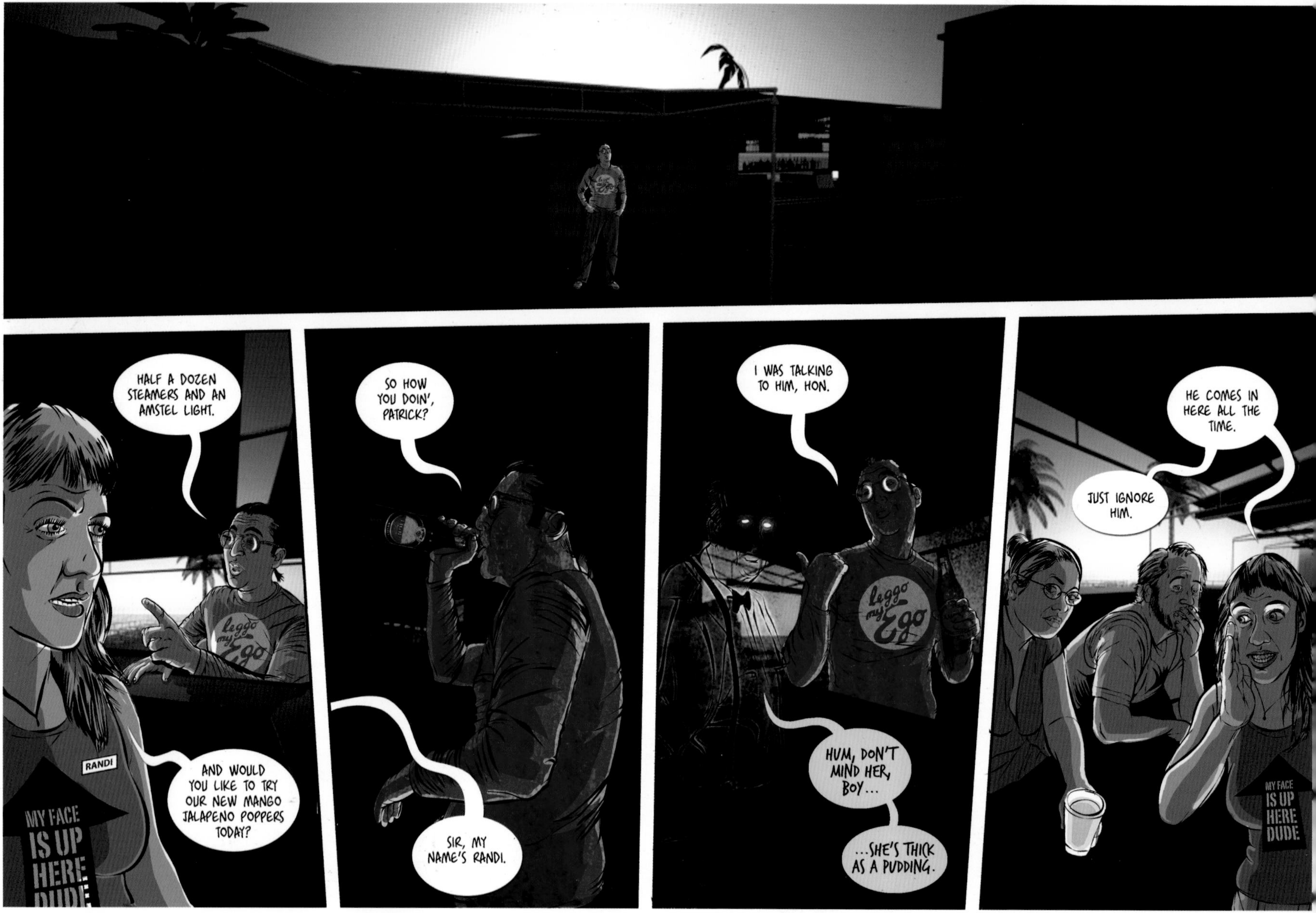
HALF A DOZEN STEAMERS AND AN AMSTEL LIGHT.
leggo my Ego
RANDI
MY FACE IS UP HERE
AND WOULD YOU LIKE TO TRY OUR NEW MANGO JALAPENO POPPERS TODAY?
SO HOW YOU DOIN', PATRICK?
SIR, MY NAME'S RANDI.
I WAS TALKING TO HIM, HON.
leggo my Ego
HUM, DON'T MIND HER, BOY...
...SHE'S THICK AS A PUDDING.
HE COMES IN HERE ALL THE TIME.
JUST IGNORE HIM.
MY FACE IS UP HERE DUDE

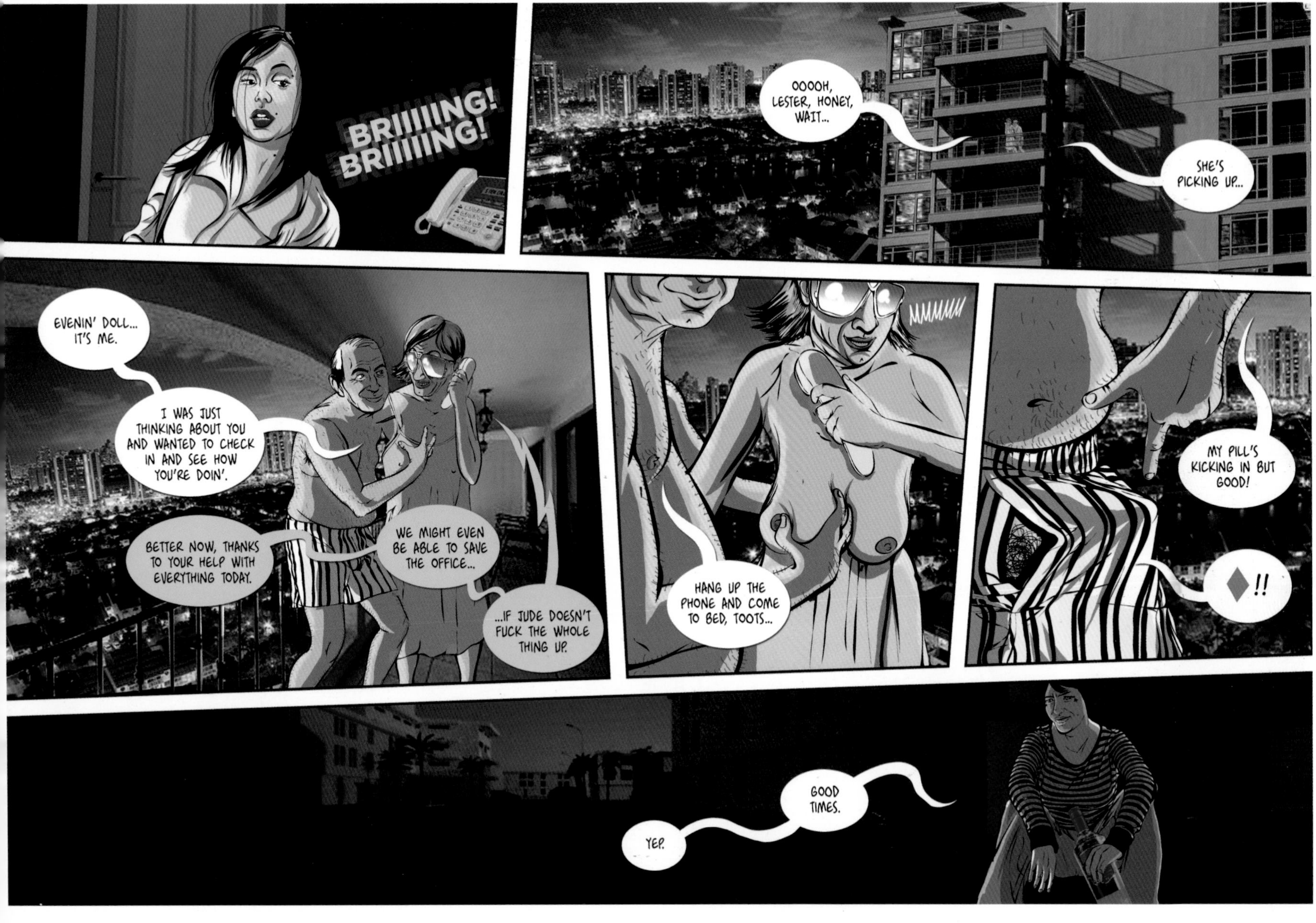
BRIIIIING!
BRIIIIING!
OOOOH, LESTER, HONEY, WAIT...
SHE'S PICKING UP...
EVENIN' DOLL... IT'S ME.
I WAS JUST THINKING ABOUT YOU AND WANTED TO CHECK IN AND SEE HOW YOU'RE DOIN'.
BETTER NOW, THANKS TO YOUR HELP WITH EVERYTHING TODAY.
WE MIGHT EVEN BE ABLE TO SAVE THE OFFICE...
...IF JUDE DOESN'T FUCK THE WHOLE THING UP.
MMMMMM
HANG UP THE PHONE AND COME TO BED, TOOTS...
MY PILL'S KICKING IN BUT GOOD!
♦!!
GOOD TIMES.
YEP.

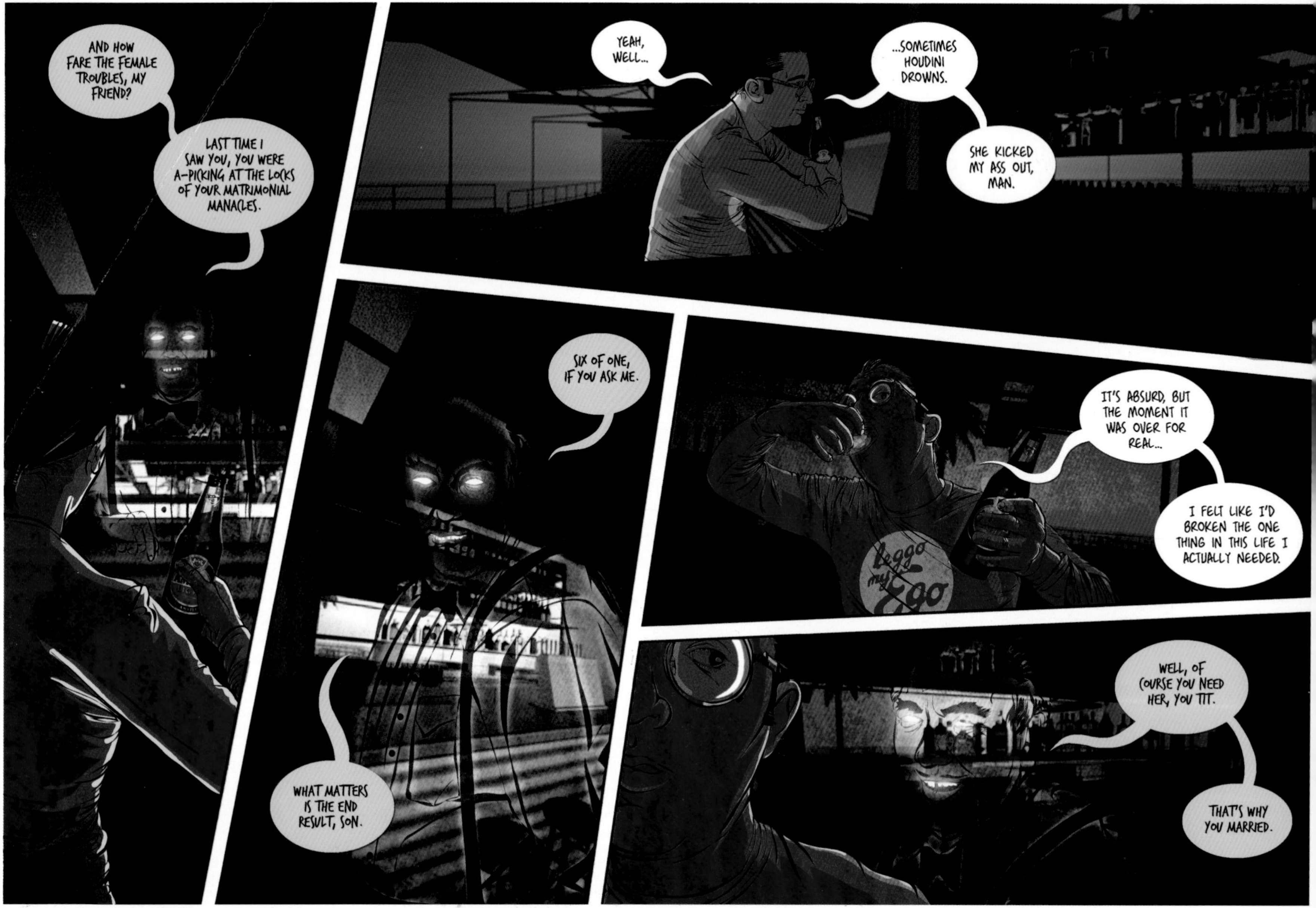
AND HOW FARE THE FEMALE TROUBLES, MY FRIEND?
LAST TIME I SAW YOU, YOU WERE A-PICKING AT THE LOCKS OF YOUR MATRIMONIAL MANACLES.
YEAH, WELL...
...SOMETIMES HOUDINI DROWNS.
SHE KICKED MY ASS OUT, MAN.
SIX OF ONE, IF YOU ASK ME.
WHAT MATTERS IS THE END RESULT, SON.
IT'S ABSURD, BUT THE MOMENT IT WAS OVER FOR REAL...
I FELT LIKE I'D BROKEN THE ONE THING IN THIS LIFE I ACTUALLY NEEDED.
leggo my Ego
WELL, OF COURSE YOU NEED HER, YOU TIT.
THAT'S WHY YOU MARRIED.

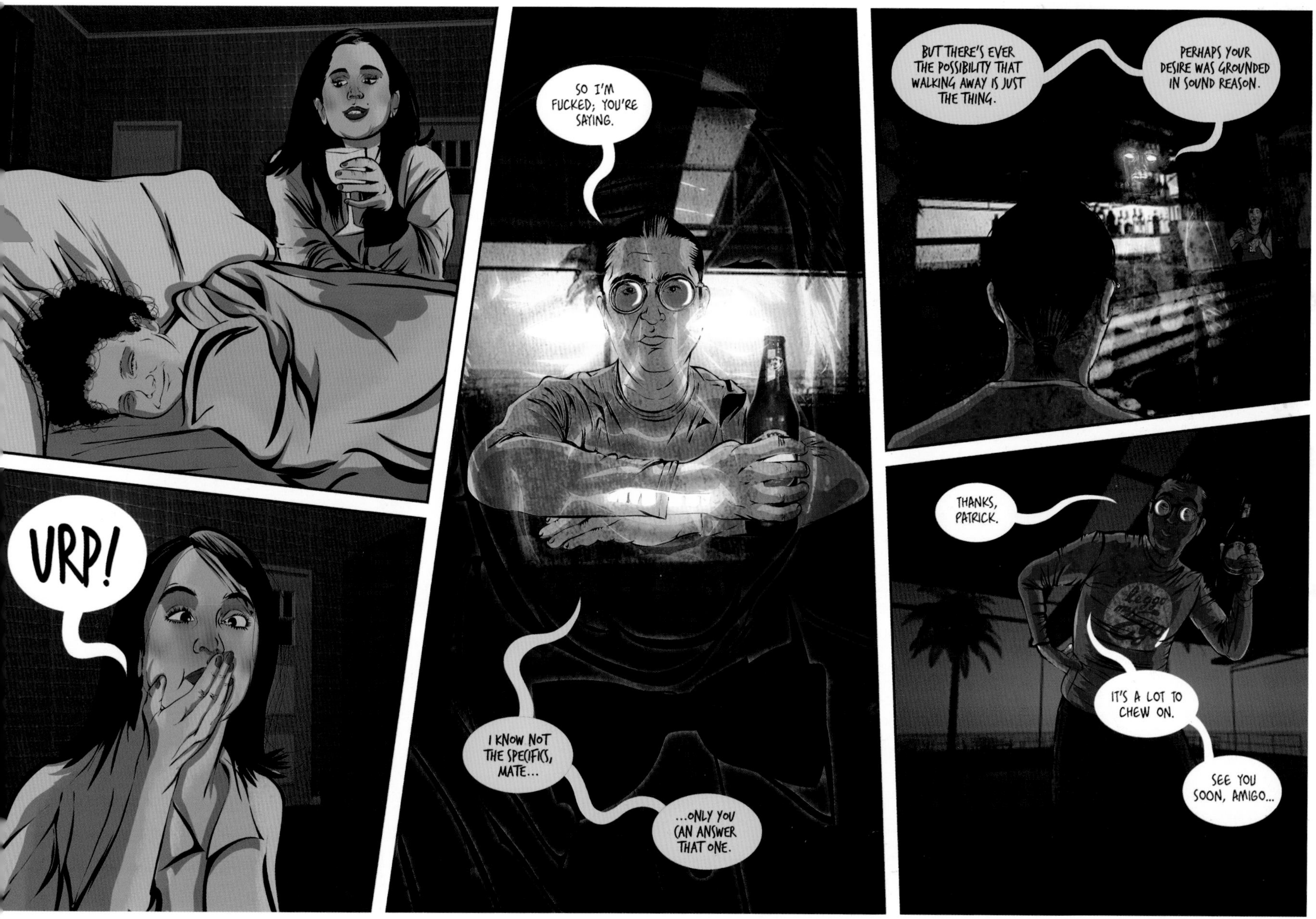
URP!
SO I'M FUCKED; YOU'RE SAYING.
I KNOW NOT THE SPECIFICS, MATE...
...ONLY YOU CAN ANSWER THAT ONE.
BUT THERE'S EVER THE POSSIBILITY THAT WALKING AWAY IS JUST THE THING.
PERHAPS YOUR DESIRE WAS GROUNDED IN SOUND REASON.
THANKS, PATRICK.
IT'S A LOT TO CHEW ON.
SEE YOU SOON, AMIGO...

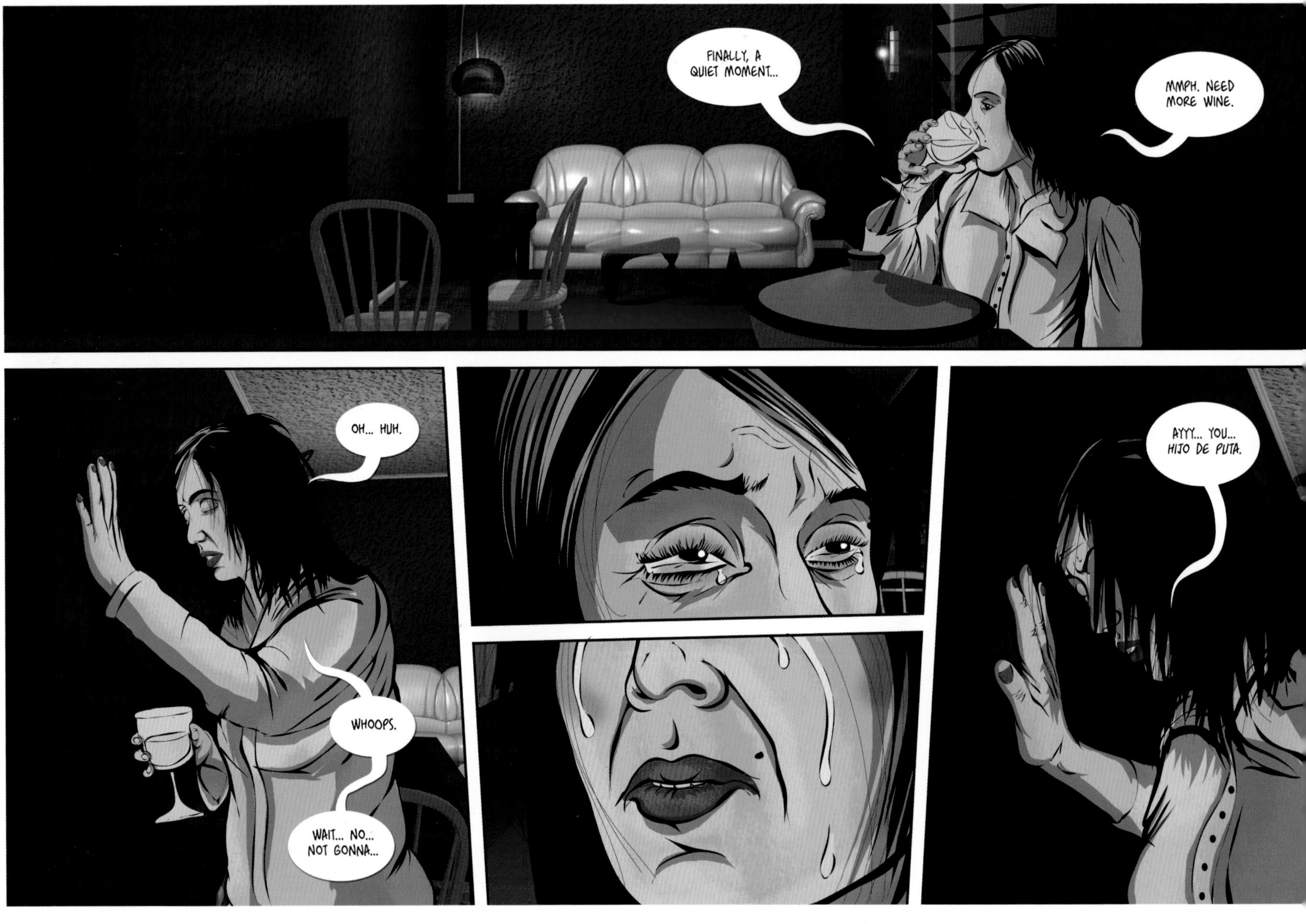
FINALLY, A QUIET MOMENT...
MMPH. NEED MORE WINE.
OH... HUH.
WHOOPS.
WAIT... NO... NOT GONNA...
AYYY... YOU... HIJO DE PUTA.

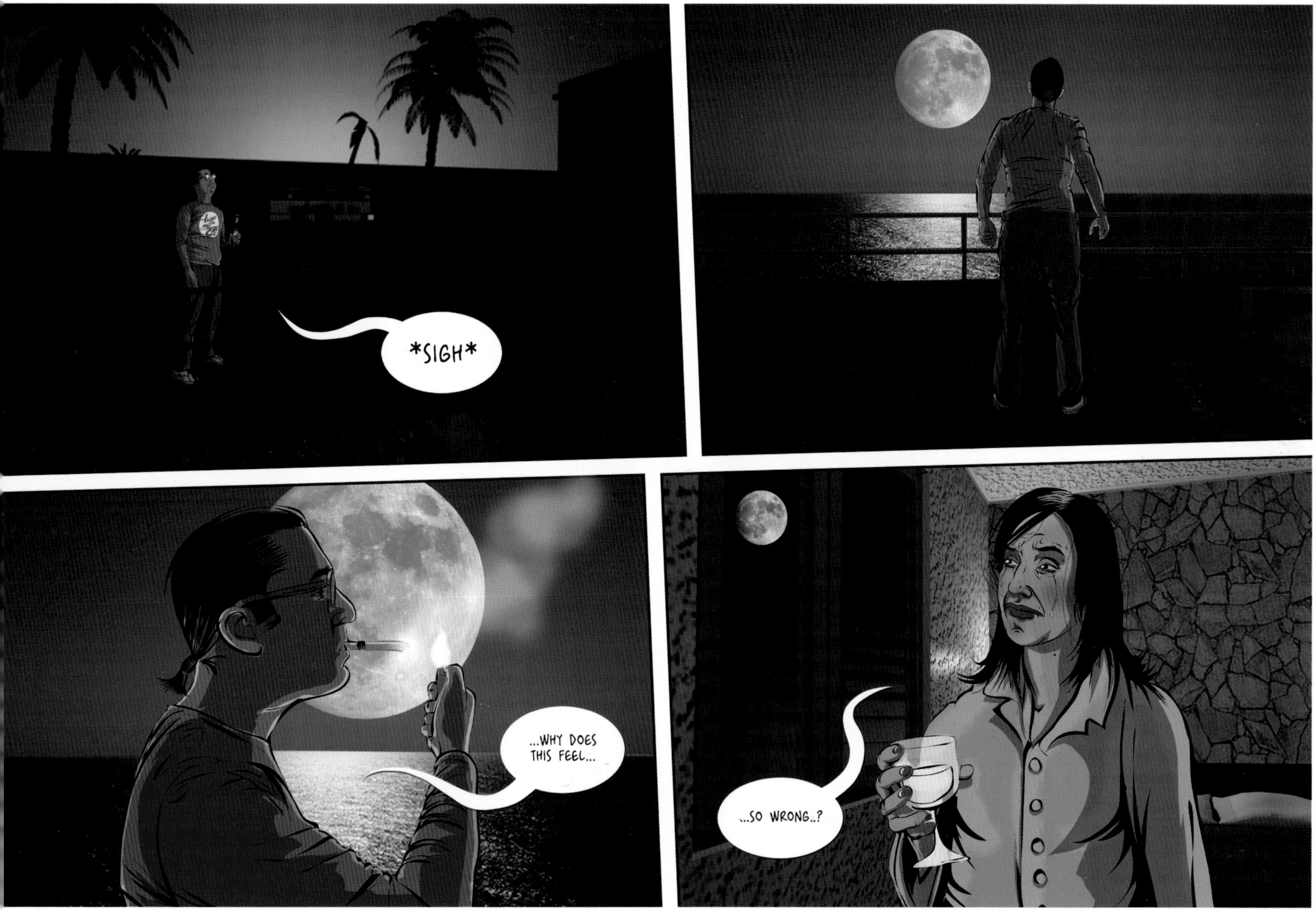
SIGH
...WHY DOES THIS FEEL...
...SO WRONG..?

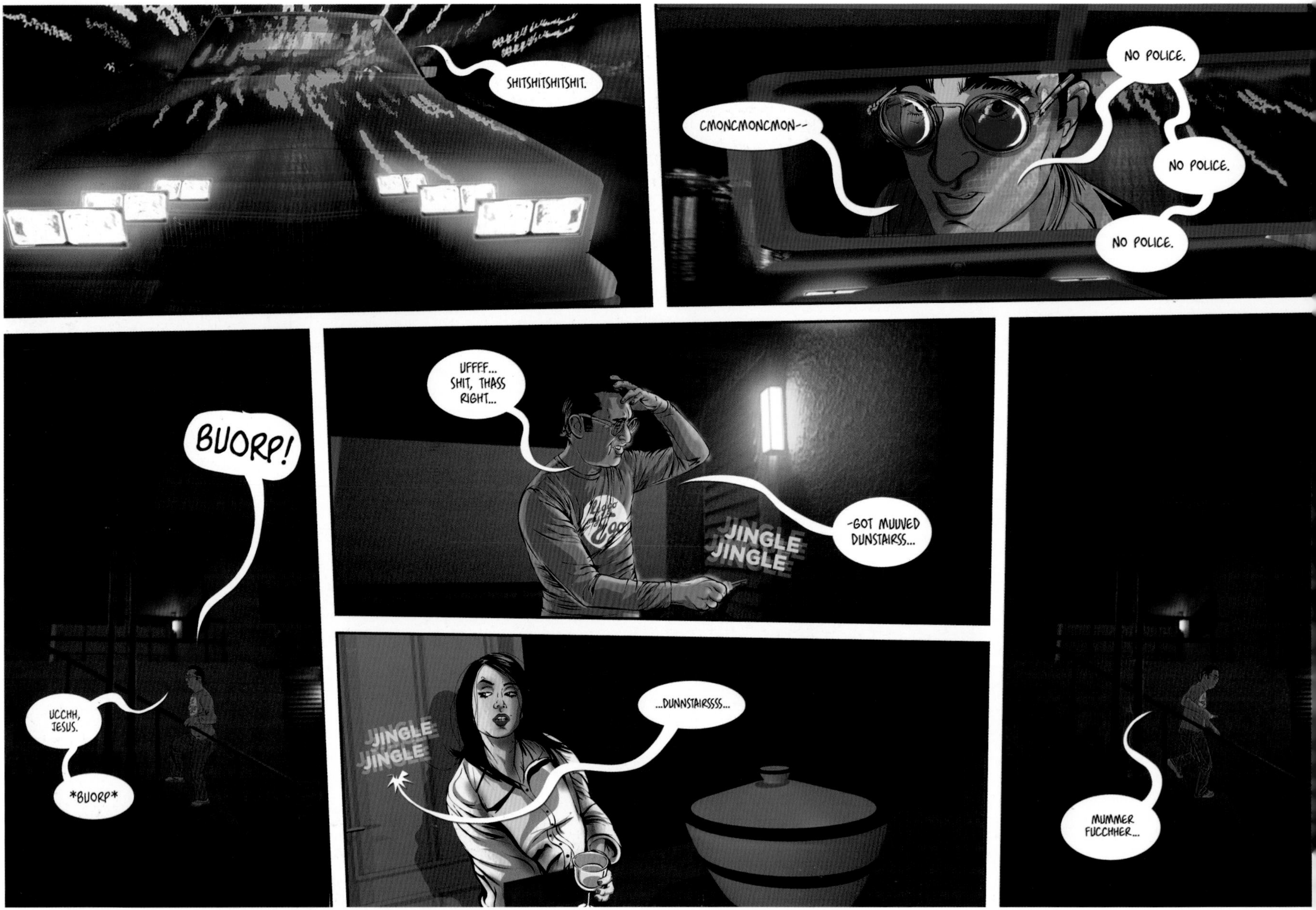
SHITSHITSHITSHIT.
CMONCMONCMON--
NO POLICE.
NO POLICE.
NO POLICE.
BUORP!
UCCHH, JESUS.
BUORP
UFFFF... SHIT, THASS RIGHT...
-GOT MUUVED DUNSTAIRSS...
JINGLE JINGLE
JINGLE JINGLE
...DUNNSTAIRSSSS...
MUMMER FUCCHHER...

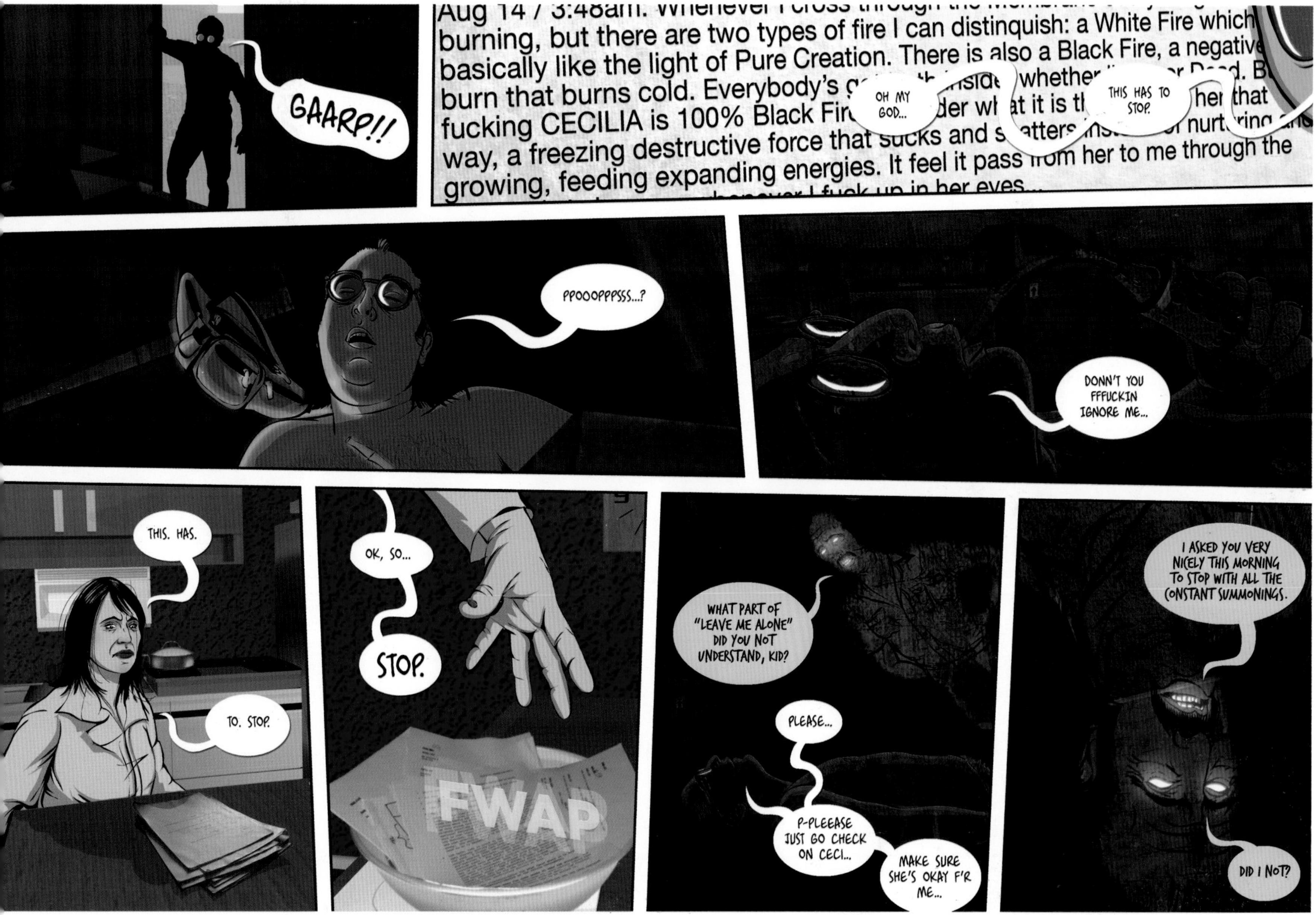
GAARP!!
burning, but there are two types of fire I can distinquish: a White Fire which
basically like the light of Pure Creation. There is also a Black Fire, a negative
burn that burns cold. Everybody's
fucking CECILIA is 100% Black Fir
way, a freezing destructive force that sucks and
growing, feeding expanding energies. It feel it pass
OH MY GOD...
THIS HAS TO STOP.
PPOOOPPPSSS...?
DONN'T YOU FFFUCKIN IGNORE ME...
THIS. HAS.
TO. STOP.
OK, SO...
STOP.
FWAP
WHAT PART OF "LEAVE ME ALONE" DID YOU NOT UNDERSTAND, KID?
PLEASE...
P-PLEEASE JUST GO CHECK ON CECI...
MAKE SURE SHE'S OKAY F'R ME...
I ASKED YOU VERY NICELY THIS MORNING TO STOP WITH ALL THE CONSTANT SUMMONINGS.
DID I NOT?

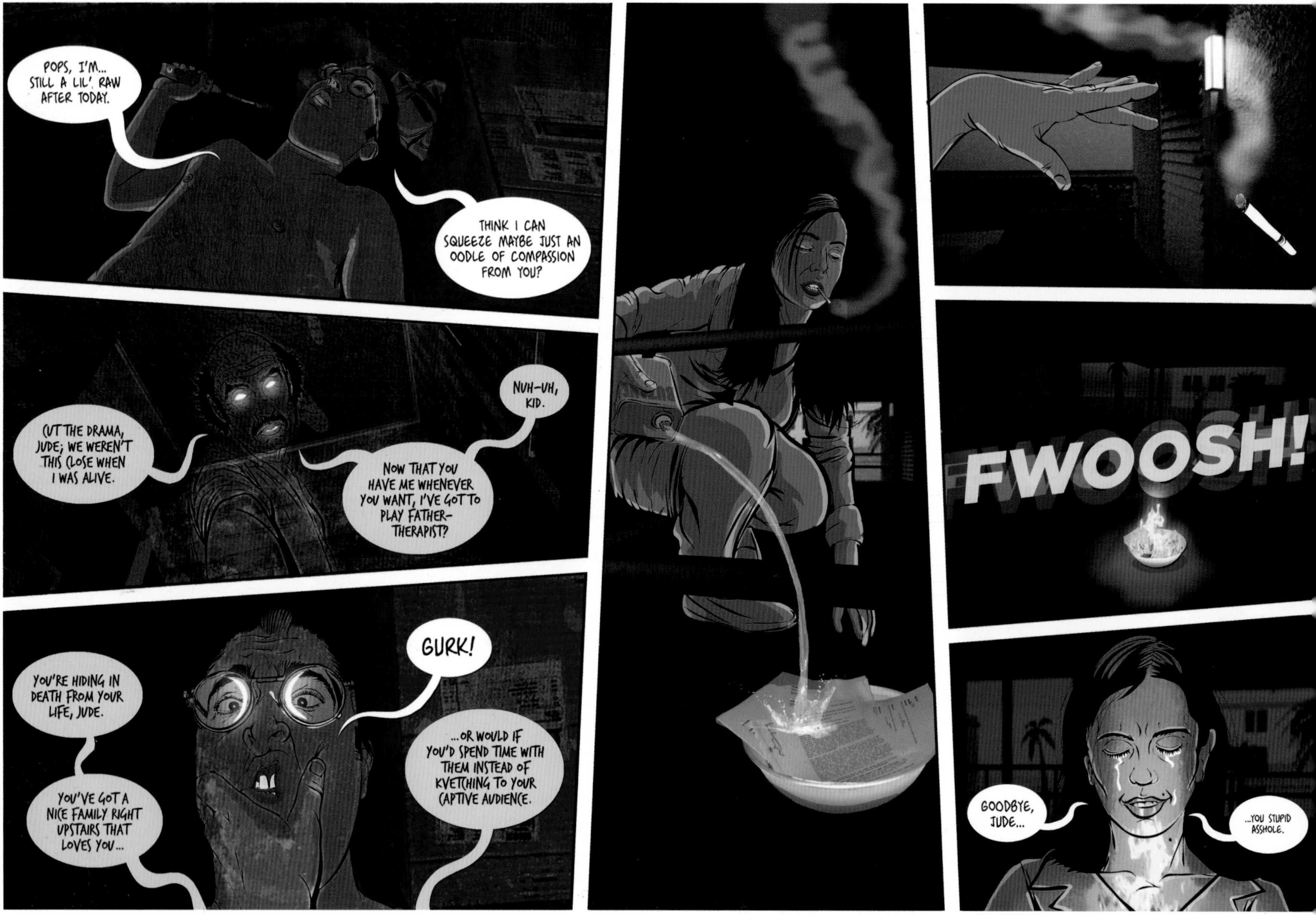
POPS, I'M... STILL A LIL' RAW AFTER TODAY.
THINK I CAN SQUEEZE MAYBE JUST AN OODLE OF COMPASSION FROM YOU?
NUH-UH, KID.
CUT THE DRAMA, JUDE; WE WEREN'T THIS CLOSE WHEN I WAS ALIVE.
NOW THAT YOU HAVE ME WHENEVER YOU WANT, I'VE GOT TO PLAY FATHER-THERAPIST?
YOU'RE HIDING IN DEATH FROM YOUR LIFE, JUDE.
GURK!
YOU'VE GOT A NICE FAMILY RIGHT UPSTAIRS THAT LOVES YOU...
...OR WOULD IF YOU'D SPEND TIME WITH THEM INSTEAD OF KVETCHING TO YOUR CAPTIVE AUDIENCE.
FWOOSH!
GOODBYE, JUDE...
...YOU STUPID ASSHOLE.

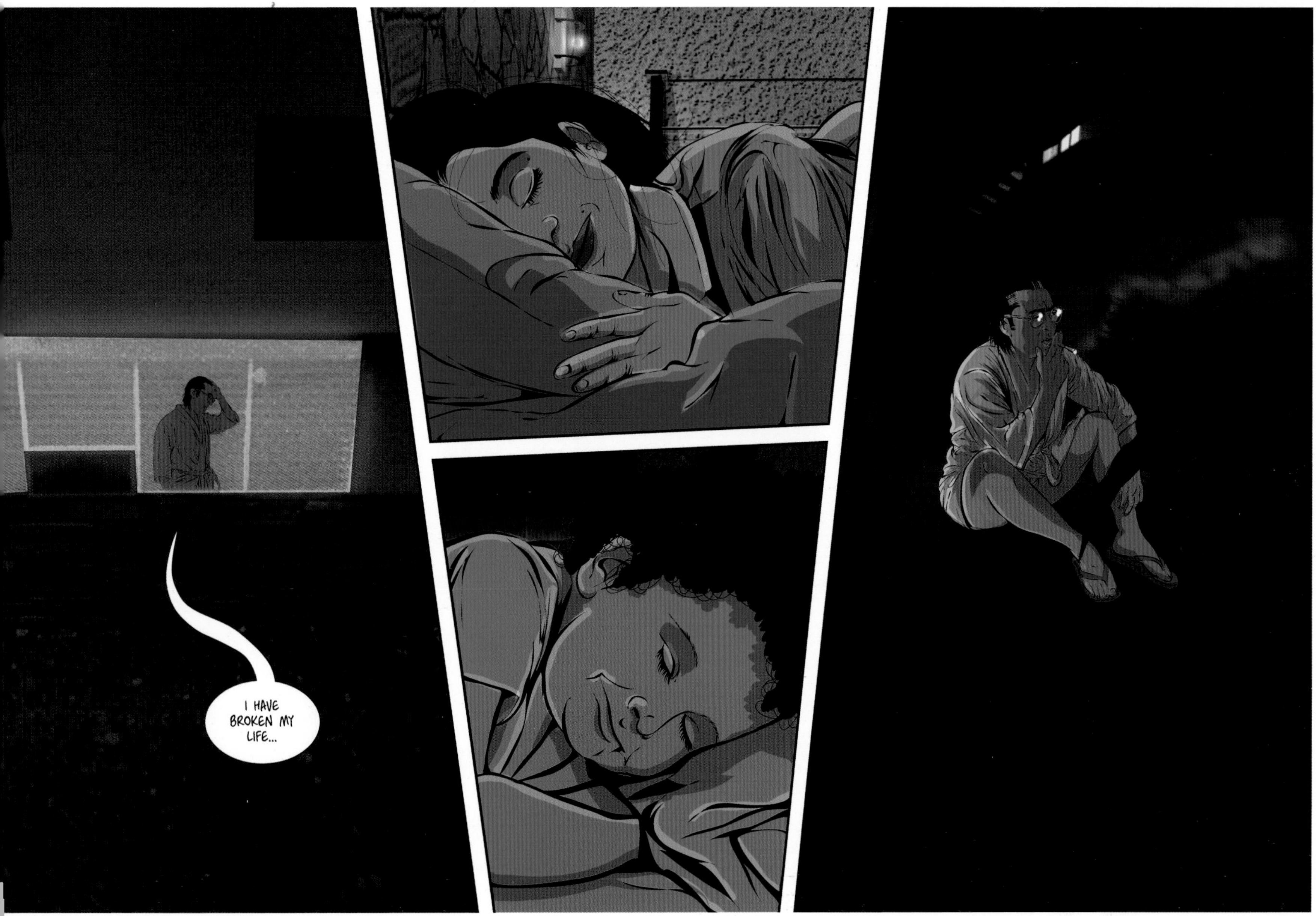
I HAVE BROKEN MY LIFE...

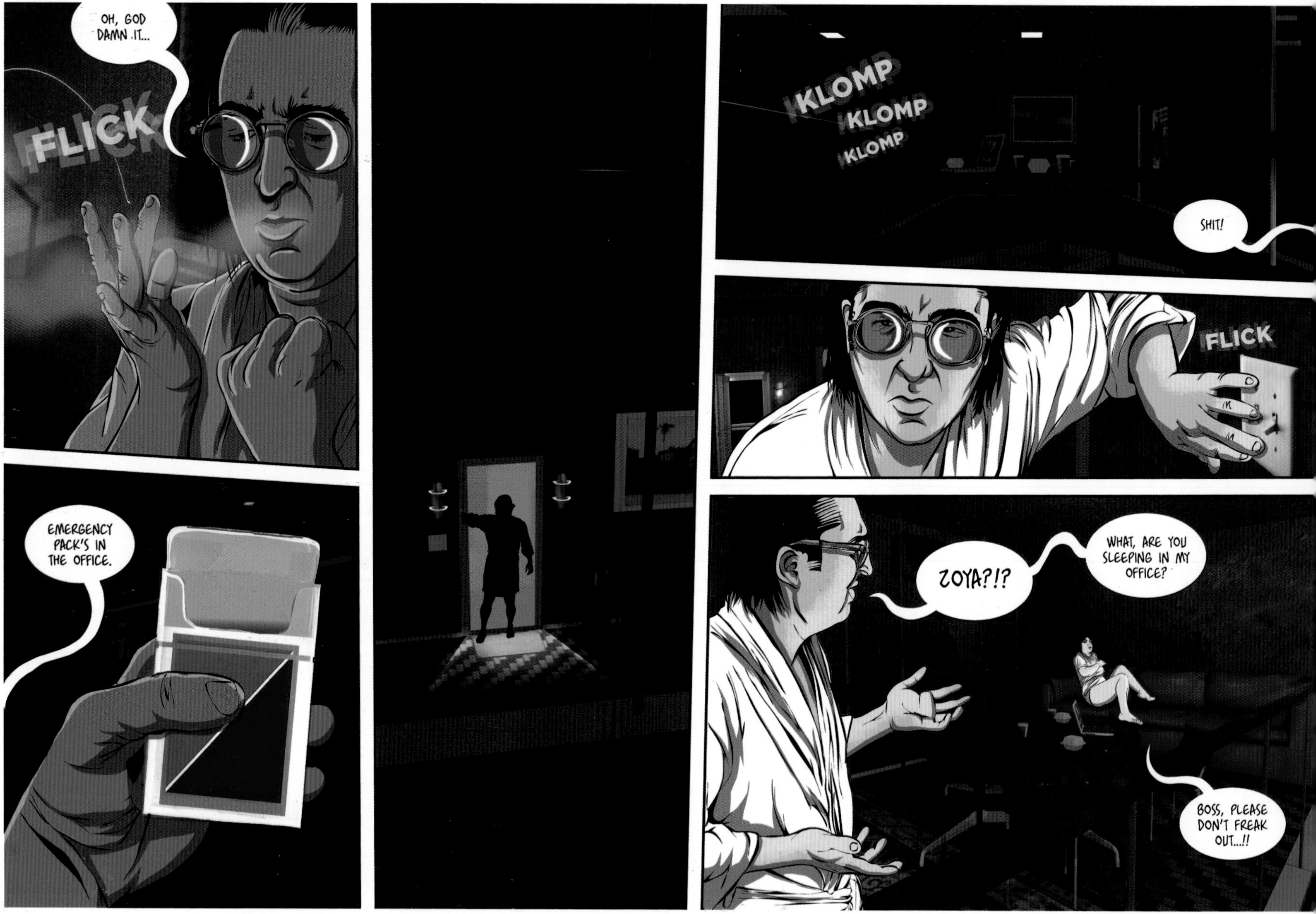
OH, GOD DAMN IT...
FLICK
EMERGENCY PACK'S IN THE OFFICE.
KLOMP
KLOMP
KLOMP
SHIT!
FLICK
ZOYA?!?
WHAT, ARE YOU SLEEPING IN MY OFFICE?
BOSS, PLEASE DON'T FREAK OUT...!!

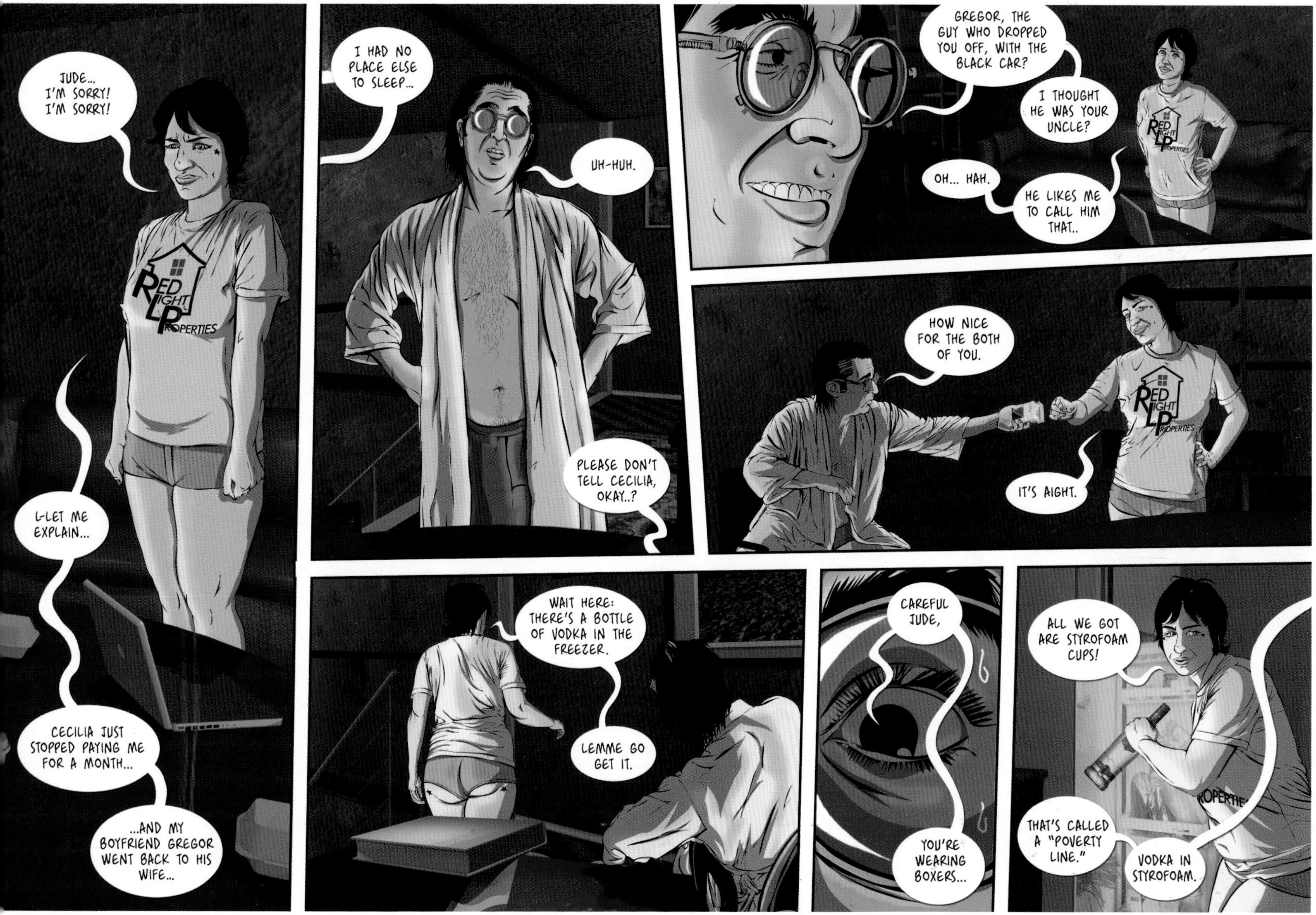
JUDE... I'M SORRY! I'M SORRY!
L-LET ME EXPLAIN...
CECILIA JUST STOPPED PAYING ME FOR A MONTH...
...AND MY BOYFRIEND GREGOR WENT BACK TO HIS WIFE...
I HAD NO PLACE ELSE TO SLEEP...
UH-HUH.
PLEASE DON'T TELL CECILIA, OKAY..?
GREGOR, THE GUY WHO DROPPED YOU OFF, WITH THE BLACK CAR?
I THOUGHT HE WAS YOUR UNCLE?
OH... HAH.
HE LIKES ME TO CALL HIM THAT..
HOW NICE FOR THE BOTH OF YOU.
IT'S AIGHT.
WAIT HERE: THERE'S A BOTTLE OF VODKA IN THE FREEZER.
LEMME GO GET IT.
CAREFUL JUDE,
YOU'RE WEARING BOXERS...
ALL WE GOT ARE STYROFOAM CUPS!
THAT'S CALLED A "POVERTY LINE."
VODKA IN STYROFOAM.

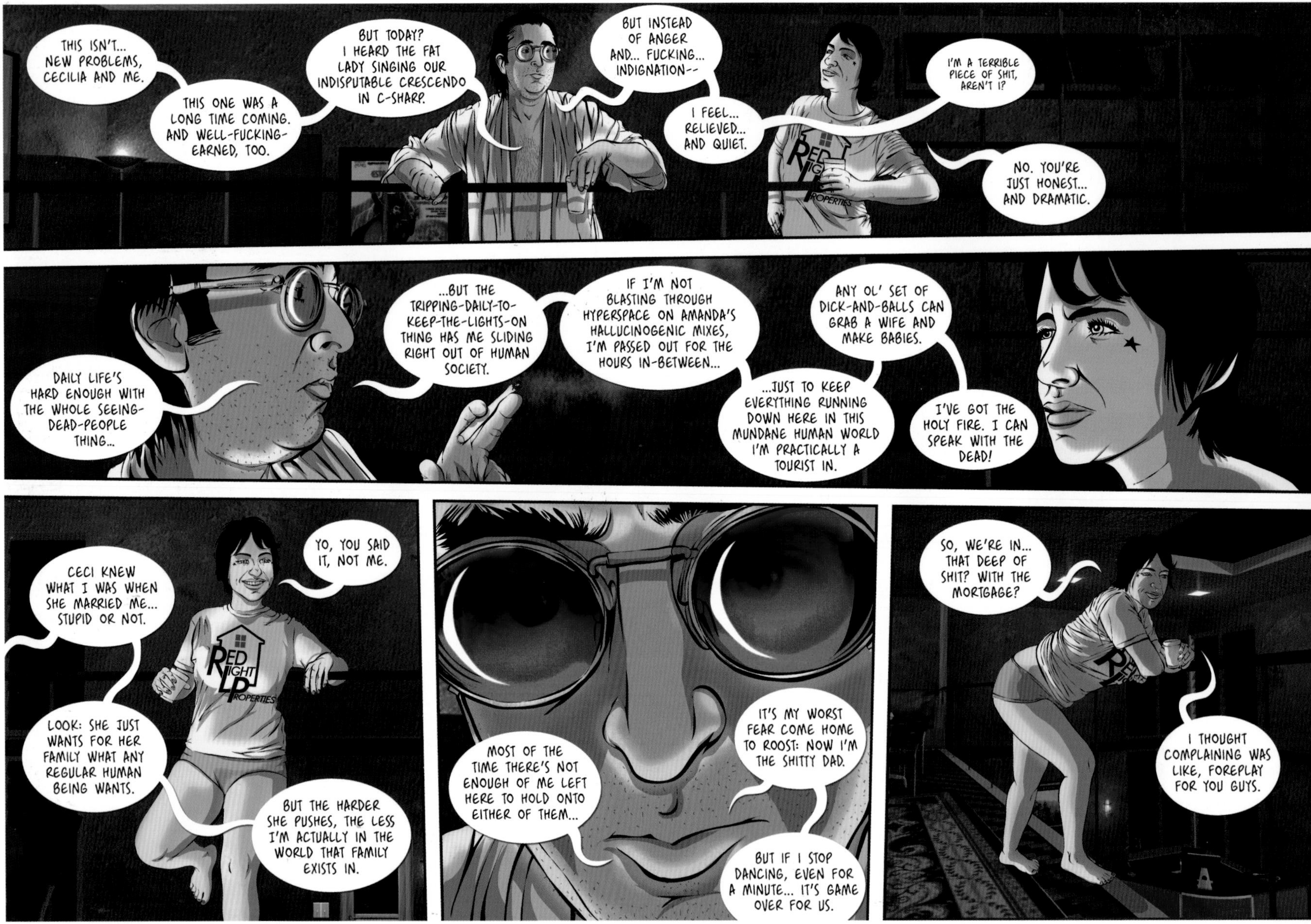
THIS ISN'T... NEW PROBLEMS, CECILIA AND ME.
THIS ONE WAS A LONG TIME COMING. AND WELL-FUCKING-EARNED, TOO.
BUT TODAY? I HEARD THE FAT LADY SINGING OUR INDISPUTABLE CRESCENDO IN C-SHARP.
BUT INSTEAD OF ANGER AND... FUCKING... INDIGNATION--
I FEEL... RELIEVED... AND QUIET.
I'M A TERRIBLE PIECE OF SHIT, AREN'T I?
NO. YOU'RE JUST HONEST... AND DRAMATIC.
DAILY LIFE'S HARD ENOUGH WITH THE WHOLE SEEING-DEAD-PEOPLE THING...
...BUT THE TRIPPING-DAILY-TO-KEEP-THE-LIGHTS-ON THING HAS ME SLIDING RIGHT OUT OF HUMAN SOCIETY.
IF I'M NOT BLASTING THROUGH HYPERSPACE ON AMANDA'S HALLUCINOGENIC MIXES, I'M PASSED OUT FOR THE HOURS IN-BETWEEN...
...JUST TO KEEP EVERYTHING RUNNING DOWN HERE IN THIS MUNDANE HUMAN WORLD I'M PRACTICALLY A TOURIST IN.
ANY OL' SET OF DICK-AND-BALLS CAN GRAB A WIFE AND MAKE BABIES.
I'VE GOT THE HOLY FIRE. I CAN SPEAK WITH THE DEAD!
CECI KNEW WHAT I WAS WHEN SHE MARRIED ME... STUPID OR NOT.
YO, YOU SAID IT, NOT ME.
LOOK: SHE JUST WANTS FOR HER FAMILY WHAT ANY REGULAR HUMAN BEING WANTS.
BUT THE HARDER SHE PUSHES, THE LESS I'M ACTUALLY IN THE WORLD THAT FAMILY EXISTS IN.
MOST OF THE TIME THERE'S NOT ENOUGH OF ME LEFT HERE TO HOLD ONTO EITHER OF THEM...
IT'S MY WORST FEAR COME HOME TO ROOST: NOW I'M THE SHITTY DAD.
BUT IF I STOP DANCING, EVEN FOR A MINUTE... IT'S GAME OVER FOR US.
SO, WE'RE IN... THAT DEEP OF SHIT? WITH THE MORTGAGE?
I THOUGHT COMPLAINING WAS LIKE, FOREPLAY FOR YOU GUYS.

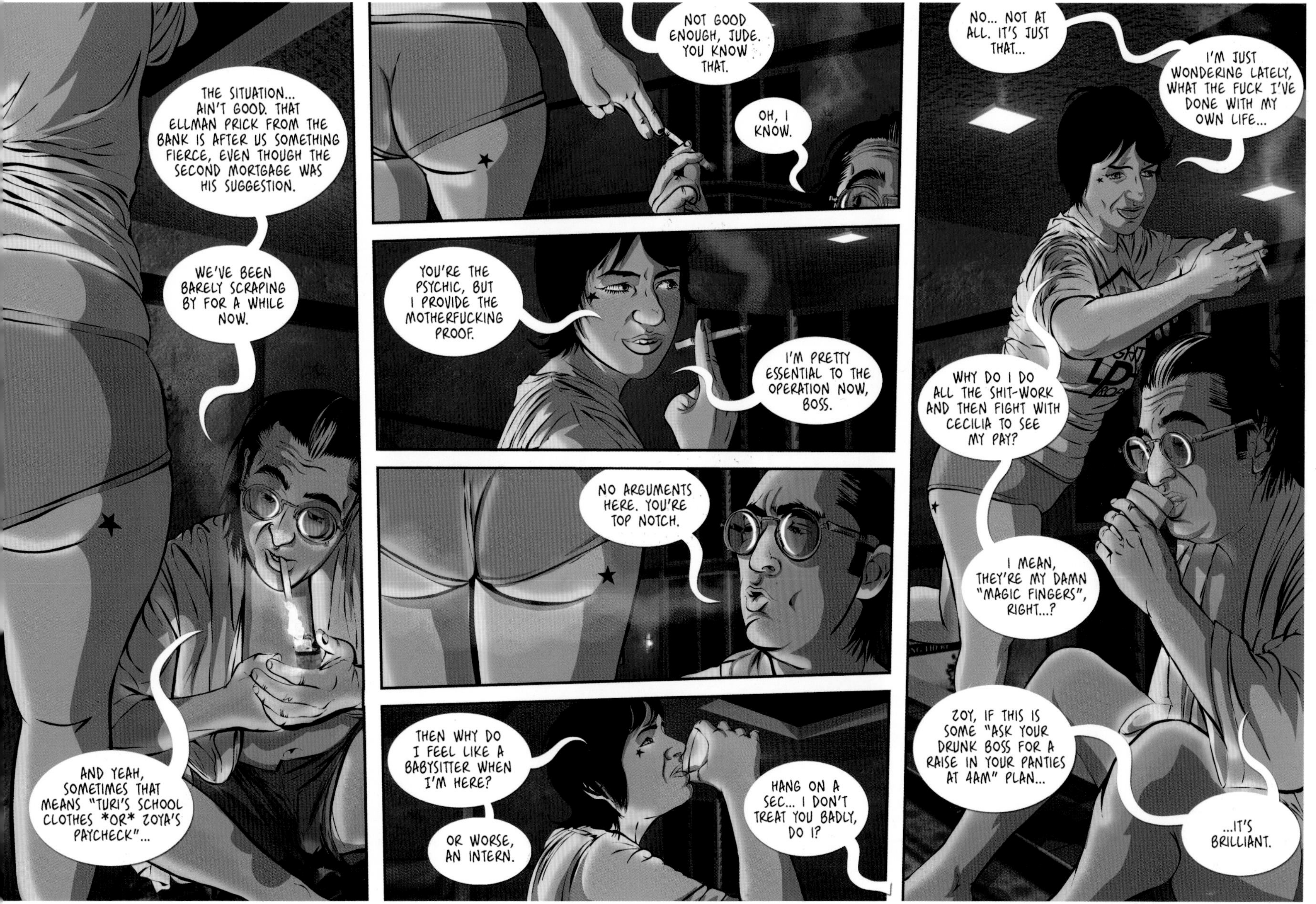
THE SITUATION... AIN'T GOOD. THAT ELLMAN PRICK FROM THE BANK IS AFTER US SOMETHING FIERCE, EVEN THOUGH THE SECOND MORTGAGE WAS HIS SUGGESTION.
WE'VE BEEN BARELY SCRAPING BY FOR A WHILE NOW.
AND YEAH, SOMETIMES THAT MEANS "TURI'S SCHOOL CLOTHES *OR* ZOYA'S PAYCHECK"...
NOT GOOD ENOUGH, JUDE. YOU KNOW THAT.
OH, I KNOW.
YOU'RE THE PSYCHIC, BUT I PROVIDE THE MOTHERFUCKING PROOF.
I'M PRETTY ESSENTIAL TO THE OPERATION NOW, BOSS.
NO ARGUMENTS HERE. YOU'RE TOP NOTCH.
THEN WHY DO I FEEL LIKE A BABYSITTER WHEN I'M HERE?
OR WORSE, AN INTERN.
HANG ON A SEC... I DON'T TREAT YOU BADLY, DO I?
NO... NOT AT ALL. IT'S JUST THAT...
I'M JUST WONDERING LATELY, WHAT THE FUCK I'VE DONE WITH MY OWN LIFE...
WHY DO I DO ALL THE SHIT-WORK AND THEN FIGHT WITH CECILIA TO SEE MY PAY?
I MEAN, THEY'RE MY DAMN "MAGIC FINGERS", RIGHT...?
ZOY, IF THIS IS SOME "ASK YOUR DRUNK BOSS FOR A RAISE IN YOUR PANTIES AT 4AM" PLAN...
...IT'S BRILLIANT.

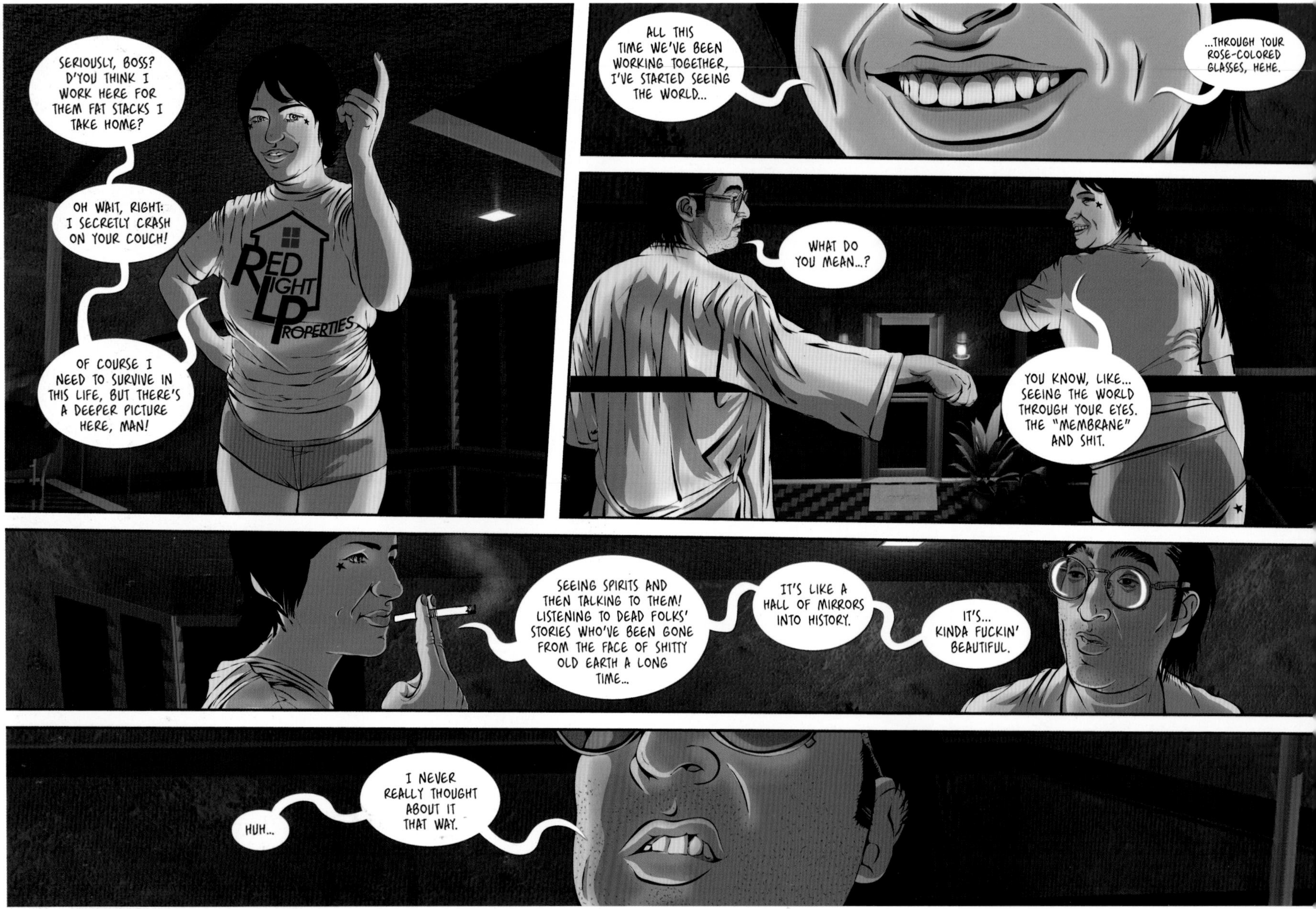
SERIOUSLY, BOSS? D'YOU THINK I WORK HERE FOR THEM FAT STACKS I TAKE HOME?
OH WAIT, RIGHT: I SECRETLY CRASH ON YOUR COUCH!
OF COURSE I NEED TO SURVIVE IN THIS LIFE, BUT THERE'S A DEEPER PICTURE HERE, MAN!
RED LIGHT PROPERTIES
ALL THIS TIME WE'VE BEEN WORKING TOGETHER, I'VE STARTED SEEING THE WORLD...
...THROUGH YOUR ROSE-COLORED GLASSES, HEHE.
WHAT DO YOU MEAN...?
YOU KNOW, LIKE... SEEING THE WORLD THROUGH YOUR EYES. THE "MEMBRANE" AND SHIT.
SEEING SPIRITS AND THEN TALKING TO THEM! LISTENING TO DEAD FOLKS' STORIES WHO'VE BEEN GONE FROM THE FACE OF SHITTY OLD EARTH A LONG TIME...
IT'S LIKE A HALL OF MIRRORS INTO HISTORY.
IT'S... KINDA FUCKIN' BEAUTIFUL.
HUH...
I NEVER REALLY THOUGHT ABOUT IT THAT WAY.

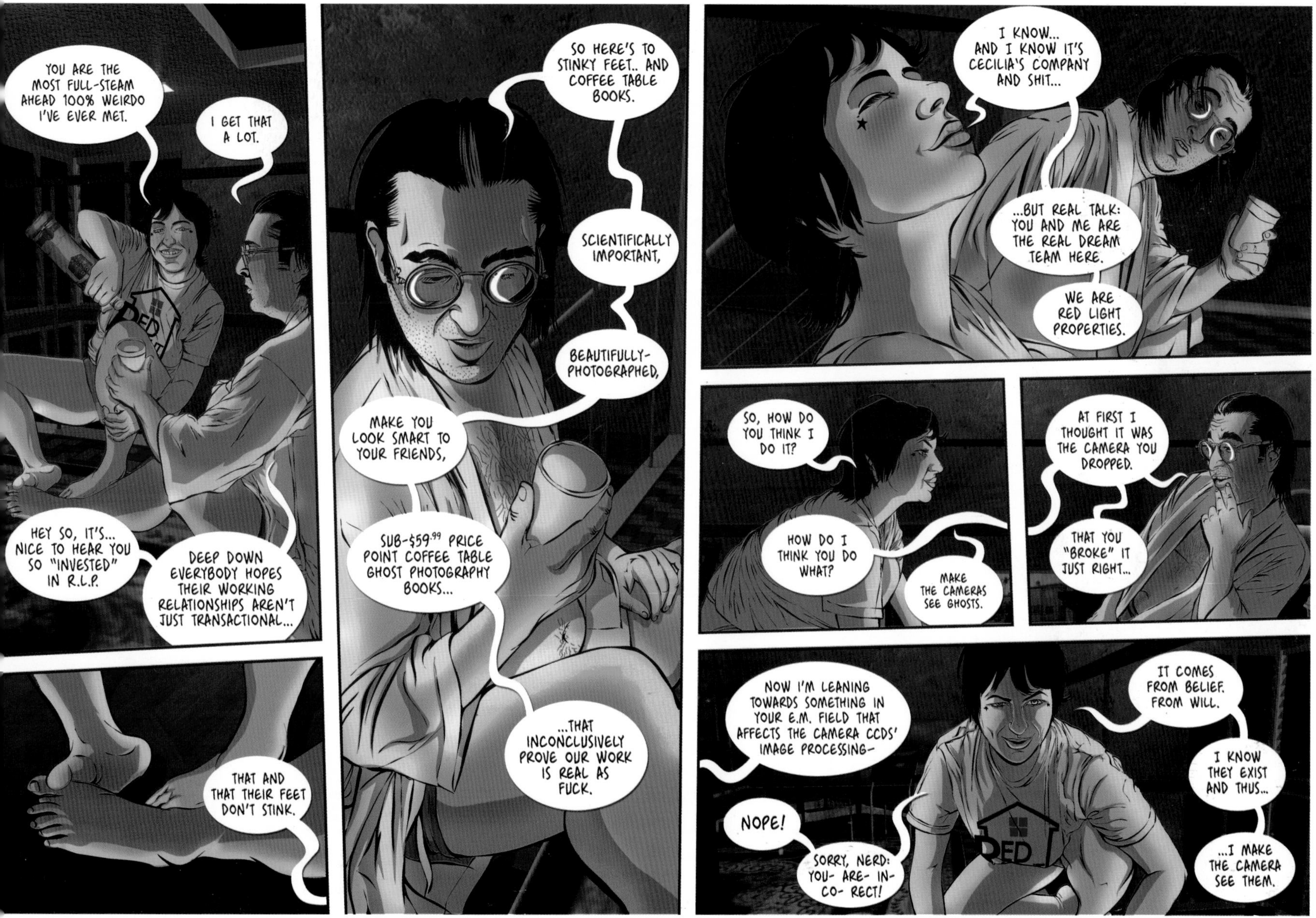
YOU ARE THE MOST FULL-STEAM AHEAD 100% WEIRDO I'VE EVER MET.
I GET THAT A LOT.
HEY SO, IT'S... NICE TO HEAR YOU SO "INVESTED" IN R.L.P.
DEEP DOWN EVERYBODY HOPES THEIR WORKING RELATIONSHIPS AREN'T JUST TRANSACTIONAL...
THAT AND THAT THEIR FEET DON'T STINK.
SO HERE'S TO STINKY FEET.. AND COFFEE TABLE BOOKS.
SCIENTIFICALLY IMPORTANT,
BEAUTIFULLY-PHOTOGRAPHED,
MAKE YOU LOOK SMART TO YOUR FRIENDS,
SUB-$59.99 PRICE POINT COFFEE TABLE GHOST PHOTOGRAPHY BOOKS...
...THAT INCONCLUSIVELY PROVE OUR WORK IS REAL AS FUCK.
I KNOW... AND I KNOW IT'S CECILIA'S COMPANY AND SHIT...
...BUT REAL TALK: YOU AND ME ARE THE REAL DREAM TEAM HERE.
WE ARE RED LIGHT PROPERTIES.
SO, HOW DO YOU THINK I DO IT?
HOW DO I THINK YOU DO WHAT?
MAKE THE CAMERAS SEE GHOSTS.
AT FIRST I THOUGHT IT WAS THE CAMERA YOU DROPPED.
THAT YOU "BROKE" IT JUST RIGHT...
NOW I'M LEANING TOWARDS SOMETHING IN YOUR E.M. FIELD THAT AFFECTS THE CAMERA CCDS' IMAGE PROCESSING-
NOPE!
SORRY, NERD: YOU- ARE- IN- CO- RECT!
IT COMES FROM BELIEF. FROM WILL.
I KNOW THEY EXIST AND THUS...
...I MAKE THE CAMERA SEE THEM.

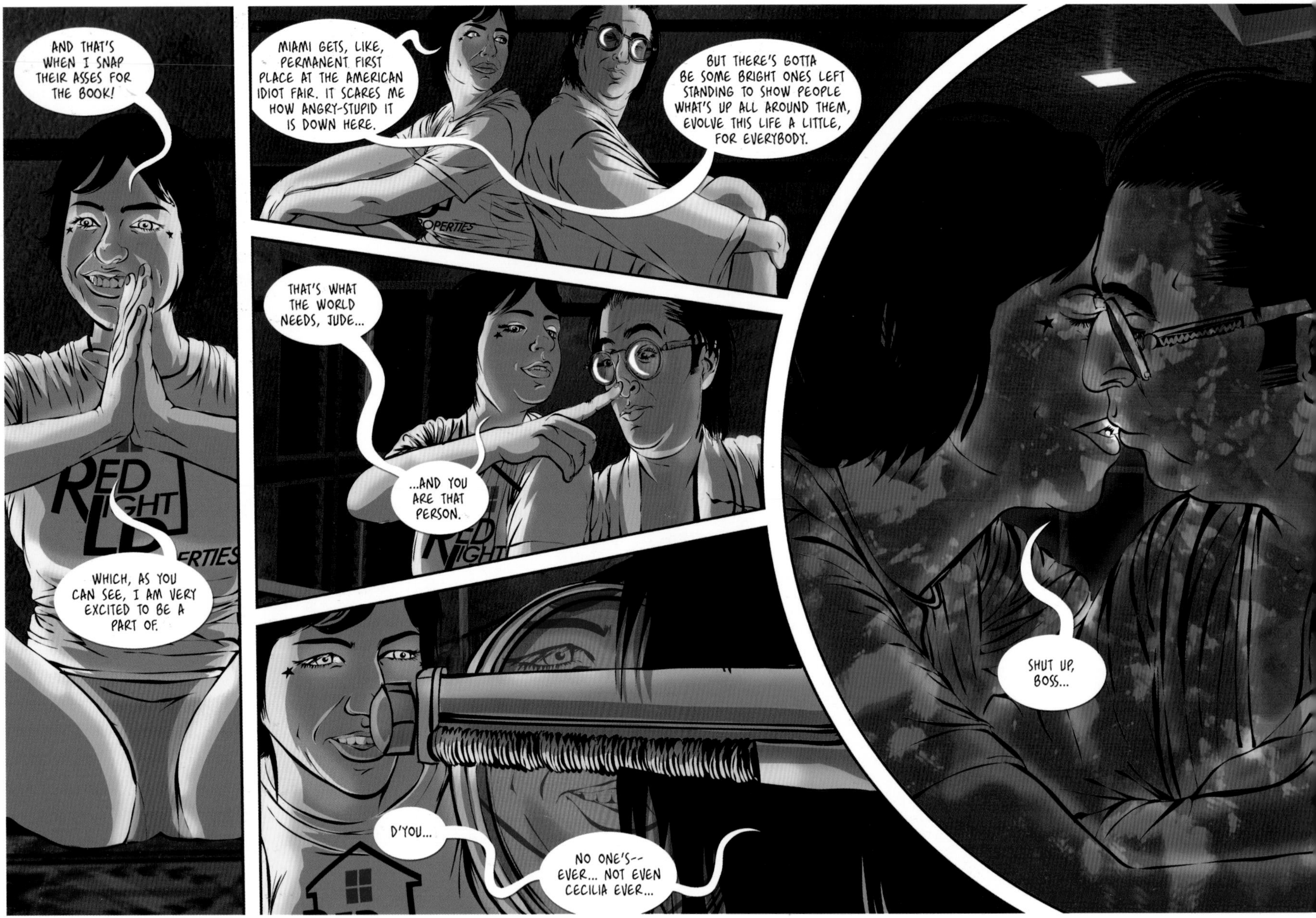
AND THAT'S WHEN I SNAP THEIR ASSES FOR THE BOOK!
WHICH, AS YOU CAN SEE, I AM VERY EXCITED TO BE A PART OF.
MIAMI GETS, LIKE, PERMANENT FIRST PLACE AT THE AMERICAN IDIOT FAIR. IT SCARES ME HOW ANGRY-STUPID IT IS DOWN HERE.
BUT THERE'S GOTTA BE SOME BRIGHT ONES LEFT STANDING TO SHOW PEOPLE WHAT'S UP ALL AROUND THEM, EVOLVE THIS LIFE A LITTLE, FOR EVERYBODY.
THAT'S WHAT THE WORLD NEEDS, JUDE...
...AND YOU ARE THAT PERSON.
D'YOU...
NO ONE'S-- EVER... NOT EVEN CECILIA EVER...
SHUT UP, BOSS...

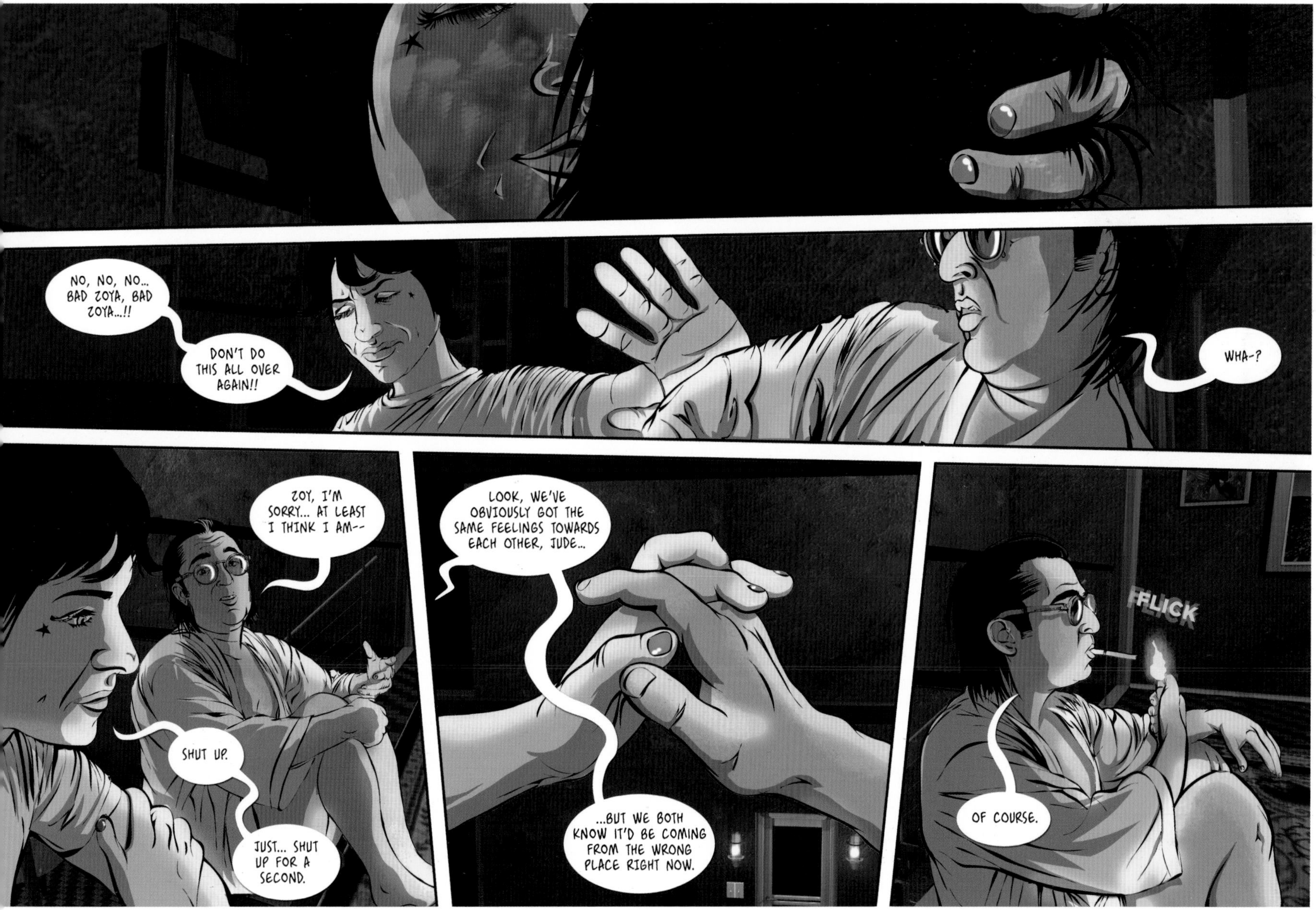
NO, NO, NO... BAD ZOYA, BAD ZOYA...!!
DON'T DO THIS ALL OVER AGAIN!!
WHA-?
ZOY, I'M SORRY... AT LEAST I THINK I AM--
SHUT UP.
JUST... SHUT UP FOR A SECOND.
LOOK, WE'VE OBVIOUSLY GOT THE SAME FEELINGS TOWARDS EACH OTHER, JUDE...
...BUT WE BOTH KNOW IT'D BE COMING FROM THE WRONG PLACE RIGHT NOW.
FFLICK
OF COURSE.

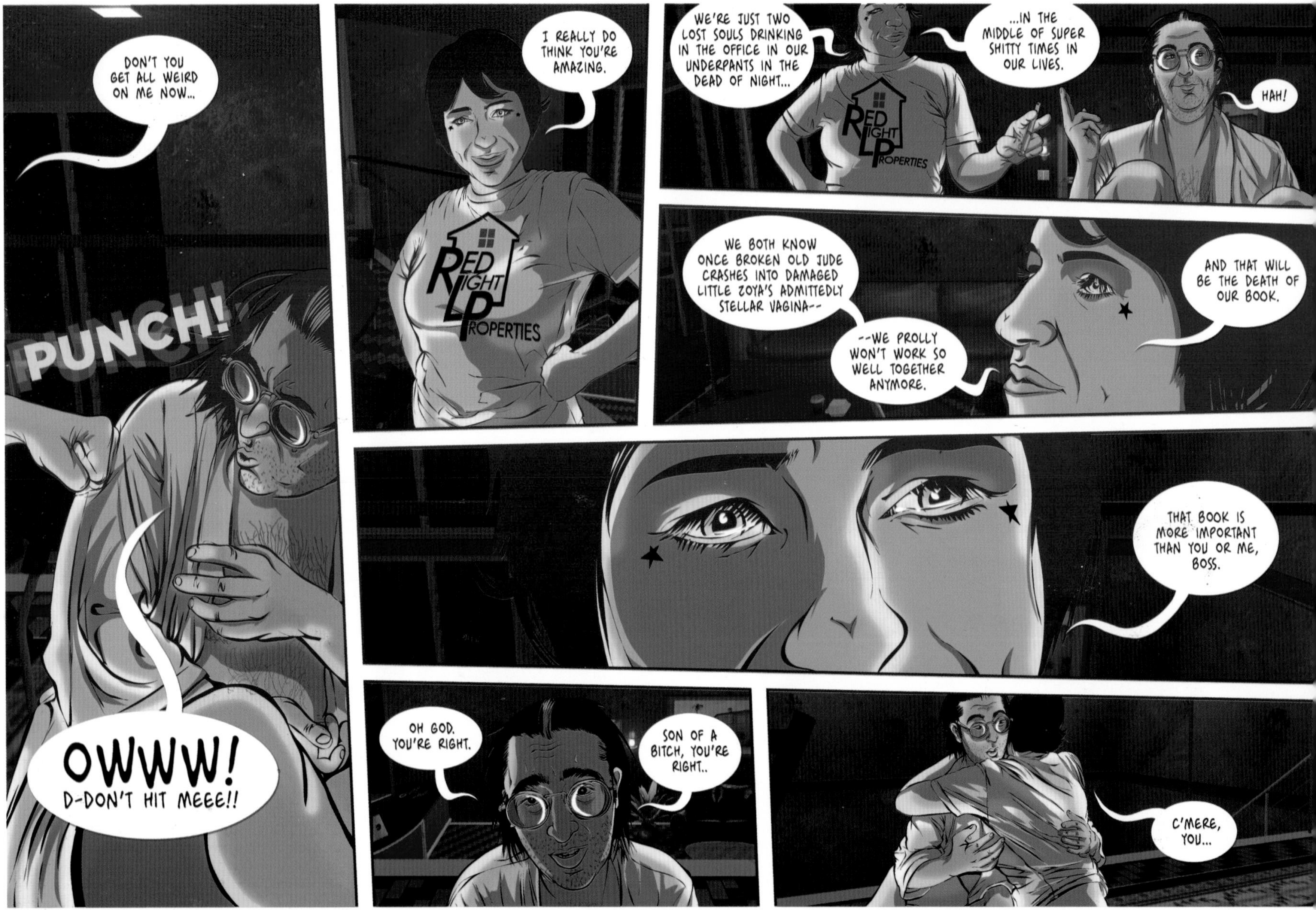
DON'T YOU GET ALL WEIRD ON ME NOW...
PUNCH!
OWWW! D-DON'T HIT MEEE!!
I REALLY DO THINK YOU'RE AMAZING.
RED RIGHT LP PROPERTIES
WE'RE JUST TWO LOST SOULS DRINKING IN THE OFFICE IN OUR UNDERPANTS IN THE DEAD OF NIGHT...
...IN THE MIDDLE OF SUPER SHITTY TIMES IN OUR LIVES.
HAH!
WE BOTH KNOW ONCE BROKEN OLD JUDE CRASHES INTO DAMAGED LITTLE ZOYA'S ADMITTEDLY STELLAR VAGINA--
--WE PROLLY WON'T WORK SO WELL TOGETHER ANYMORE.
AND THAT WILL BE THE DEATH OF OUR BOOK.
THAT BOOK IS MORE IMPORTANT THAN YOU OR ME, BOSS.
OH GOD. YOU'RE RIGHT.
SON OF A BITCH, YOU'RE RIGHT..
C'MERE, YOU...

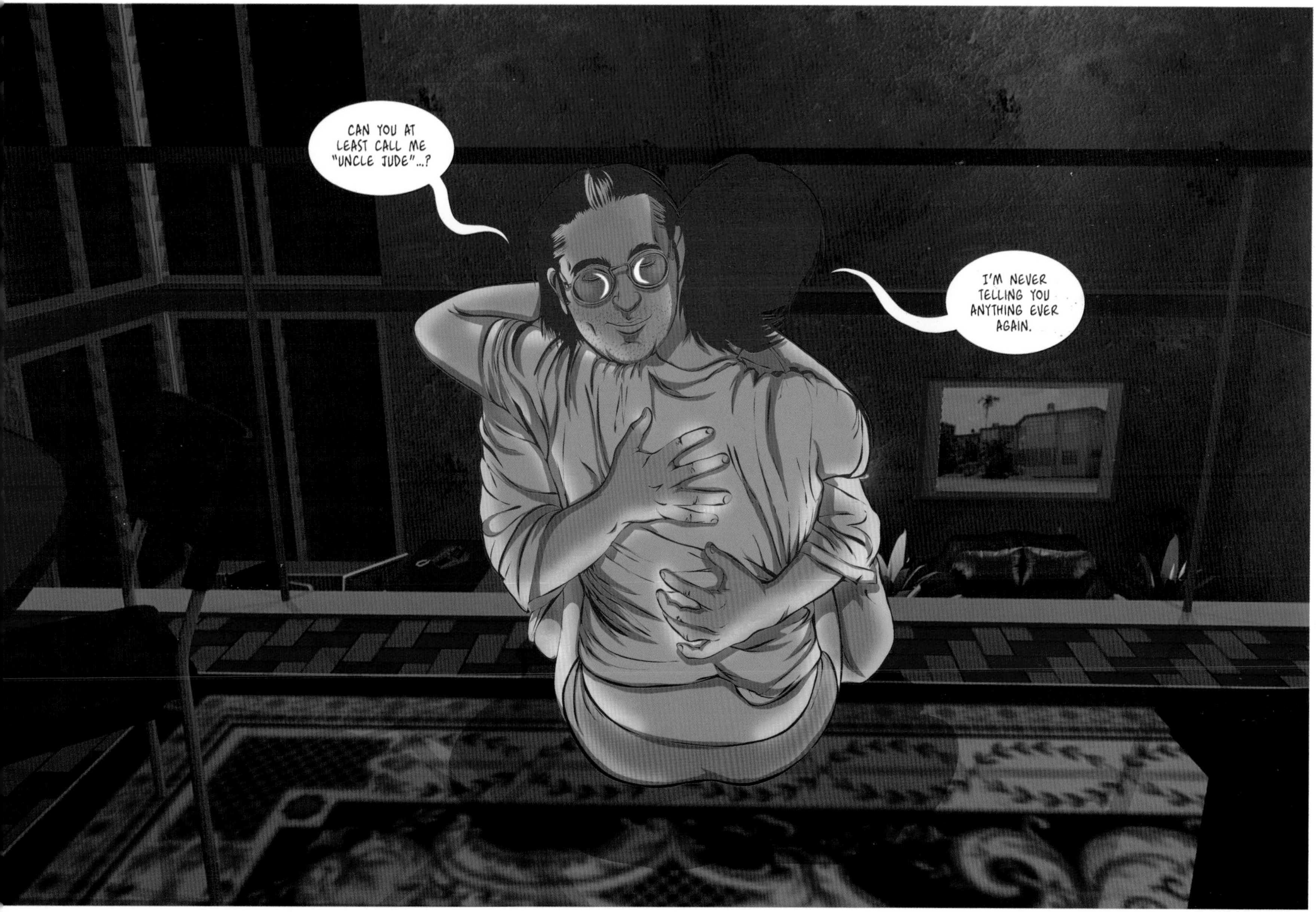
CAN YOU AT LEAST CALL ME "UNCLE JUDE"...?
I'M NEVER TELLING YOU ANYTHING EVER AGAIN.

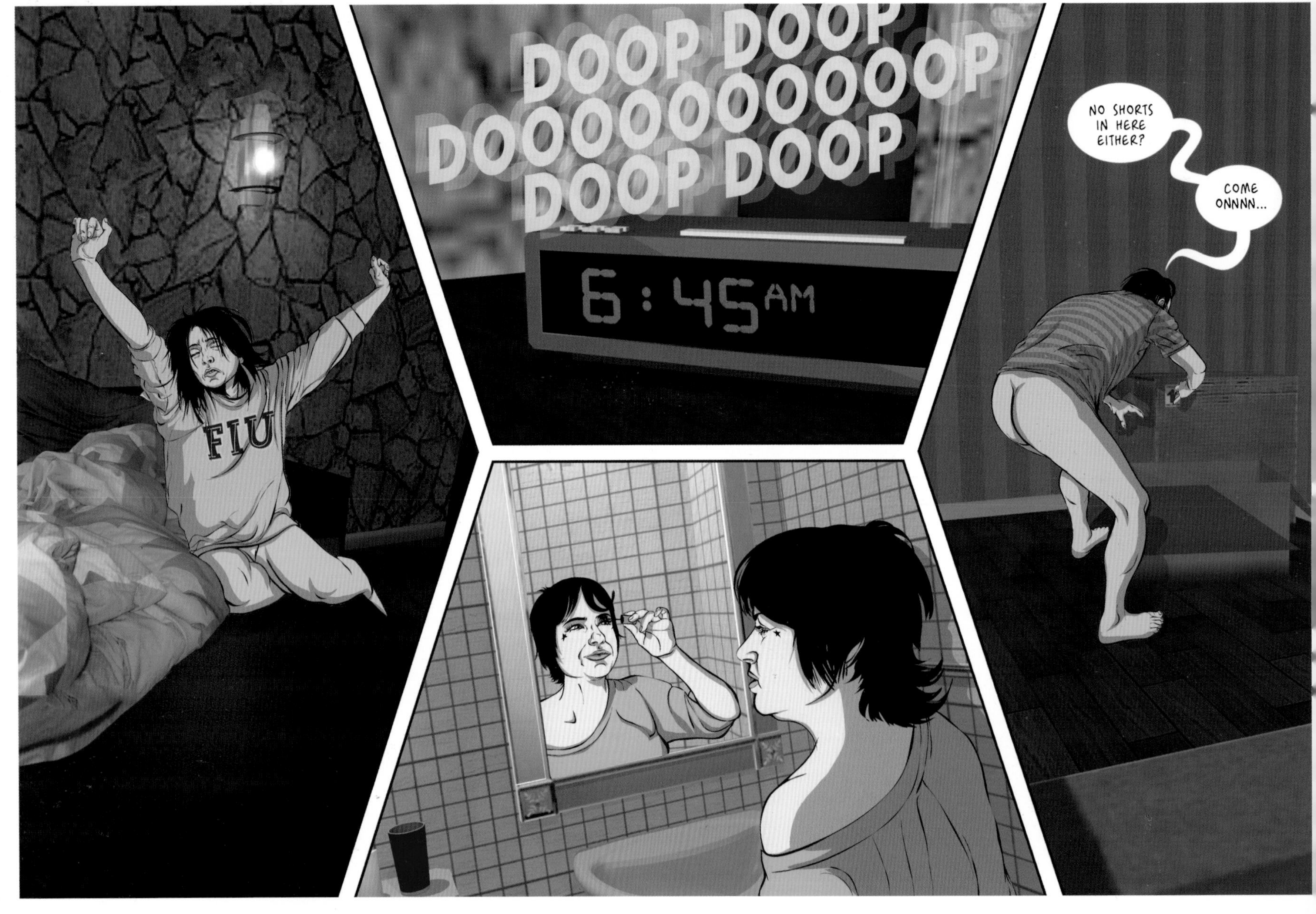
DOOP DOOP
DOOOOOOOOOOP
DOOP DOOP
6:45AM
NO SHORTS IN HERE EITHER?
COME ONNNN...
FIU

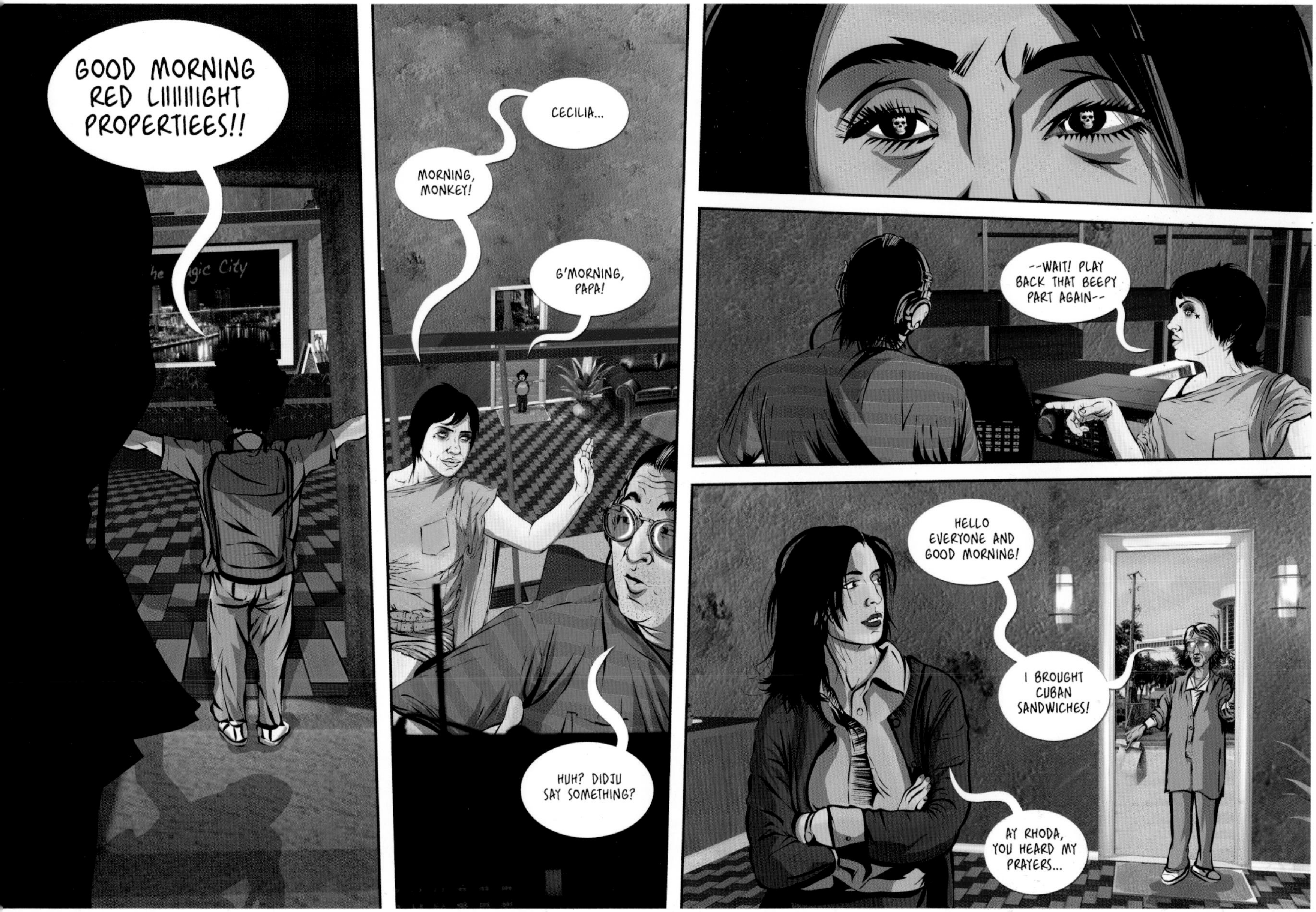
GOOD MORNING RED LIIIIIIIIGHT PROPERTIEES!!
CECILIA...
MORNING, MONKEY!
G'MORNING, PAPA!
HUH? DIDJU SAY SOMETHING?
--WAIT! PLAY BACK THAT BEEPY PART AGAIN--
HELLO EVERYONE AND GOOD MORNING!
I BROUGHT CUBAN SANDWICHES!
AY RHODA, YOU HEARD MY PRAYERS...

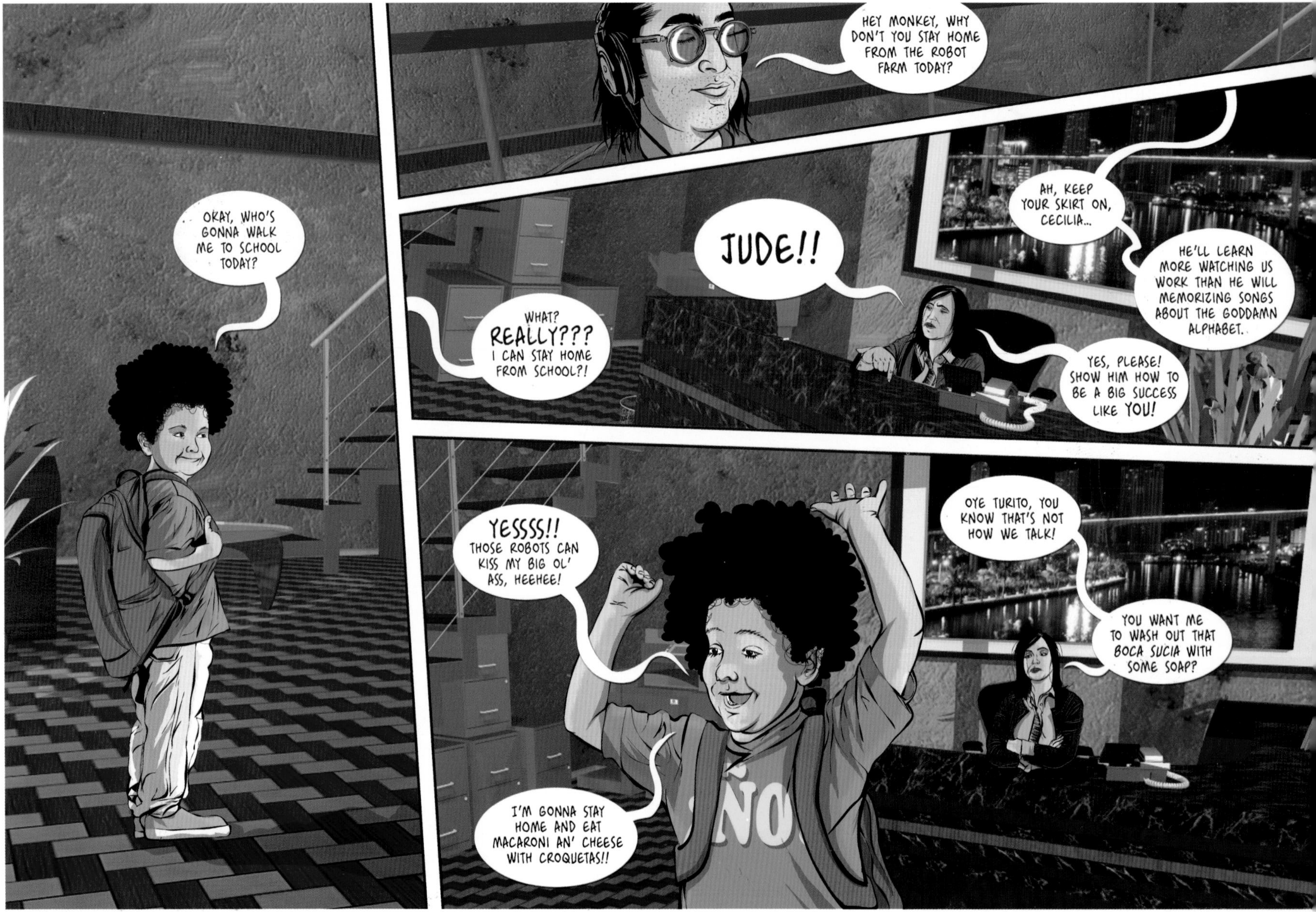
OKAY, WHO'S GONNA WALK ME TO SCHOOL TODAY?
HEY MONKEY, WHY DON'T YOU STAY HOME FROM THE ROBOT FARM TODAY?
JUDE!!
WHAT? REALLY??? I CAN STAY HOME FROM SCHOOL?!
AH, KEEP YOUR SKIRT ON, CECILIA...
HE'LL LEARN MORE WATCHING US WORK THAN HE WILL MEMORIZING SONGS ABOUT THE GODDAMN ALPHABET.
YES, PLEASE! SHOW HIM HOW TO BE A BIG SUCCESS LIKE YOU!
YESSSS!! THOSE ROBOTS CAN KISS MY BIG OL' ASS, HEEHEE!
I'M GONNA STAY HOME AND EAT MACARONI AN' CHEESE WITH CROQUETAS!!
OYE TURITO, YOU KNOW THAT'S NOT HOW WE TALK!
YOU WANT ME TO WASH OUT THAT BOCA SUCIA WITH SOME SOAP?

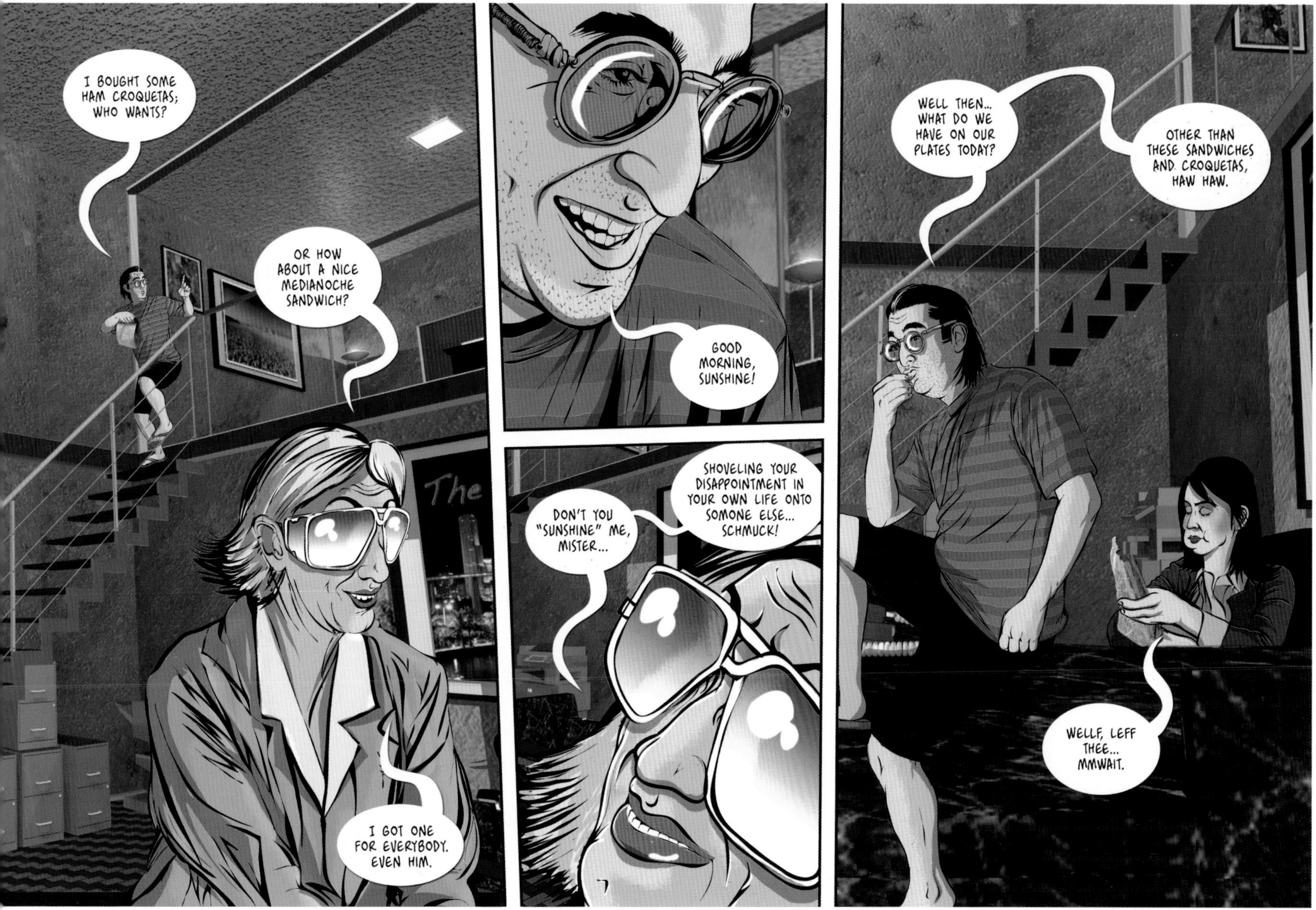
I BOUGHT SOME HAM CROQUETAS; WHO WANTS?
OR HOW ABOUT A NICE MEDIANOCHE SANDWICH?
I GOT ONE FOR EVERYBODY. EVEN HIM.
GOOD MORNING, SUNSHINE!
DON'T YOU "SUNSHINE" ME, MISTER...
SHOVELING YOUR DISAPPOINTMENT IN YOUR OWN LIFE ONTO SOMONE ELSE... SCHMUCK!
WELL THEN... WHAT DO WE HAVE ON OUR PLATES TODAY?
OTHER THAN THESE SANDWICHES AND CROQUETAS, HAW HAW.
WELLF, LEFF THEE... MMWAIT.

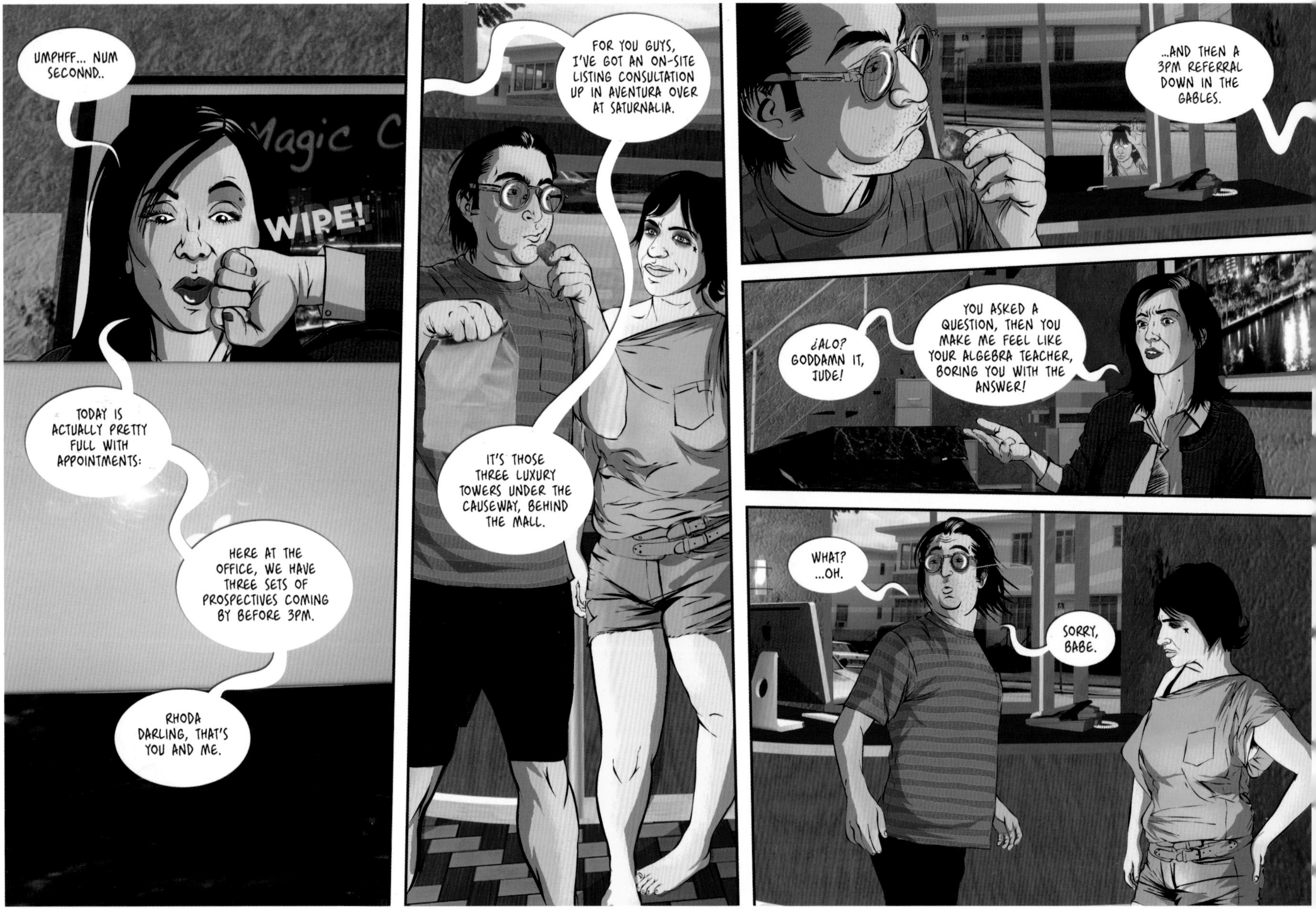
UMPHFF... NUM SECONND..
Magic C
WIPE!
TODAY IS ACTUALLY PRETTY FULL WITH APPOINTMENTS:
HERE AT THE OFFICE, WE HAVE THREE SETS OF PROSPECTIVES COMING BY BEFORE 3PM.
RHODA DARLING, THAT'S YOU AND ME.
FOR YOU GUYS, I'VE GOT AN ON-SITE LISTING CONSULTATION UP IN AVENTURA OVER AT SATURNALIA.
IT'S THOSE THREE LUXURY TOWERS UNDER THE CAUSEWAY, BEHIND THE MALL.
...AND THEN A 3PM REFERRAL DOWN IN THE GABLES.
¿ALO? GODDAMN IT, JUDE!
YOU ASKED A QUESTION, THEN YOU MAKE ME FEEL LIKE YOUR ALGEBRA TEACHER, BORING YOU WITH THE ANSWER!
WHAT? ...OH.
SORRY, BABE.

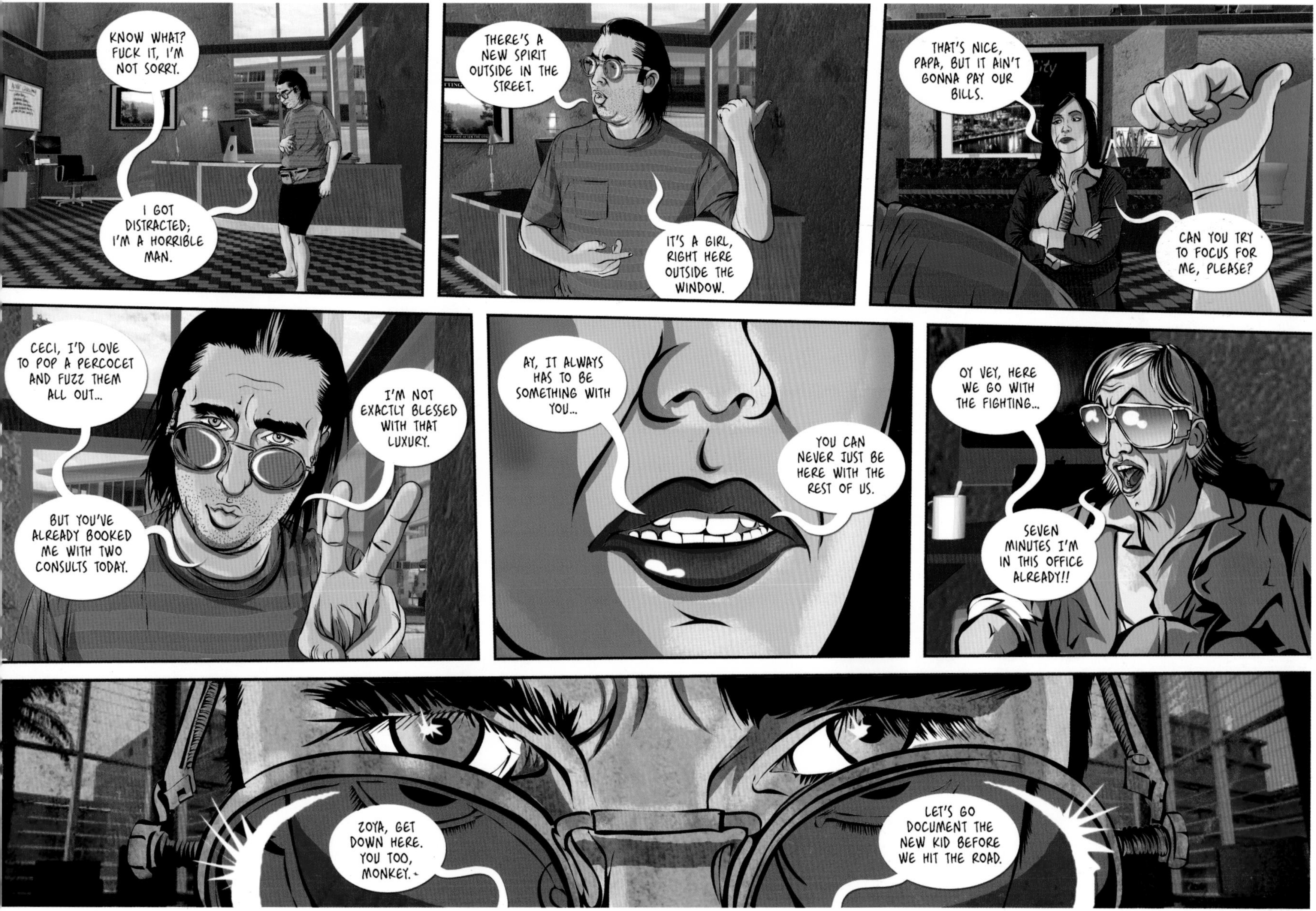
KNOW WHAT? FUCK IT, I'M NOT SORRY.
I GOT DISTRACTED; I'M A HORRIBLE MAN.
THERE'S A NEW SPIRIT OUTSIDE IN THE STREET.
IT'S A GIRL, RIGHT HERE OUTSIDE THE WINDOW.
THAT'S NICE, PAPA, BUT IT AIN'T GONNA PAY OUR BILLS.
CAN YOU TRY TO FOCUS FOR ME, PLEASE?
CECI, I'D LOVE TO POP A PERCOCET AND FUZZ THEM ALL OUT...
BUT YOU'VE ALREADY BOOKED ME WITH TWO CONSULTS TODAY.
I'M NOT EXACTLY BLESSED WITH THAT LUXURY.
AY, IT ALWAYS HAS TO BE SOMETHING WITH YOU...
YOU CAN NEVER JUST BE HERE WITH THE REST OF US.
OY VEY, HERE WE GO WITH THE FIGHTING...
SEVEN MINUTES I'M IN THIS OFFICE ALREADY!!
ZOYA, GET DOWN HERE. YOU TOO, MONKEY.
LET'S GO DOCUMENT THE NEW KID BEFORE WE HIT THE ROAD.

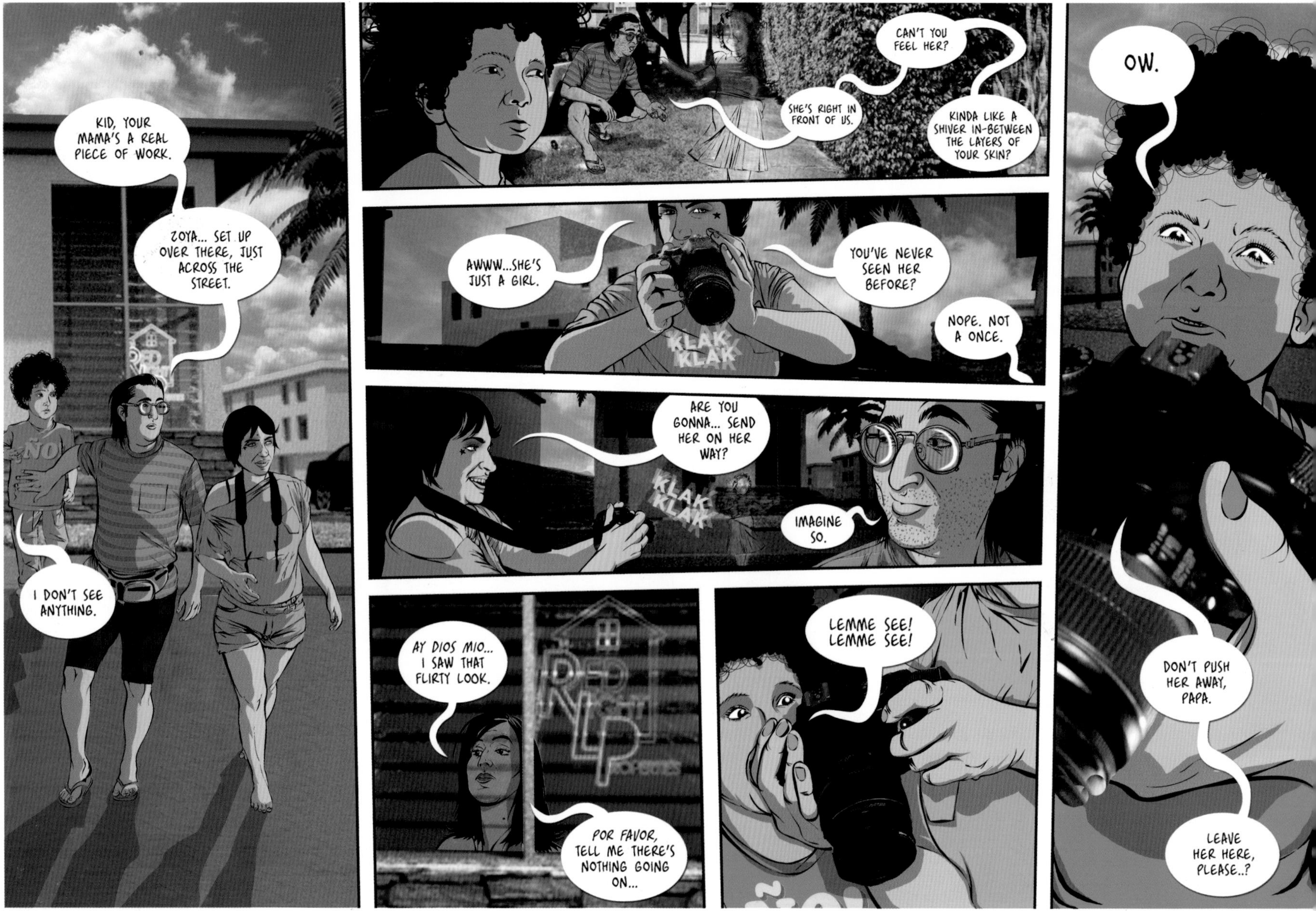
KID, YOUR MAMA'S A REAL PIECE OF WORK.
ZOYA... SET UP OVER THERE, JUST ACROSS THE STREET.
I DON'T SEE ANYTHING.
SHE'S RIGHT IN FRONT OF US.
CAN'T YOU FEEL HER?
KINDA LIKE A SHIVER IN-BETWEEN THE LAYERS OF YOUR SKIN?
AWWW...SHE'S JUST A GIRL.
KLAK KLAK
YOU'VE NEVER SEEN HER BEFORE?
NOPE. NOT A ONCE.
ARE YOU GONNA... SEND HER ON HER WAY?
KLAK KLAK
IMAGINE SO.
AY DIOS MIO... I SAW THAT FLIRTY LOOK.
POR FAVOR, TELL ME THERE'S NOTHING GOING ON...
LEMME SEE! LEMME SEE!
OW.
DON'T PUSH HER AWAY, PAPA.
LEAVE HER HERE, PLEASE..?

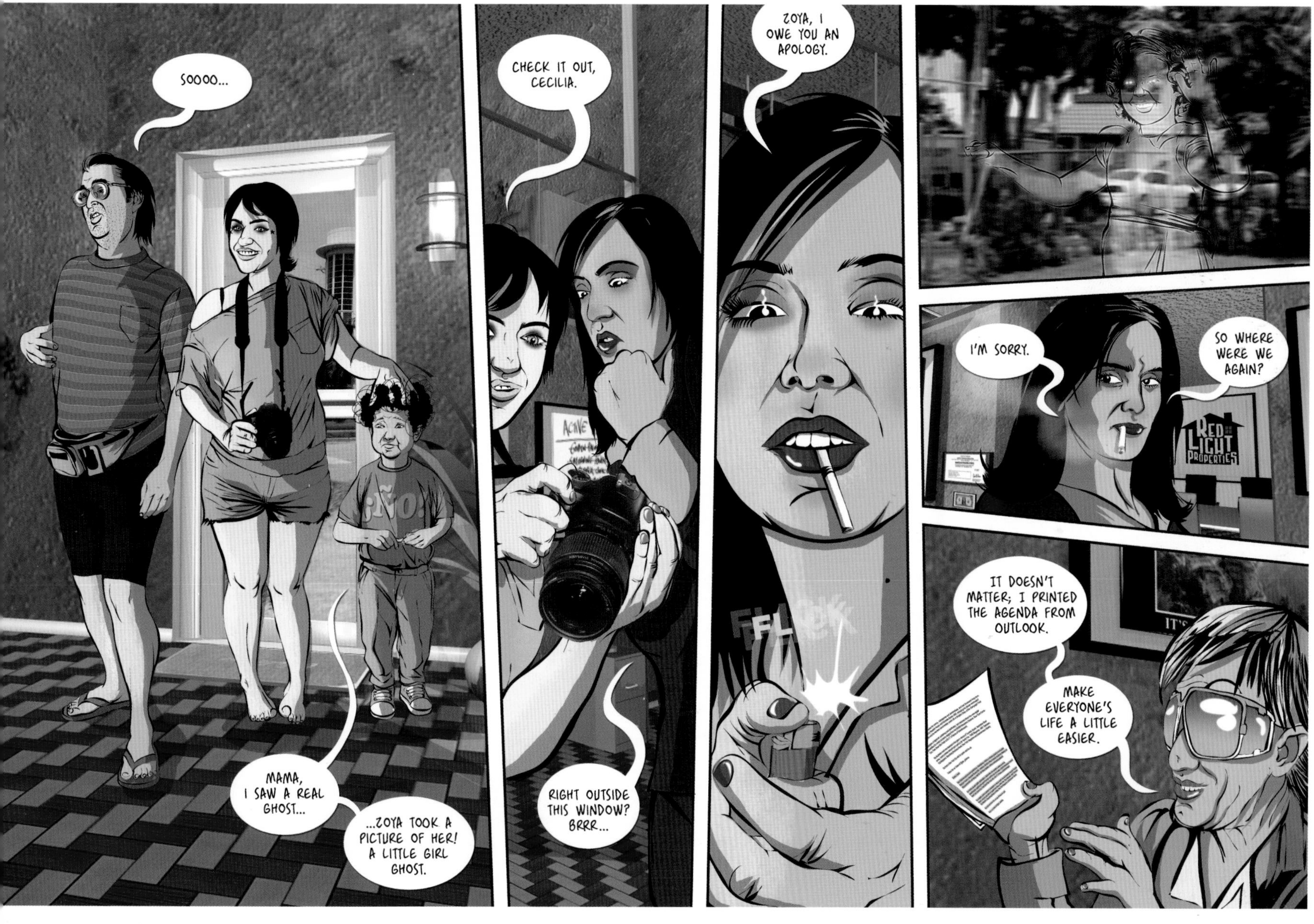
SOOOO...
MAMA, I SAW A REAL GHOST...
...ZOYA TOOK A PICTURE OF HER! A LITTLE GIRL GHOST.
CHECK IT OUT, CECILIA.
RIGHT OUTSIDE THIS WINDOW? BRRR...
ZOYA, I OWE YOU AN APOLOGY.
I'M SORRY.
SO WHERE WERE WE AGAIN?
RED LIGHT PROPERTIES
IT DOESN'T MATTER; I PRINTED THE AGENDA FROM OUTLOOK.
MAKE EVERYONE'S LIFE A LITTLE EASIER.
IT'S

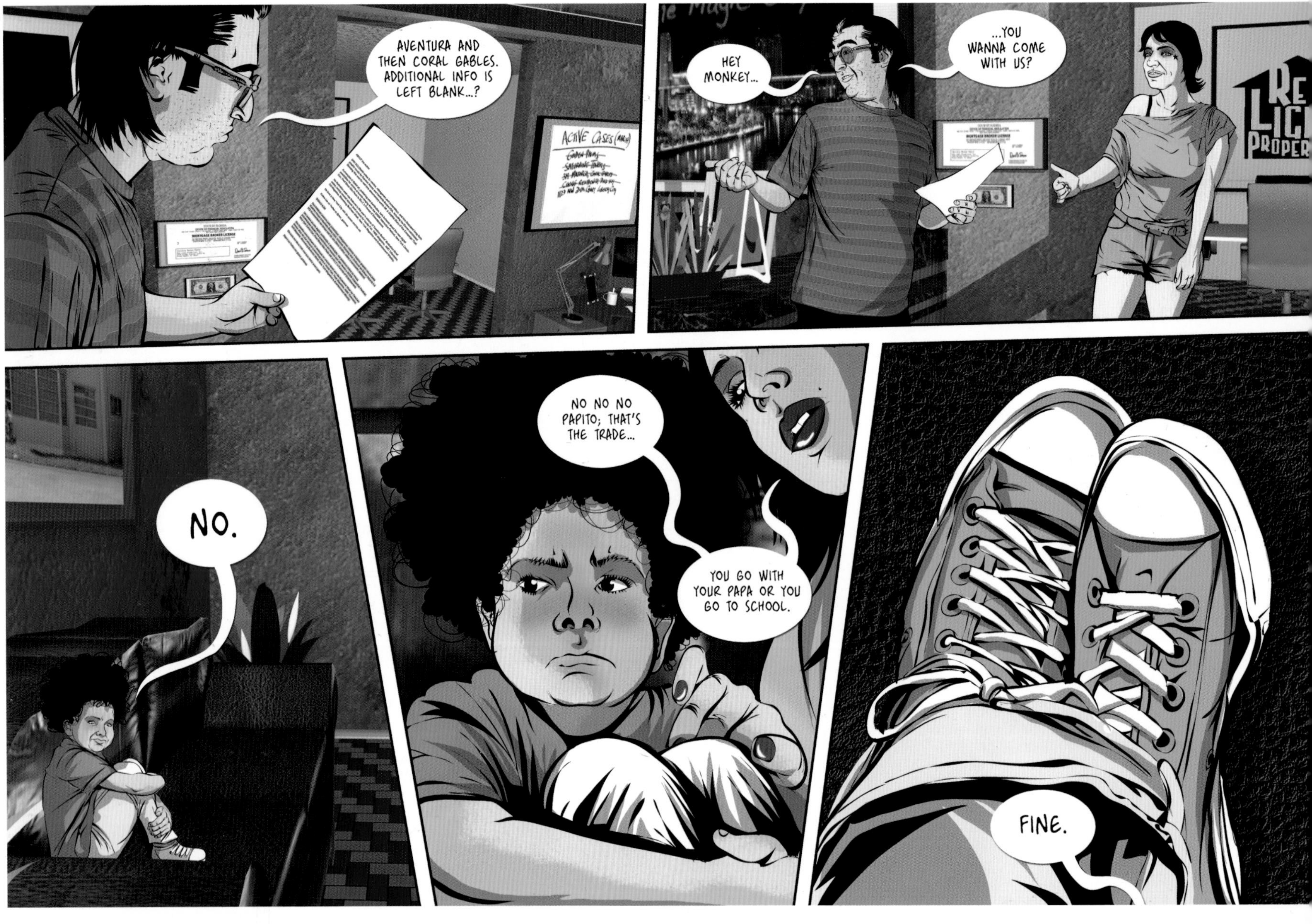
AVENTURA AND THEN CORAL GABLES. ADDITIONAL INFO IS LEFT BLANK...?
HEY MONKEY...
...YOU WANNA COME WITH US?
NO.
NO NO NO PAPITO; THAT'S THE TRADE...
YOU GO WITH YOUR PAPA OR YOU GO TO SCHOOL.
FINE.

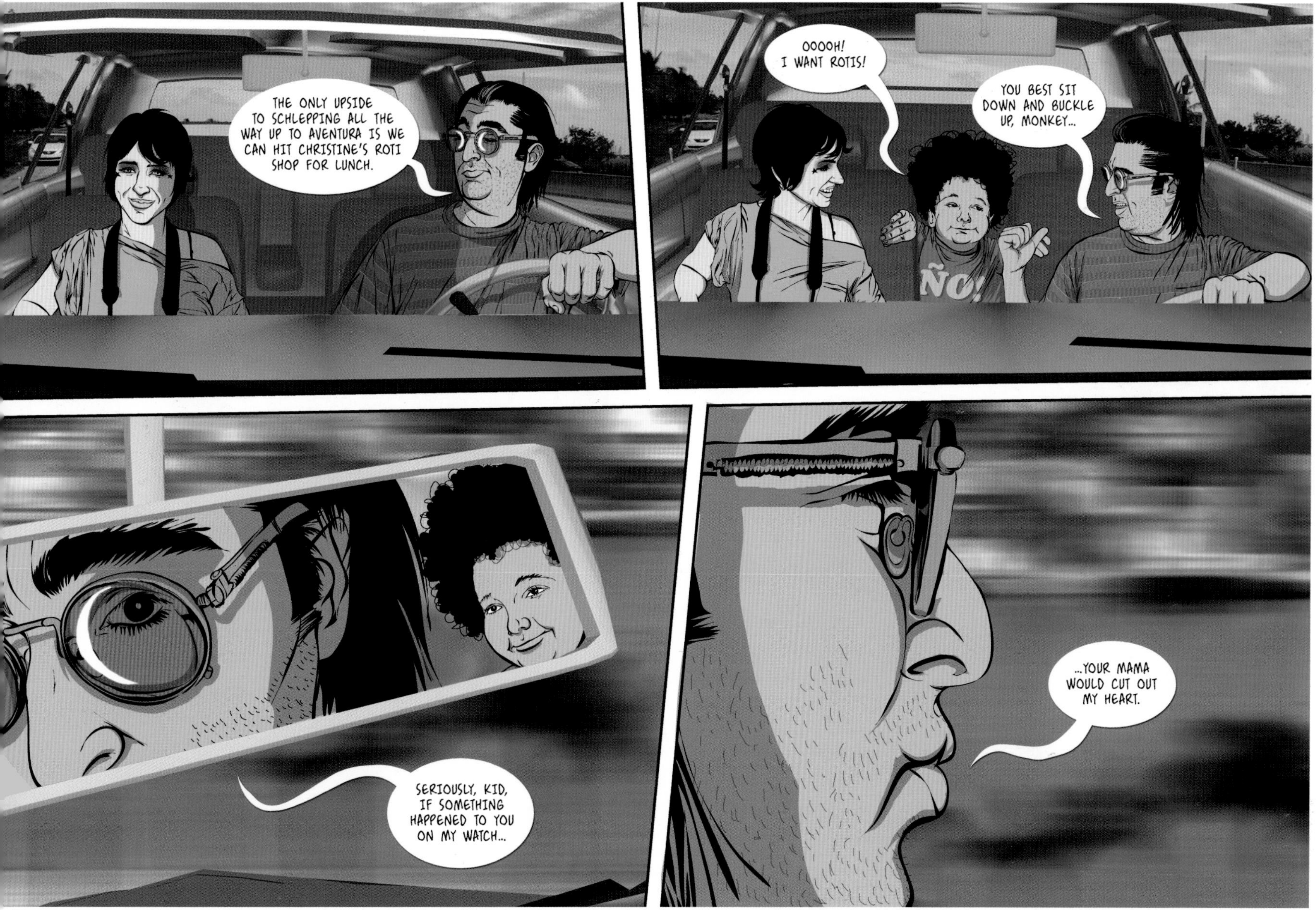
THE ONLY UPSIDE TO SCHLEPPING ALL THE WAY UP TO AVENTURA IS WE CAN HIT CHRISTINE'S ROTI SHOP FOR LUNCH.
OOOOH! I WANT ROTIS!
YOU BEST SIT DOWN AND BUCKLE UP, MONKEY...
ÑO!
SERIOUSLY, KID, IF SOMETHING HAPPENED TO YOU ON MY WATCH...
...YOUR MAMA WOULD CUT OUT MY HEART.

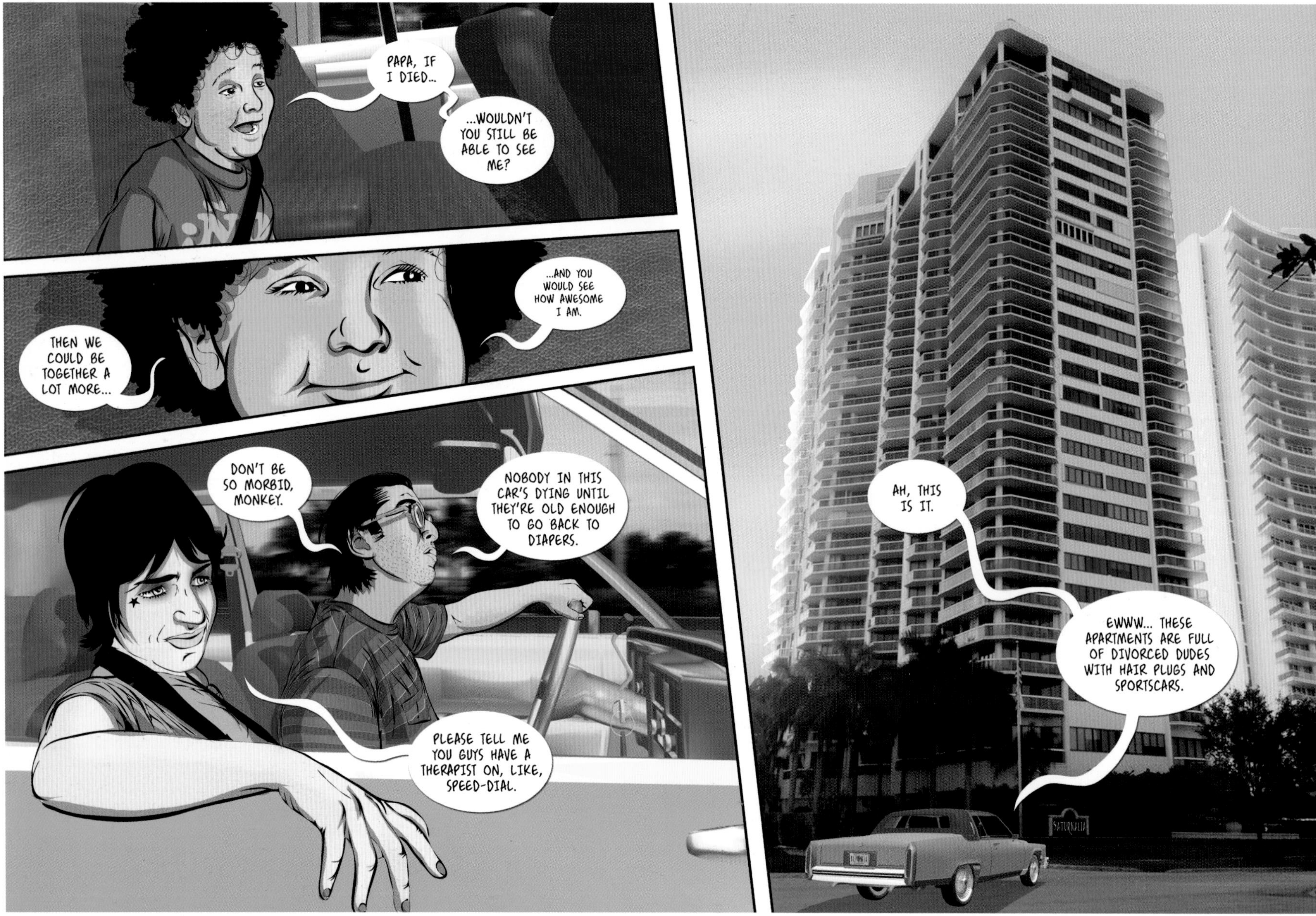
PAPA, IF I DIED...
...WOULDN'T YOU STILL BE ABLE TO SEE ME?
...AND YOU WOULD SEE HOW AWESOME I AM.
THEN WE COULD BE TOGETHER A LOT MORE...
DON'T BE SO MORBID, MONKEY.
NOBODY IN THIS CAR'S DYING UNTIL THEY'RE OLD ENOUGH TO GO BACK TO DIAPERS.
PLEASE TELL ME YOU GUYS HAVE A THERAPIST ON, LIKE, SPEED-DIAL.
AH, THIS IS IT.
EWWW... THESE APARTMENTS ARE FULL OF DIVORCED DUDES WITH HAIR PLUGS AND SPORTSCARS.

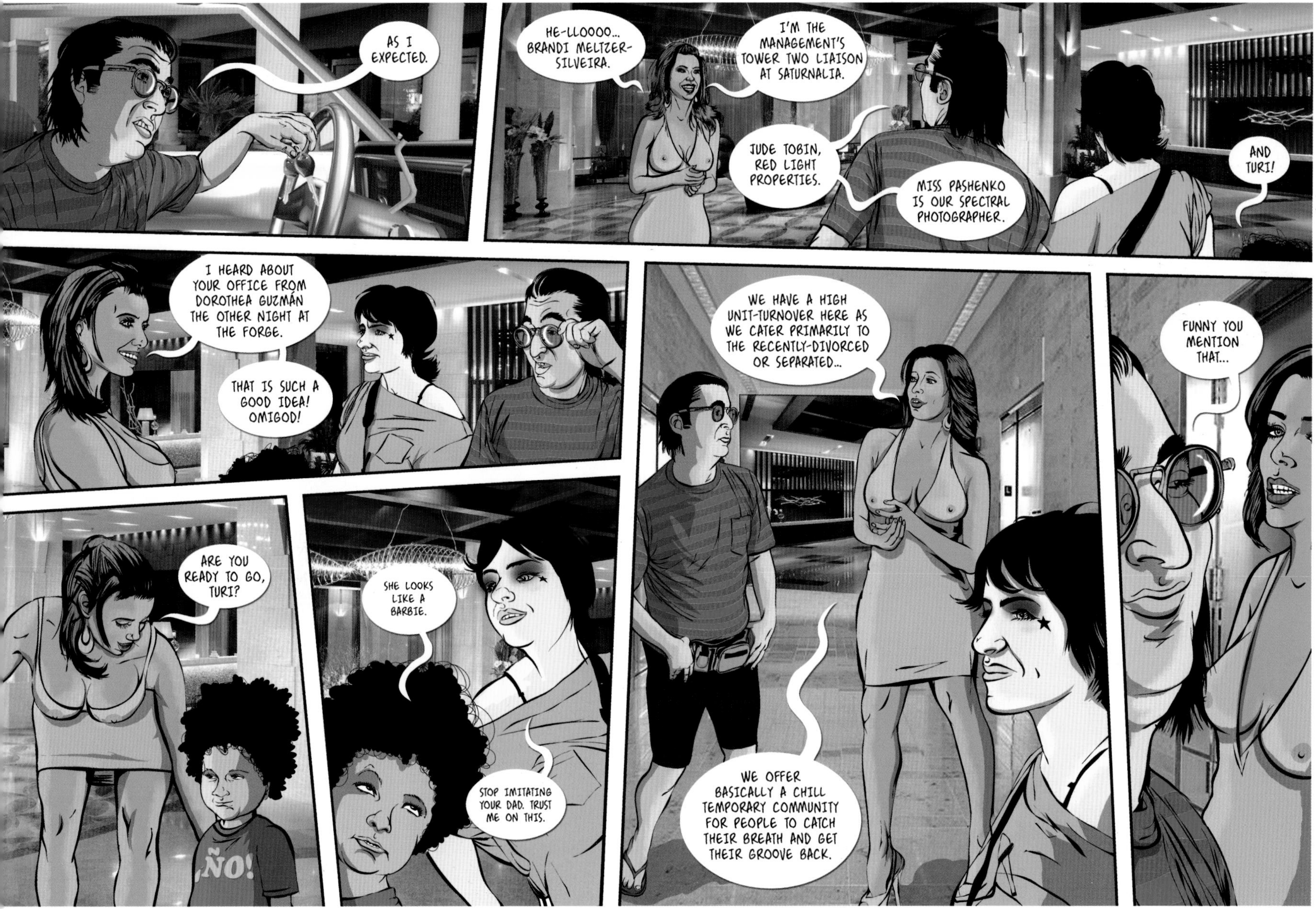
AS I EXPECTED.
HE-LLOOOO... BRANDI MELTZER-SILVEIRA.
I'M THE MANAGEMENT'S TOWER TWO LIAISON AT SATURNALIA.
JUDE TOBIN, RED LIGHT PROPERTIES.
MISS PASHENKO IS OUR SPECTRAL PHOTOGRAPHER.
AND TURI!
I HEARD ABOUT YOUR OFFICE FROM DOROTHEA GUZMÁN THE OTHER NIGHT AT THE FORGE.
THAT IS SUCH A GOOD IDEA! OMIGOD!
ARE YOU READY TO GO, TURI?
¡NO!
SHE LOOKS LIKE A BARBIE.
STOP IMITATING YOUR DAD. TRUST ME ON THIS.
WE HAVE A HIGH UNIT-TURNOVER HERE AS WE CATER PRIMARILY TO THE RECENTLY-DIVORCED OR SEPARATED...
WE OFFER BASICALLY A CHILL TEMPORARY COMMUNITY FOR PEOPLE TO CATCH THEIR BREATH AND GET THEIR GROOVE BACK.
FUNNY YOU MENTION THAT...

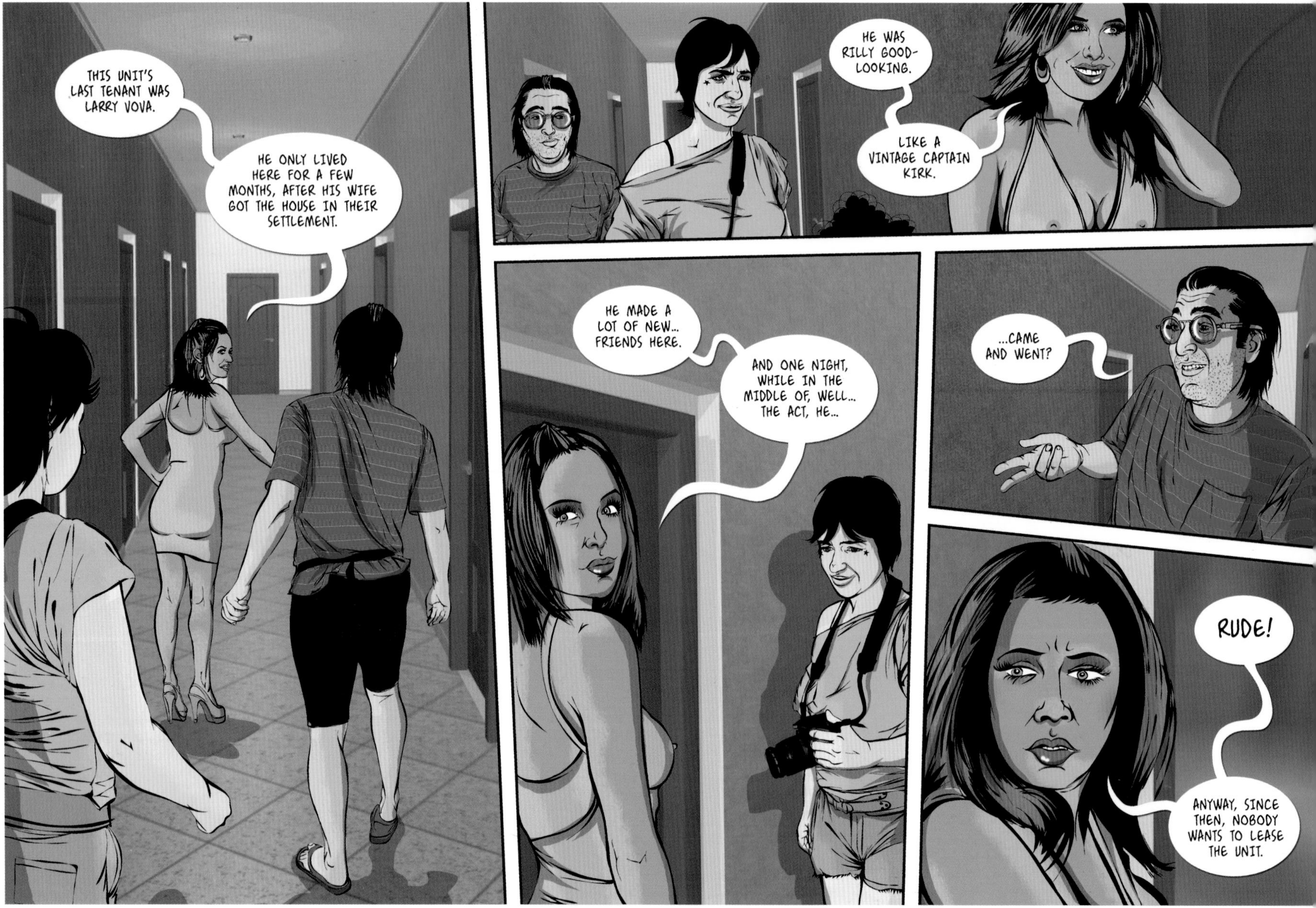
THIS UNIT'S LAST TENANT WAS LARRY VOVA.
HE ONLY LIVED HERE FOR A FEW MONTHS, AFTER HIS WIFE GOT THE HOUSE IN THEIR SETTLEMENT.
HE WAS RILLY GOOD-LOOKING.
LIKE A VINTAGE CAPTAIN KIRK.
HE MADE A LOT OF NEW... FRIENDS HERE.
AND ONE NIGHT, WHILE IN THE MIDDLE OF, WELL... THE ACT, HE...
...CAME AND WENT?
RUDE!
ANYWAY, SINCE THEN, NOBODY WANTS TO LEASE THE UNIT.

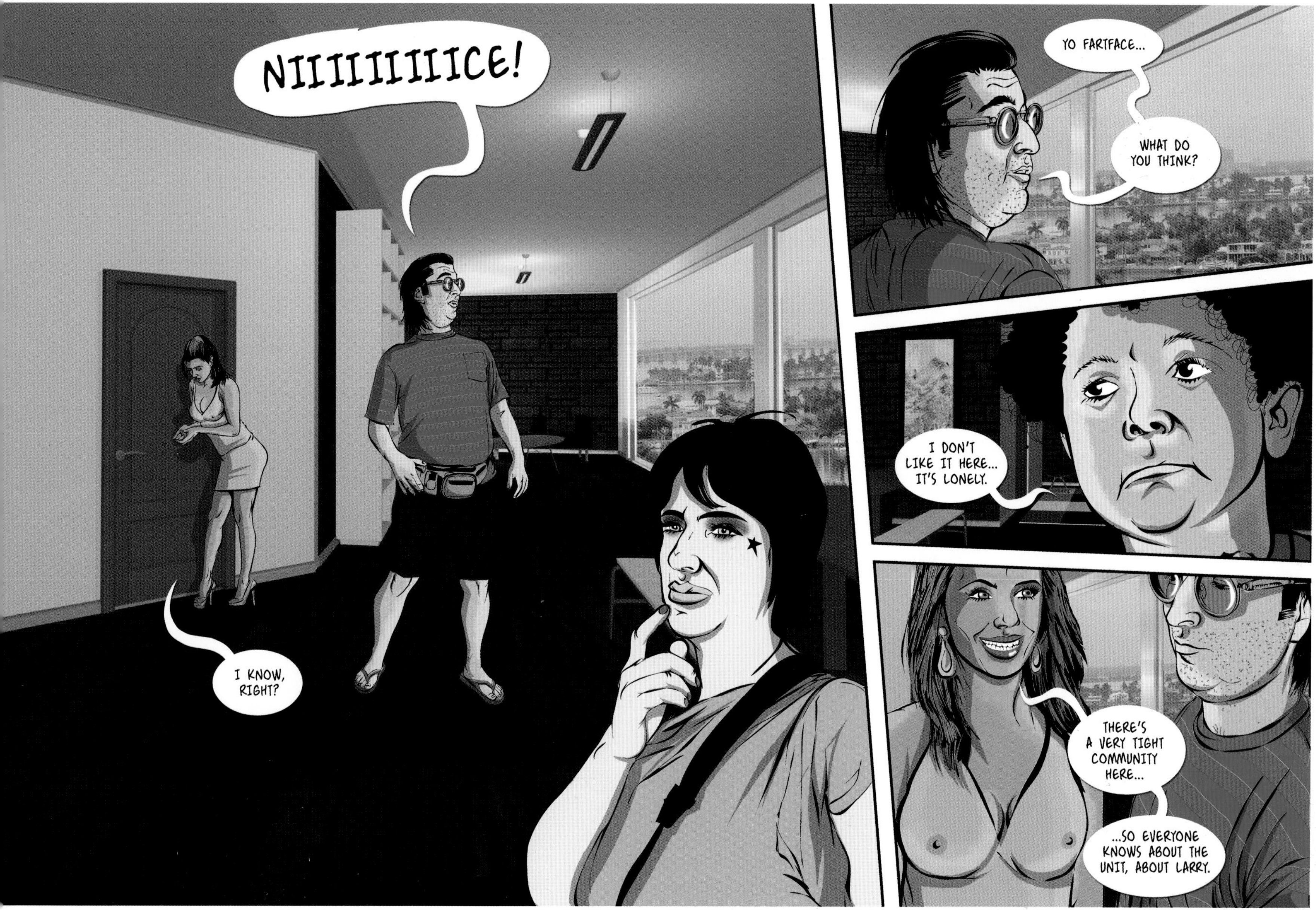
NIIIIIIIICE!
I KNOW, RIGHT?
YO FARTFACE...
WHAT DO YOU THINK?
I DON'T LIKE IT HERE... IT'S LONELY.
THERE'S A VERY TIGHT COMMUNITY HERE...
...SO EVERYONE KNOWS ABOUT THE UNIT, ABOUT LARRY.

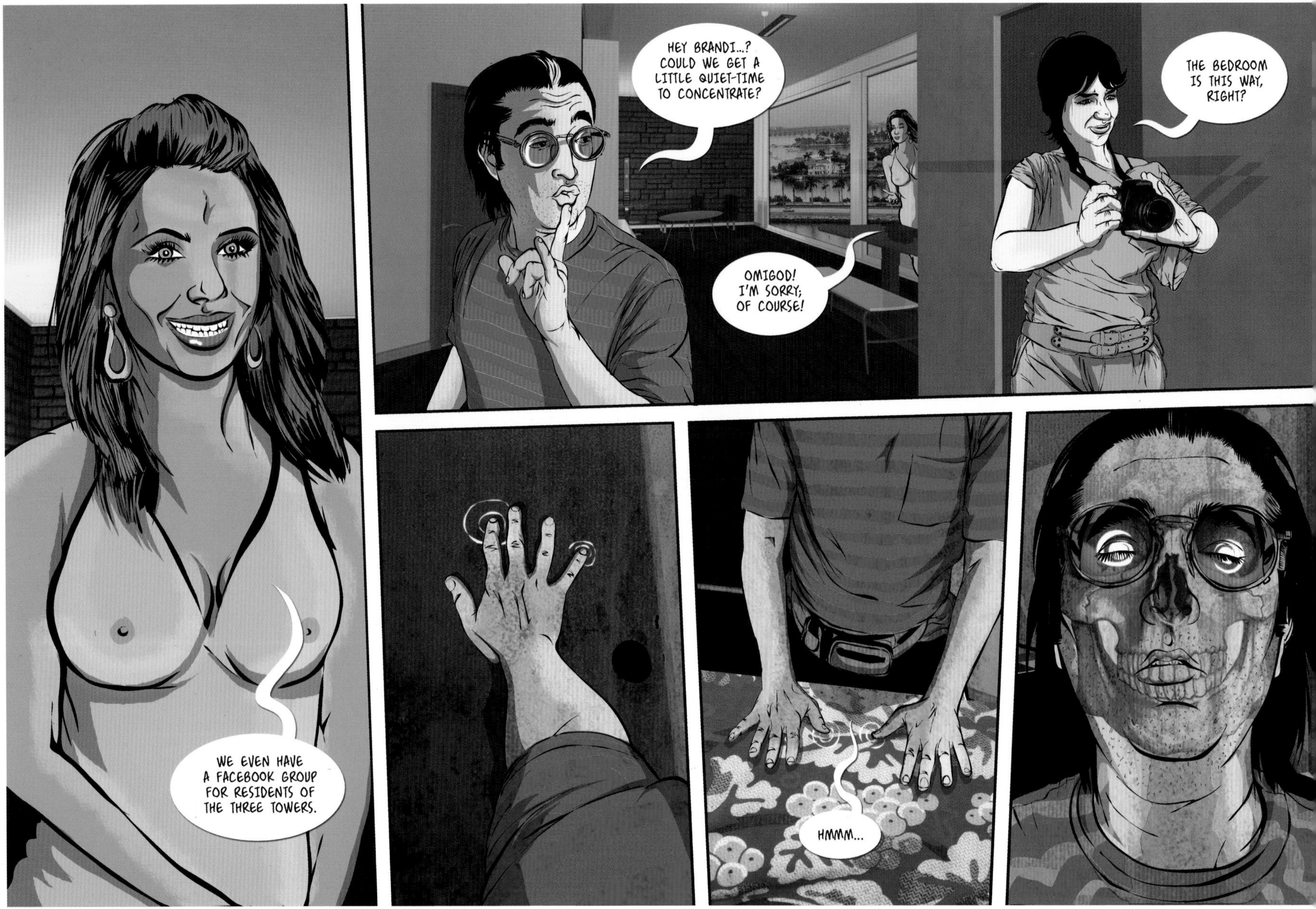
WE EVEN HAVE A FACEBOOK GROUP FOR RESIDENTS OF THE THREE TOWERS.
HEY BRANDI...? COULD WE GET A LITTLE QUIET-TIME TO CONCENTRATE?
OMIGOD! I'M SORRY; OF COURSE!
THE BEDROOM IS THIS WAY, RIGHT?
HMMM...

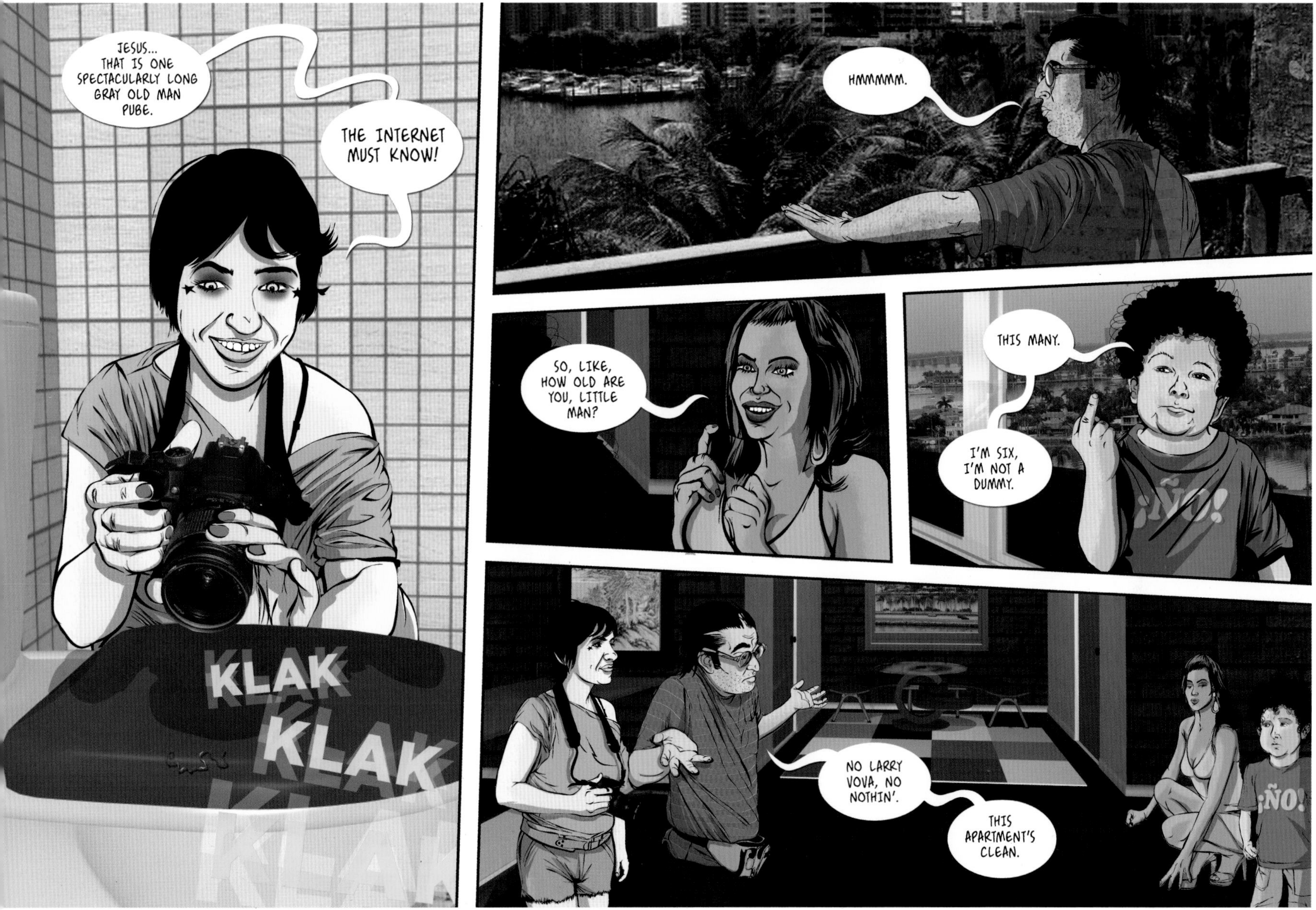
JESUS... THAT IS ONE SPECTACULARLY LONG GRAY OLD MAN PUBE.
THE INTERNET MUST KNOW!
KLAK
KLAK
KLAK
KLAK
HMMMMM.
SO, LIKE, HOW OLD ARE YOU, LITTLE MAN?
THIS MANY.
I'M SIX, I'M NOT A DUMMY.
¡ÑO!
NO LARRY VOVA, NO NOTHIN'.
THIS APARTMENT'S CLEAN.
¡ÑO!

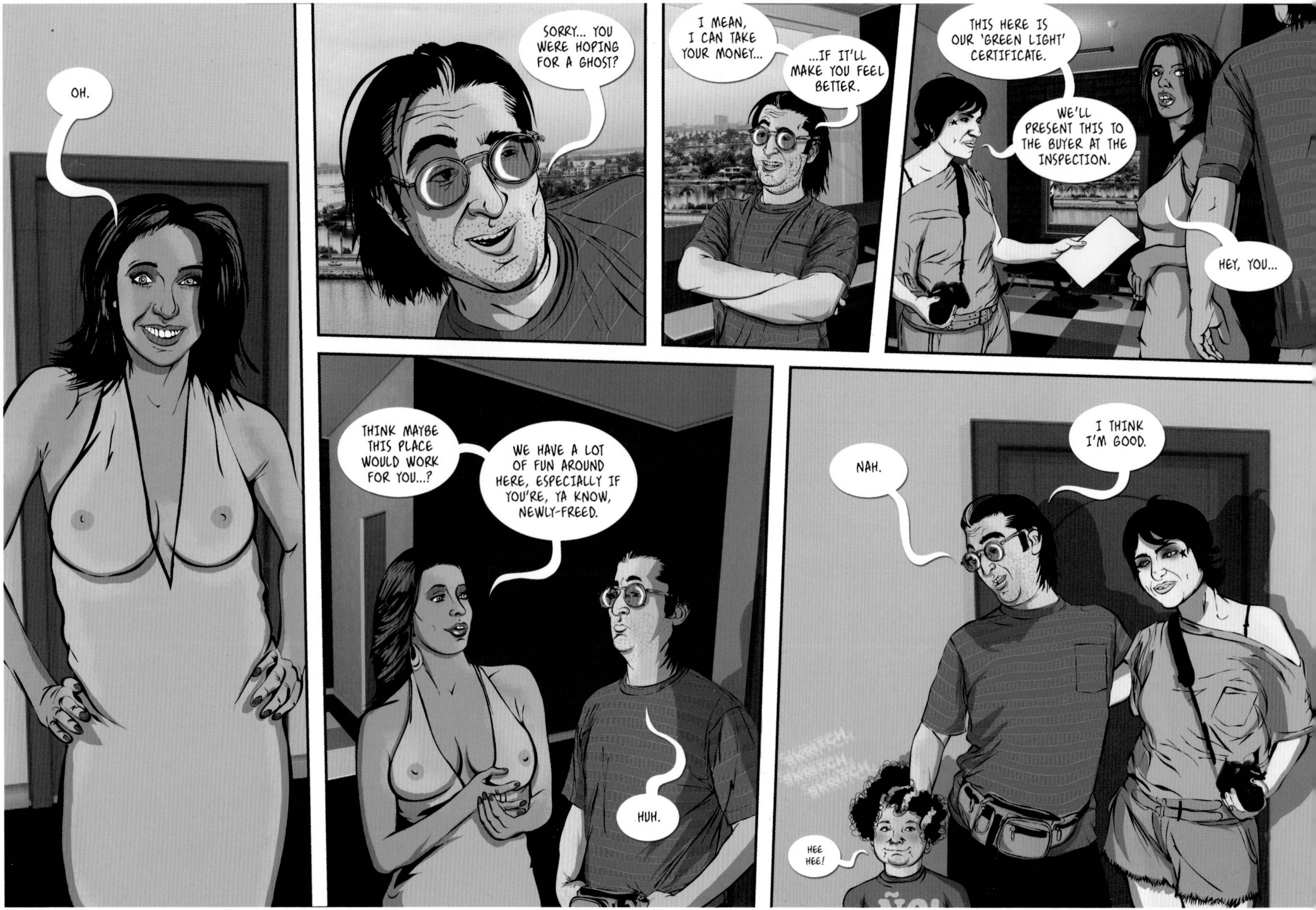
OH.
SORRY... YOU WERE HOPING FOR A GHOST?
I MEAN, I CAN TAKE YOUR MONEY...
...IF IT'LL MAKE YOU FEEL BETTER.
THIS HERE IS OUR 'GREEN LIGHT' CERTIFICATE.
WE'LL PRESENT THIS TO THE BUYER AT THE INSPECTION.
HEY, YOU...
THINK MAYBE THIS PLACE WOULD WORK FOR YOU...?
WE HAVE A LOT OF FUN AROUND HERE, ESPECIALLY IF YOU'RE, YA KNOW, NEWLY-FREED.
HUH.
NAH.
I THINK I'M GOOD.
SKRITCH SKRITCH SKRITCH
HEE HEE!

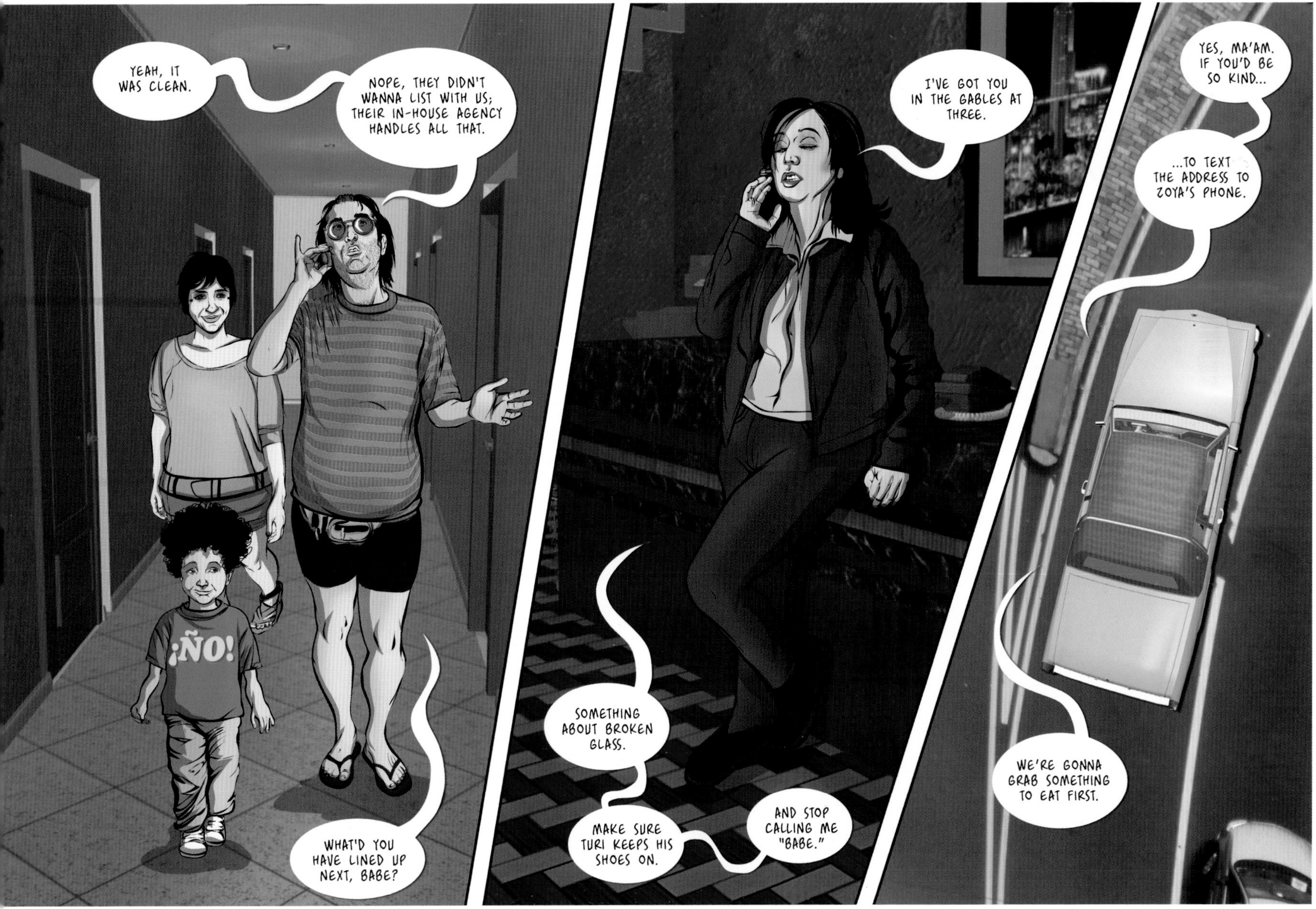
YEAH, IT WAS CLEAN.
NOPE, THEY DIDN'T WANNA LIST WITH US; THEIR IN-HOUSE AGENCY HANDLES ALL THAT.
¡ÑO!
WHAT'D YOU HAVE LINED UP NEXT, BABE?
I'VE GOT YOU IN THE GABLES AT THREE.
SOMETHING ABOUT BROKEN GLASS.
MAKE SURE TURI KEEPS HIS SHOES ON.
AND STOP CALLING ME "BABE."
YES, MA'AM. IF YOU'D BE SO KIND...
...TO TEXT THE ADDRESS TO ZOYA'S PHONE.
WE'RE GONNA GRAB SOMETHING TO EAT FIRST.

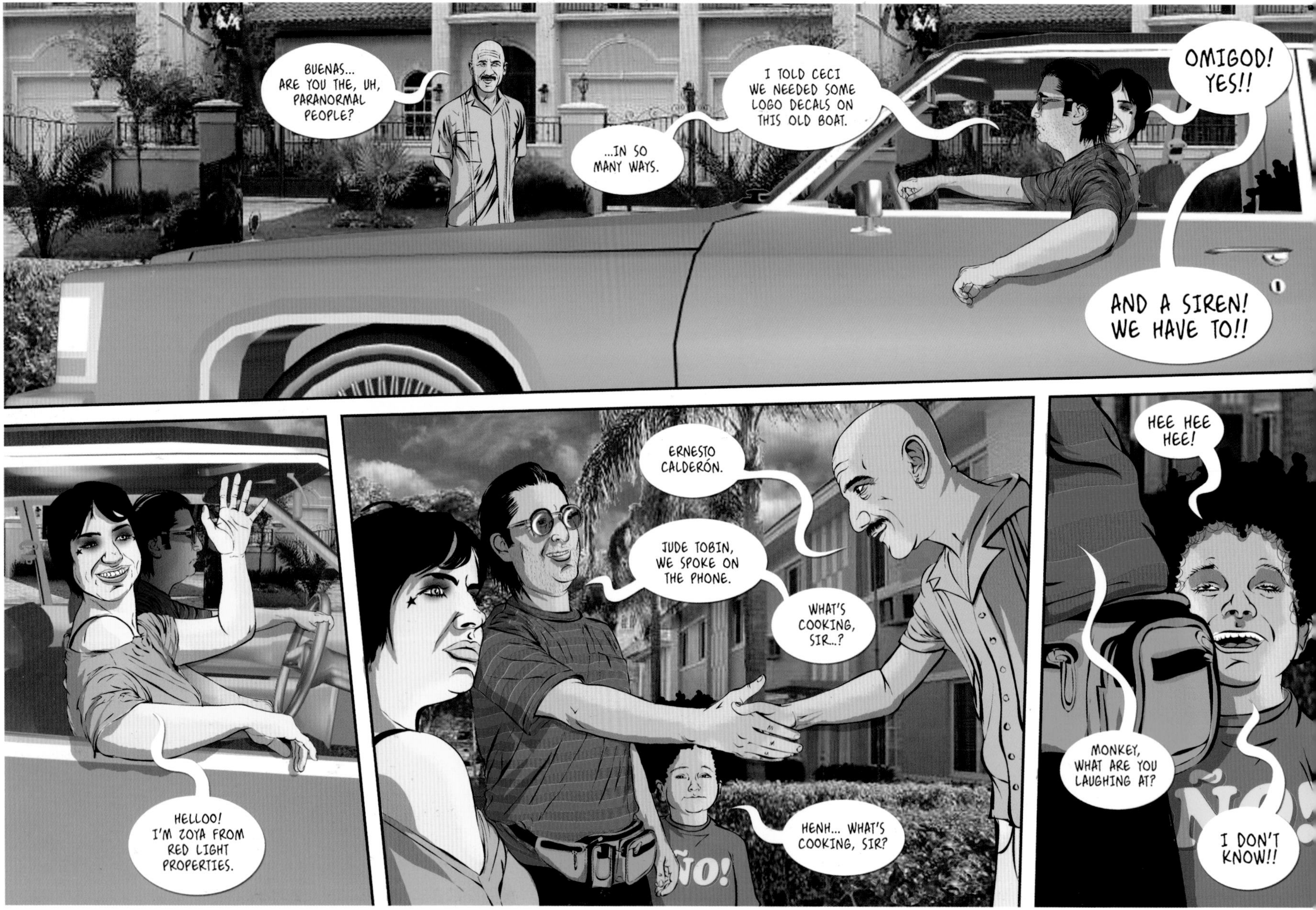
BUENAS... ARE YOU THE, UH, PARANORMAL PEOPLE?
I TOLD CECI WE NEEDED SOME LOGO DECALS ON THIS OLD BOAT.
...IN SO MANY WAYS.
OMIGOD! YES!!
AND A SIREN! WE HAVE TO!!
HELLOO! I'M ZOYA FROM RED LIGHT PROPERTIES.
ERNESTO CALDERÓN.
JUDE TOBIN, WE SPOKE ON THE PHONE.
WHAT'S COOKING, SIR...?
HENH... WHAT'S COOKING, SIR?
ÑO!
HEE HEE HEE!
MONKEY, WHAT ARE YOU LAUGHING AT?
I DON'T KNOW!!
ÑO!

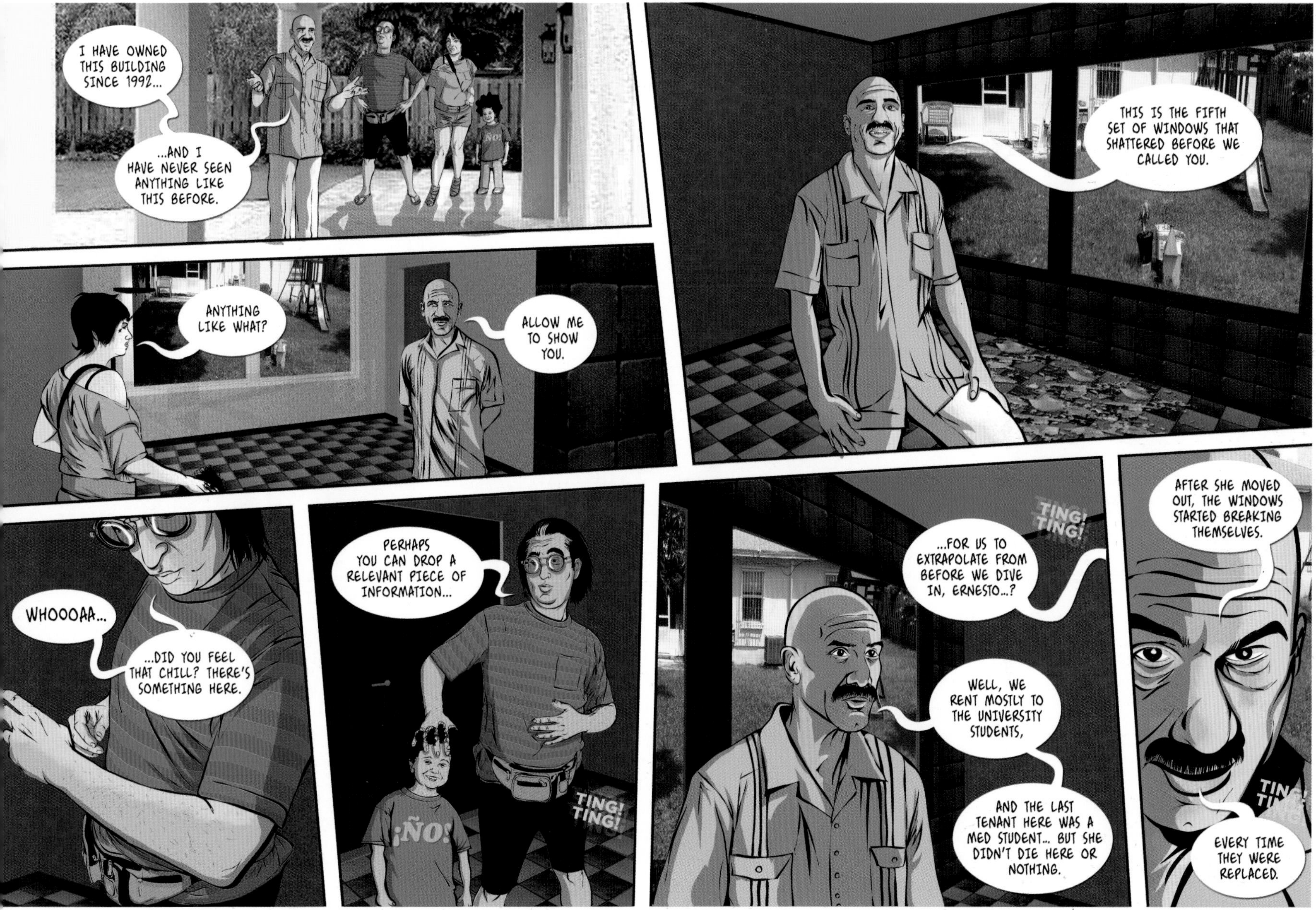
I HAVE OWNED THIS BUILDING SINCE 1992...
...AND I HAVE NEVER SEEN ANYTHING LIKE THIS BEFORE.
THIS IS THE FIFTH SET OF WINDOWS THAT SHATTERED BEFORE WE CALLED YOU.
ANYTHING LIKE WHAT?
ALLOW ME TO SHOW YOU.
WHOOOAA...
...DID YOU FEEL THAT CHILL? THERE'S SOMETHING HERE.
PERHAPS YOU CAN DROP A RELEVANT PIECE OF INFORMATION...
¡ÑO!
TING! TING!
...FOR US TO EXTRAPOLATE FROM BEFORE WE DIVE IN, ERNESTO...?
TING! TING!
WELL, WE RENT MOSTLY TO THE UNIVERSITY STUDENTS,
AND THE LAST TENANT HERE WAS A MED STUDENT... BUT SHE DIDN'T DIE HERE OR NOTHING.
AFTER SHE MOVED OUT, THE WINDOWS STARTED BREAKING THEMSELVES.
EVERY TIME THEY WERE REPLACED.

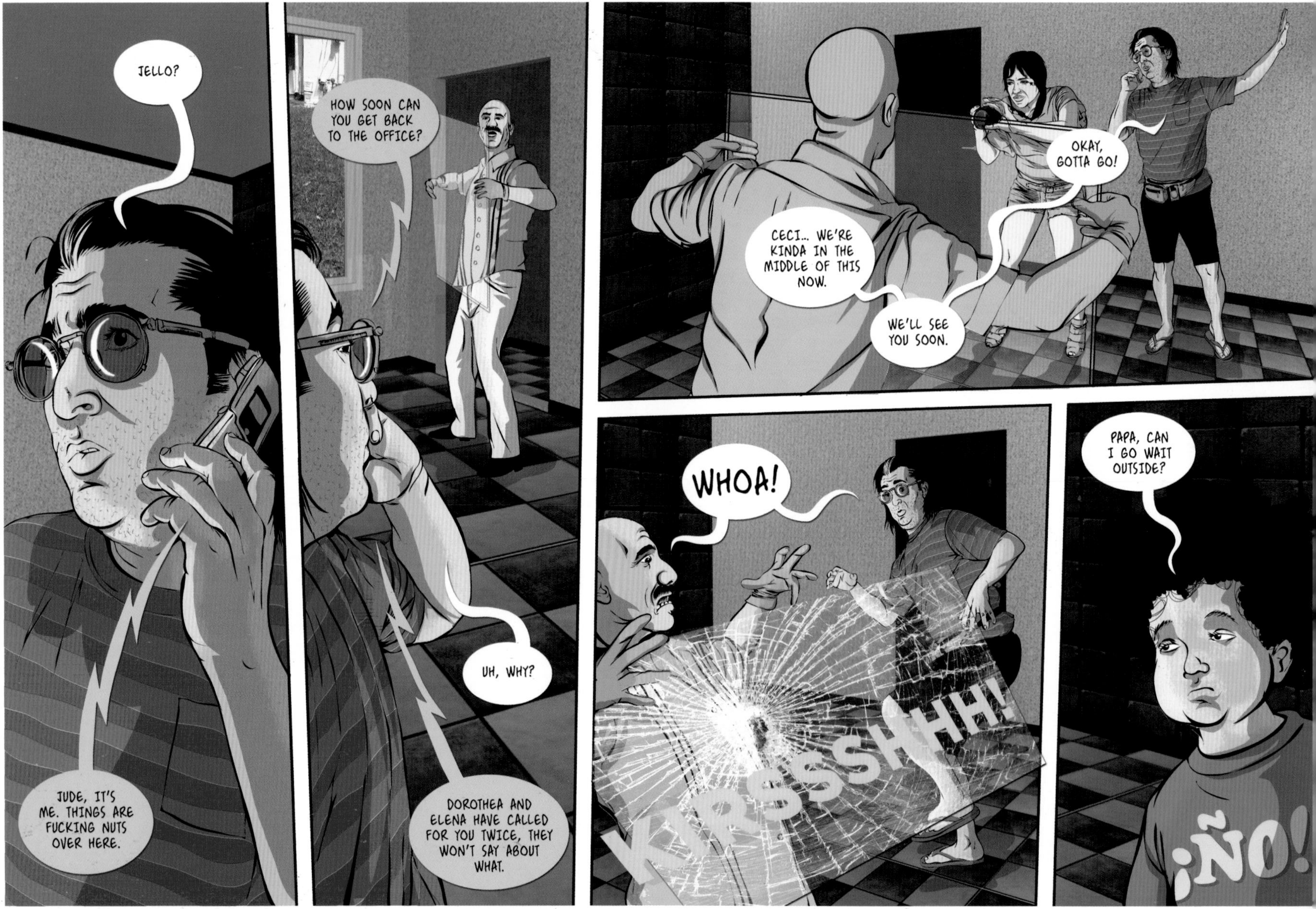
JELLO?
JUDE, IT'S ME. THINGS ARE FUCKING NUTS OVER HERE.
HOW SOON CAN YOU GET BACK TO THE OFFICE?
UH, WHY?
DOROTHEA AND ELENA HAVE CALLED FOR YOU TWICE, THEY WON'T SAY ABOUT WHAT.
CECI... WE'RE KINDA IN THE MIDDLE OF THIS NOW.
WE'LL SEE YOU SOON.
OKAY, GOTTA GO!
WHOA!
KRSSSHHH!
PAPA, CAN I GO WAIT OUTSIDE?
¡ÑO!

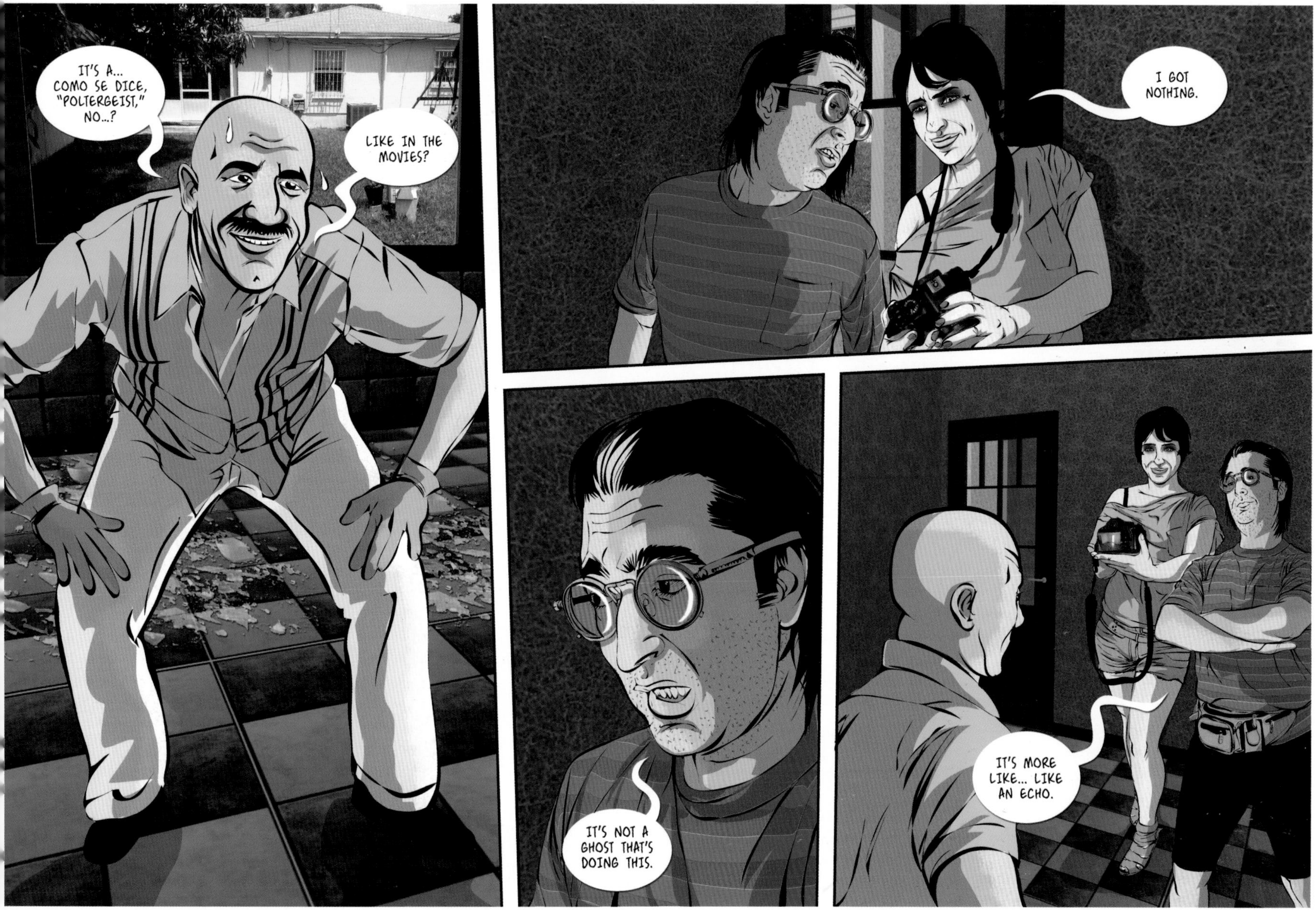
IT'S A... COMO SE DICE, "POLTERGEIST," NO...?
LIKE IN THE MOVIES?
I GOT NOTHING.
IT'S NOT A GHOST THAT'S DOING THIS.
IT'S MORE LIKE... LIKE AN ECHO.

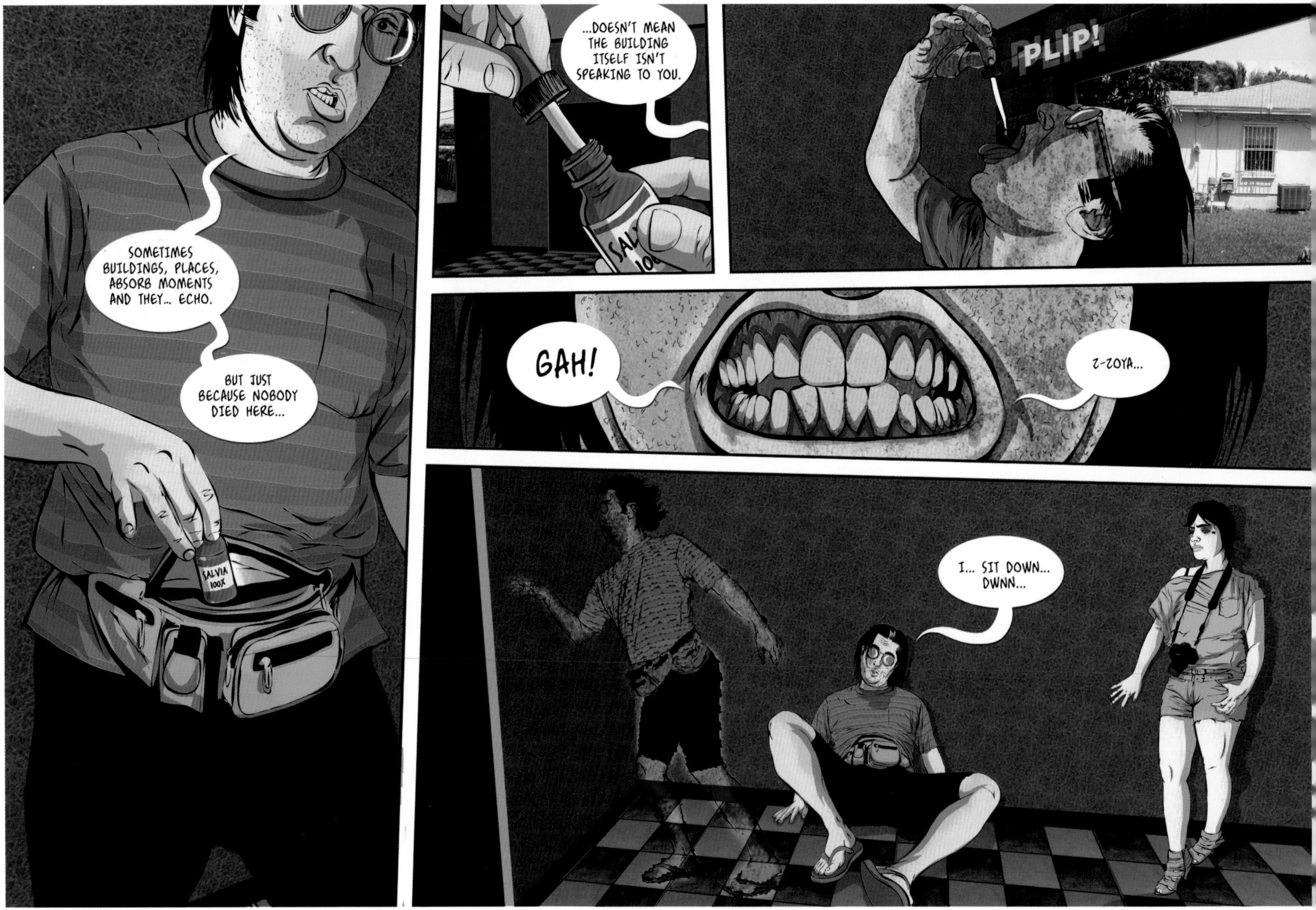
SOMETIMES BUILDINGS, PLACES, ABSORB MOMENTS AND THEY... ECHO.
BUT JUST BECAUSE NOBODY DIED HERE...
SALVIA 100X
...DOESN'T MEAN THE BUILDING ITSELF ISN'T SPEAKING TO YOU.
PLIP!
GAH!
Z-ZOYA...
I... SIT DOWN... DWNN...

OH.
O WOW.
I SAW HIM TAKE A SIP FROM THAT LITTLE BOTTLE!
WAS THAT DRUGS?
THIS SANTERO SHIT IS BAD ENOUGH BUT DON'T YOU BE BRINGING DRUGS INTO MY BUILDING, BRO... NAH-AH!
THAT BOTTLE CONTAINS EXTRACT OF AN HERB CALLED SALVIA DIVINORUM,
IT'S BEEN USED BY SHAMANS FOR CENTURIES...
JUDE ISN'T JUST A PRO... HE'S THE TITS.

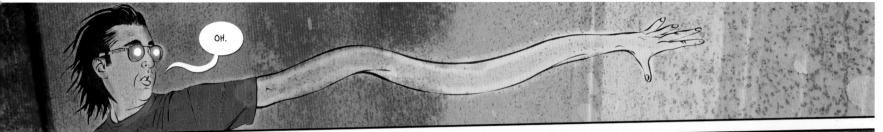

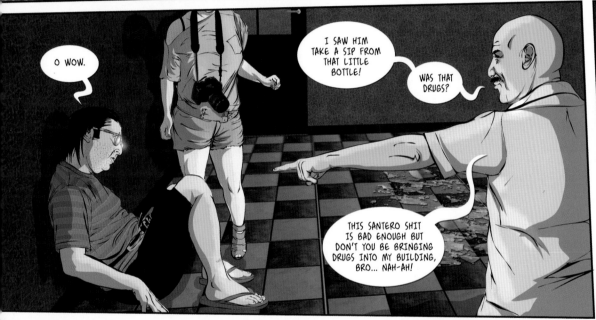

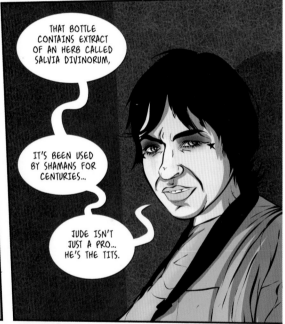

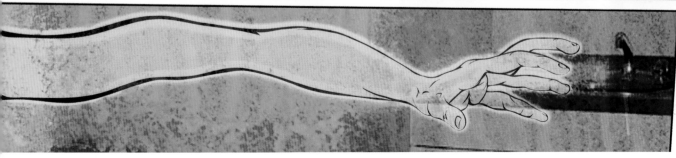

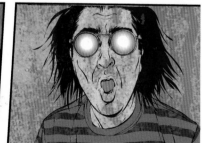

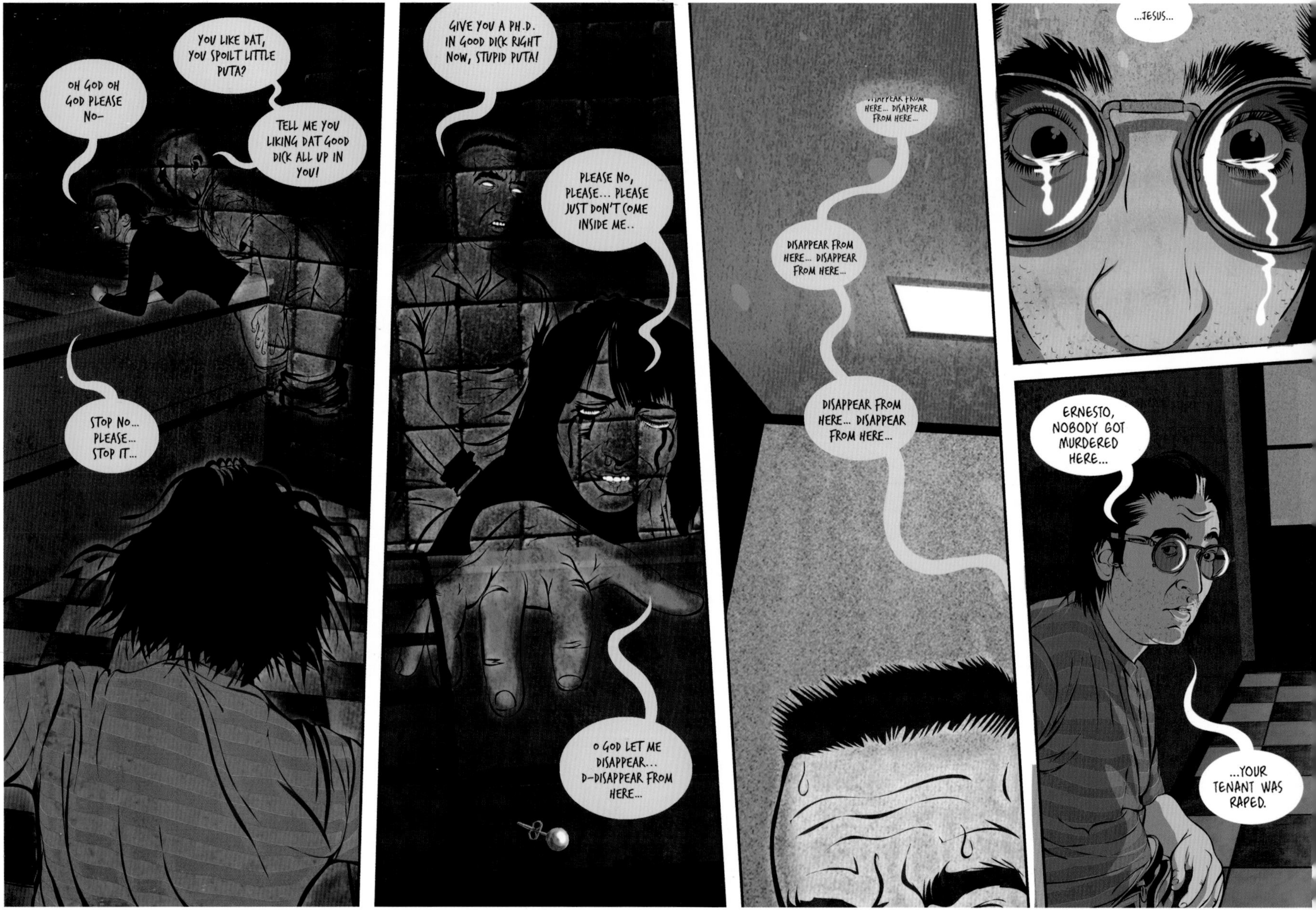

YOU LIKE DAT, YOU SPOILT LITTLE PUTA?
OH GOD OH GOD PLEASE NO–
TELL ME YOU LIKING DAT GOOD DICK ALL UP IN YOU!
STOP NO... PLEASE... STOP IT...
GIVE YOU A PH.D. IN GOOD DICK RIGHT NOW, STUPID PUTA!
PLEASE NO, PLEASE... PLEASE JUST DON'T COME INSIDE ME..
O GOD LET ME DISAPPEAR... D-DISAPPEAR FROM HERE...
HERE... DISAPPEAR FROM HERE...
DISAPPEAR FROM HERE... DISAPPEAR FROM HERE...
DISAPPEAR FROM HERE... DISAPPEAR FROM HERE...
...JESUS...
ERNESTO, NOBODY GOT MURDERED HERE...
...YOUR TENANT WAS RAPED.

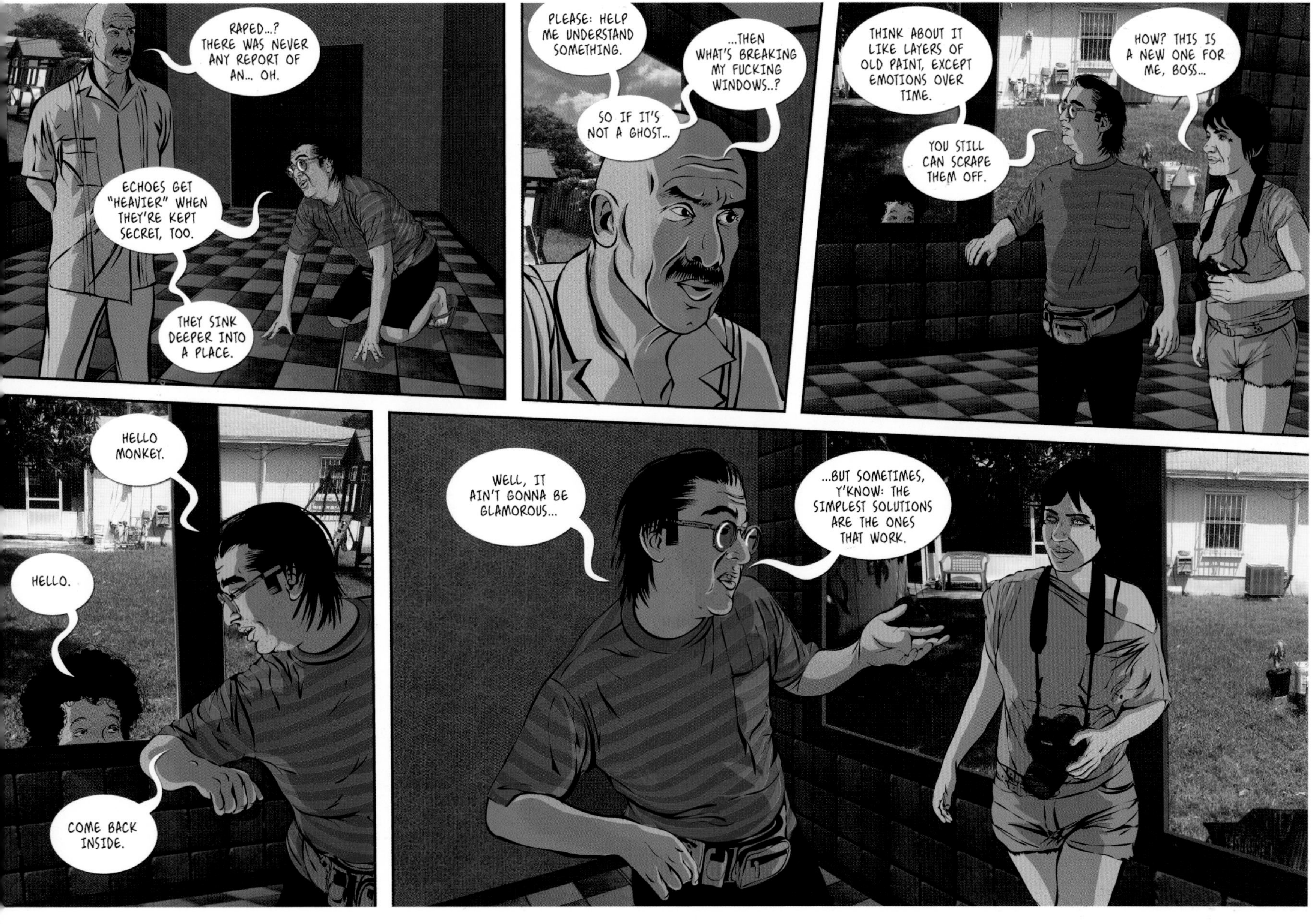
RAPED...? THERE WAS NEVER ANY REPORT OF AN... OH.
ECHOES GET "HEAVIER" WHEN THEY'RE KEPT SECRET, TOO.
THEY SINK DEEPER INTO A PLACE.
PLEASE: HELP ME UNDERSTAND SOMETHING.
SO IF IT'S NOT A GHOST...
...THEN WHAT'S BREAKING MY FUCKING WINDOWS..?
THINK ABOUT IT LIKE LAYERS OF OLD PAINT, EXCEPT EMOTIONS OVER TIME.
YOU STILL CAN SCRAPE THEM OFF.
HOW? THIS IS A NEW ONE FOR ME, BOSS...
HELLO MONKEY.
HELLO.
COME BACK INSIDE.
WELL, IT AIN'T GONNA BE GLAMOROUS...
...BUT SOMETIMES, Y'KNOW: THE SIMPLEST SOLUTIONS ARE THE ONES THAT WORK.

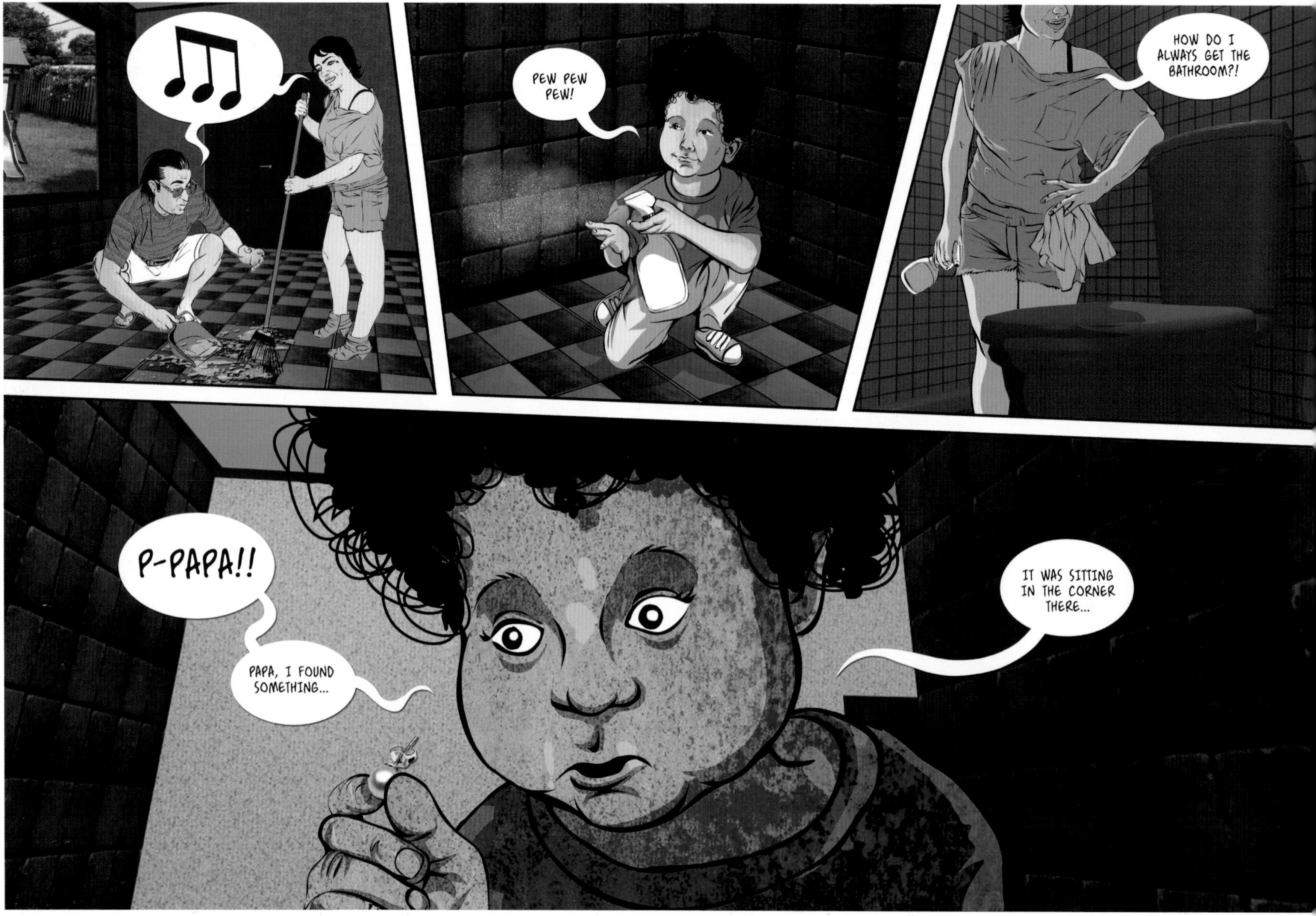
PEW PEW PEW!
HOW DO I ALWAYS GET THE BATHROOM?!
P-PAPA!!
PAPA, I FOUND SOMETHING...
IT WAS SITTING IN THE CORNER THERE...

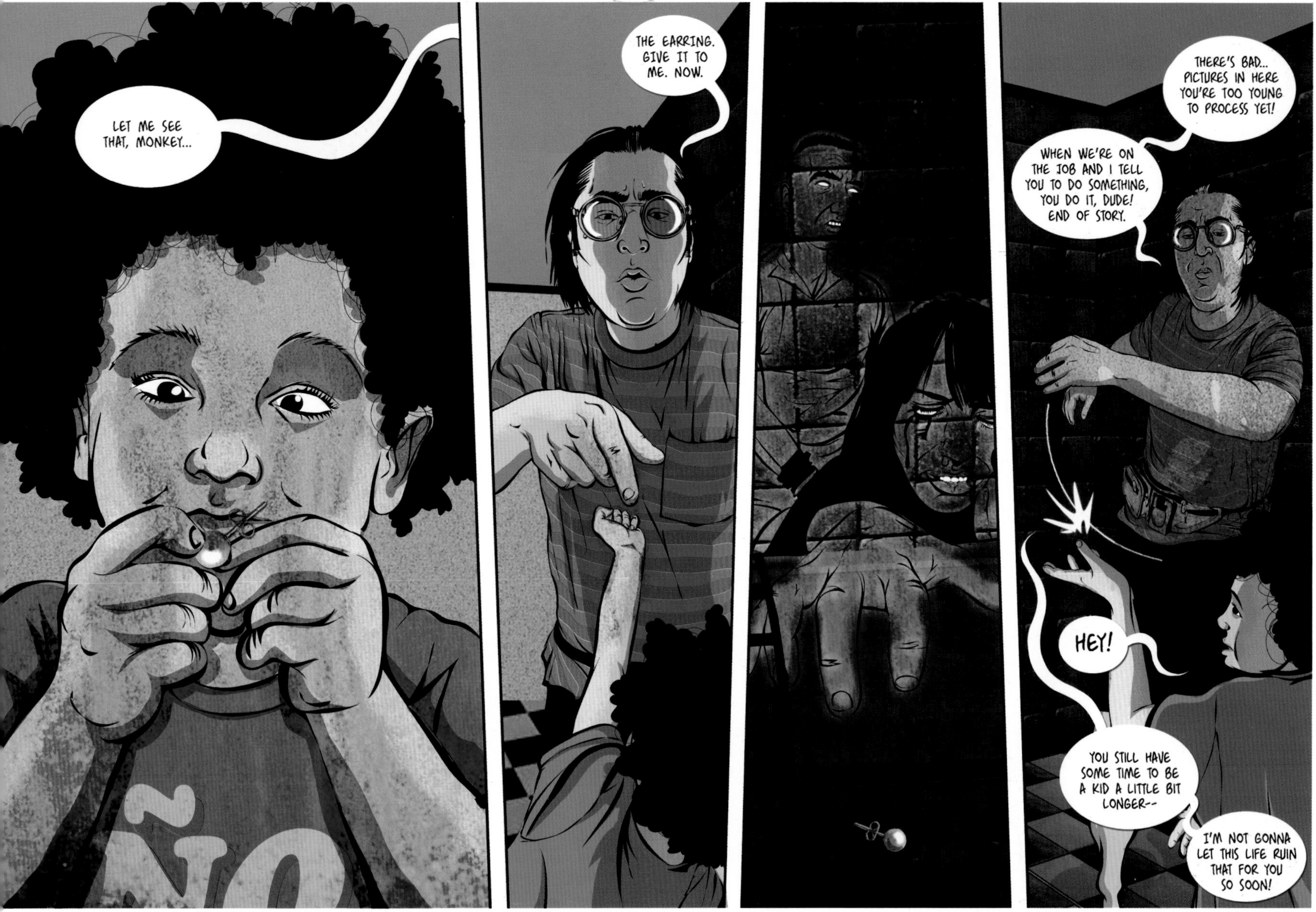
LET ME SEE THAT, MONKEY...
THE EARRING. GIVE IT TO ME. NOW.
THERE'S BAD... PICTURES IN HERE YOU'RE TOO YOUNG TO PROCESS YET!
WHEN WE'RE ON THE JOB AND I TELL YOU TO DO SOMETHING, YOU DO IT, DUDE! END OF STORY.
HEY!
YOU STILL HAVE SOME TIME TO BE A KID A LITTLE BIT LONGER--
I'M NOT GONNA LET THIS LIFE RUIN THAT FOR YOU SO SOON!
ÑO

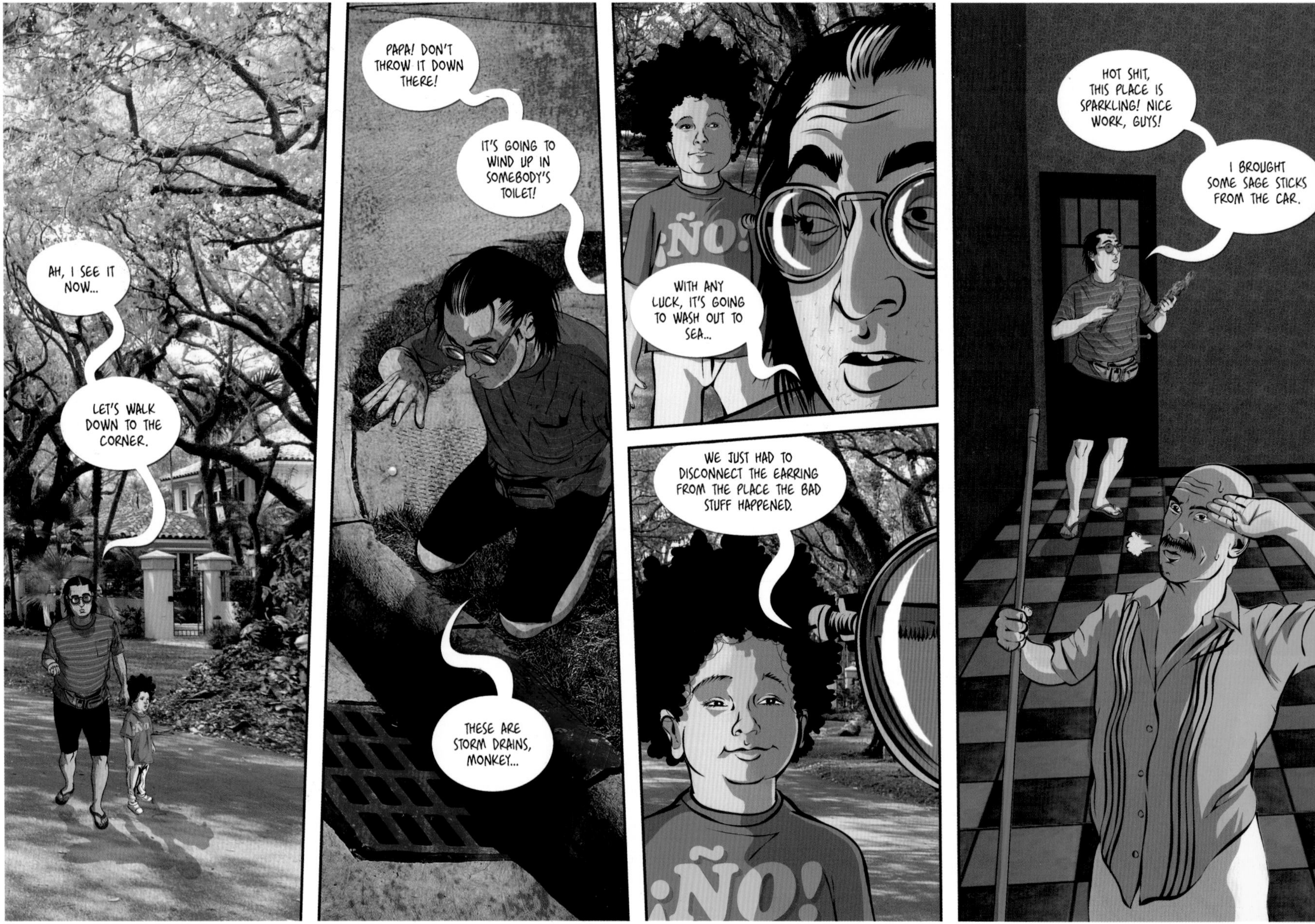
AH, I SEE IT NOW...
LET'S WALK DOWN TO THE CORNER.
PAPA! DON'T THROW IT DOWN THERE!
IT'S GOING TO WIND UP IN SOMEBODY'S TOILET!
THESE ARE STORM DRAINS, MONKEY...
¡ÑO!
WITH ANY LUCK, IT'S GOING TO WASH OUT TO SEA...
WE JUST HAD TO DISCONNECT THE EARRING FROM THE PLACE THE BAD STUFF HAPPENED.
¡ÑO!
HOT SHIT, THIS PLACE IS SPARKLING! NICE WORK, GUYS!
I BROUGHT SOME SAGE STICKS FROM THE CAR.

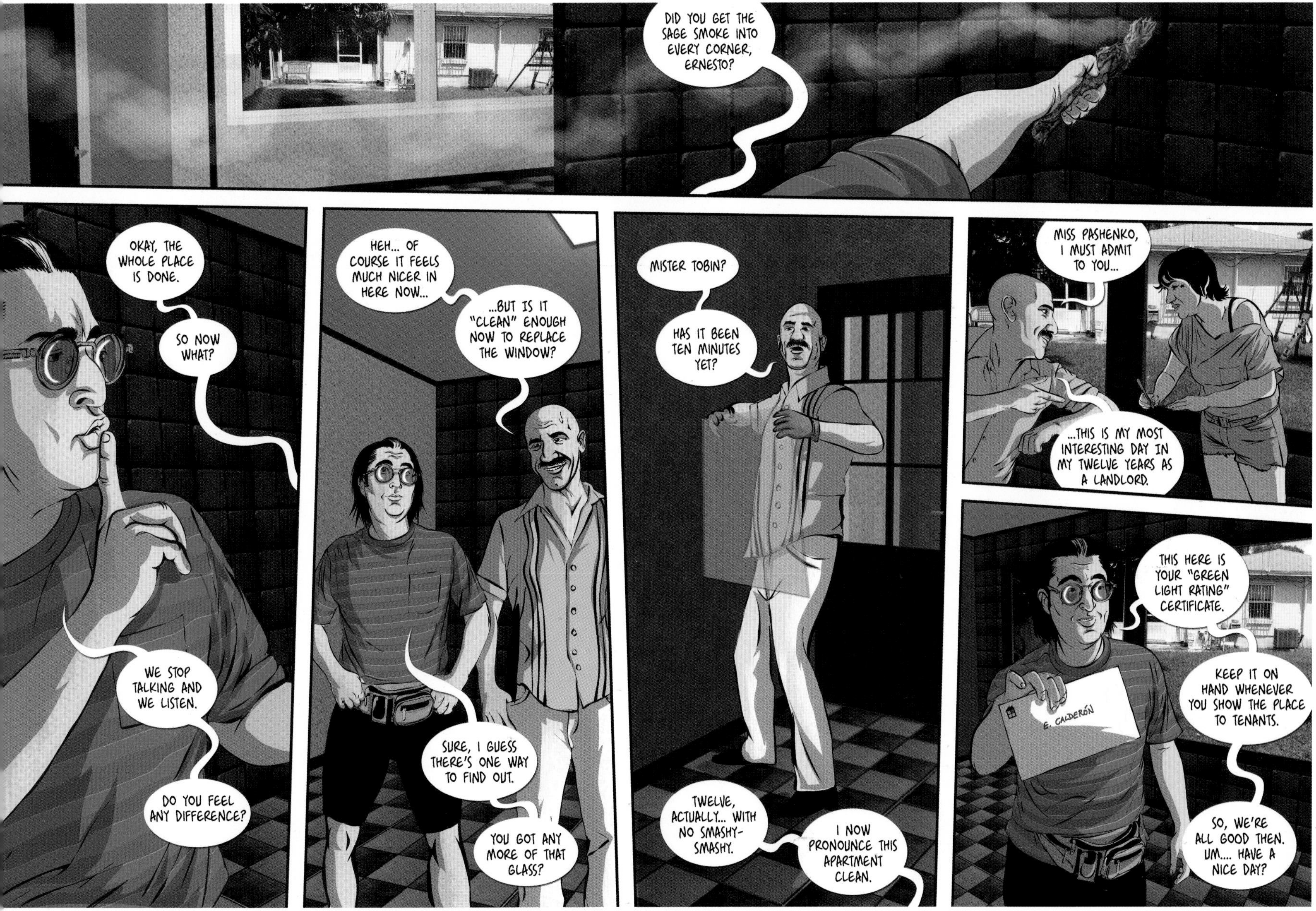
DID YOU GET THE SAGE SMOKE INTO EVERY CORNER, ERNESTO?
OKAY, THE WHOLE PLACE IS DONE.
SO NOW WHAT?
WE STOP TALKING AND WE LISTEN.
DO YOU FEEL ANY DIFFERENCE?
HEH... OF COURSE IT FEELS MUCH NICER IN HERE NOW...
...BUT IS IT "CLEAN" ENOUGH NOW TO REPLACE THE WINDOW?
SURE, I GUESS THERE'S ONE WAY TO FIND OUT.
YOU GOT ANY MORE OF THAT GLASS?
MISTER TOBIN?
HAS IT BEEN TEN MINUTES YET?
TWELVE, ACTUALLY... WITH NO SMASHY-SMASHY.
I NOW PRONOUNCE THIS APARTMENT CLEAN.
MISS PASHENKO, I MUST ADMIT TO YOU...
...THIS IS MY MOST INTERESTING DAY IN MY TWELVE YEARS AS A LANDLORD.
THIS HERE IS YOUR "GREEN LIGHT RATING" CERTIFICATE.
E. CALDERÓN
KEEP IT ON HAND WHENEVER YOU SHOW THE PLACE TO TENANTS.
SO, WE'RE ALL GOOD THEN. UM.... HAVE A NICE DAY?

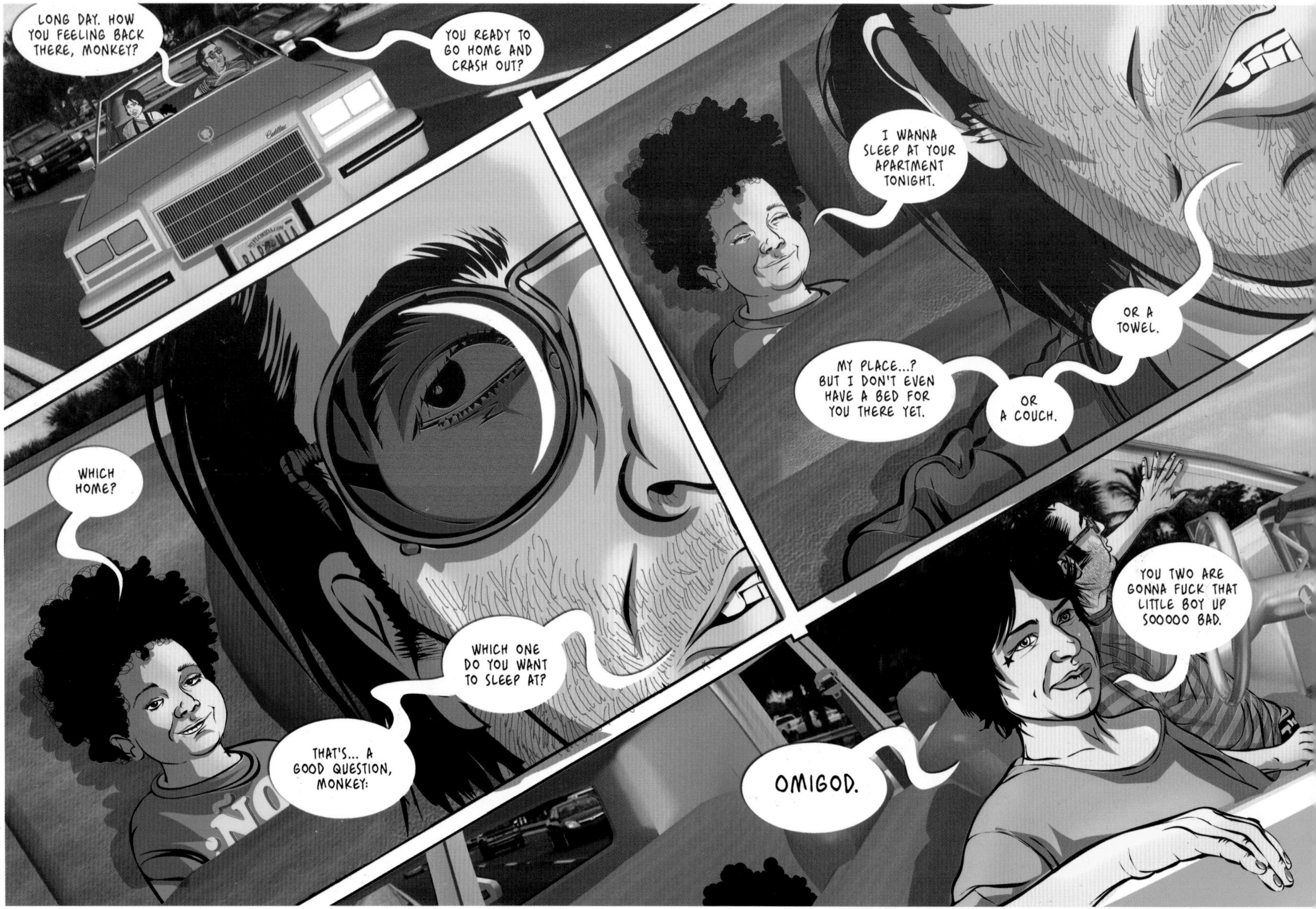

LONG DAY. HOW YOU FEELING BACK THERE, MONKEY?
YOU READY TO GO HOME AND CRASH OUT?
WHICH HOME?
WHICH ONE DO YOU WANT TO SLEEP AT?
THAT'S... A GOOD QUESTION, MONKEY:
I WANNA SLEEP AT YOUR APARTMENT TONIGHT.
MY PLACE...? BUT I DON'T EVEN HAVE A BED FOR YOU THERE YET.
OR A COUCH.
OR A TOWEL.
YOU TWO ARE GONNA FUCK THAT LITTLE BOY UP SOOOOO BAD.
OMIGOD.

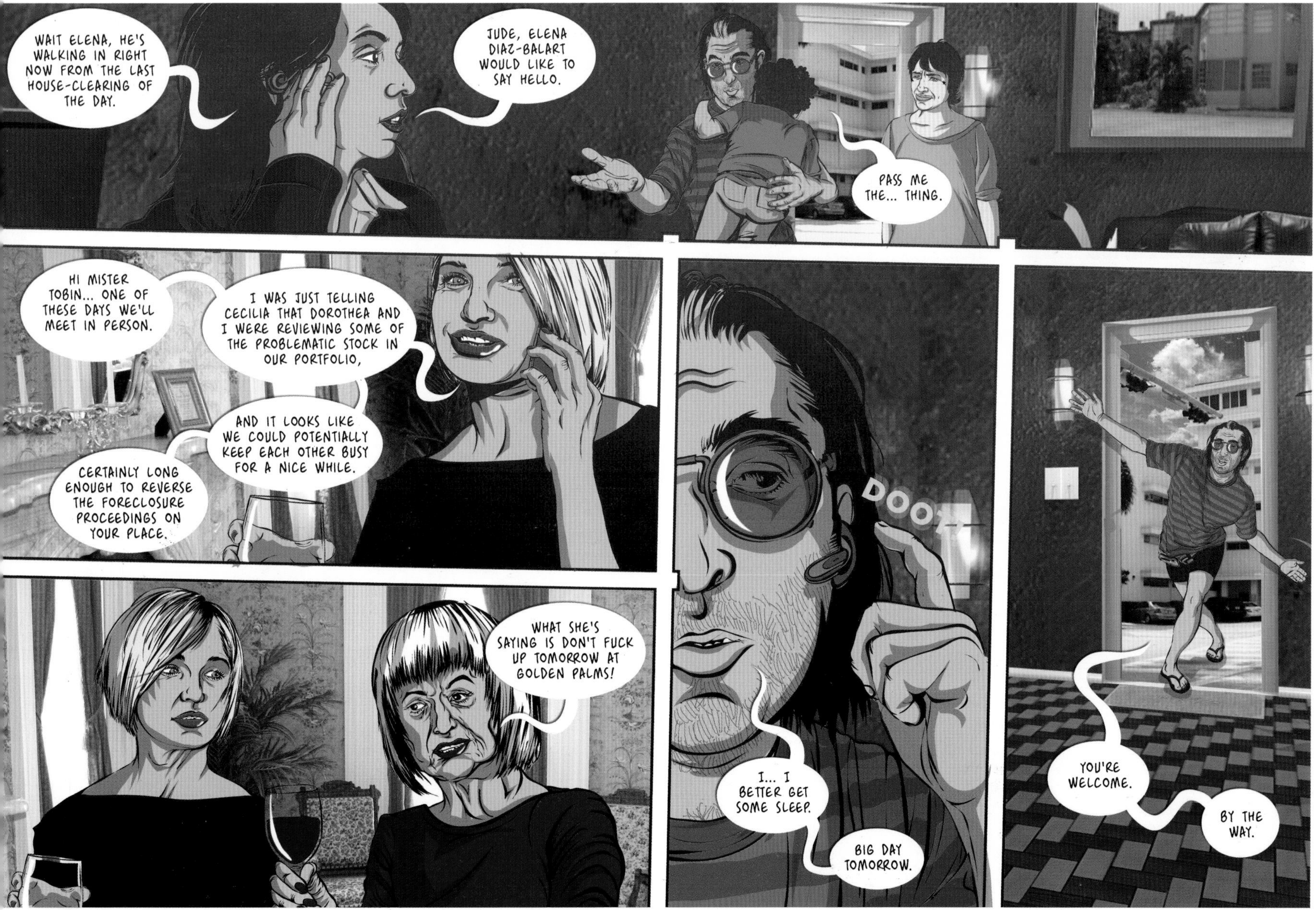
WAIT ELENA, HE'S WALKING IN RIGHT NOW FROM THE LAST HOUSE-CLEARING OF THE DAY.
JUDE, ELENA DIAZ-BALART WOULD LIKE TO SAY HELLO.
PASS ME THE... THING.
HI MISTER TOBIN... ONE OF THESE DAYS WE'LL MEET IN PERSON.
I WAS JUST TELLING CECILIA THAT DOROTHEA AND I WERE REVIEWING SOME OF THE PROBLEMATIC STOCK IN OUR PORTFOLIO,
AND IT LOOKS LIKE WE COULD POTENTIALLY KEEP EACH OTHER BUSY FOR A NICE WHILE.
CERTAINLY LONG ENOUGH TO REVERSE THE FORECLOSURE PROCEEDINGS ON YOUR PLACE.
WHAT SHE'S SAYING IS DON'T FUCK UP TOMORROW AT GOLDEN PALMS!
DOOT
I... I BETTER GET SOME SLEEP.
BIG DAY TOMORROW.
YOU'RE WELCOME.
BY THE WAY.

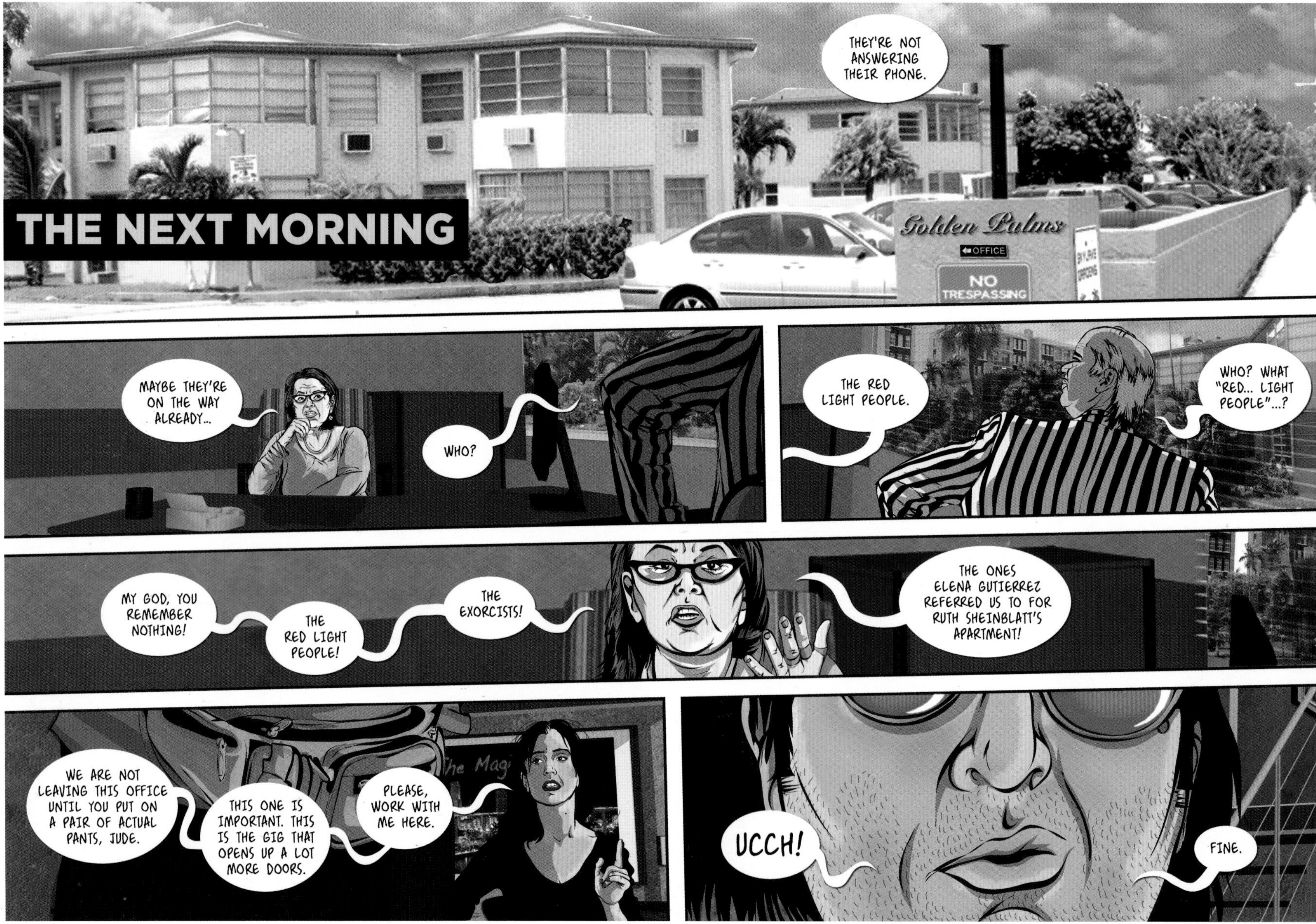
THE NEXT MORNING
THEY'RE NOT ANSWERING THEIR PHONE.
Golden Palms
OFFICE
NO TRESPASSING
MAYBE THEY'RE ON THE WAY ALREADY...
WHO?
THE RED LIGHT PEOPLE.
WHO? WHAT "RED... LIGHT PEOPLE"...?
MY GOD, YOU REMEMBER NOTHING!
THE RED LIGHT PEOPLE!
THE EXORCISTS!
THE ONES ELENA GUTIERREZ REFERRED US TO FOR RUTH SHEINBLATT'S APARTMENT!
WE ARE NOT LEAVING THIS OFFICE UNTIL YOU PUT ON A PAIR OF ACTUAL PANTS, JUDE.
THIS ONE IS IMPORTANT. THIS IS THE GIG THAT OPENS UP A LOT MORE DOORS.
PLEASE, WORK WITH ME HERE.
UCCH!
FINE.

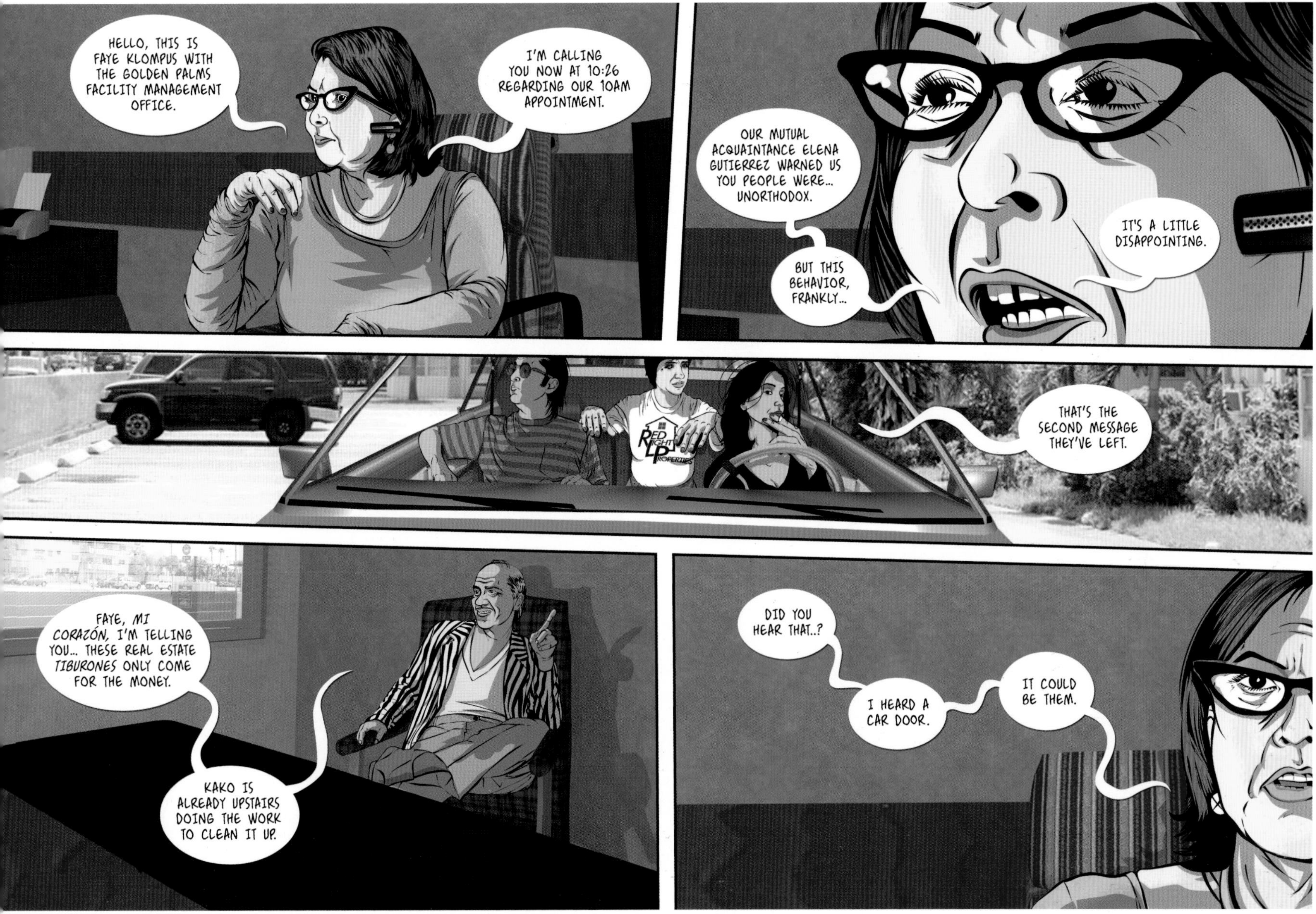
HELLO, THIS IS FAYE KLOMPUS WITH THE GOLDEN PALMS FACILITY MANAGEMENT OFFICE.
I'M CALLING YOU NOW AT 10:26 REGARDING OUR 10AM APPOINTMENT.
OUR MUTUAL ACQUAINTANCE ELENA GUTIERREZ WARNED US YOU PEOPLE WERE... UNORTHODOX.
BUT THIS BEHAVIOR, FRANKLY...
IT'S A LITTLE DISAPPOINTING.
RED LIGHT PROPERTIES
THAT'S THE SECOND MESSAGE THEY'VE LEFT.
FAYE, *MI CORAZÓN*, I'M TELLING YOU... THESE REAL ESTATE *TIBURONES* ONLY COME FOR THE MONEY.
KAKO IS ALREADY UPSTAIRS DOING THE WORK TO CLEAN IT UP.
DID YOU HEAR THAT..?
I HEARD A CAR DOOR.
IT COULD BE THEM.

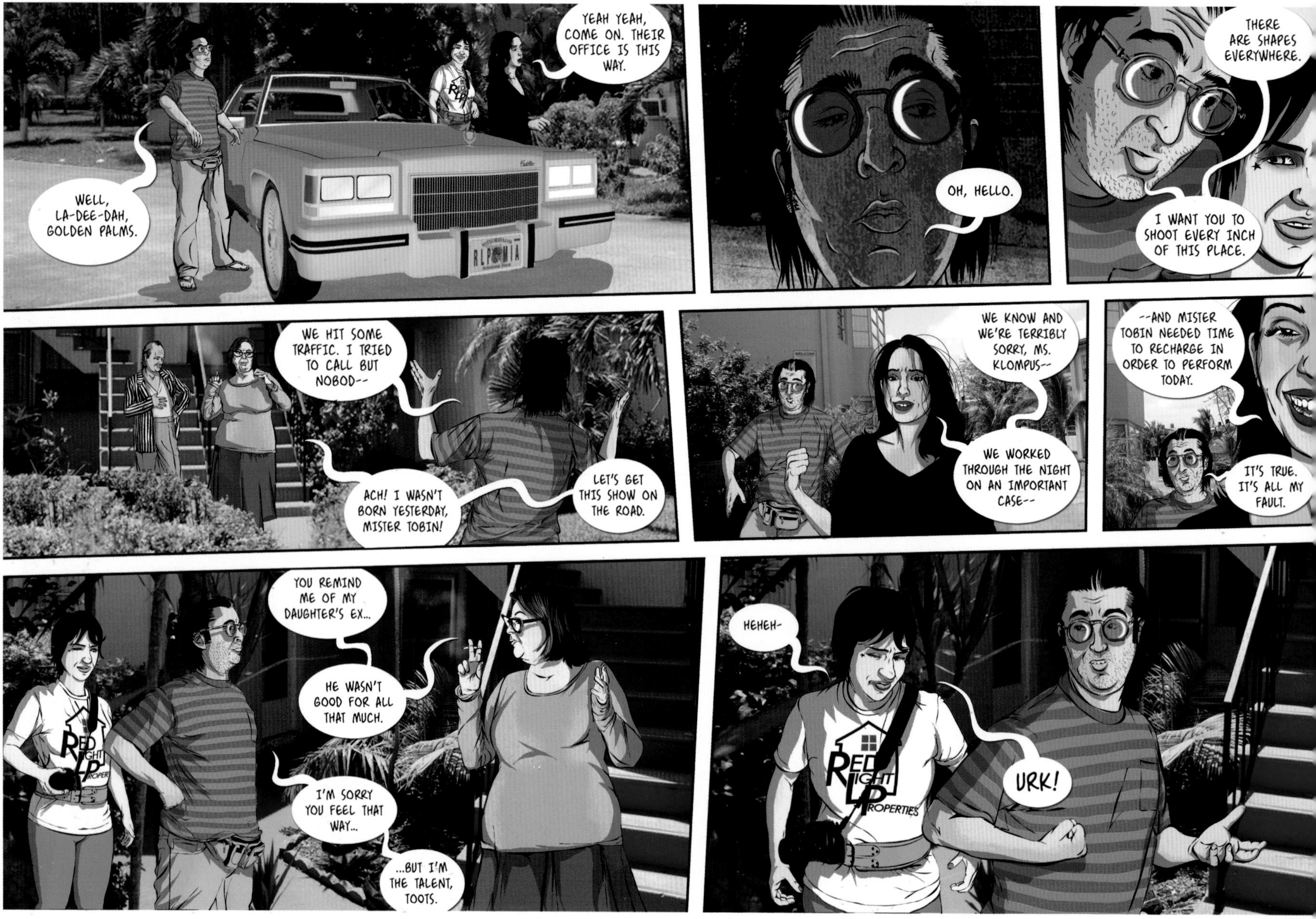

WELL, LA-DEE-DAH, GOLDEN PALMS.
YEAH YEAH, COME ON. THEIR OFFICE IS THIS WAY.
OH, HELLO.
THERE ARE SHAPES EVERYWHERE.
I WANT YOU TO SHOOT EVERY INCH OF THIS PLACE.
WE HIT SOME TRAFFIC. I TRIED TO CALL BUT NOBOD--
ACH! I WASN'T BORN YESTERDAY, MISTER TOBIN!
LET'S GET THIS SHOW ON THE ROAD.
WE KNOW AND WE'RE TERRIBLY SORRY, MS. KLOMPUS--
WE WORKED THROUGH THE NIGHT ON AN IMPORTANT CASE--
--AND MISTER TOBIN NEEDED TIME TO RECHARGE IN ORDER TO PERFORM TODAY.
IT'S TRUE. IT'S ALL MY FAULT.
YOU REMIND ME OF MY DAUGHTER'S EX...
HE WASN'T GOOD FOR ALL THAT MUCH.
I'M SORRY YOU FEEL THAT WAY...
...BUT I'M THE TALENT, TOOTS.
HEHEH-
URK!

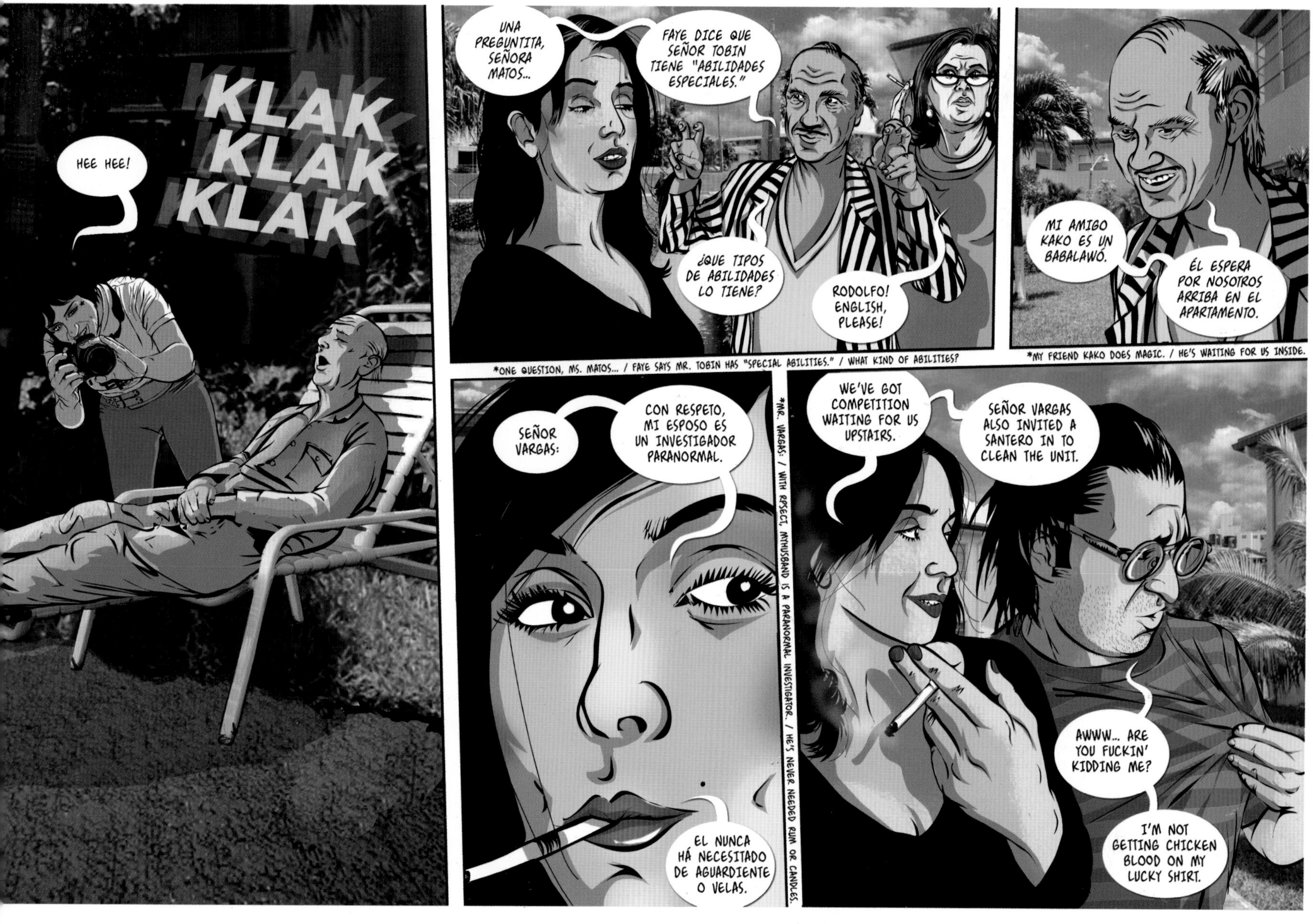
KLAK KLAK KLAK
HEE HEE!
UNA PREGUNTITA, SEÑORA MATOS...
FAYE DICE QUE SEÑOR TOBIN TIENE "ABILIDADES ESPECIALES."
¿QUE TIPOS DE ABILIDADES LO TIENE?
RODOLFO! ENGLISH, PLEASE!
MI AMIGO KAKO ES UN BABALAWÓ.
ÉL ESPERA POR NOSOTROS ARRIBA EN EL APARTAMENTO.
*ONE QUESTION, MS. MATOS... / FAYE SAYS MR. TOBIN HAS "SPECIAL ABILITIES." / WHAT KIND OF ABILITIES?
*MY FRIEND KAKO DOES MAGIC. / HE'S WAITING FOR US INSIDE.
SEÑOR VARGAS:
CON RESPETO, MI ESPOSO ES UN INVESTIGADOR PARANORMAL.
EL NUNCA HÁ NECESITADO DE AGUARDIENTE O VELAS.
*MR. VARGAS: / WITH RPSECT, MYHUSBAND IS A PARANORMAL INVESTIGATOR. / HE'S NEVER NEEDED RUM OR CANDLES.
WE'VE GOT COMPETITION WAITING FOR US UPSTAIRS.
SEÑOR VARGAS ALSO INVITED A SANTERO IN TO CLEAN THE UNIT.
AWWW... ARE YOU FUCKIN' KIDDING ME?
I'M NOT GETTING CHICKEN BLOOD ON MY LUCKY SHIRT.

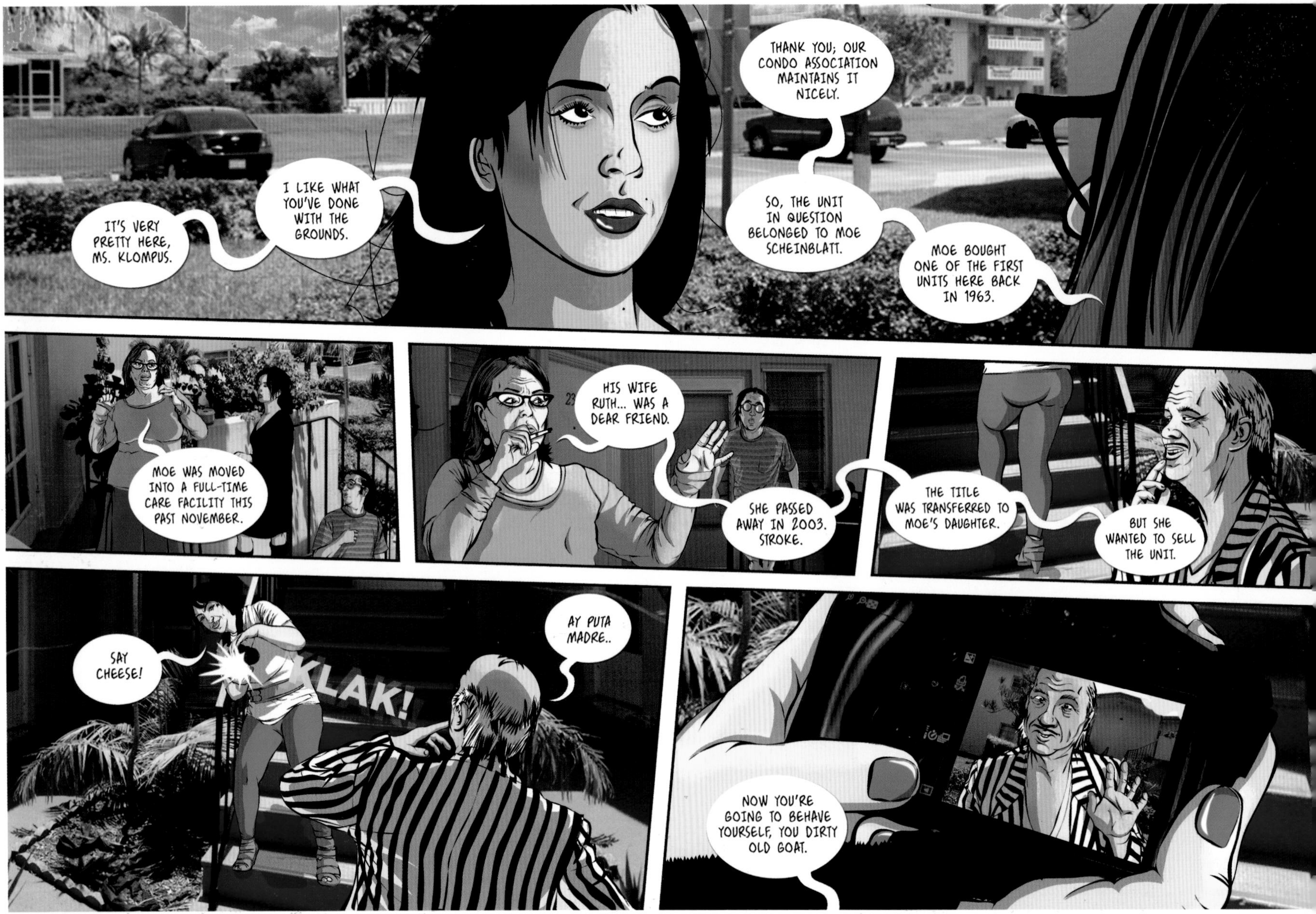
IT'S VERY PRETTY HERE, MS. KLOMPUS.
I LIKE WHAT YOU'VE DONE WITH THE GROUNDS.
THANK YOU; OUR CONDO ASSOCIATION MAINTAINS IT NICELY.
SO, THE UNIT IN QUESTION BELONGED TO MOE SCHEINBLATT.
MOE BOUGHT ONE OF THE FIRST UNITS HERE BACK IN 1963.
MOE WAS MOVED INTO A FULL-TIME CARE FACILITY THIS PAST NOVEMBER.
HIS WIFE RUTH... WAS A DEAR FRIEND.
SHE PASSED AWAY IN 2003. STROKE.
THE TITLE WAS TRANSFERRED TO MOE'S DAUGHTER.
BUT SHE WANTED TO SELL THE UNIT.
SAY CHEESE!
KLAK!
AY PUTA MADRE..
NOW YOU'RE GOING TO BEHAVE YOURSELF, YOU DIRTY OLD GOAT.

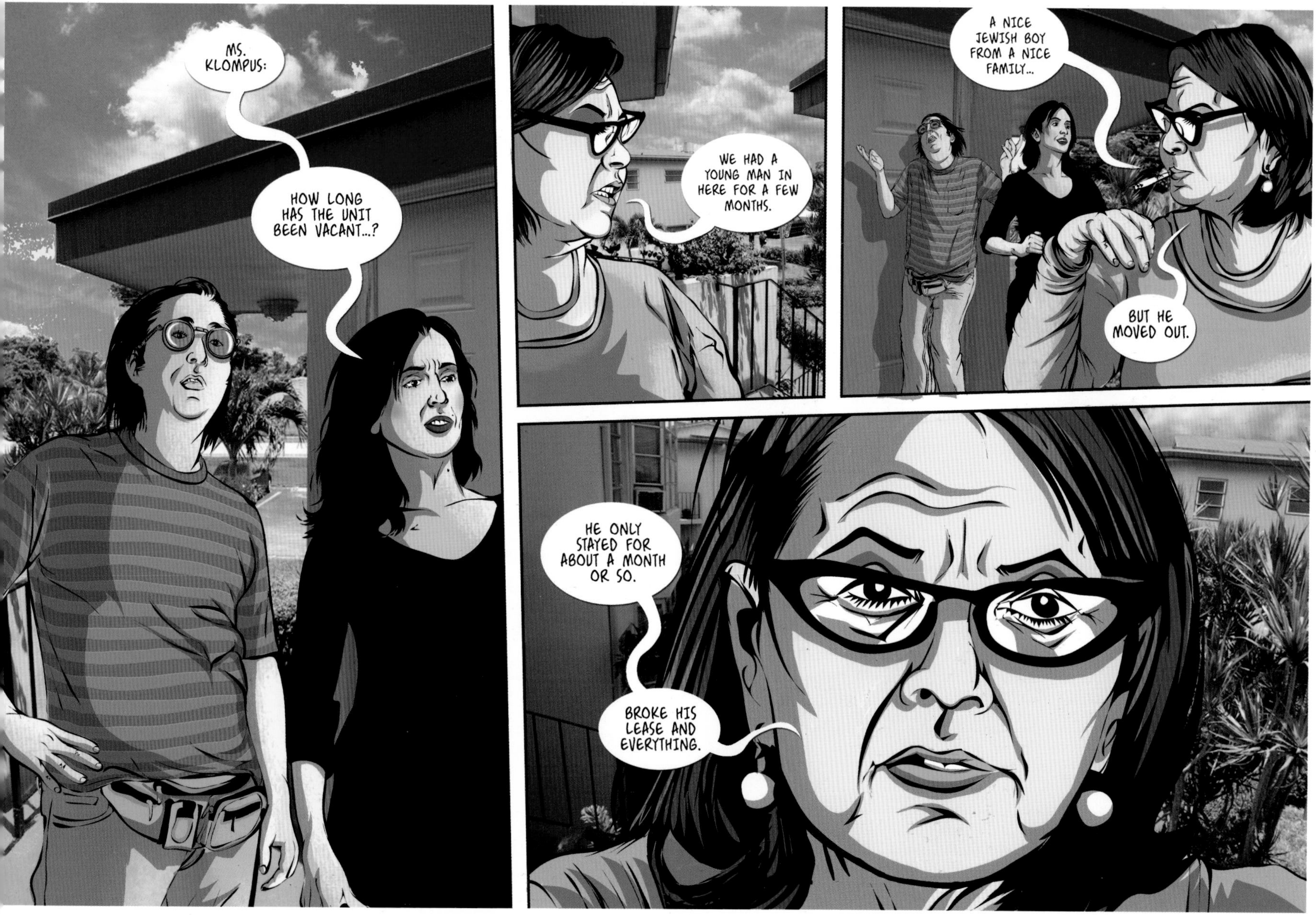
MS. KLOMPUS:
HOW LONG HAS THE UNIT BEEN VACANT...?
WE HAD A YOUNG MAN IN HERE FOR A FEW MONTHS.
A NICE JEWISH BOY FROM A NICE FAMILY...
BUT HE MOVED OUT.
HE ONLY STAYED FOR ABOUT A MONTH OR SO.
BROKE HIS LEASE AND EVERYTHING.

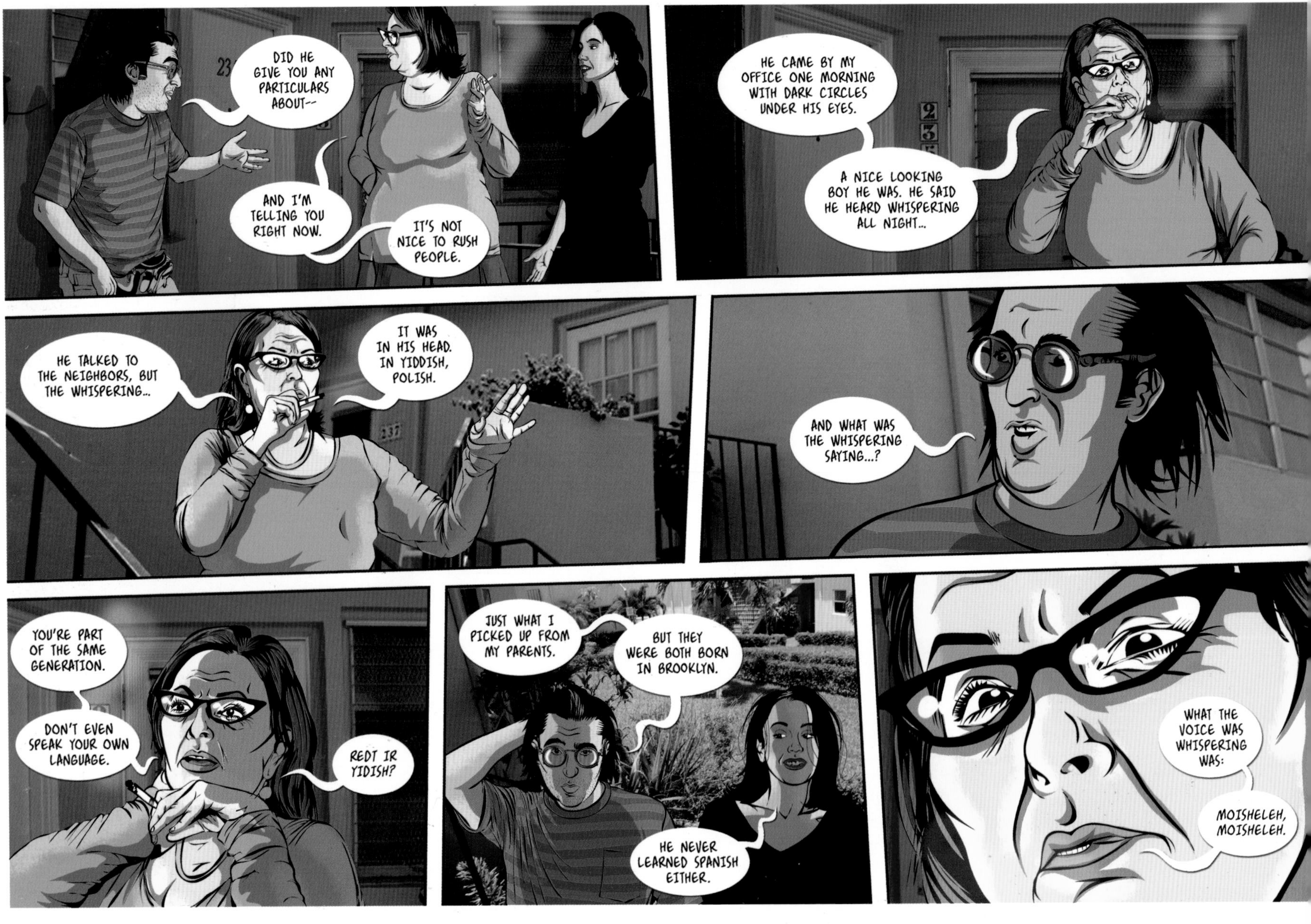
DID HE GIVE YOU ANY PARTICULARS ABOUT--
AND I'M TELLING YOU RIGHT NOW.
IT'S NOT NICE TO RUSH PEOPLE.
HE CAME BY MY OFFICE ONE MORNING WITH DARK CIRCLES UNDER HIS EYES.
A NICE LOOKING BOY HE WAS. HE SAID HE HEARD WHISPERING ALL NIGHT...
HE TALKED TO THE NEIGHBORS, BUT THE WHISPERING...
IT WAS IN HIS HEAD. IN YIDDISH, POLISH.
AND WHAT WAS THE WHISPERING SAYING...?
YOU'RE PART OF THE SAME GENERATION.
DON'T EVEN SPEAK YOUR OWN LANGUAGE.
REDT IR YIDISH?
JUST WHAT I PICKED UP FROM MY PARENTS.
BUT THEY WERE BOTH BORN IN BROOKLYN.
HE NEVER LEARNED SPANISH EITHER.
WHAT THE VOICE WAS WHISPERING WAS:
MOISHELEH, MOISHELEH.

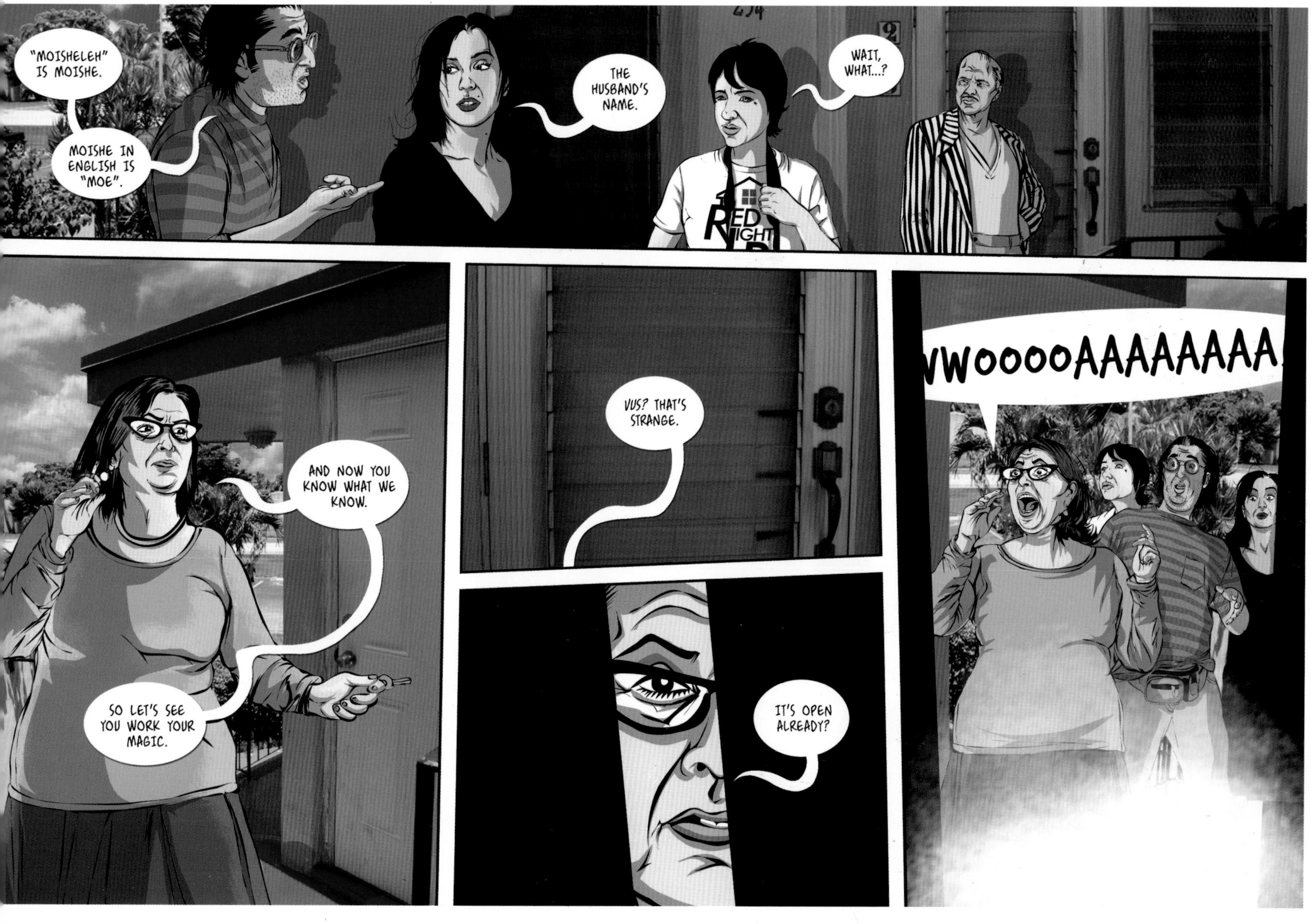
"MOISHELEH" IS MOISHE.
MOISHE IN ENGLISH IS "MOE".
THE HUSBAND'S NAME.
WAIT, WHAT...?
AND NOW YOU KNOW WHAT WE KNOW.
SO LET'S SEE YOU WORK YOUR MAGIC.
VUS? THAT'S STRANGE.
IT'S OPEN ALREADY?
WOOOOAAAAAAAA

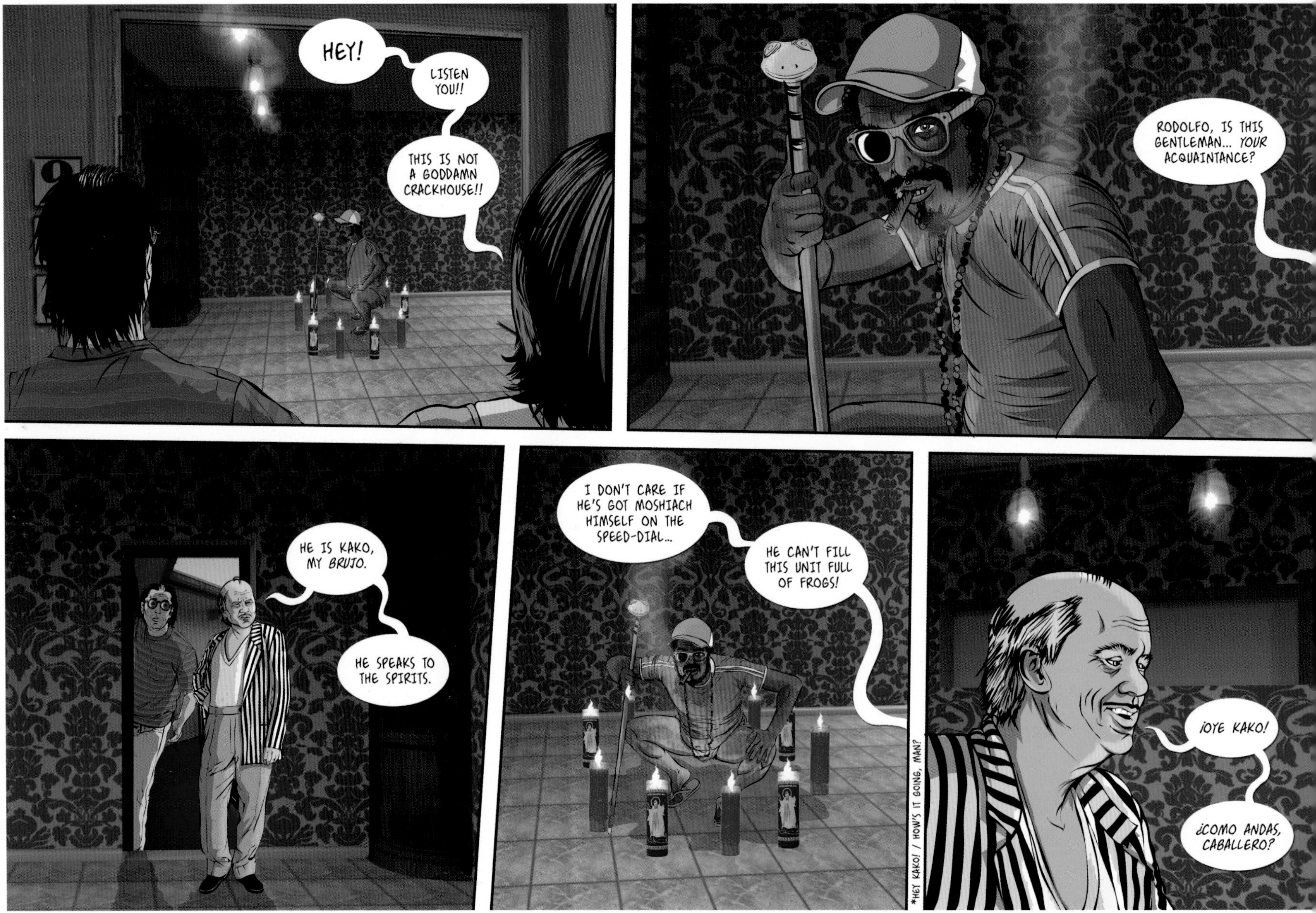
HEY!
LISTEN YOU!!
THIS IS NOT A GODDAMN CRACKHOUSE!!
RODOLFO, IS THIS GENTLEMAN... YOUR ACQUAINTANCE?
HE IS KAKO, MY BRUJO.
HE SPEAKS TO THE SPIRITS.
I DON'T CARE IF HE'S GOT MOSHIACH HIMSELF ON THE SPEED-DIAL...
HE CAN'T FILL THIS UNIT FULL OF FROGS!
¡OYE KAKO!
¿COMO ANDAS, CABALLERO?
*HEY KAKO! / HOW'S IT GOING, MAN?

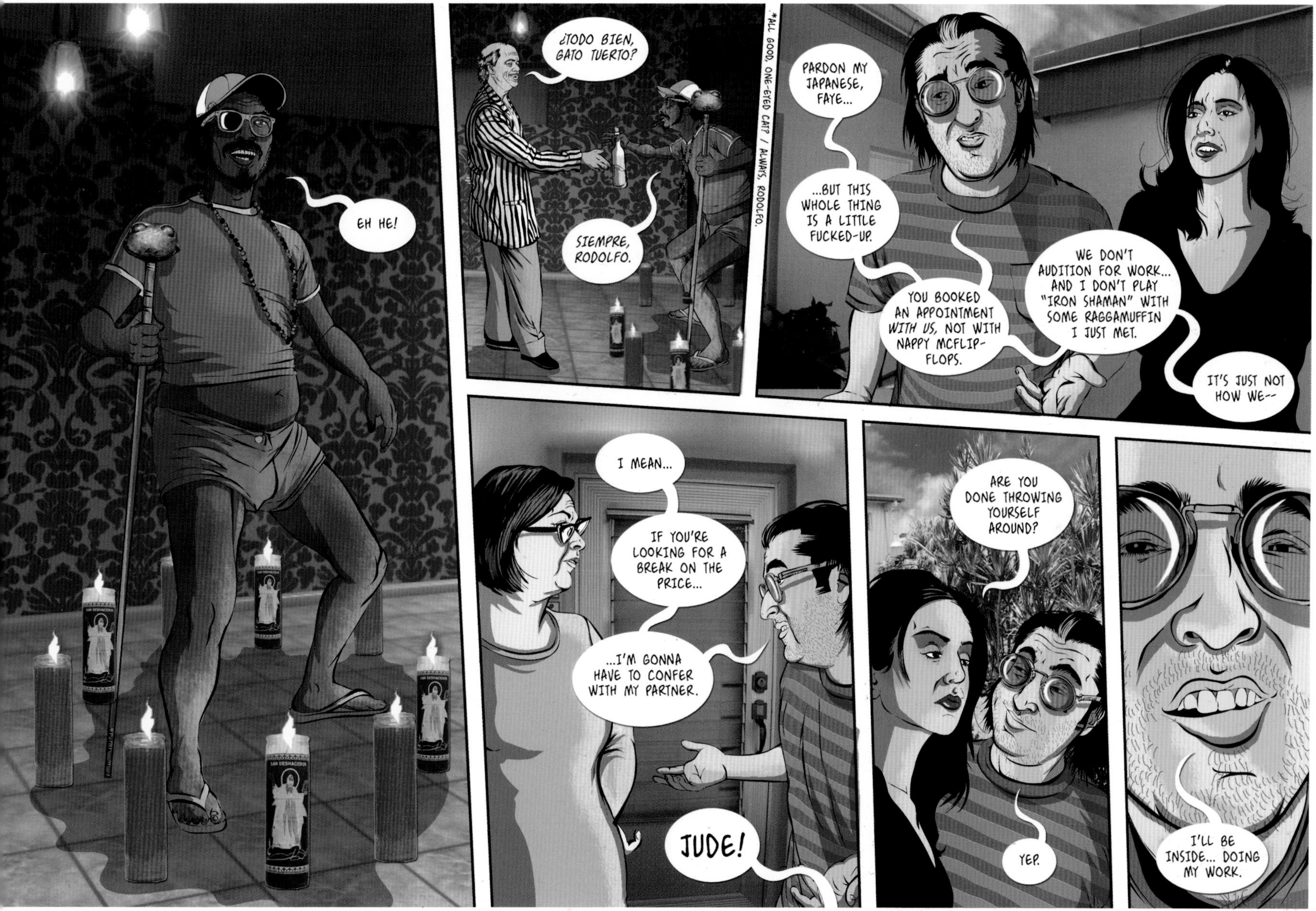
EH HE!
¿TODO BIEN, GATO TUERTO?
SIEMPRE, RODOLFO.
*ALL GOOD, ONE-EYED CAT? / ALWAYS, RODOLFO.
PARDON MY JAPANESE, FAYE...
...BUT THIS WHOLE THING IS A LITTLE FUCKED-UP.
YOU BOOKED AN APPOINTMENT WITH US, NOT WITH NAPPY MCFLIP-FLOPS.
WE DON'T AUDITION FOR WORK... AND I DON'T PLAY "IRON SHAMAN" WITH SOME RAGGAMUFFIN I JUST MET.
IT'S JUST NOT HOW WE--
I MEAN...
IF YOU'RE LOOKING FOR A BREAK ON THE PRICE...
...I'M GONNA HAVE TO CONFER WITH MY PARTNER.
JUDE!
ARE YOU DONE THROWING YOURSELF AROUND?
YEP.
I'LL BE INSIDE... DOING MY WORK.

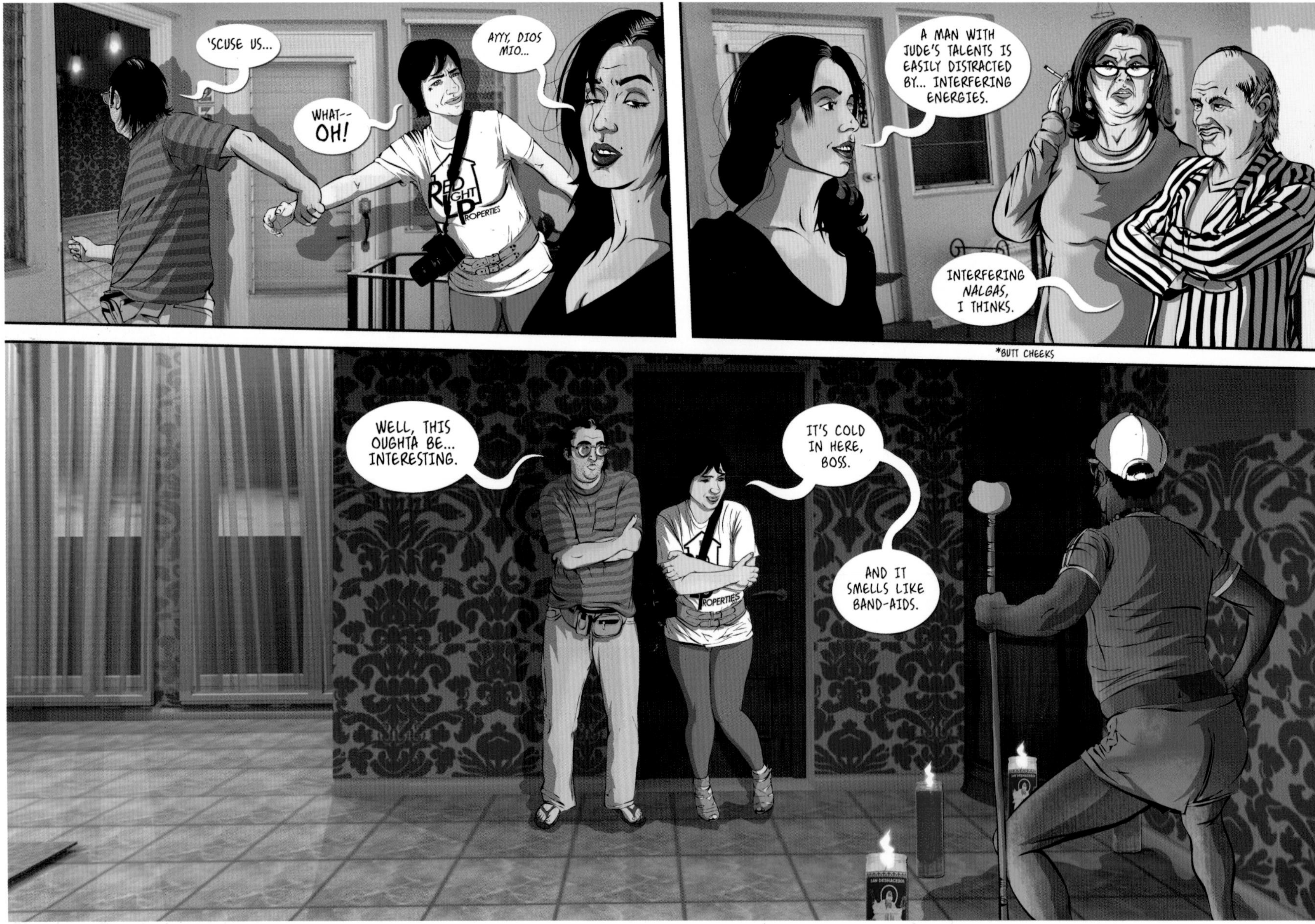
'SCUSE US...
WHAT--
OH!
AYYY, DIOS MIO...
A MAN WITH JUDE'S TALENTS IS EASILY DISTRACTED BY... INTERFERING ENERGIES.
INTERFERING NALGAS, I THINKS.
*BUTT CHEEKS
WELL, THIS OUGHTA BE... INTERESTING.
IT'S COLD IN HERE, BOSS.
AND IT SMELLS LIKE BAND-AIDS.

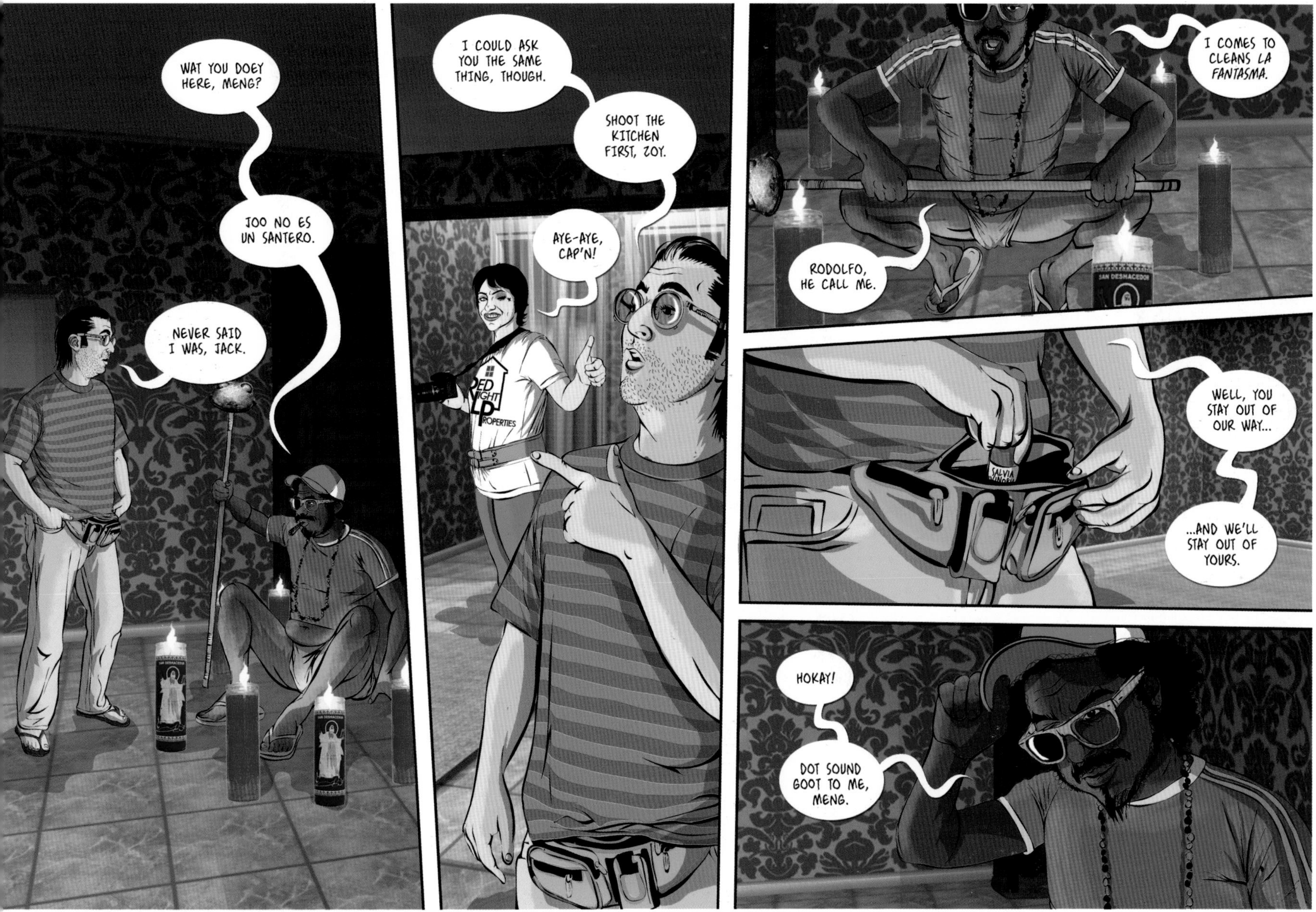
WAT YOU DOEY HERE, MENG?
JOO NO ES UN SANTERO.
NEVER SAID I WAS, JACK.
I COULD ASK YOU THE SAME THING, THOUGH.
SHOOT THE KITCHEN FIRST, ZOY.
AYE-AYE, CAP'N!
RED LIGHT PROPERTIES
I COMES TO CLEANS *LA FANTASMA.*
RODOLFO, HE CALL ME.
SAN DESHACEDOR
WELL, YOU STAY OUT OF OUR WAY...
...AND WE'LL STAY OUT OF YOURS.
HOKAY!
DOT SOUND GOOT TO ME, MENG.

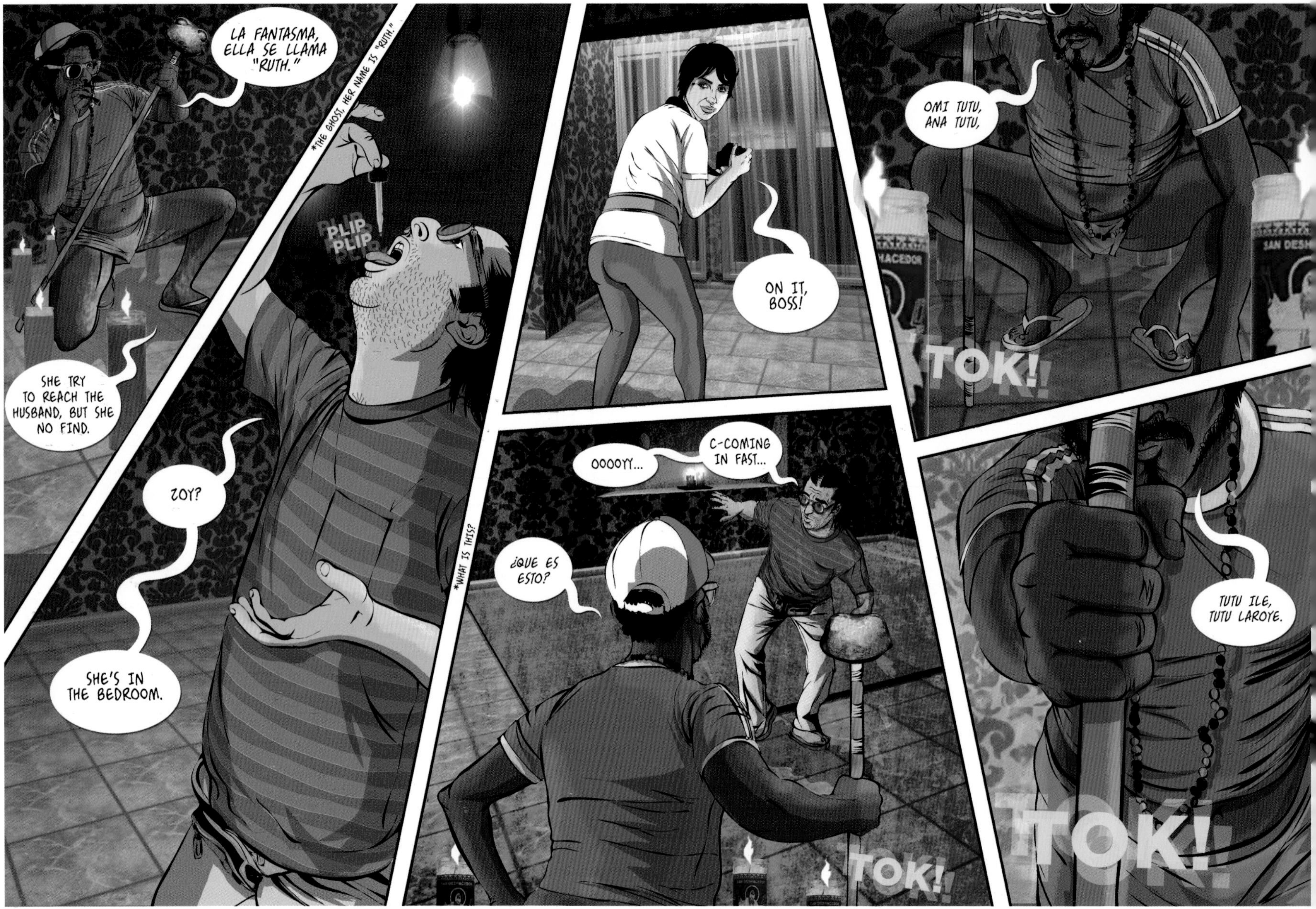
LA FANTASMA, ELLA SE LLAMA "RUTH."
*THE GHOST, HER NAME IS "RUTH."
SHE TRY TO REACH THE HUSBAND, BUT SHE NO FIND.
PLIP PLIP
¿OY?
SHE'S IN THE BEDROOM.
ON IT, BOSS!
OMI TUTU, ANA TUTU,
TOK!
OOOOYY...
C-COMING IN FAST...
¿QUE ES ESTO?
*WHAT IS THIS?
TOK!
TUTU ILE, TUTU LAROYE.
TOK!

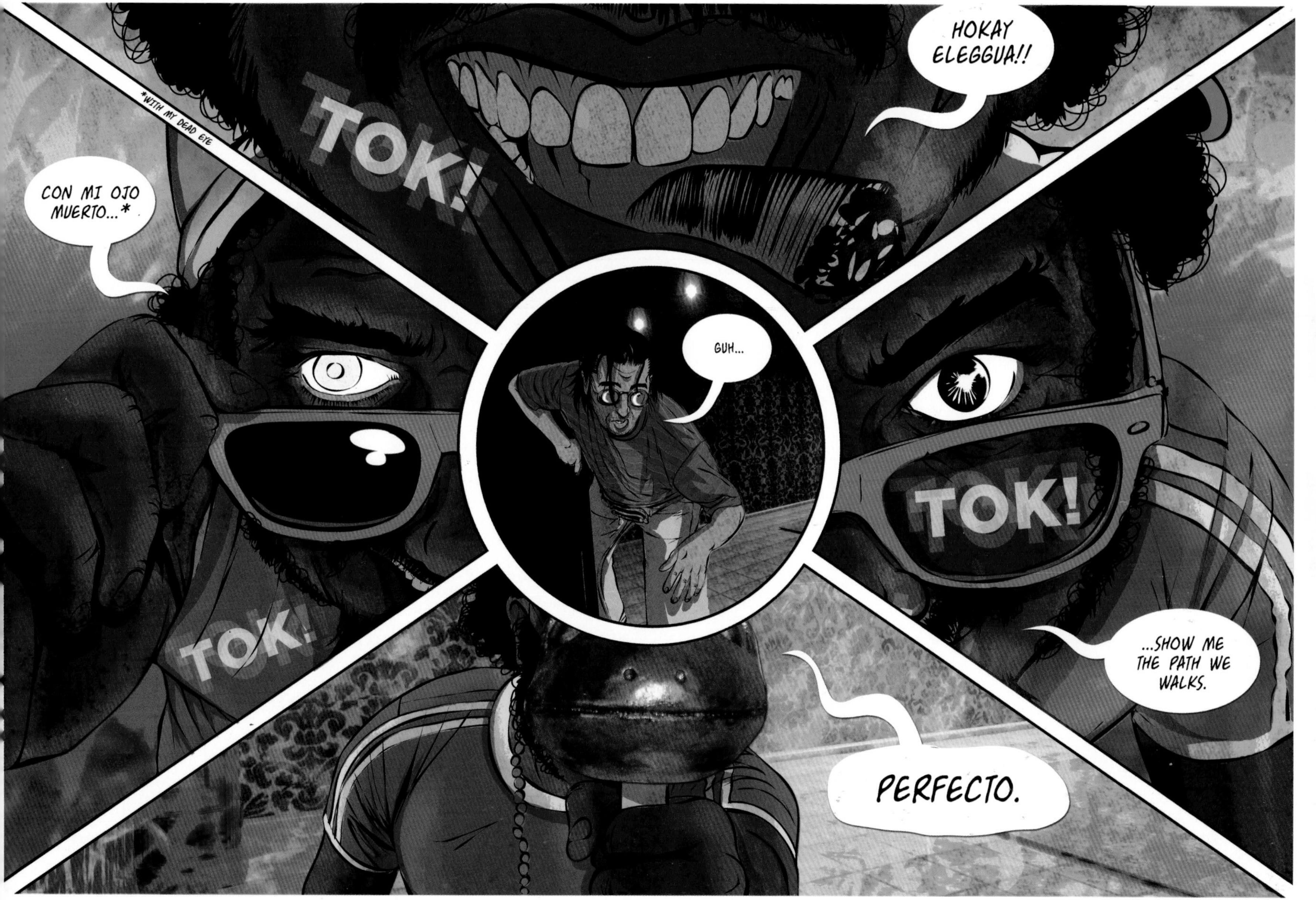
TOK!
HOKAY ELEGGUA!!
CON MI OJO MUERTO...*
*WITH MY DEAD EYE
TOK!
GUH...
TOK!
...SHOW ME THE PATH WE WALKS.
PERFECTO.

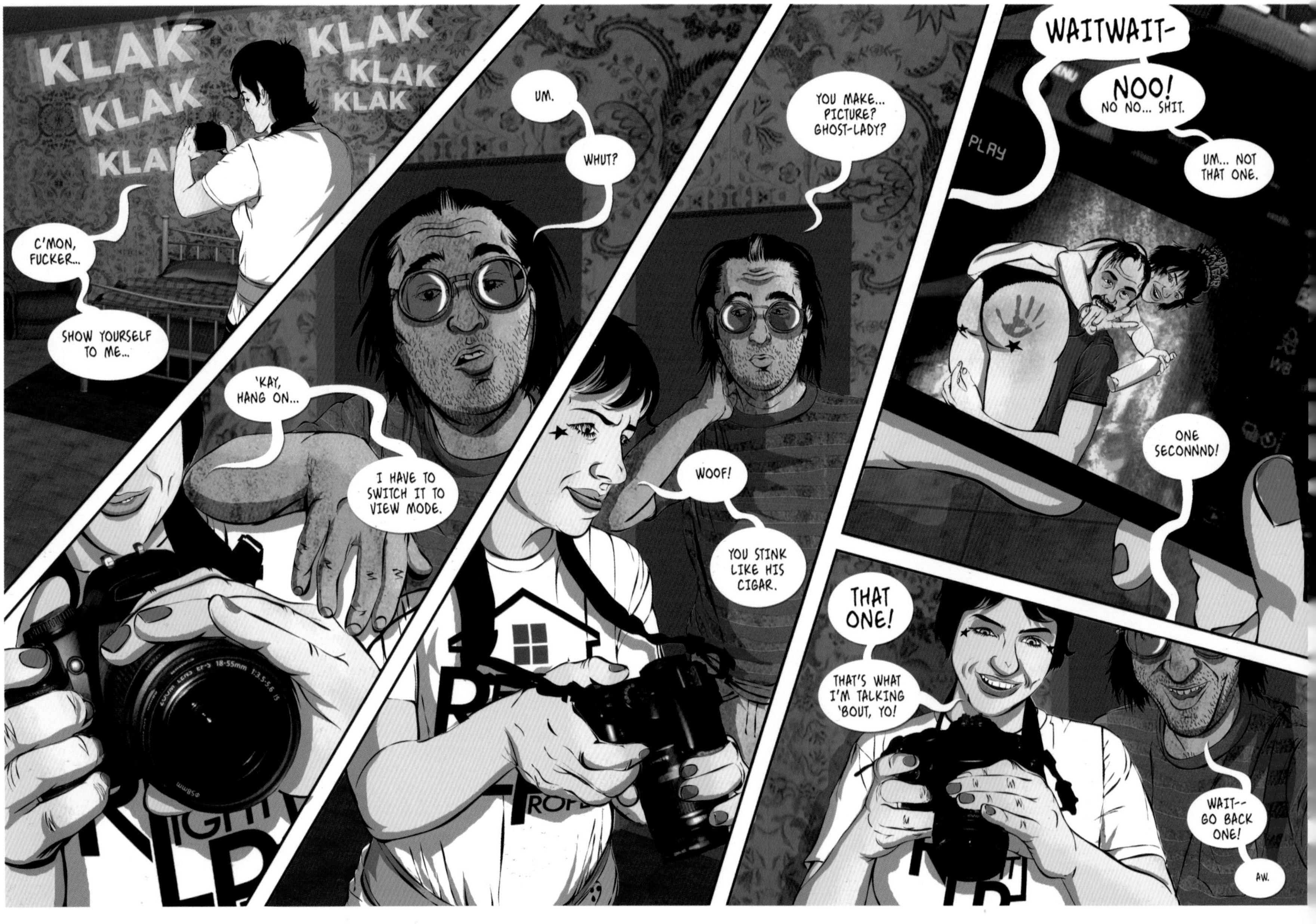
KLAK KLAK KLAK KLAK KLAK KLAK
C'MON, FUCKER...
SHOW YOURSELF TO ME...
UM.
WHUT?
'KAY, HANG ON...
I HAVE TO SWITCH IT TO VIEW MODE.
YOU MAKE... PICTURE? GHOST-LADY?
WOOF!
YOU STINK LIKE HIS CIGAR.
WAITWAIT-
NOO! NO NO... SHIT.
UM... NOT THAT ONE.
PLAY
ONE SECONNND!
THAT ONE!
THAT'S WHAT I'M TALKING 'BOUT, YO!
WAIT-- GO BACK ONE!
AW.

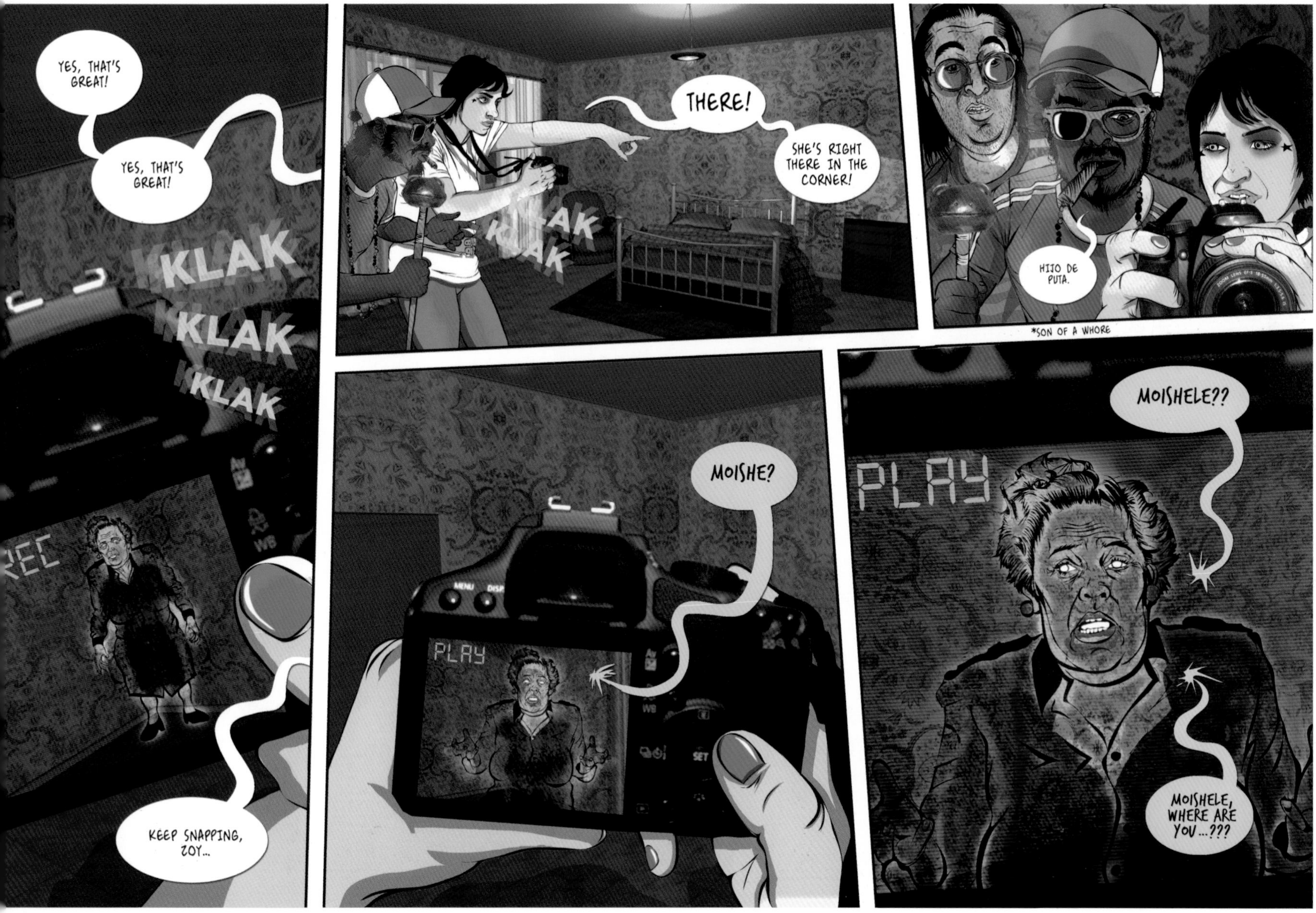
YES, THAT'S GREAT!
YES, THAT'S GREAT!
KLAK
KLAK
KLAK
REC
KEEP SNAPPING, ZOY...
THERE!
SHE'S RIGHT THERE IN THE CORNER!
KLAK
KLAK
HIJO DE PUTA.
*SON OF A WHORE
MOISHE?
PLAY
MOISHELE??
PLAY
MOISHELE, WHERE ARE YOU...???

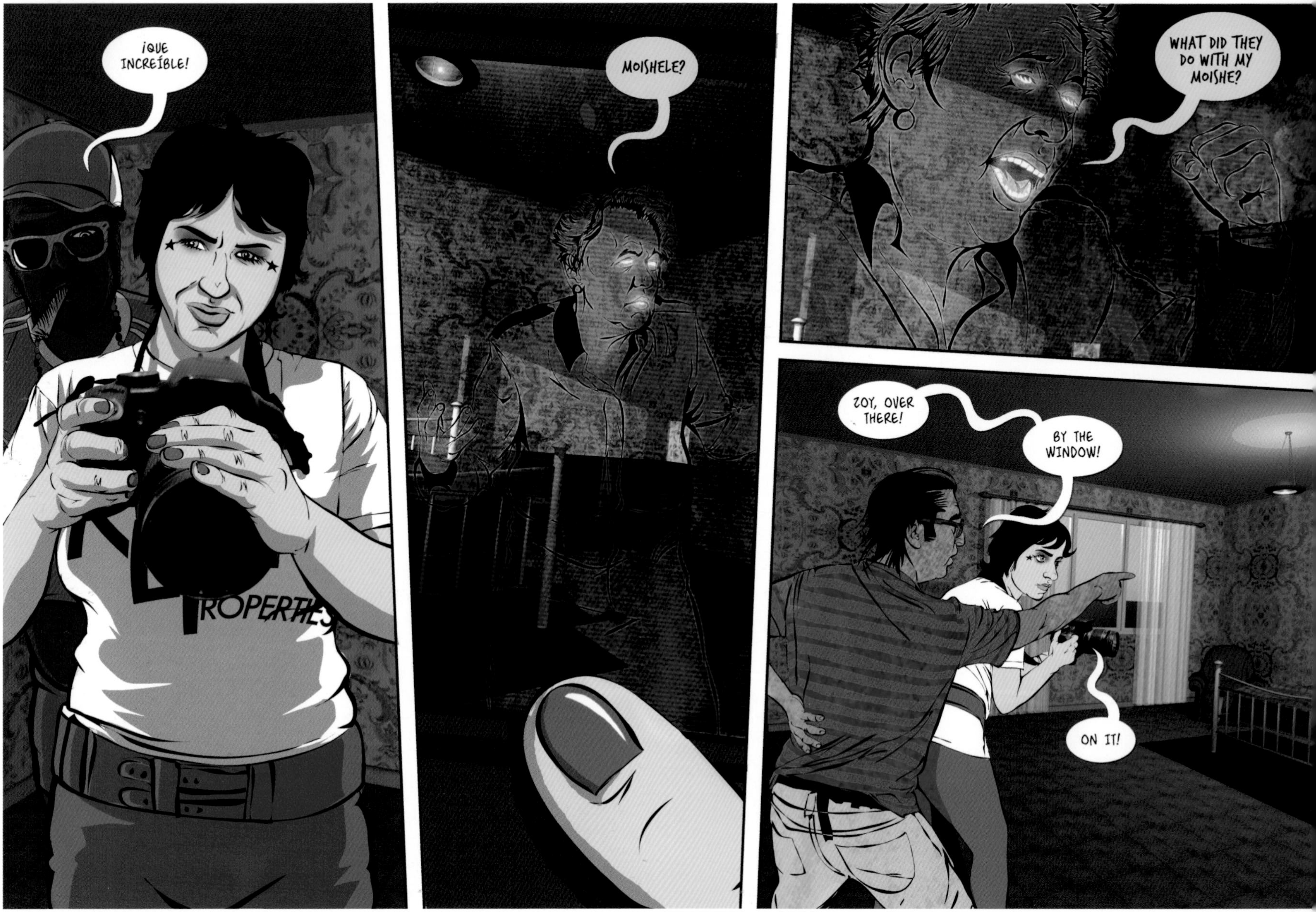
¡QUE INCREÍBLE!
MOISHELE?
WHAT DID THEY DO WITH MY MOISHE?
ZOY, OVER THERE!
BY THE WINDOW!
ON IT!
PROPERTIES

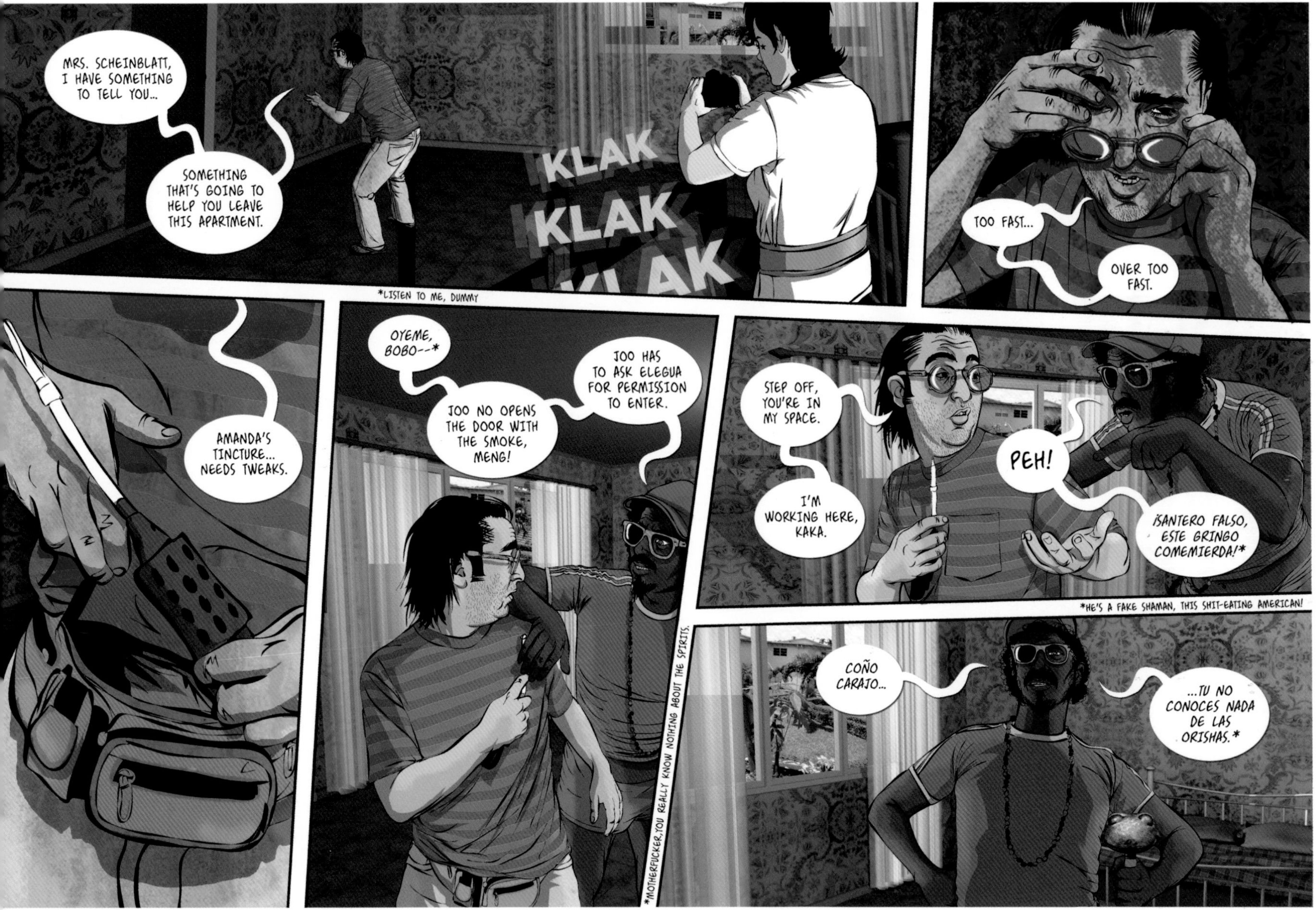
MRS. SCHEINBLATT, I HAVE SOMETHING TO TELL YOU...
SOMETHING THAT'S GOING TO HELP YOU LEAVE THIS APARTMENT.
KLAK
KLAK
KLAK
TOO FAST...
OVER TOO FAST.
AMANDA'S TINCTURE... NEEDS TWEAKS.
OYEME, BOBO--*
JOO NO OPENS THE DOOR WITH THE SMOKE, MENG!
JOO HAS TO ASK ELEGUA FOR PERMISSION TO ENTER.
*LISTEN TO ME, DUMMY
*MOTHERFUCKER, YOU REALLY KNOW NOTHING ABOUT THE SPIRITS.
STEP OFF, YOU'RE IN MY SPACE.
I'M WORKING HERE, KAKA.
PEH!
¡SANTERO FALSO, ESTE GRINGO COMEMIERDA!*
*HE'S A FAKE SHAMAN, THIS SHIT-EATING AMERICAN!
COÑO CARAJO...
...TU NO CONOCES NADA DE LAS ORISHAS.*

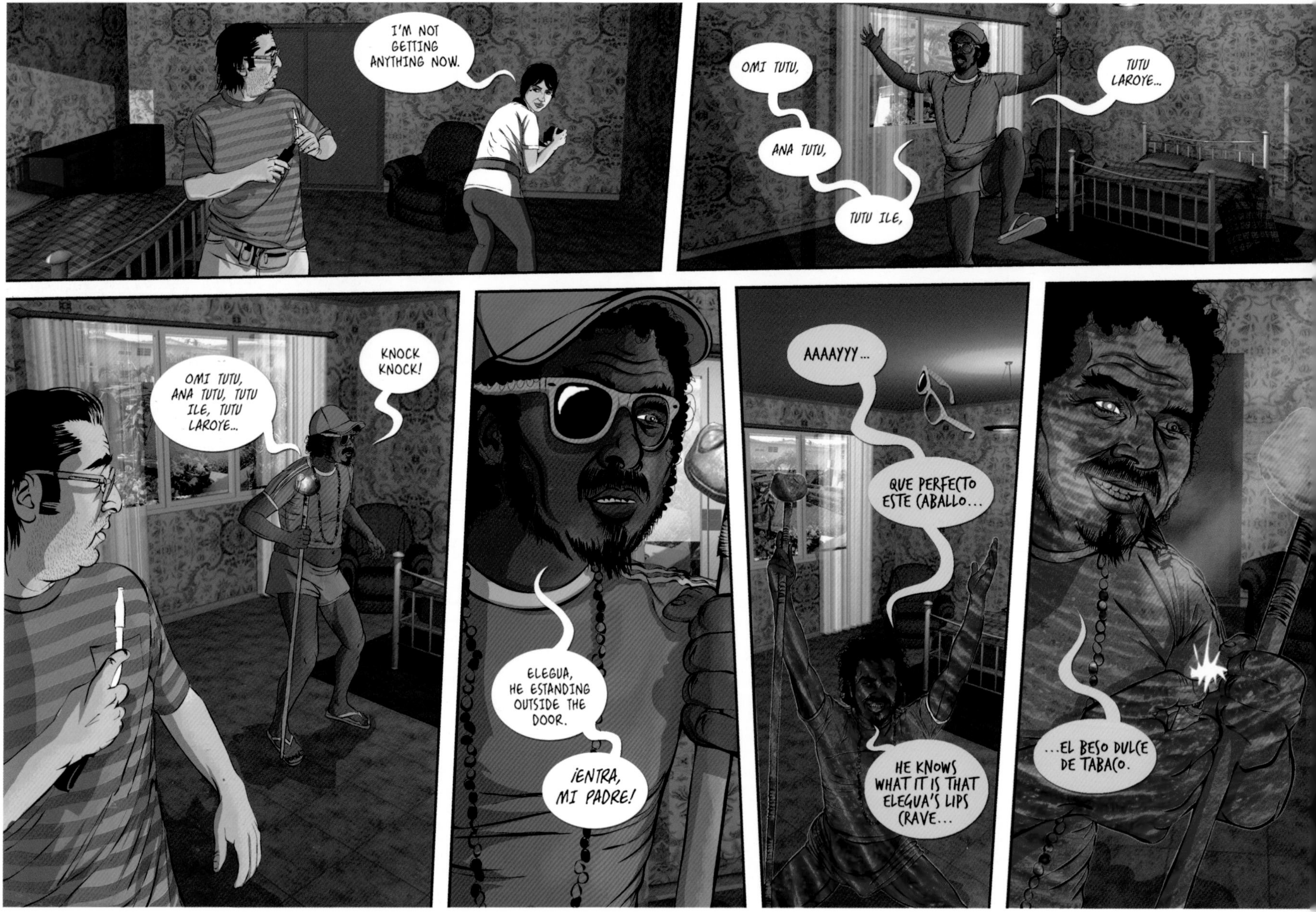
I'M NOT GETTING ANYTHING NOW.
OMI TUTU,
ANA TUTU,
TUTU ILE,
TUTU LAROYE...
OMI TUTU, ANA TUTU, TUTU ILE, TUTU LAROYE...
KNOCK KNOCK!
ELEGUA, HE ESTANDING OUTSIDE THE DOOR.
¡ENTRA, MI PADRE!
AAAAYYY...
QUE PERFECTO ESTE CABALLO...
HE KNOWS WHAT IT IS THAT ELEGUA'S LIPS CRAVE...
...EL BESO DULCE DE TABACO.

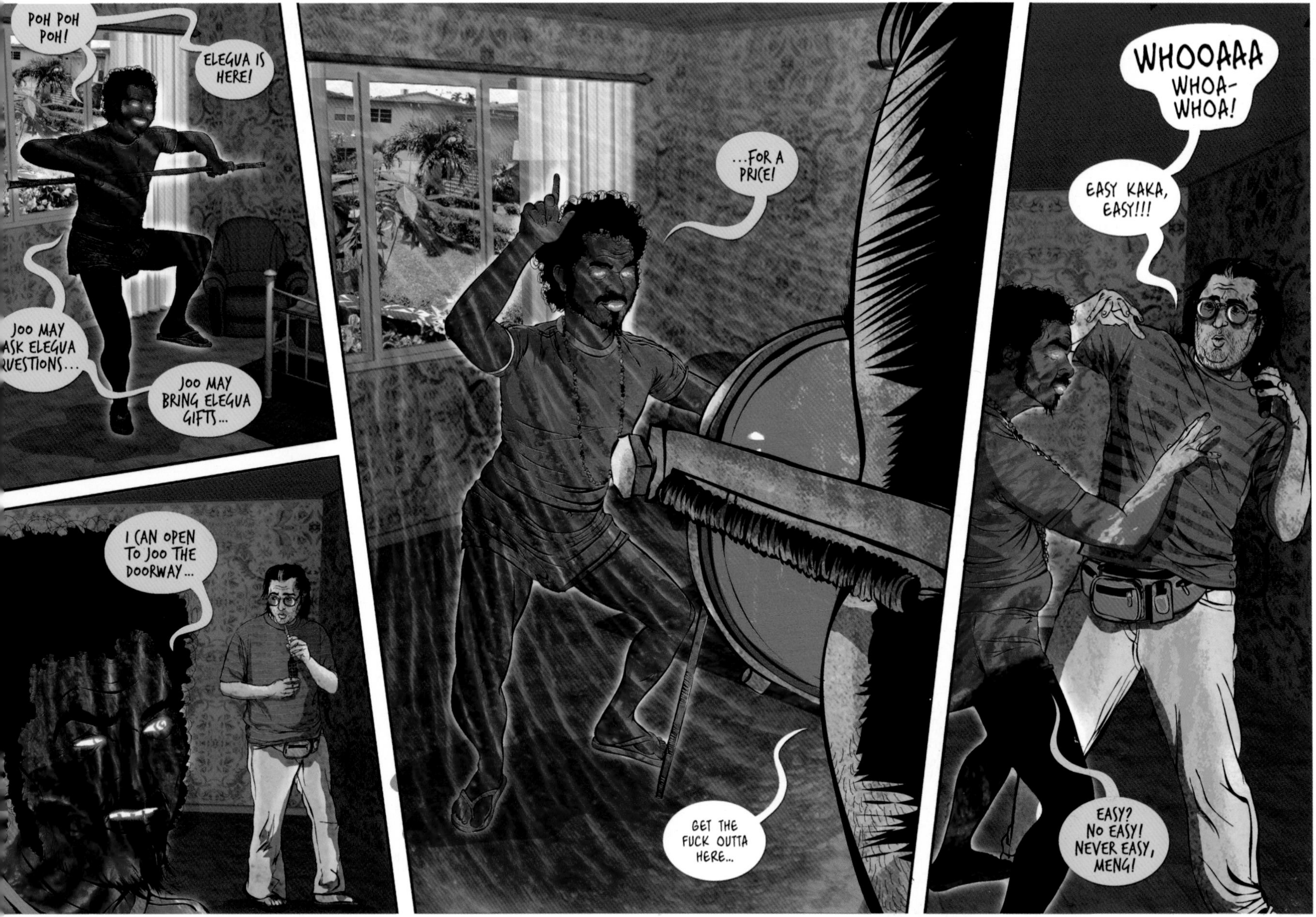
POH POH POH!
ELEGUA IS HERE!
JOO MAY ASK ELEGUA QUESTIONS...
JOO MAY BRING ELEGUA GIFTS...
I CAN OPEN TO JOO THE DOORWAY...
...FOR A PRICE!
GET THE FUCK OUTTA HERE...
WHOOAAA WHOA-WHOA!
EASY KAKA, EASY!!!
EASY? NO EASY! NEVER EASY, MENG!

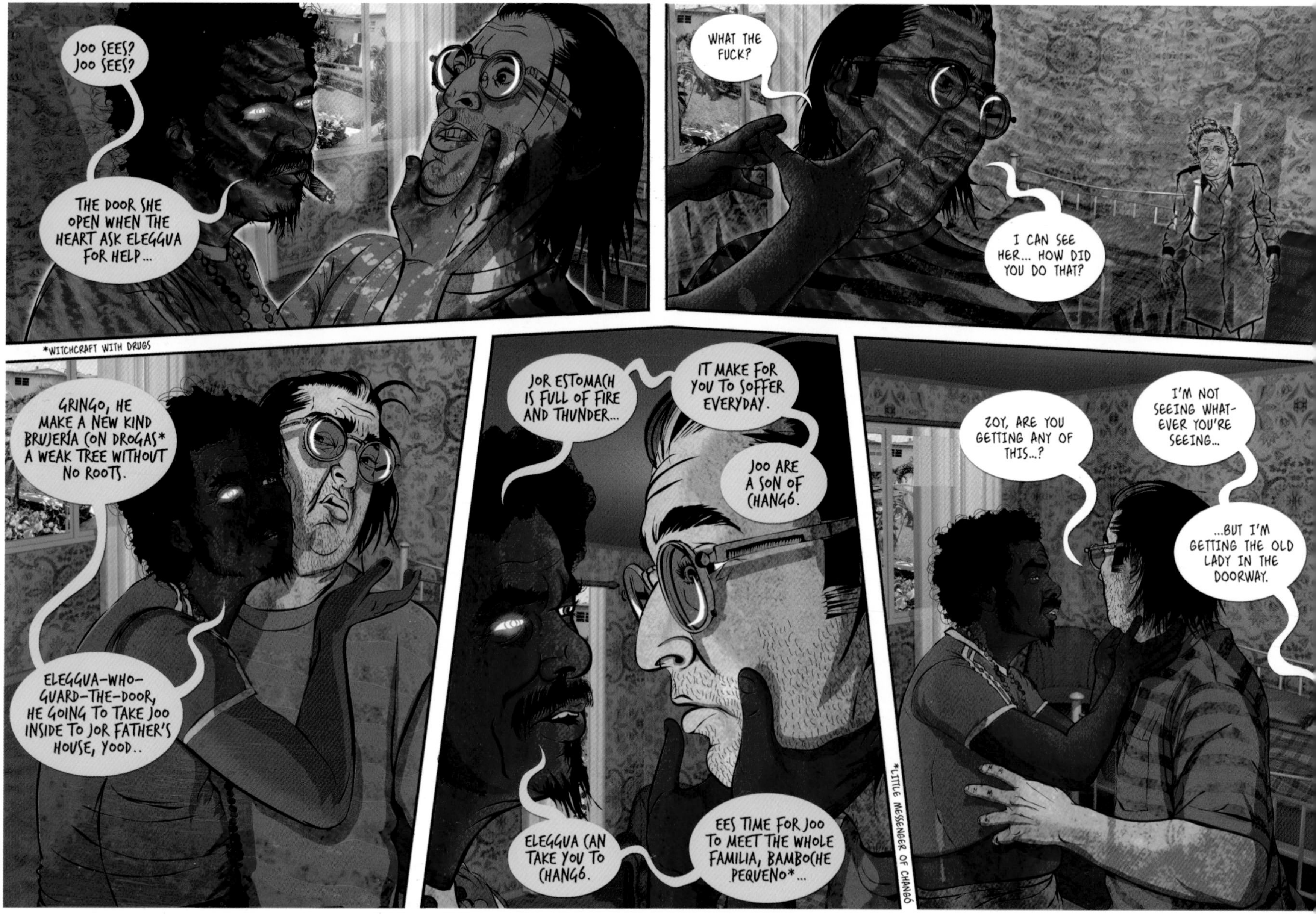

JOO SEES? JOO SEES?
THE DOOR SHE OPEN WHEN THE HEART ASK ELEGGUA FOR HELP...
WHAT THE FUCK?
I CAN SEE HER... HOW DID YOU DO THAT?
*WITCHCRAFT WITH DRUGS
GRINGO, HE MAKE A NEW KIND BRUJERÍA CON DROGAS* A WEAK TREE WITHOUT NO ROOTS.
ELEGGUA-WHO-GUARD-THE-DOOR, HE GOING TO TAKE JOO INSIDE TO JOR FATHER'S HOUSE, YOOD..
JOR ESTOMACH IS FULL OF FIRE AND THUNDER...
IT MAKE FOR YOU TO SOFFER EVERYDAY.
JOO ARE A SON OF CHANGÓ.
ELEGGUA CAN TAKE YOU TO CHANGÓ.
EES TIME FOR JOO TO MEET THE WHOLE FAMILIA, BAMBOCHE PEQUENO*...
*LITTLE MESSENGER OF CHANGÓ
ZOY, ARE YOU GETTING ANY OF THIS...?
I'M NOT SEEING WHAT-EVER YOU'RE SEEING...
...BUT I'M GETTING THE OLD LADY IN THE DOORWAY.

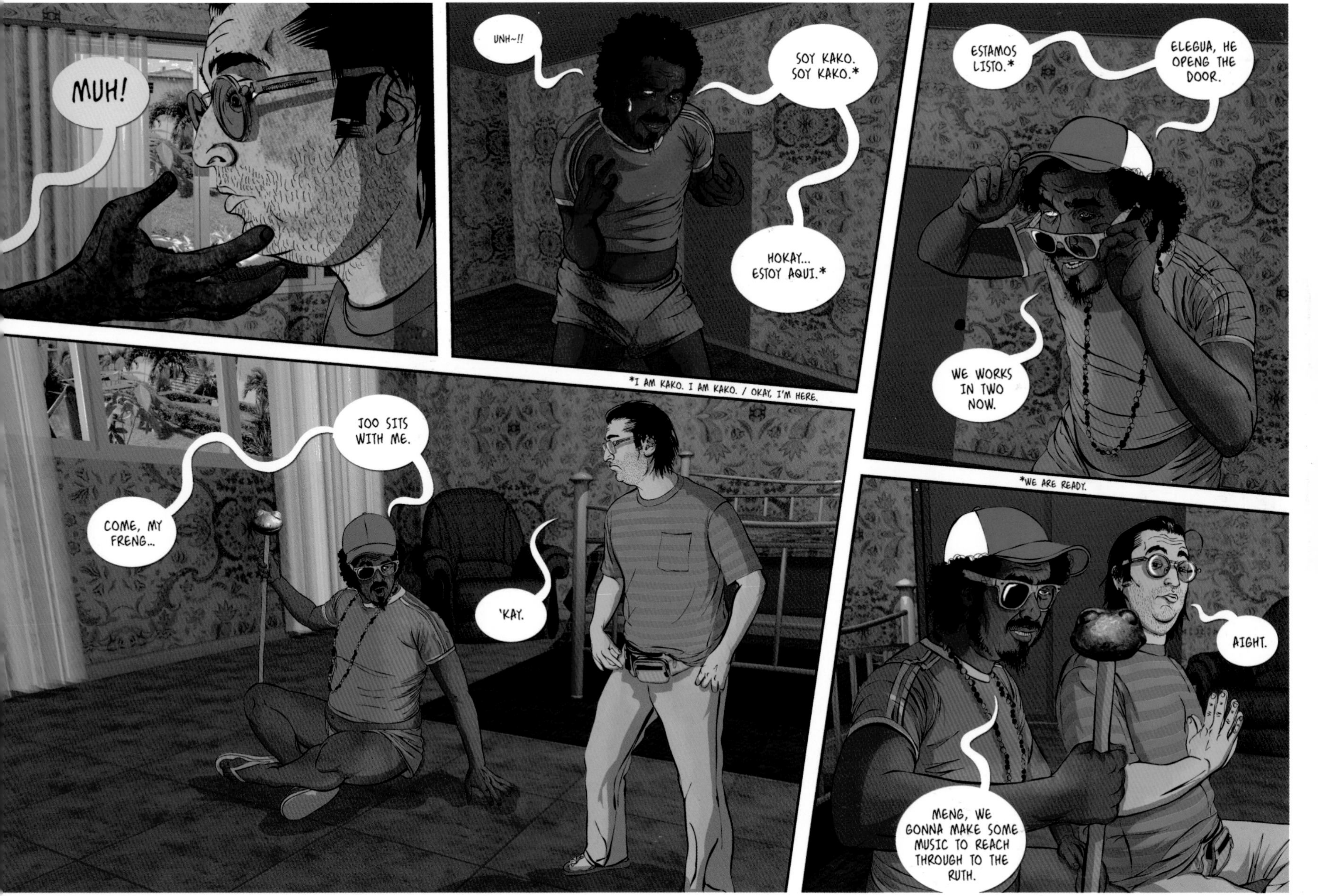
MUH!
UNH~!!
SOY KAKO. SOY KAKO.*
HOKAY... ESTOY AQUI.*
*I AM KAKO. I AM KAKO. / OKAY, I'M HERE.
ESTAMOS LISTO.*
ELEGUA, HE OPENG THE DOOR.
WE WORKS IN TWO NOW.
*WE ARE READY.
COME, MY FRENG...
JOO SITS WITH ME.
'KAY.
MENG, WE GONNA MAKE SOME MUSIC TO REACH THROUGH TO THE RUTH.
AIGHT.

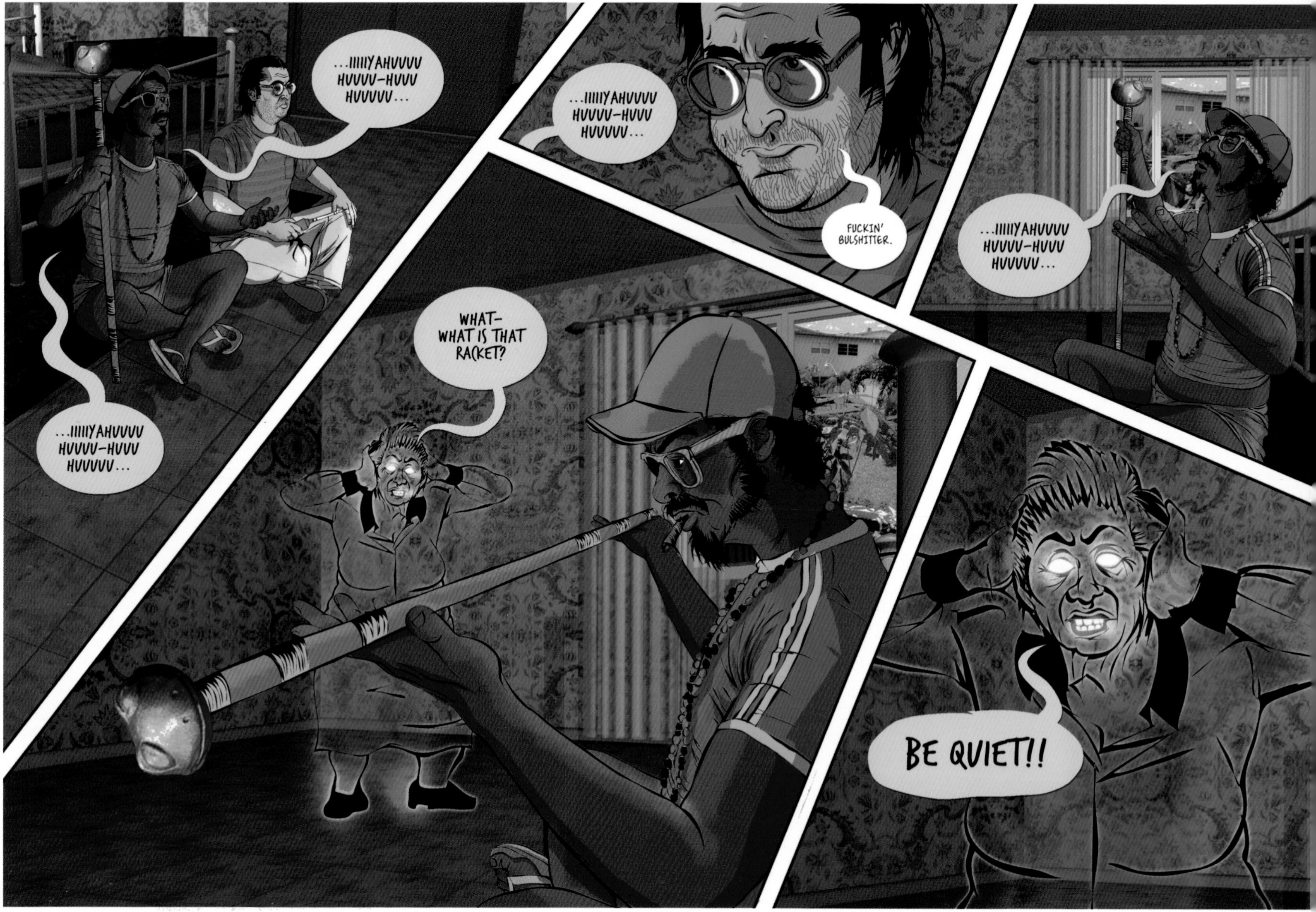
...IIIIIYAHUVVV HUVVV–HUVV HUVVVV...
...IIIIIYAHUVVV HUVVV–HUVV HUVVVV...
...IIIIIYAHUVVV HUVVV–HUVV HUVVVV...
FUCKIN' BULSHITTER.
...IIIIIYAHUVVV HUVVV–HUVV HUVVVV...
WHAT- WHAT IS THAT RACKET?
BE QUIET!!

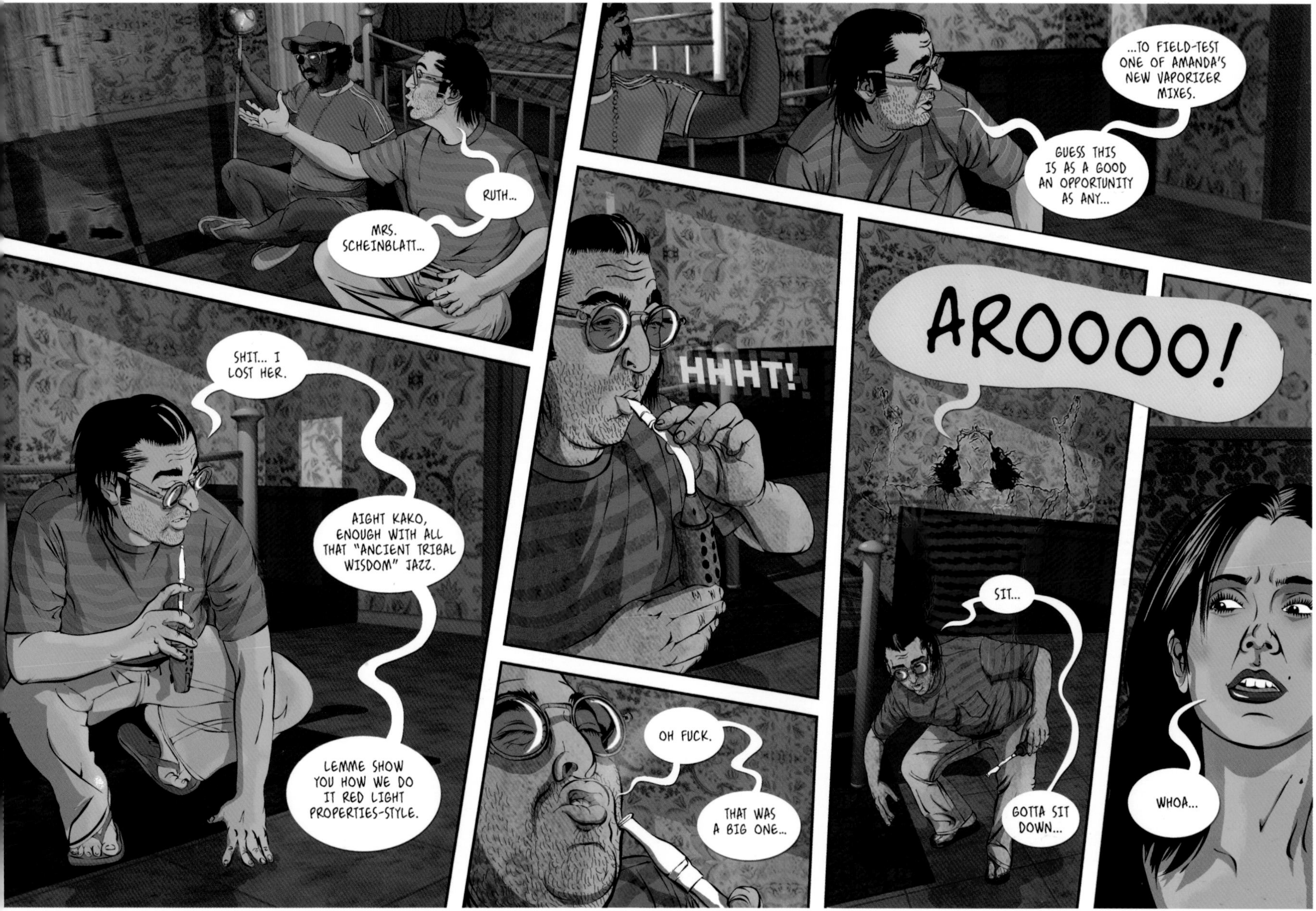
RUTH...
MRS. SCHEINBLATT...
...TO FIELD-TEST ONE OF AMANDA'S NEW VAPORIZER MIXES.
GUESS THIS IS AS A GOOD AN OPPORTUNITY AS ANY...
SHIT... I LOST HER.
AIGHT KAKO, ENOUGH WITH ALL THAT "ANCIENT TRIBAL WISDOM" JAZZ.
LEMME SHOW YOU HOW WE DO IT RED LIGHT PROPERTIES-STYLE.
HHHT!
OH FUCK.
THAT WAS A BIG ONE...
AROOOO!
SIT...
GOTTA SIT DOWN...
WHOA...

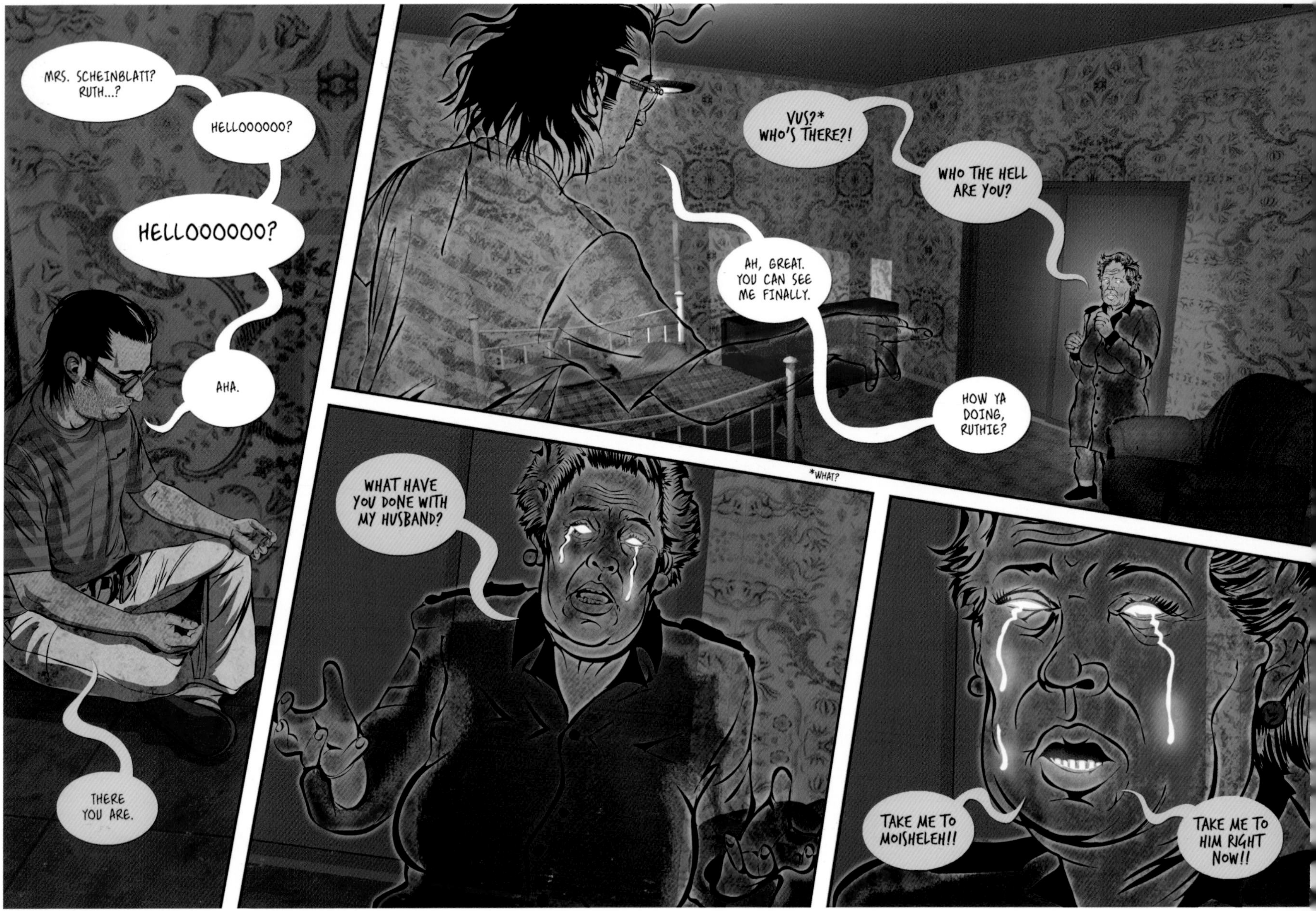
MRS. SCHEINBLATT? RUTH...?
HELLOOOOOO?
HELLOOOOOO?
AHA.
THERE YOU ARE.
VUS?* WHO'S THERE?!
WHO THE HELL ARE YOU?
AH, GREAT. YOU CAN SEE ME FINALLY.
HOW YA DOING, RUTHIE?
*WHAT?
WHAT HAVE YOU DONE WITH MY HUSBAND?
TAKE ME TO MOISHELEH!!
TAKE ME TO HIM RIGHT NOW!!

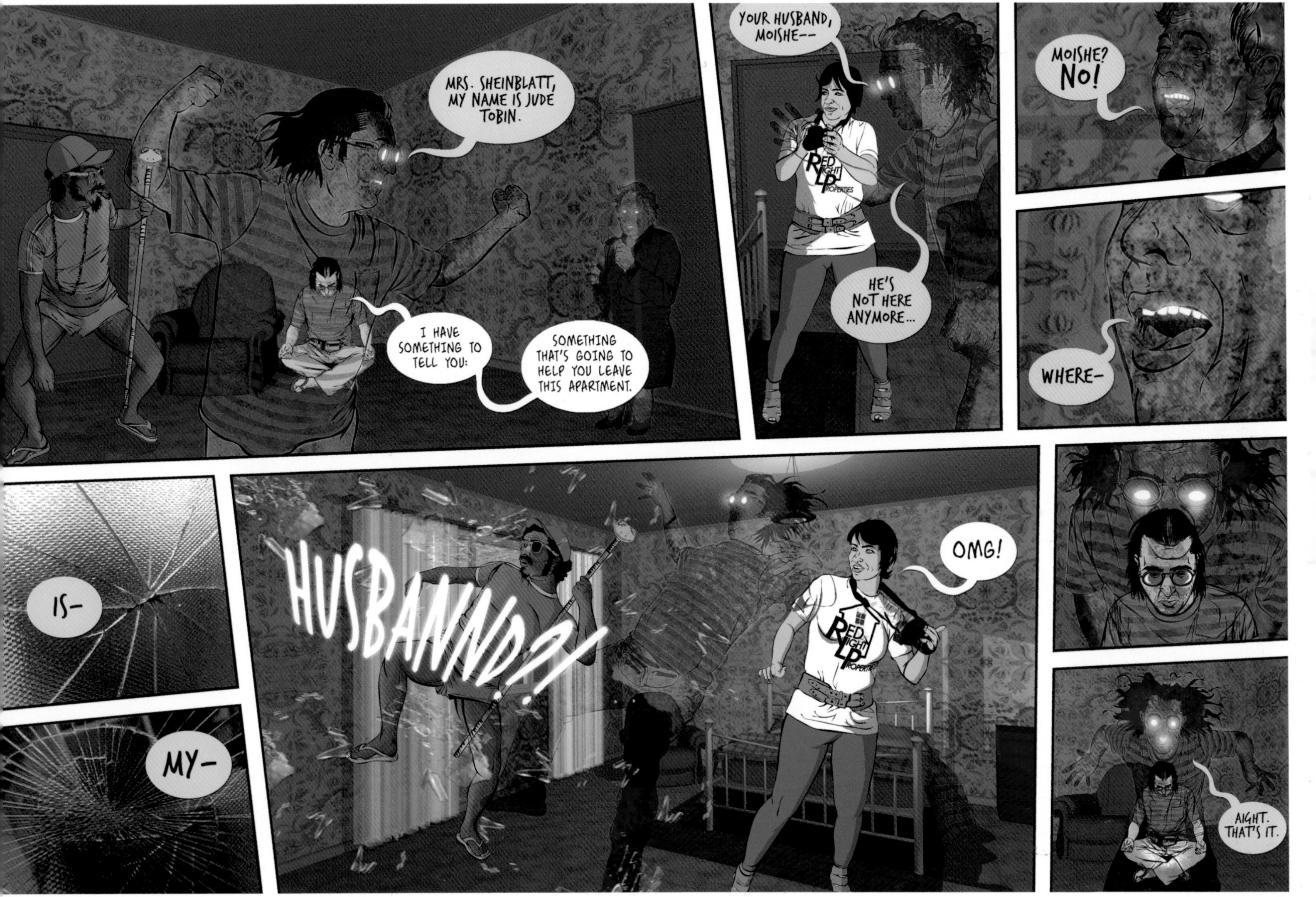
MRS. SHEINBLATT, MY NAME IS JUDE TOBIN.
I HAVE SOMETHING TO TELL YOU:
SOMETHING THAT'S GOING TO HELP YOU LEAVE THIS APARTMENT.
YOUR HUSBAND, MOISHE--
HE'S NOT HERE ANYMORE...
MOISHE? NO!
WHERE-
IS-
MY-
HUSBANND?!
OMG!
AIGHT. THAT'S IT.

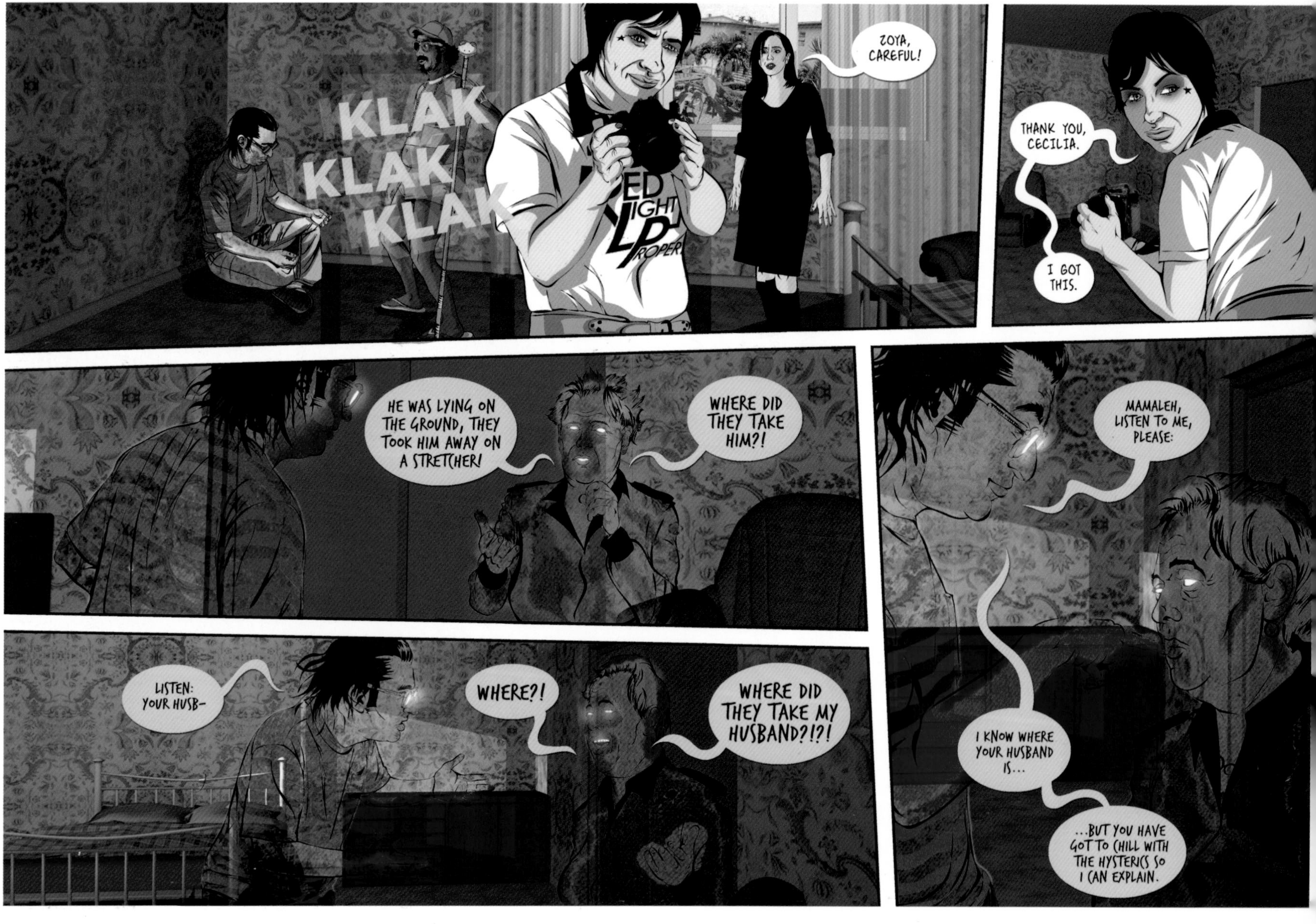
KLAK KLAK KLAK
RED LIGHT PROPERTIES
ZOYA, CAREFUL!
THANK YOU, CECILIA.
I GOT THIS.
HE WAS LYING ON THE GROUND, THEY TOOK HIM AWAY ON A STRETCHER!
WHERE DID THEY TAKE HIM?!
MAMALEH, LISTEN TO ME, PLEASE:
I KNOW WHERE YOUR HUSBAND IS...
...BUT YOU HAVE GOT TO CHILL WITH THE HYSTERICS SO I CAN EXPLAIN.
LISTEN: YOUR HUSB–
WHERE?!
WHERE DID THEY TAKE MY HUSBAND?!?!

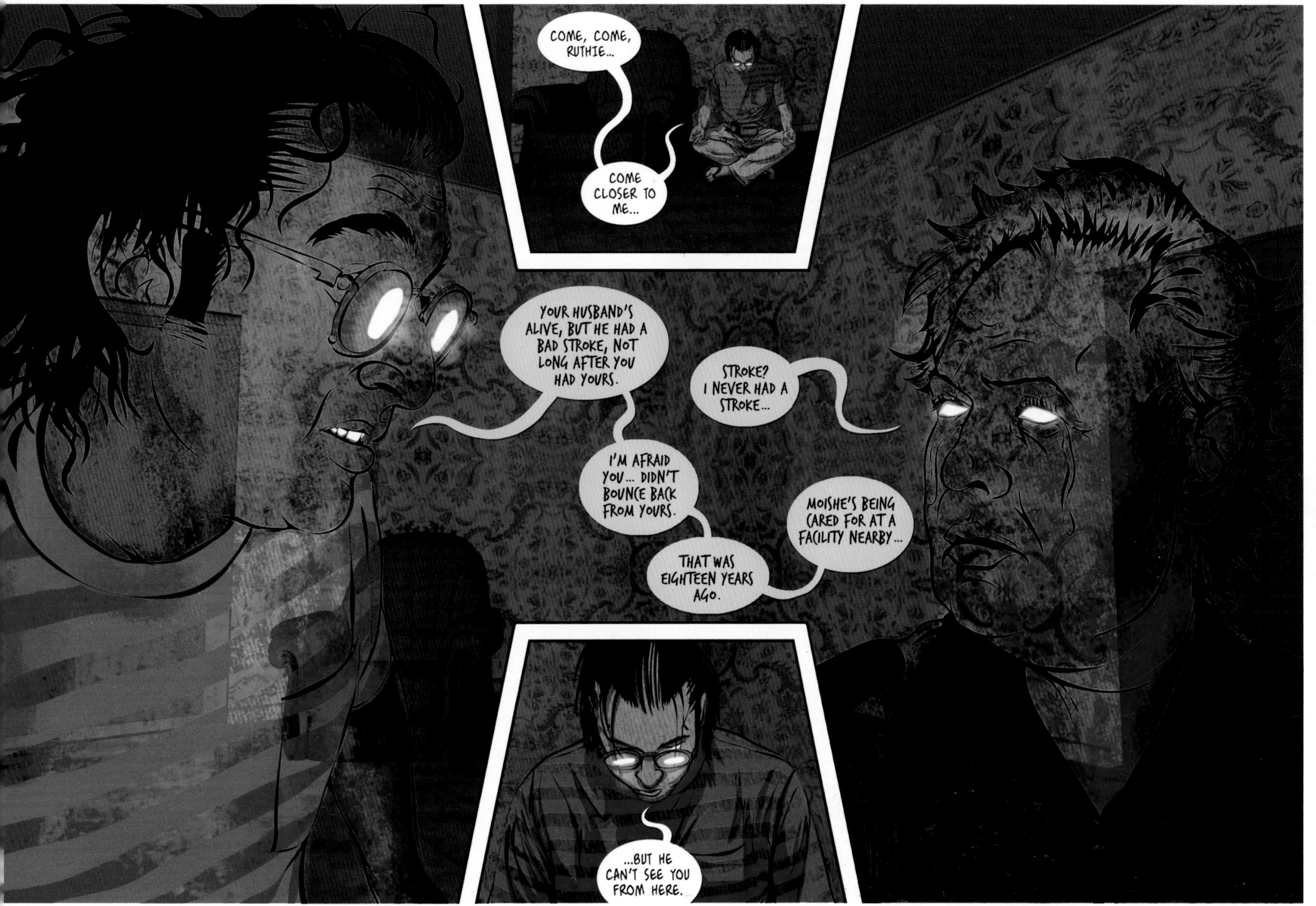
COME, COME, RUTHIE...
COME CLOSER TO ME...
YOUR HUSBAND'S ALIVE, BUT HE HAD A BAD STROKE, NOT LONG AFTER YOU HAD YOURS.
STROKE? I NEVER HAD A STROKE...
I'M AFRAID YOU... DIDN'T BOUNCE BACK FROM YOURS.
THAT WAS EIGHTEEN YEARS AGO.
MOISHE'S BEING CARED FOR AT A FACILITY NEARBY...
...BUT HE CAN'T SEE YOU FROM HERE.

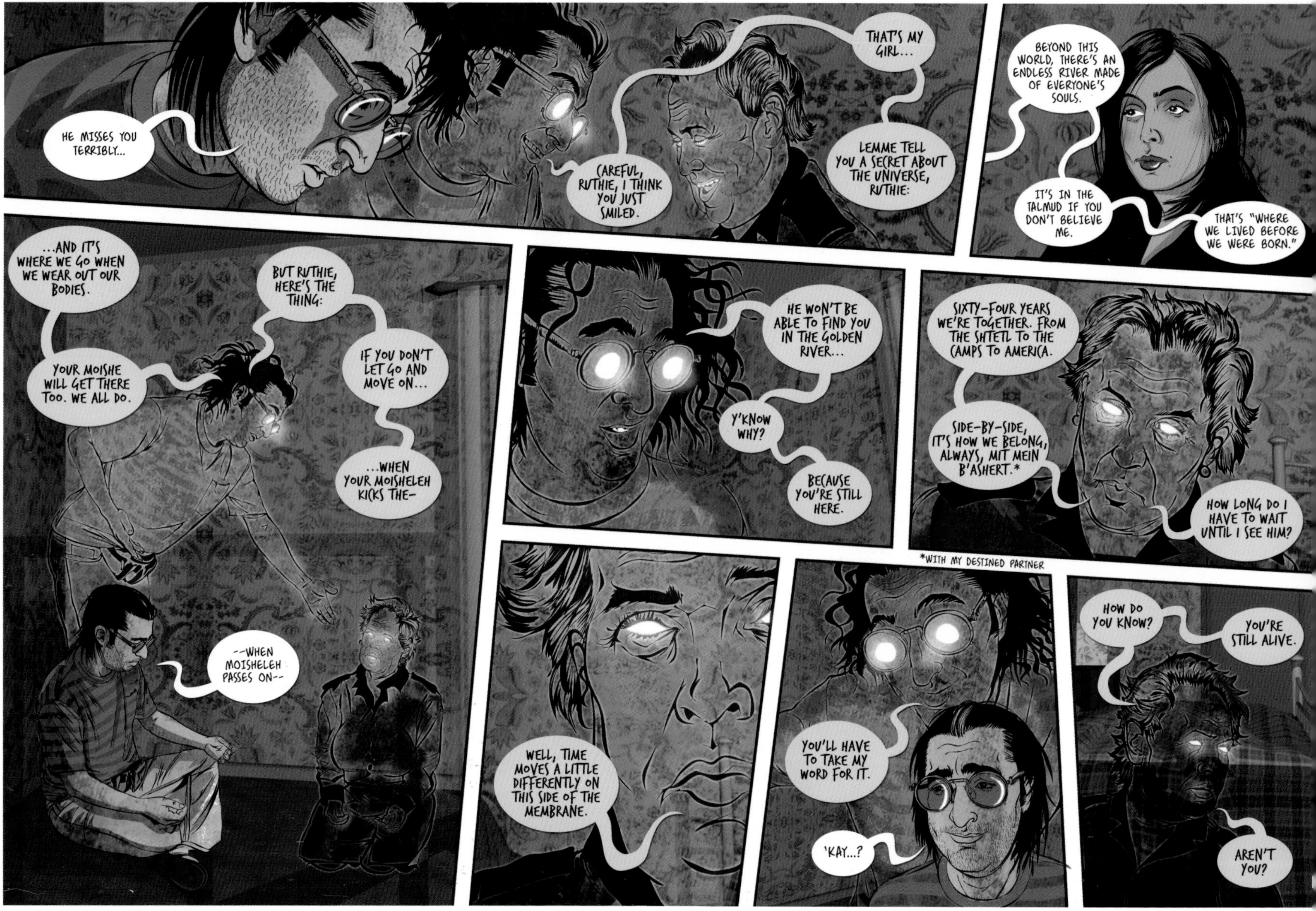
HE MISSES YOU TERRIBLY...
CAREFUL, RUTHIE, I THINK YOU JUST SMILED.
THAT'S MY GIRL...
LEMME TELL YOU A SECRET ABOUT THE UNIVERSE, RUTHIE:
BEYOND THIS WORLD, THERE'S AN ENDLESS RIVER MADE OF EVERYONE'S SOULS.
IT'S IN THE TALMUD IF YOU DON'T BELIEVE ME.
THAT'S "WHERE WE LIVED BEFORE WE WERE BORN."
...AND IT'S WHERE WE GO WHEN WE WEAR OUT OUR BODIES.
YOUR MOISHE WILL GET THERE TOO. WE ALL DO.
BUT RUTHIE, HERE'S THE THING:
IF YOU DON'T LET GO AND MOVE ON...
...WHEN YOUR MOISHELEH KICKS THE-
--WHEN MOISHELEH PASSES ON--
HE WON'T BE ABLE TO FIND YOU IN THE GOLDEN RIVER...
Y'KNOW WHY?
BECAUSE YOU'RE STILL HERE.
SIXTY-FOUR YEARS WE'RE TOGETHER. FROM THE SHTETL TO THE CAMPS TO AMERICA.
SIDE-BY-SIDE, IT'S HOW WE BELONG, ALWAYS, MIT MEIN B'ASHERT.*
HOW LONG DO I HAVE TO WAIT UNTIL I SEE HIM?
*WITH MY DESTINED PARTNER
WELL, TIME MOVES A LITTLE DIFFERENTLY ON THIS SIDE OF THE MEMBRANE.
YOU'LL HAVE TO TAKE MY WORD FOR IT.
'KAY...?
HOW DO YOU KNOW?
YOU'RE STILL ALIVE.
AREN'T YOU?

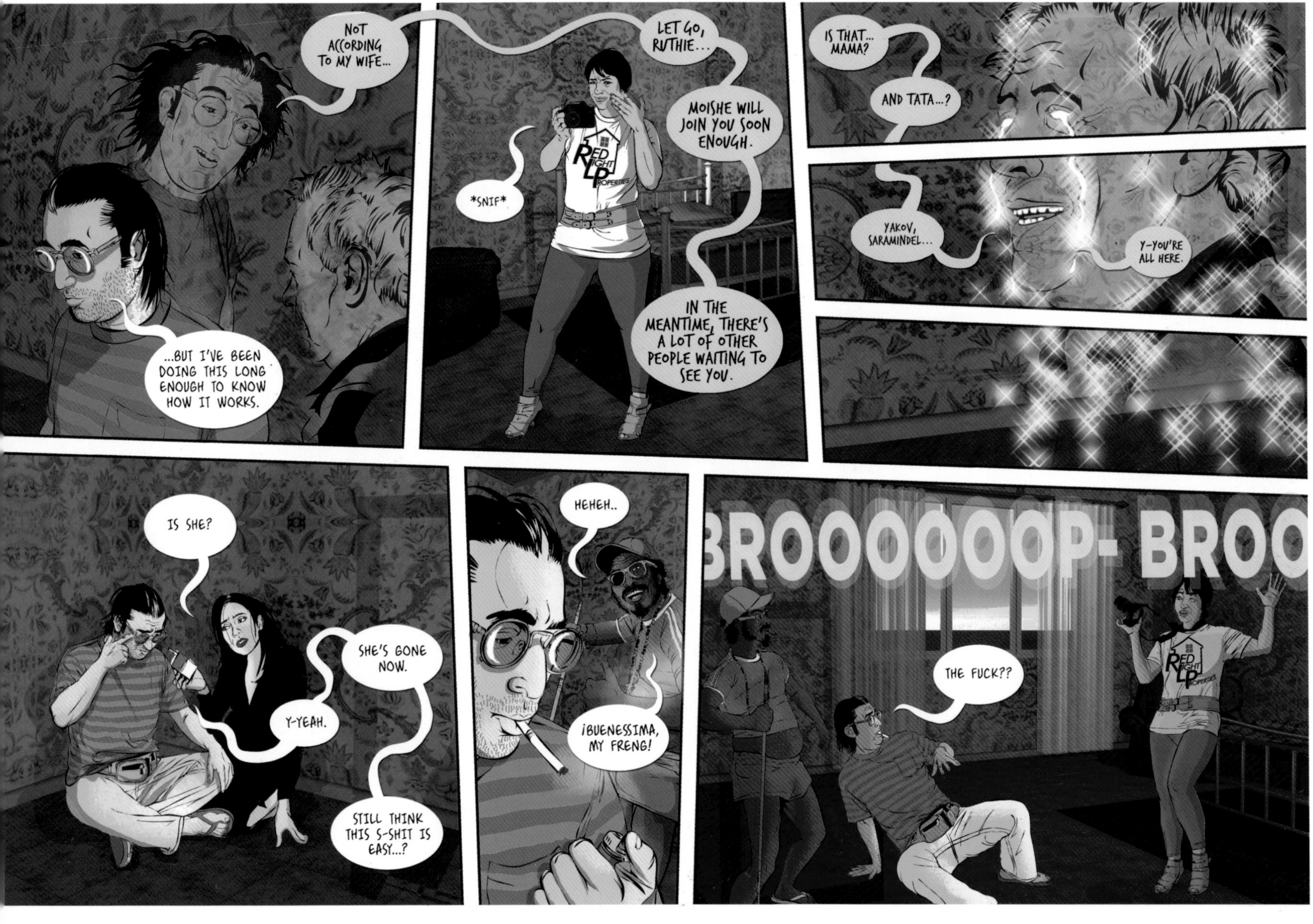
NOT ACCORDING TO MY WIFE...
...BUT I'VE BEEN DOING THIS LONG ENOUGH TO KNOW HOW IT WORKS.
LET GO, RUTHIE...
SNIF
MOISHE WILL JOIN YOU SOON ENOUGH.
IN THE MEANTIME, THERE'S A LOT OF OTHER PEOPLE WAITING TO SEE YOU.
IS THAT... MAMA?
AND TATA...?
YAKOV, SARAMINDEL...
Y-YOU'RE ALL HERE.
IS SHE?
SHE'S GONE NOW.
Y-YEAH.
STILL THINK THIS S-SHIT IS EASY...?
HEHEH..
¡BUENESSIMA, MY FRENG!
BROOOOOOOP- BROO
THE FUCK??

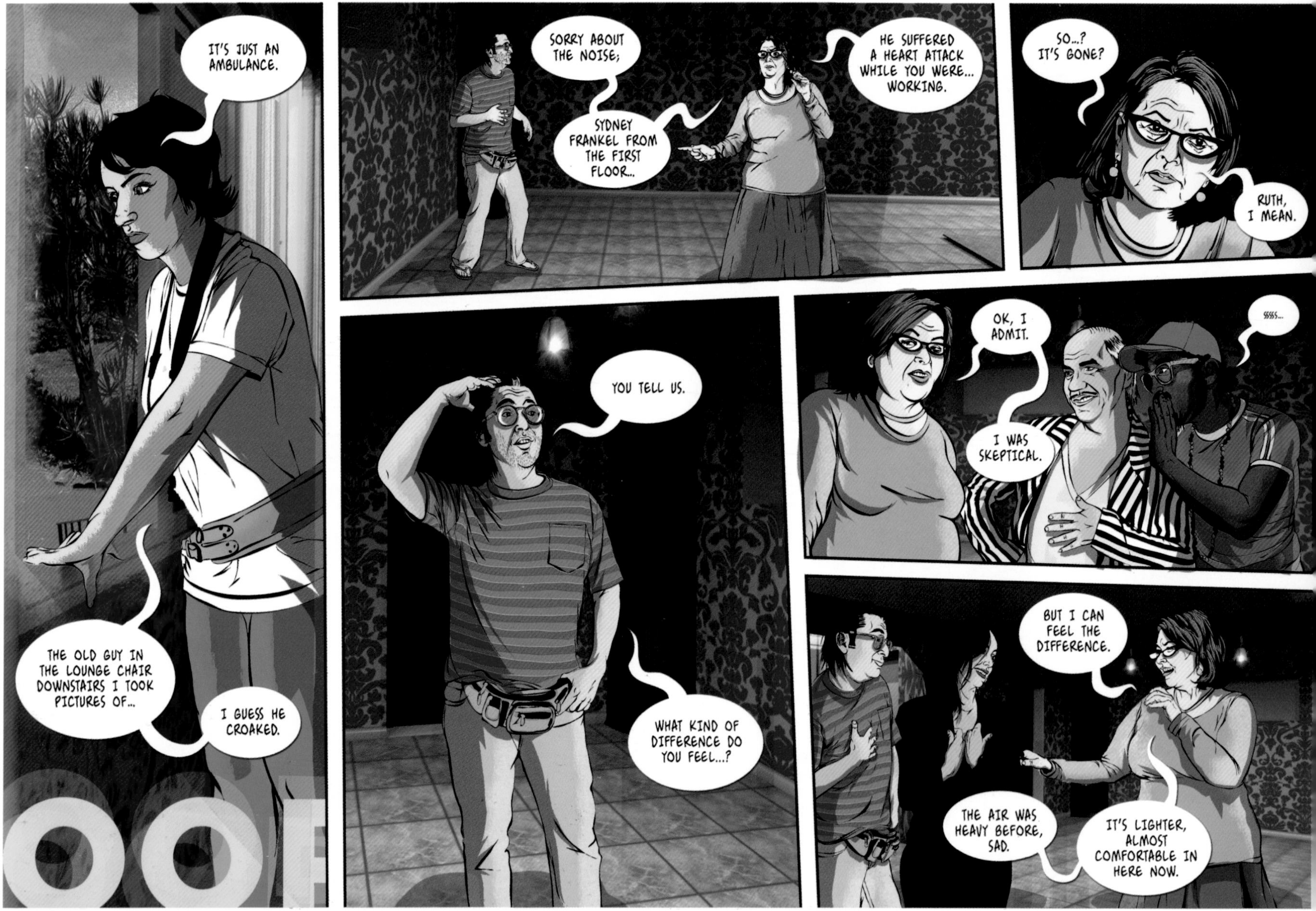
IT'S JUST AN AMBULANCE.
THE OLD GUY IN THE LOUNGE CHAIR DOWNSTAIRS I TOOK PICTURES OF...
I GUESS HE CROAKED.
OOF
SORRY ABOUT THE NOISE;
SYDNEY FRANKEL FROM THE FIRST FLOOR...
HE SUFFERED A HEART ATTACK WHILE YOU WERE... WORKING.
SO...? IT'S GONE?
RUTH, I MEAN.
YOU TELL US.
WHAT KIND OF DIFFERENCE DO YOU FEEL...?
OK, I ADMIT.
I WAS SKEPTICAL.
SSSSS...
BUT I CAN FEEL THE DIFFERENCE.
THE AIR WAS HEAVY BEFORE, SAD.
IT'S LIGHTER, ALMOST COMFORTABLE IN HERE NOW.

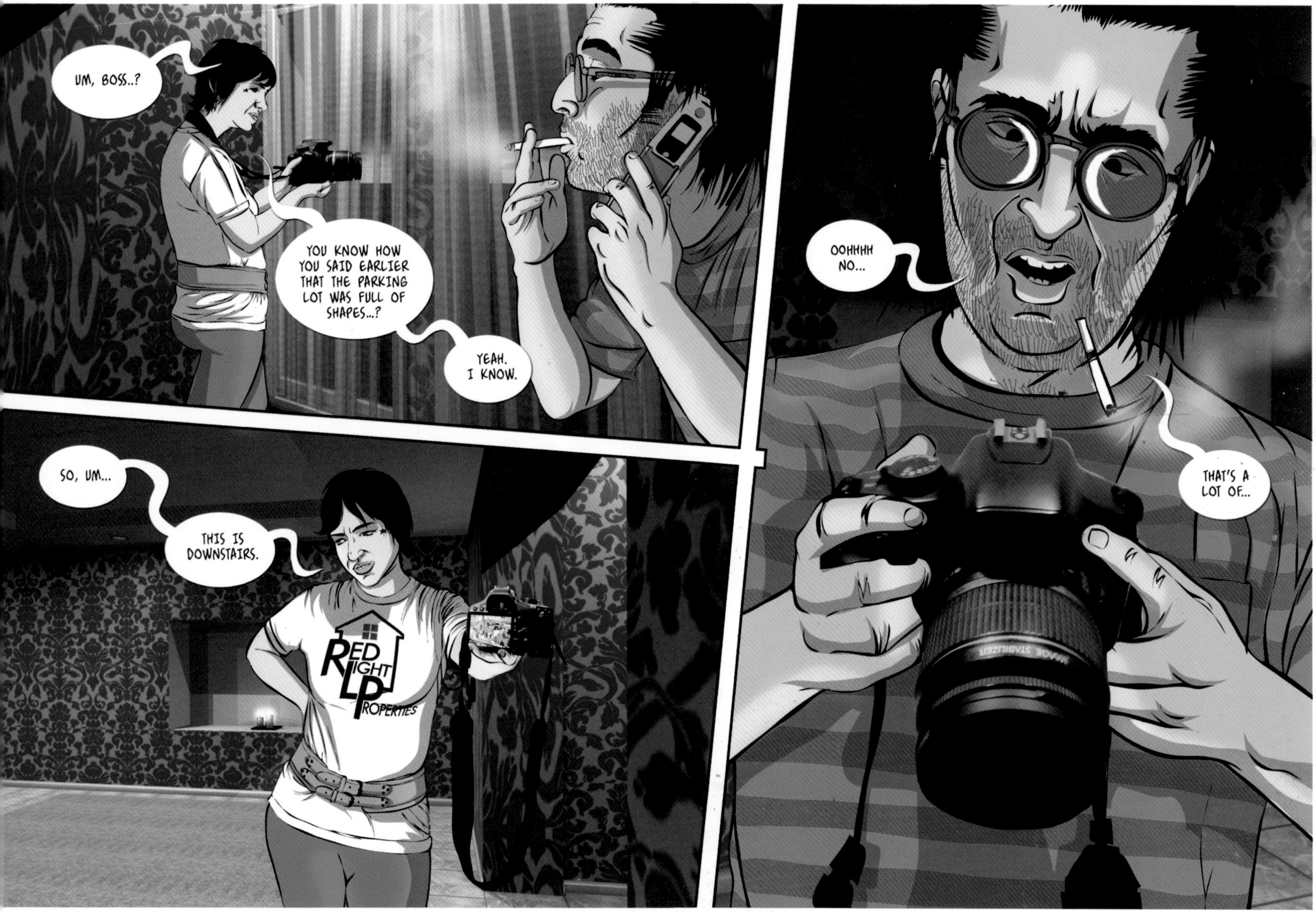
UM, BOSS..?
YOU KNOW HOW YOU SAID EARLIER THAT THE PARKING LOT WAS FULL OF SHAPES...?
YEAH. I KNOW.
SO, UM...
THIS IS DOWNSTAIRS.
RED LIGHT RLP PROPERTIES
OOHHHH NO...
THAT'S A LOT OF...
IMAGE STABILIZER

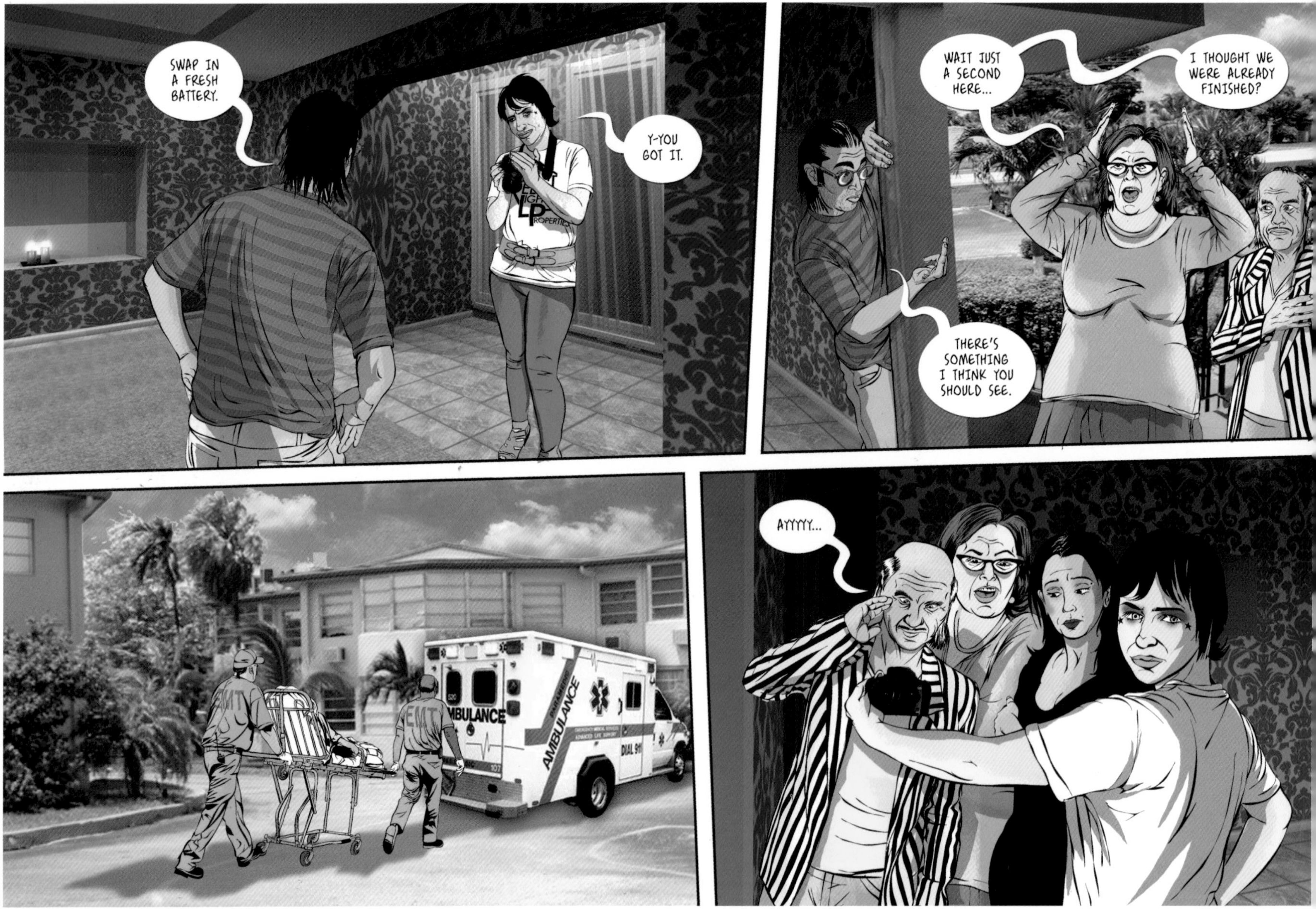
SWAP IN A FRESH BATTERY.
Y-YOU GOT IT.
WAIT JUST A SECOND HERE...
I THOUGHT WE WERE ALREADY FINISHED?
THERE'S SOMETHING I THINK YOU SHOULD SEE.
EMT
EMT
AMBULANCE
AMBULANCE
DIAL 911
AYYYYY...

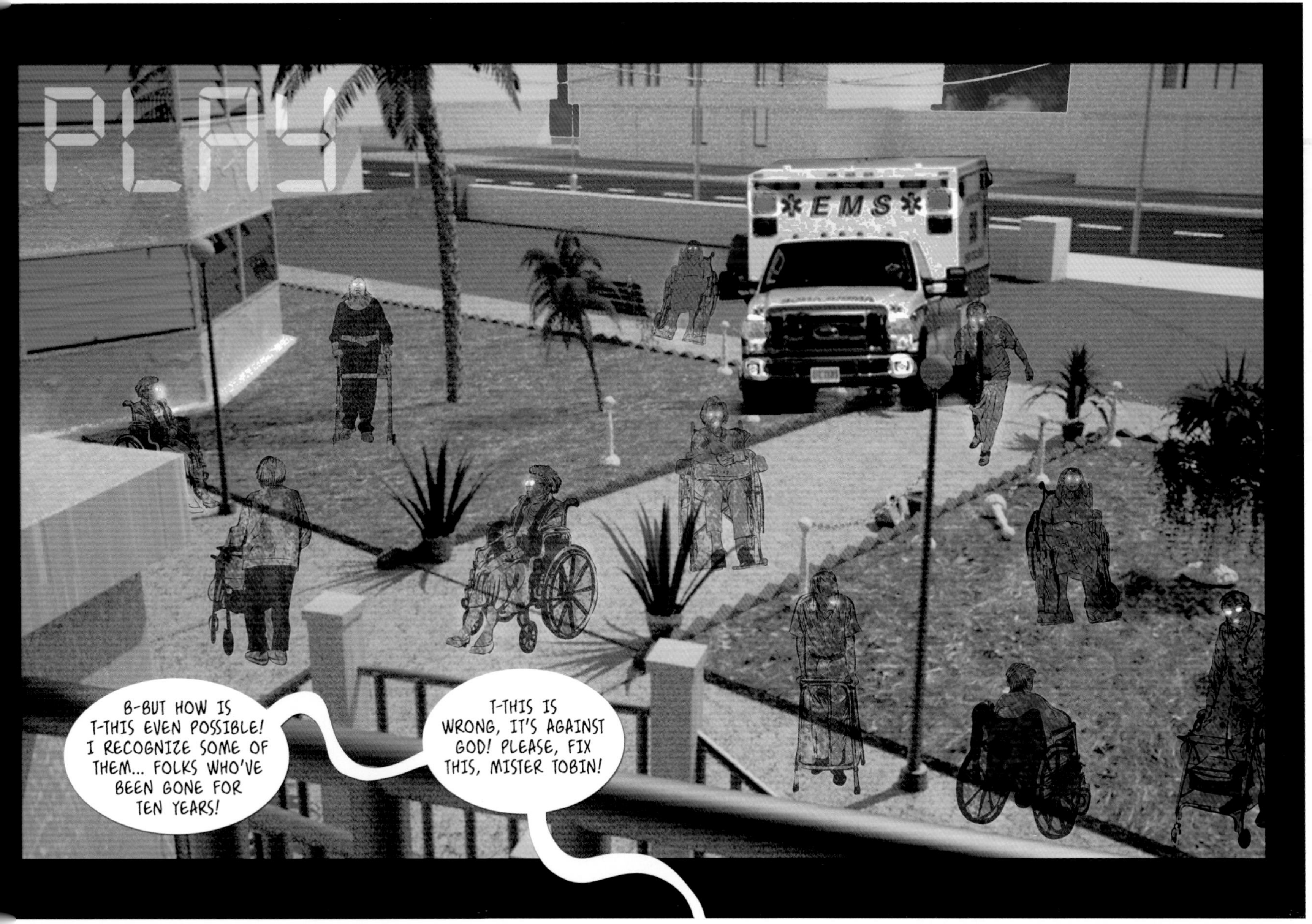
PLAY
EMS
B-BUT HOW IS T-THIS EVEN POSSIBLE! I RECOGNIZE SOME OF THEM... FOLKS WHO'VE BEEN GONE FOR TEN YEARS!
T-THIS IS WRONG, IT'S AGAINST GOD! PLEASE, FIX THIS, MISTER TOBIN!

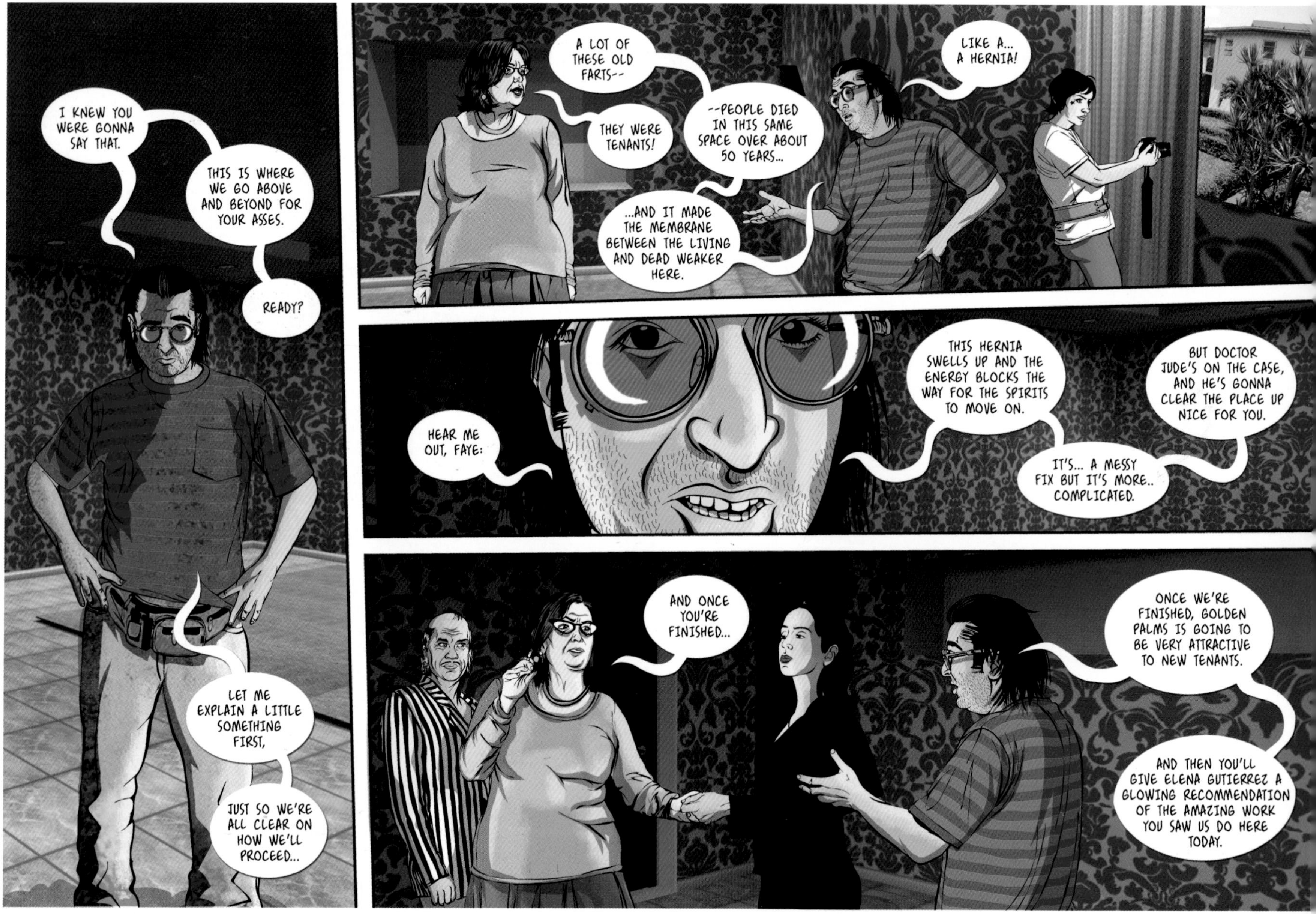
I KNEW YOU WERE GONNA SAY THAT.
THIS IS WHERE WE GO ABOVE AND BEYOND FOR YOUR ASSES.
READY?
LET ME EXPLAIN A LITTLE SOMETHING FIRST,
JUST SO WE'RE ALL CLEAR ON HOW WE'LL PROCEED...
A LOT OF THESE OLD FARTS--
THEY WERE TENANTS!
--PEOPLE DIED IN THIS SAME SPACE OVER ABOUT 50 YEARS...
...AND IT MADE THE MEMBRANE BETWEEN THE LIVING AND DEAD WEAKER HERE.
LIKE A... A HERNIA!
HEAR ME OUT, FAYE:
THIS HERNIA SWELLS UP AND THE ENERGY BLOCKS THE WAY FOR THE SPIRITS TO MOVE ON.
IT'S... A MESSY FIX BUT IT'S MORE.. COMPLICATED.
BUT DOCTOR JUDE'S ON THE CASE, AND HE'S GONNA CLEAR THE PLACE UP NICE FOR YOU.
AND ONCE YOU'RE FINISHED...
ONCE WE'RE FINISHED, GOLDEN PALMS IS GOING TO BE VERY ATTRACTIVE TO NEW TENANTS.
AND THEN YOU'LL GIVE ELENA GUTIERREZ A GLOWING RECOMMENDATION OF THE AMAZING WORK YOU SAW US DO HERE TODAY.

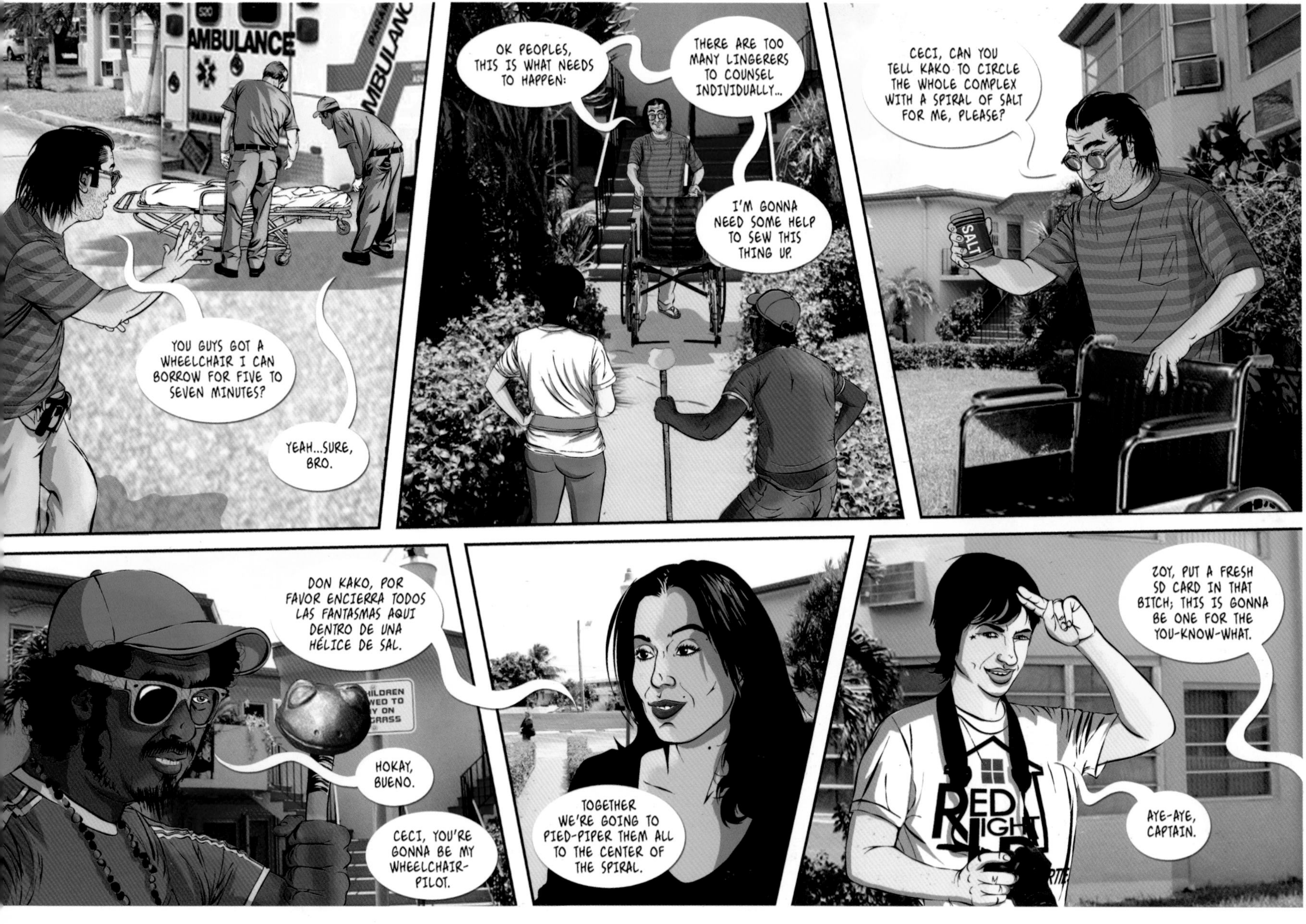
AMBULANCE
YOU GUYS GOT A WHEELCHAIR I CAN BORROW FOR FIVE TO SEVEN MINUTES?
YEAH...SURE, BRO.
OK PEOPLES, THIS IS WHAT NEEDS TO HAPPEN:
THERE ARE TOO MANY LINGERERS TO COUNSEL INDIVIDUALLY...
I'M GONNA NEED SOME HELP TO SEW THIS THING UP.
CECI, CAN YOU TELL KAKO TO CIRCLE THE WHOLE COMPLEX WITH A SPIRAL OF SALT FOR ME, PLEASE?
SALT
DON KAKO, POR FAVOR ENCIERRA TODOS LAS FANTASMAS AQUI DENTRO DE UNA HÉLICE DE SAL.
HOKAY, BUENO.
CECI, YOU'RE GONNA BE MY WHEELCHAIR-PILOT.
TOGETHER WE'RE GOING TO PIED-PIPER THEM ALL TO THE CENTER OF THE SPIRAL.
ZOY, PUT A FRESH SD CARD IN THAT BITCH; THIS IS GONNA BE ONE FOR THE YOU-KNOW-WHAT.
AYE-AYE, CAPTAIN.

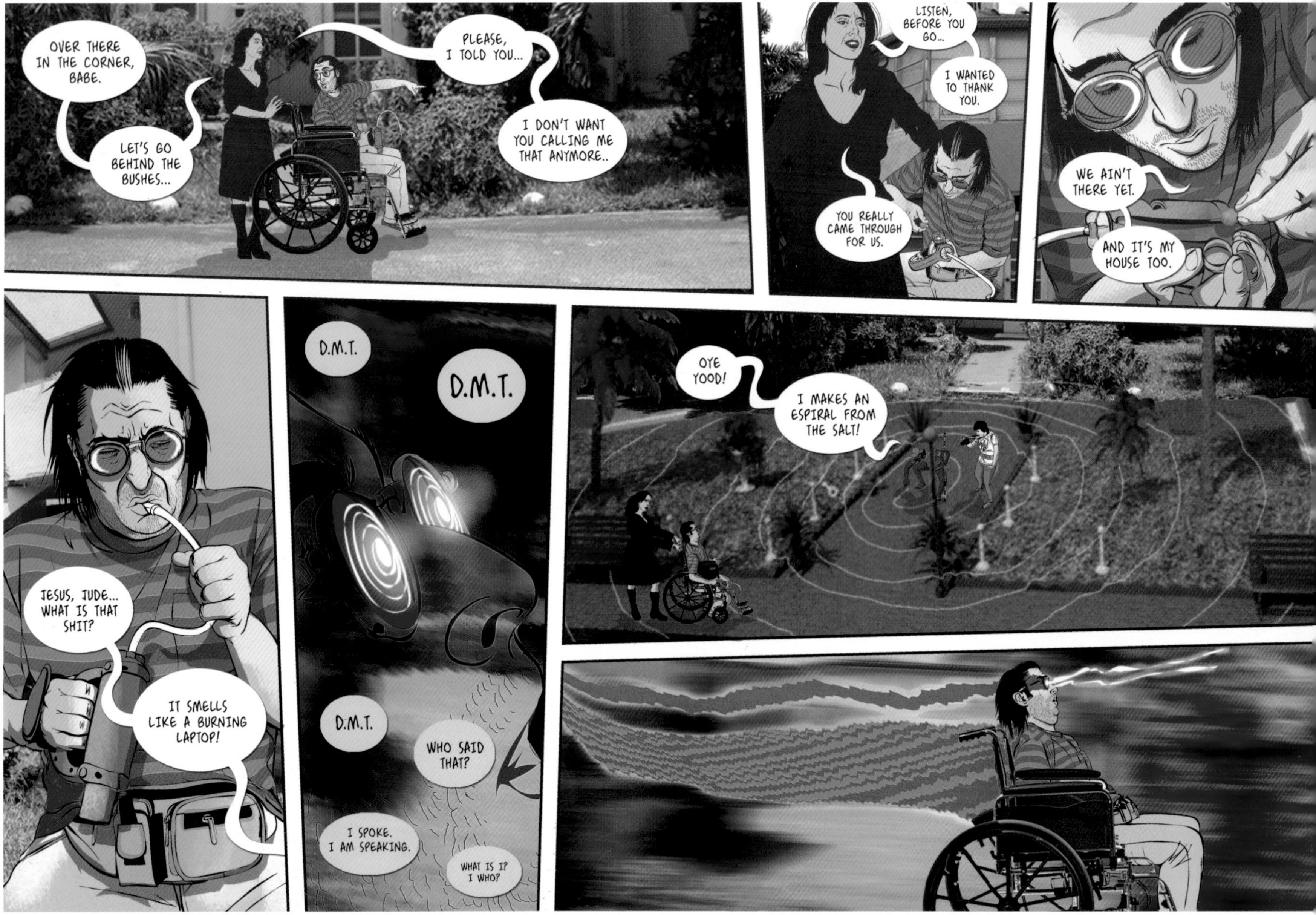

OVER THERE IN THE CORNER, BABE.
LET'S GO BEHIND THE BUSHES...
PLEASE, I TOLD YOU...
I DON'T WANT YOU CALLING ME THAT ANYMORE..
LISTEN, BEFORE YOU GO...
I WANTED TO THANK YOU.
YOU REALLY CAME THROUGH FOR US.
WE AIN'T THERE YET.
AND IT'S MY HOUSE TOO.
JESUS, JUDE... WHAT IS THAT SHIT?
IT SMELLS LIKE A BURNING LAPTOP!
D.M.T.
D.M.T.
D.M.T.
WHO SAID THAT?
I SPOKE. I AM SPEAKING.
WHAT IS I? I WHO?
OYE YOOD!
I MAKES AN ESPIRAL FROM THE SALT!

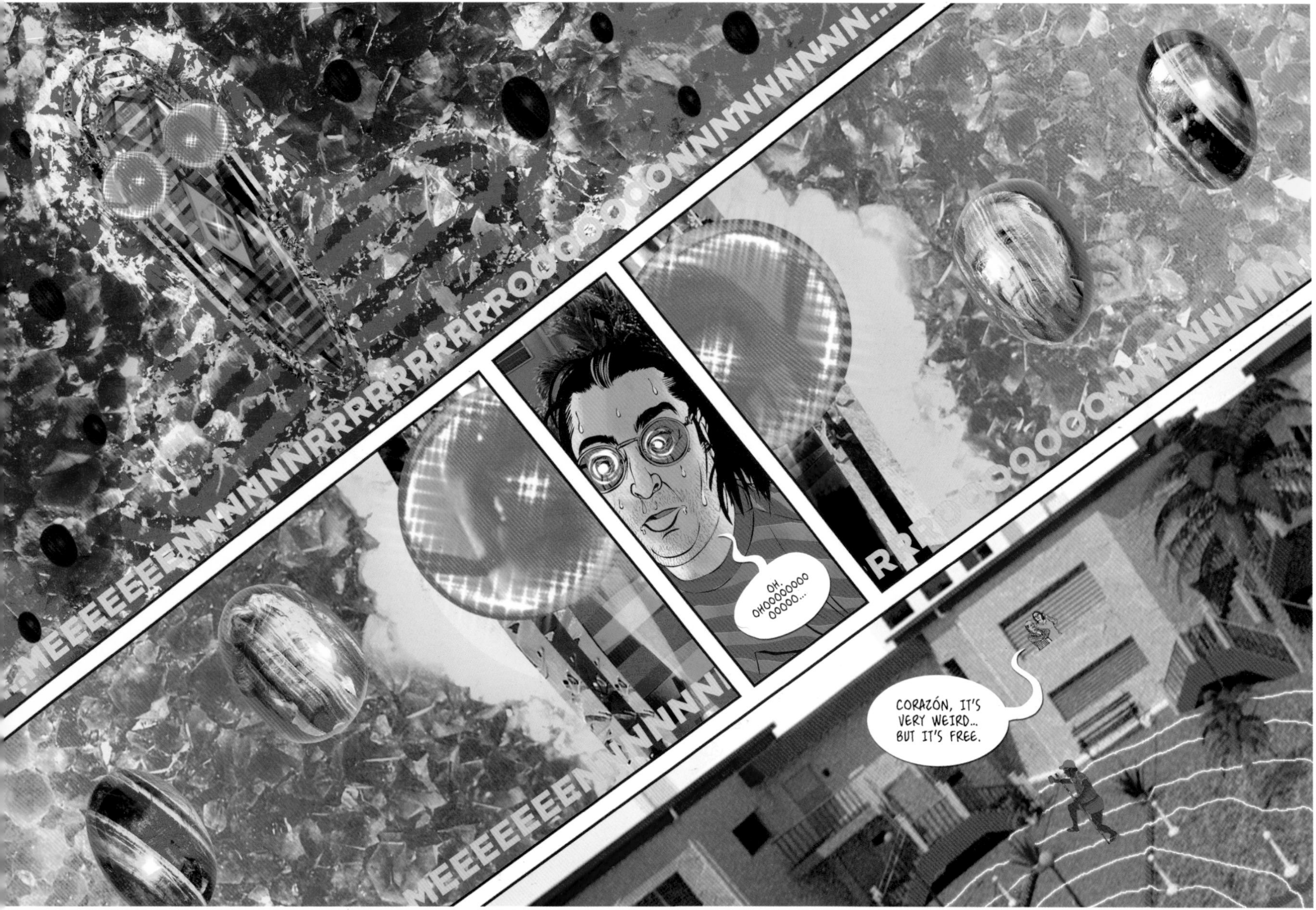
OH.
OHOOOOOOOO
OOOOO...
CORAZÓN, IT'S
VERY WEIRD...
BUT IT'S FREE.

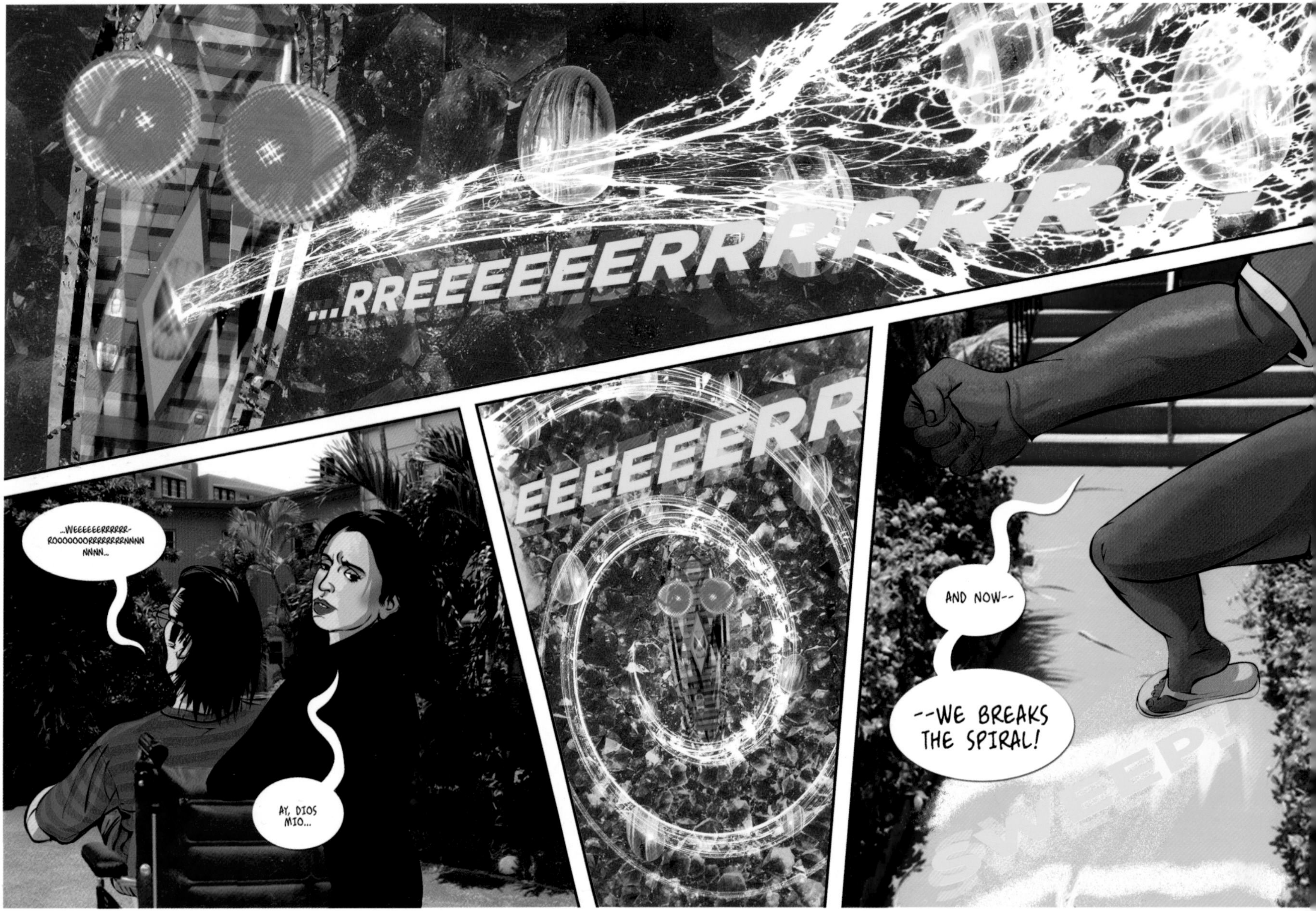
...RREEEEEEEERRRRRR...
...WEEEEEEERRRRRR-ROOOOOOORRRRRRRRNNNN NNNN...
AY, DIOS MIO...
EEEEEEERRR
AND NOW--
--WE BREAKS THE SPIRAL!
SWEEP!

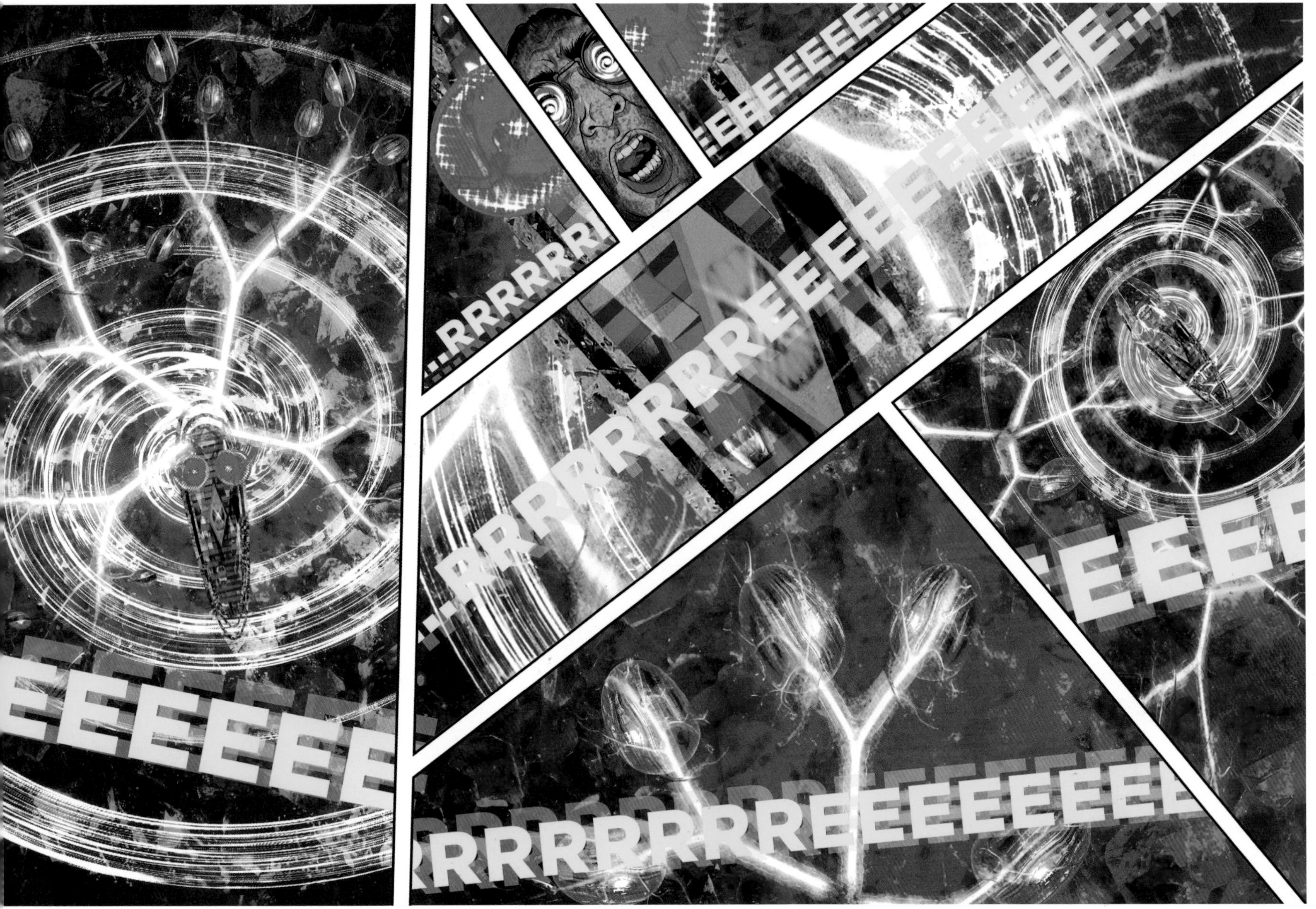

EEEEEE
...RRRRR
...EEEEEEE...
...RRRRRRRRREEEEEEEEEE...
EEEEE
RRRRRRREEEEEEEEE

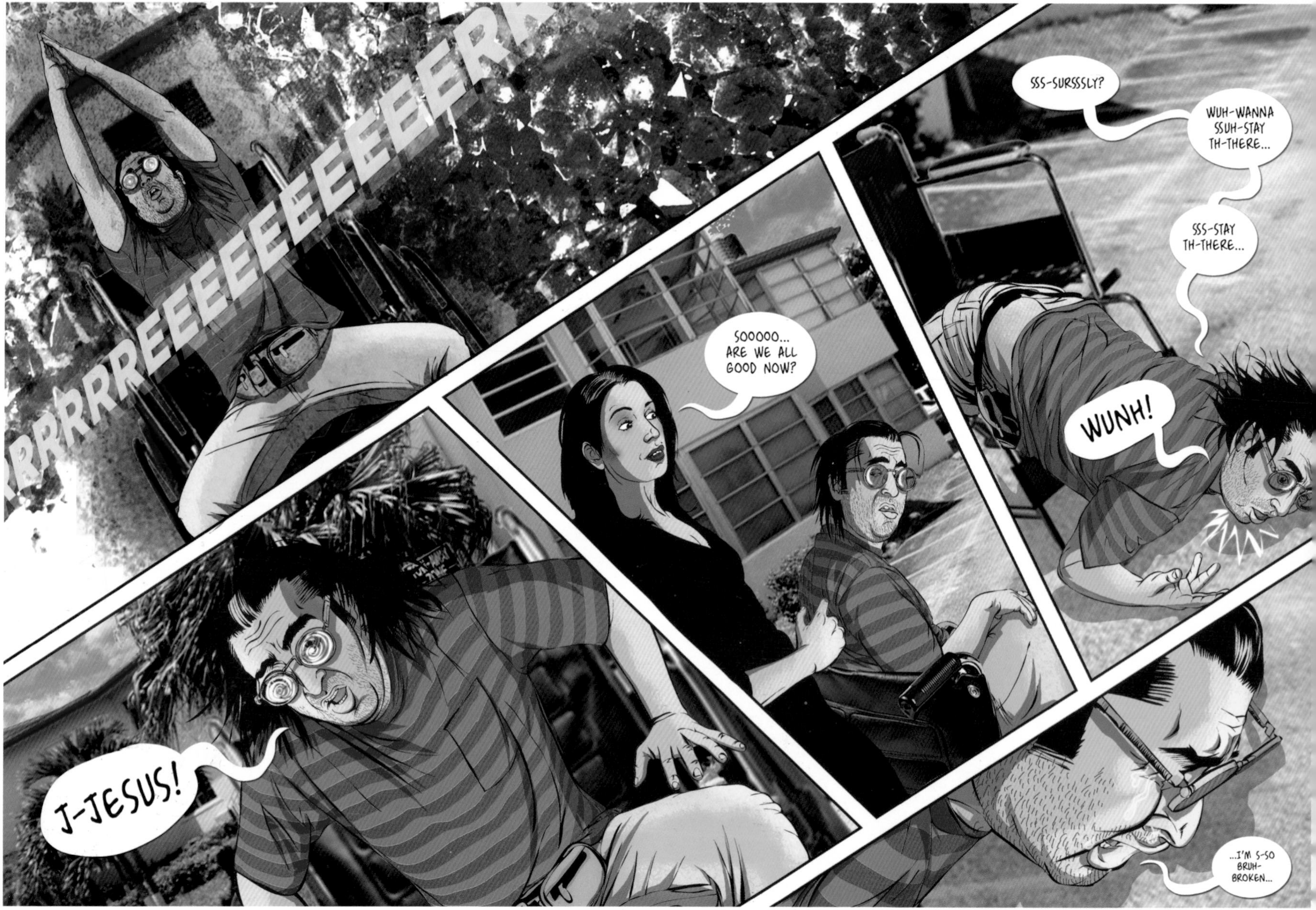
RRRRRREEEEEEEEEEEEEERR
J-JESUS!
SOOOOO... ARE WE ALL GOOD NOW?
SSS-SURSSSLY?
WUH-WANNA SSUH-STAY TH-THERE...
SSS-STAY TH-THERE...
WUNH!
...I'M S-SO BRUH-BROKEN...

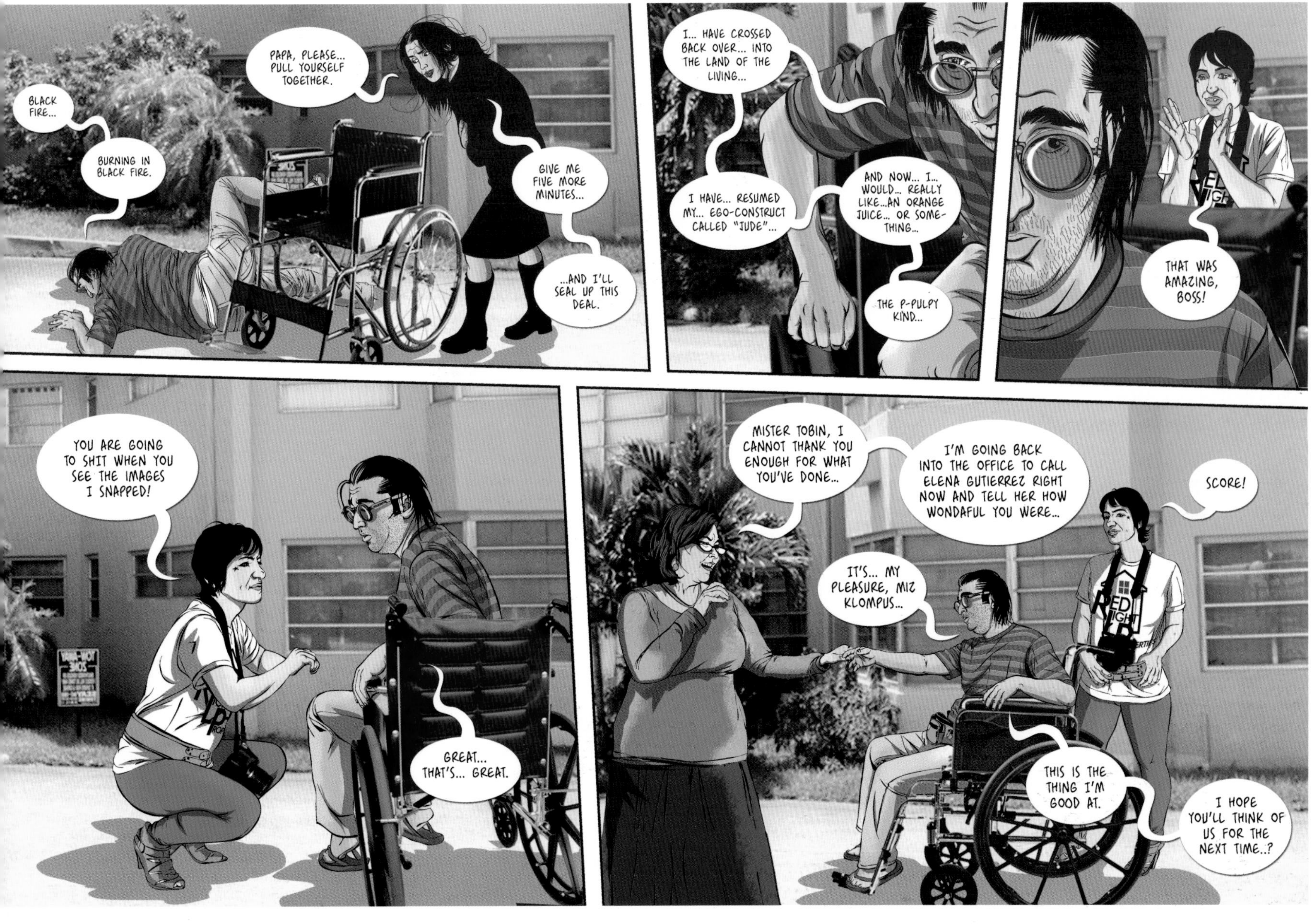
BLACK FIRE...
BURNING IN BLACK FIRE.
PAPA, PLEASE... PULL YOURSELF TOGETHER.
GIVE ME FIVE MORE MINUTES...
...AND I'LL SEAL UP THIS DEAL.
I... HAVE CROSSED BACK OVER... INTO THE LAND OF THE LIVING...
I HAVE... RESUMED MY... EGO-CONSTRUCT CALLED "JUDE"...
AND NOW... I... WOULD... REALLY LIKE...AN ORANGE JUICE... OR SOME-THING...
THE P-PULPY KIND...
THAT WAS AMAZING, BOSS!
YOU ARE GOING TO SHIT WHEN YOU SEE THE IMAGES I SNAPPED!
GREAT... THAT'S... GREAT.
MISTER TOBIN, I CANNOT THANK YOU ENOUGH FOR WHAT YOU'VE DONE...
I'M GOING BACK INTO THE OFFICE TO CALL ELENA GUTIERREZ RIGHT NOW AND TELL HER HOW WONDAFUL YOU WERE...
SCORE!
IT'S... MY PLEASURE, MIZ KLOMPUS...
THIS IS THE THING I'M GOOD AT.
I HOPE YOU'LL THINK OF US FOR THE NEXT TIME..?

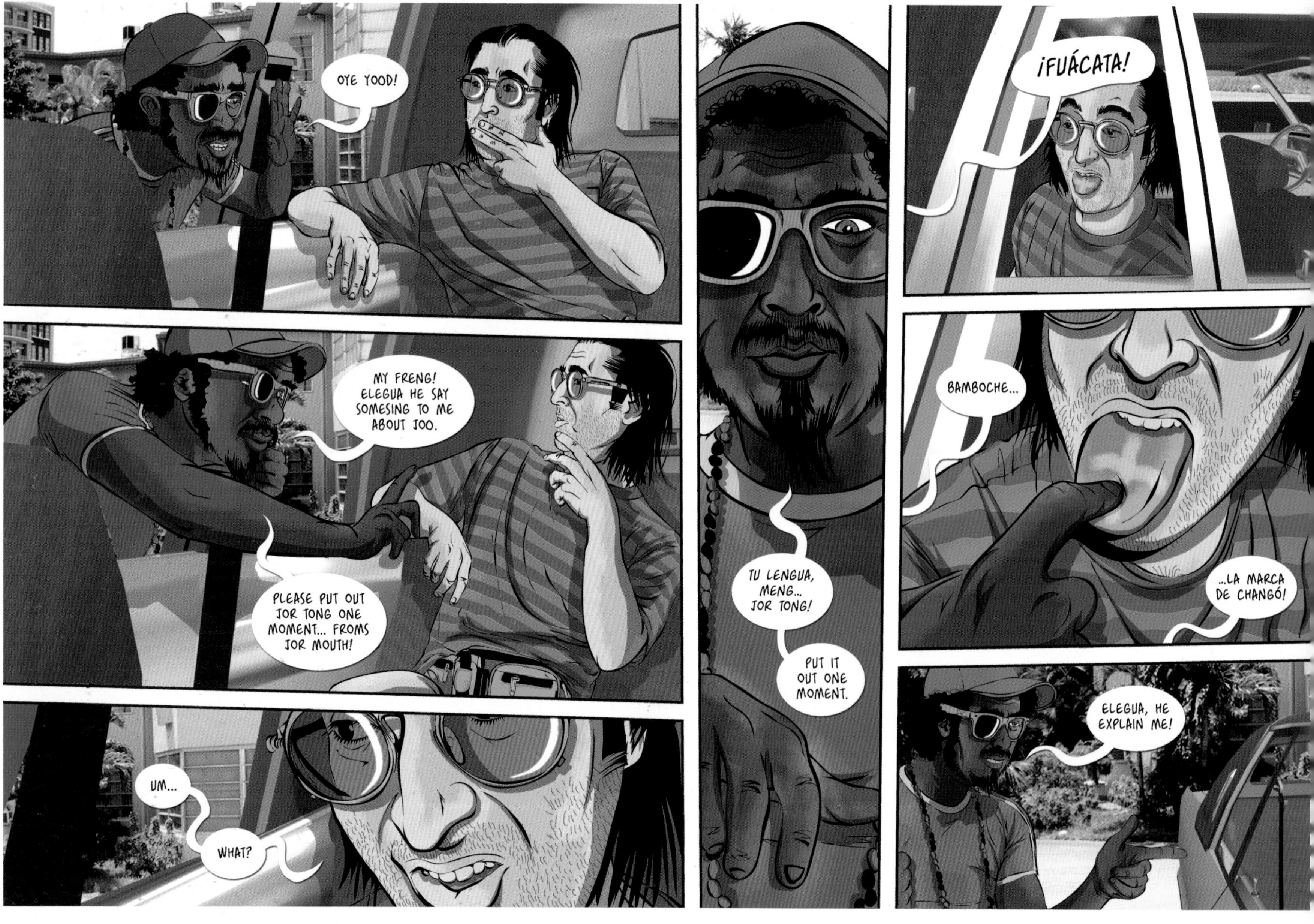
OYE YOOD!
MY FRENG! ELEGUA HE SAY SOMESING TO ME ABOUT JOO.
PLEASE PUT OUT JOR TONG ONE MOMENT... FROMS JOR MOUTH!
UM...
WHAT?
TU LENGUA, MENG... JOR TONG!
PUT IT OUT ONE MOMENT.
¡FUÁCATA!
BAMBOCHE...
...LA MARCA DE CHANGÓ!
ELEGUA, HE EXPLAIN ME!

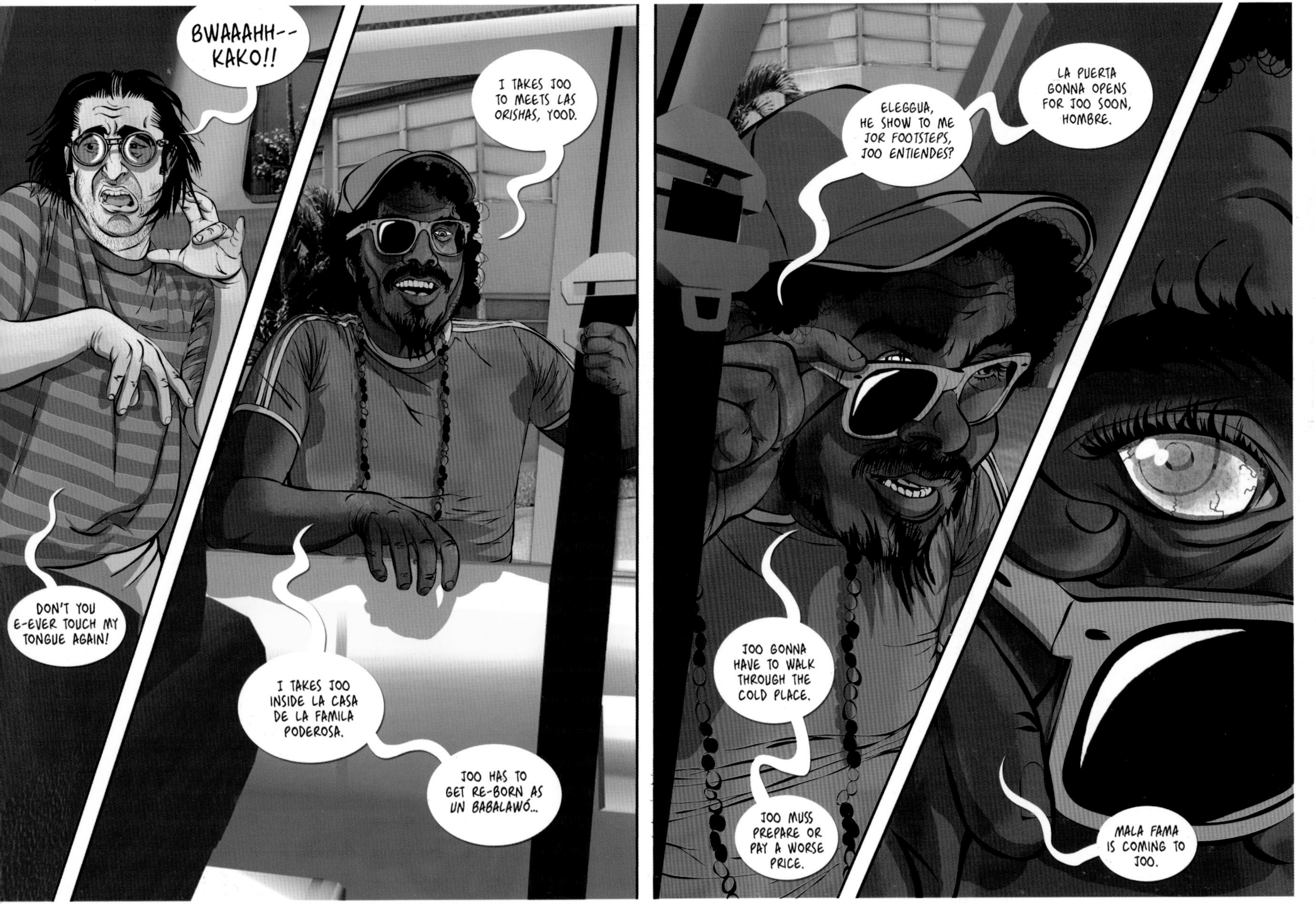
BWAAAHH--KAKO!!
DON'T YOU E-EVER TOUCH MY TONGUE AGAIN!
I TAKES JOO TO MEETS LAS ORISHAS, YOOD.
I TAKES JOO INSIDE LA CASA DE LA FAMILA PODEROSA.
JOO HAS TO GET RE-BORN AS UN BABALAWÓ...
ELEGGUA, HE SHOW TO ME JOR FOOTSTEPS, JOO ENTIENDES?
LA PUERTA GONNA OPENS FOR JOO SOON, HOMBRE.
JOO GONNA HAVE TO WALK THROUGH THE COLD PLACE.
JOO MUSS PREPARE OR PAY A WORSE PRICE.
MALA FAMA IS COMING TO JOO.

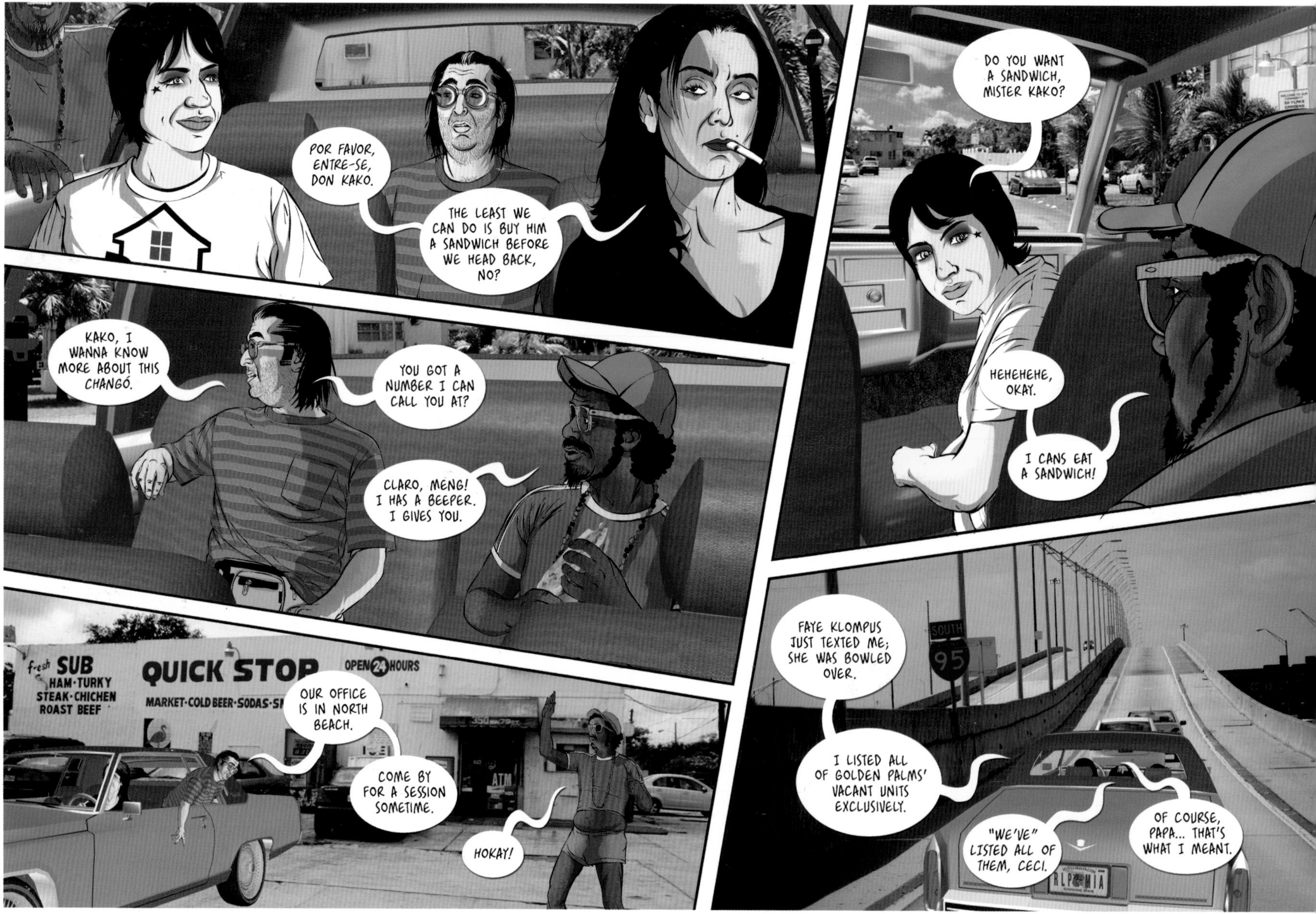
POR FAVOR, ENTRE-SE, DON KAKO.
THE LEAST WE CAN DO IS BUY HIM A SANDWICH BEFORE WE HEAD BACK, NO?
DO YOU WANT A SANDWICH, MISTER KAKO?
HEHEHEHE, OKAY.
I CANS EAT A SANDWICH!
KAKO, I WANNA KNOW MORE ABOUT THIS CHANGÓ.
YOU GOT A NUMBER I CAN CALL YOU AT?
CLARO, MENG! I HAS A BEEPER. I GIVES YOU.
fresh SUB
HAM·TURKY
STEAK·CHICHEN
ROAST BEEF
QUICK STOP
OPEN 24 HOURS
ATM
OUR OFFICE IS IN NORTH BEACH.
COME BY FOR A SESSION SOMETIME.
HOKAY!
SOUTH
95
FAYE KLOMPUS JUST TEXTED ME; SHE WAS BOWLED OVER.
I LISTED ALL OF GOLDEN PALMS' VACANT UNITS EXCLUSIVELY.
"WE'VE" LISTED ALL OF THEM, CECI.
OF COURSE, PAPA... THAT'S WHAT I MEANT.

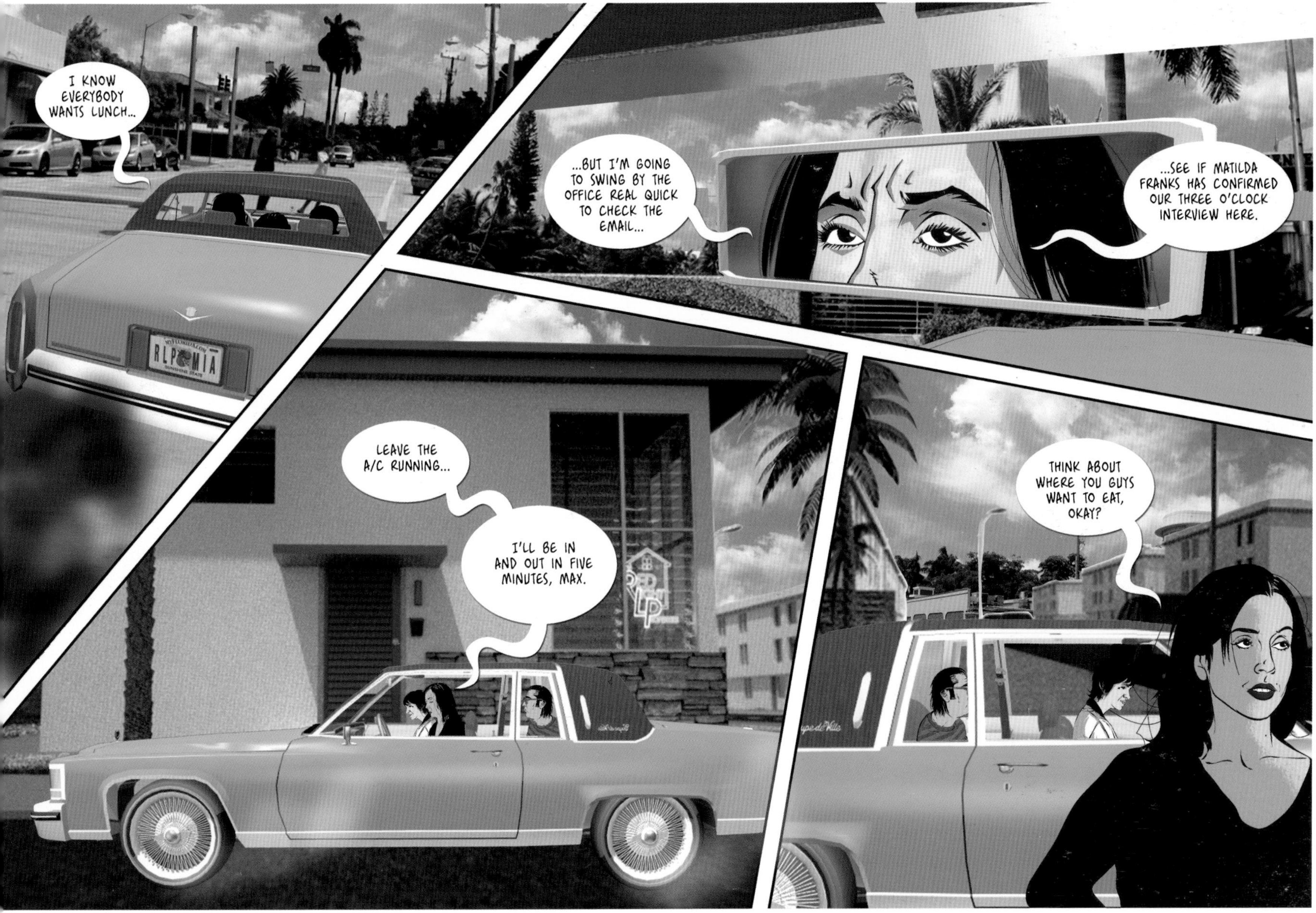
I KNOW EVERYBODY WANTS LUNCH...
RLP MIA
...BUT I'M GOING TO SWING BY THE OFFICE REAL QUICK TO CHECK THE EMAIL...
...SEE IF MATILDA FRANKS HAS CONFIRMED OUR THREE O'CLOCK INTERVIEW HERE.
LEAVE THE A/C RUNNING...
I'LL BE IN AND OUT IN FIVE MINUTES, MAX.
THINK ABOUT WHERE YOU GUYS WANT TO EAT, OKAY?

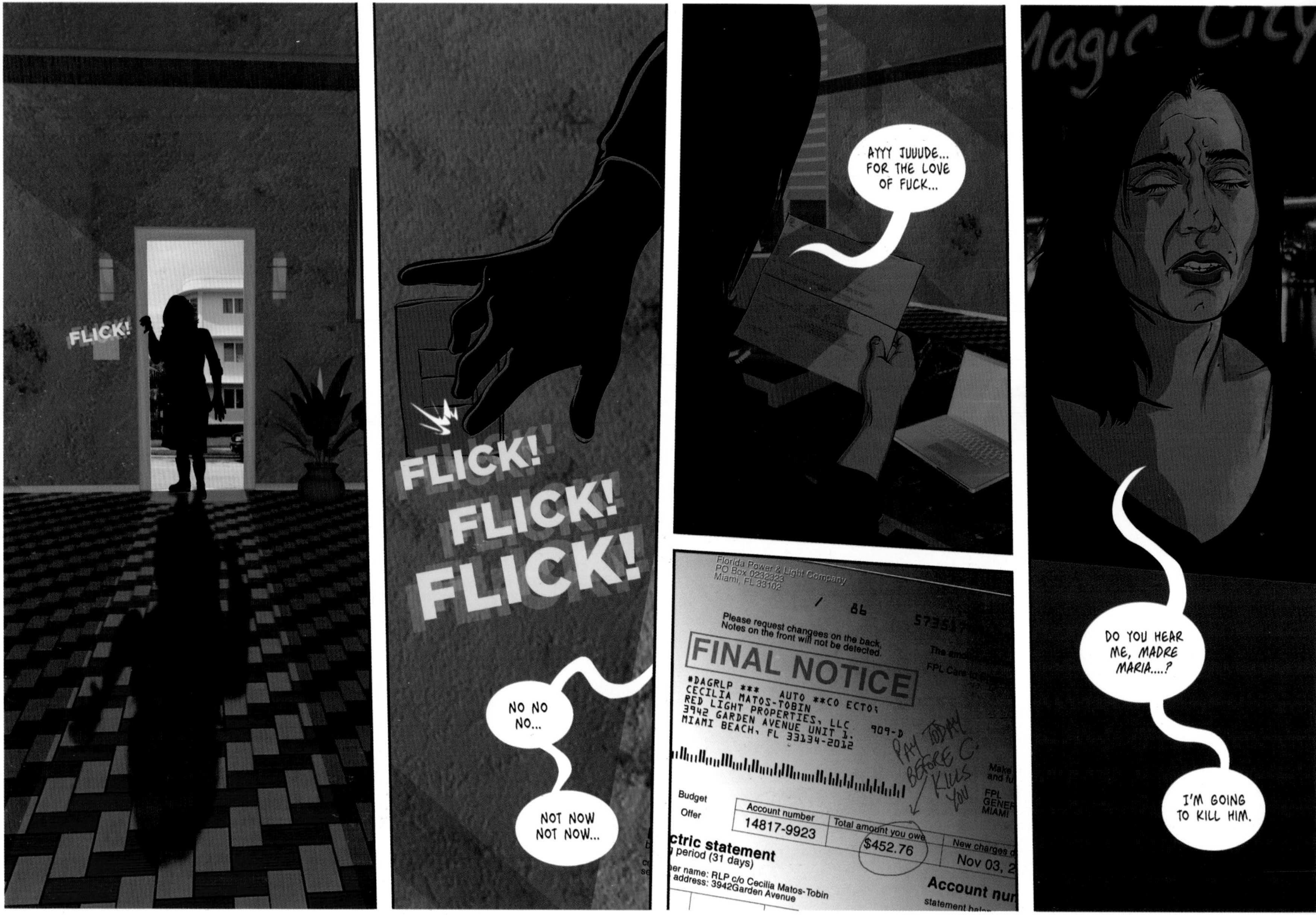
FLICK!
FLICK!
FLICK!
FLICK!
NO NO NO...
NOT NOW NOT NOW...
AYYY JUUUDE... FOR THE LOVE OF FUCK...
Florida Power & Light Company
PO Box 0232323
Miami, FL 33102
Please request changees on the back.
Notes on the front will not be detected.
FINAL NOTICE
#DAGRLP *** AUTO **CO ECTO;
CECILIA MATOS-TOBIN
RED LIGHT PROPERTIES, LLC 909-D
3942 GARDEN AVENUE UNIT 1.
MIAMI BEACH, FL 33134-2012
PAY TODAY BEFORE C. KILLS YOU
Budget Offer
Account number
14817-9923
Total amount you owe
$452.76
Nov 03,
ctric statement
period (31 days)
ner name: RLP c/o Cecilia Matos-Tobin
address: 3942Garden Avenue
Account nu
DO YOU HEAR ME, MADRE MARIA....?
I'M GOING TO KILL HIM.

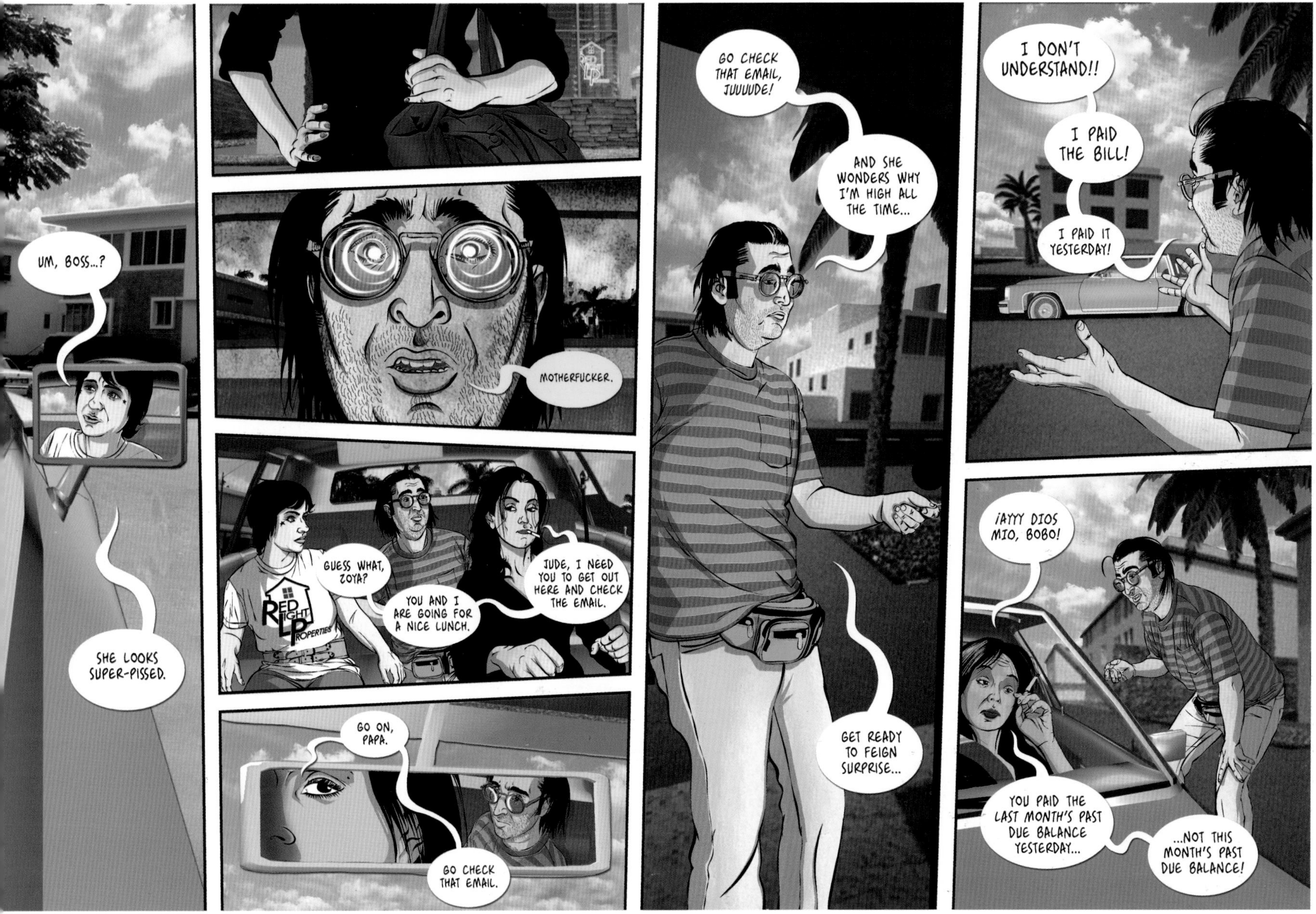
UM, BOSS...?
SHE LOOKS SUPER-PISSED.
MOTHERFUCKER.
GUESS WHAT, ZOYA?
RED LIGHT LP PROPERTIES
YOU AND I ARE GOING FOR A NICE LUNCH.
JUDE, I NEED YOU TO GET OUT HERE AND CHECK THE EMAIL.
GO ON, PAPA.
GO CHECK THAT EMAIL.
GO CHECK THAT EMAIL, JUUUUDE!
AND SHE WONDERS WHY I'M HIGH ALL THE TIME...
GET READY TO FEIGN SURPRISE...
I DON'T UNDERSTAND!!
I PAID THE BILL!
I PAID IT YESTERDAY!
¡AYYY DIOS MIO, BOBO!
YOU PAID THE LAST MONTH'S PAST DUE BALANCE YESTERDAY...
...NOT THIS MONTH'S PAST DUE BALANCE!

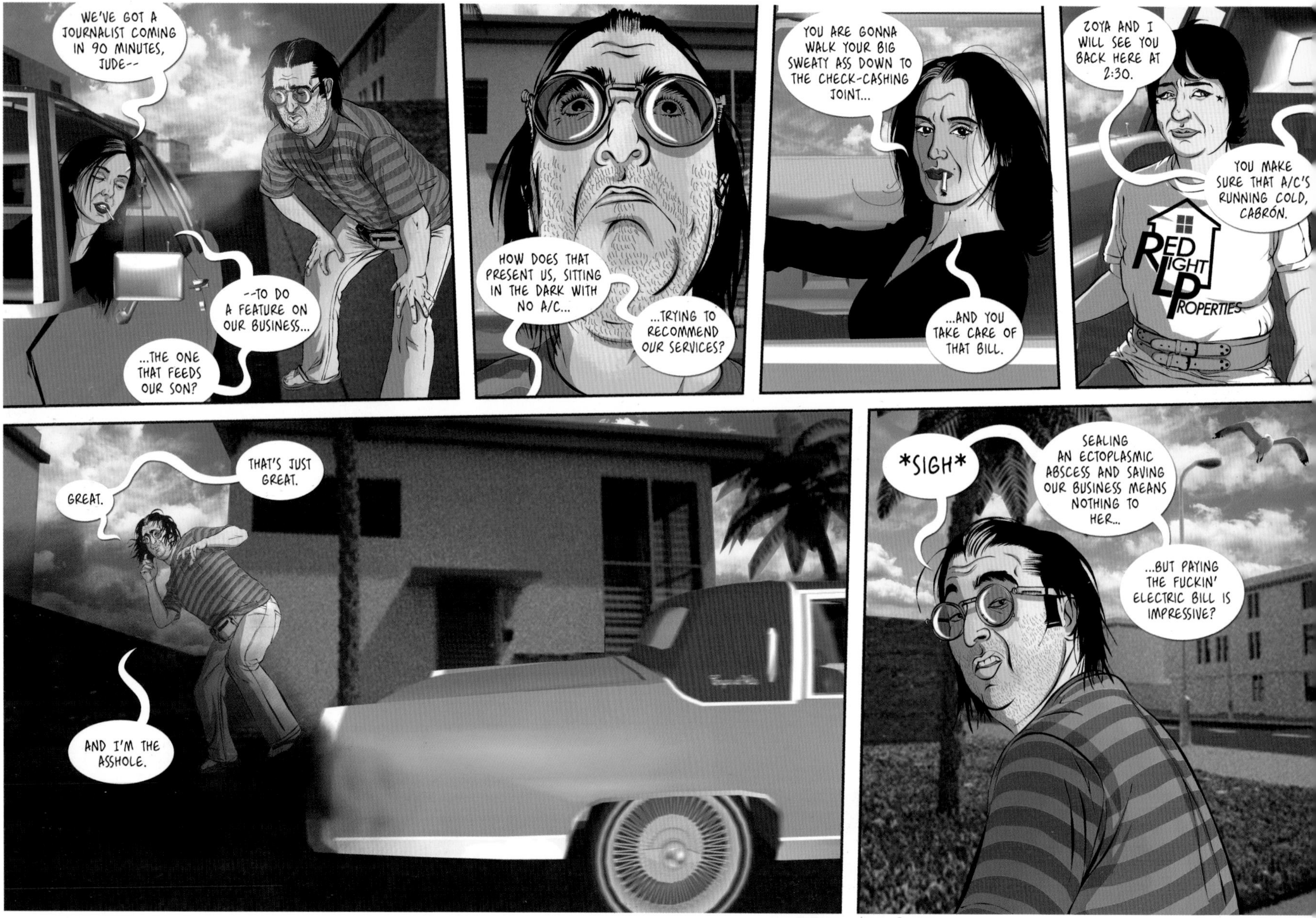
WE'VE GOT A JOURNALIST COMING IN 90 MINUTES, JUDE--
--TO DO A FEATURE ON OUR BUSINESS...
...THE ONE THAT FEEDS OUR SON?
HOW DOES THAT PRESENT US, SITTING IN THE DARK WITH NO A/C...
...TRYING TO RECOMMEND OUR SERVICES?
YOU ARE GONNA WALK YOUR BIG SWEATY ASS DOWN TO THE CHECK-CASHING JOINT...
...AND YOU TAKE CARE OF THAT BILL.
ZOYA AND I WILL SEE YOU BACK HERE AT 2:30.
YOU MAKE SURE THAT A/C'S RUNNING COLD, CABRÓN.
RED LIGHT PROPERTIES
GREAT.
THAT'S JUST GREAT.
AND I'M THE ASSHOLE.
SIGH
SEALING AN ECTOPLASMIC ABSCESS AND SAVING OUR BUSINESS MEANS NOTHING TO HER...
...BUT PAYING THE FUCKIN' ELECTRIC BILL IS IMPRESSIVE?

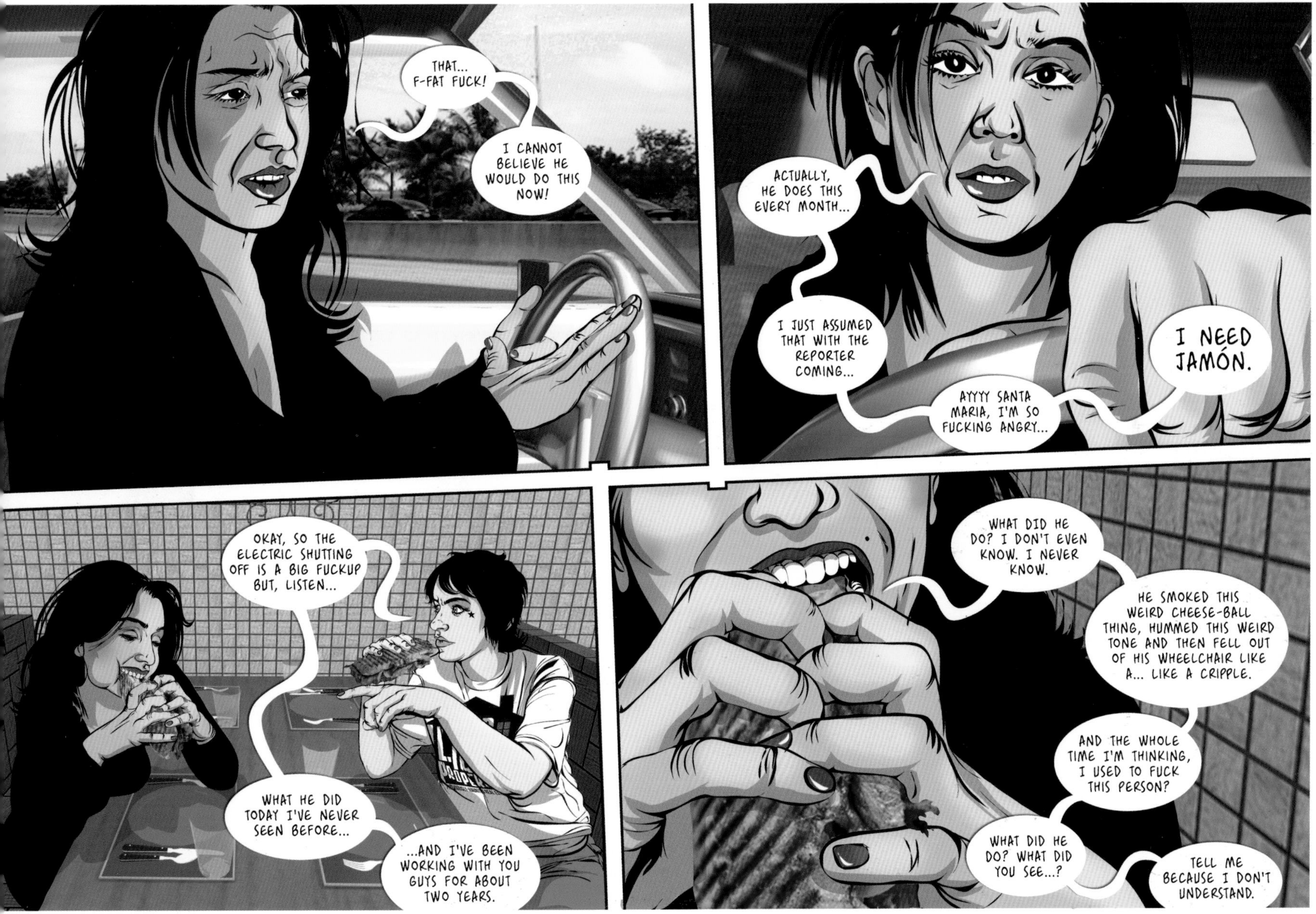
THAT... F-FAT FUCK!
I CANNOT BELIEVE HE WOULD DO THIS NOW!
ACTUALLY, HE DOES THIS EVERY MONTH...
I JUST ASSUMED THAT WITH THE REPORTER COMING...
AYYYY SANTA MARIA, I'M SO FUCKING ANGRY...
I NEED JAMÓN.
OKAY, SO THE ELECTRIC SHUTTING OFF IS A BIG FUCKUP BUT, LISTEN...
WHAT HE DID TODAY I'VE NEVER SEEN BEFORE...
...AND I'VE BEEN WORKING WITH YOU GUYS FOR ABOUT TWO YEARS.
WHAT DID HE DO? I DON'T EVEN KNOW. I NEVER KNOW.
HE SMOKED THIS WEIRD CHEESE-BALL THING, HUMMED THIS WEIRD TONE AND THEN FELL OUT OF HIS WHEELCHAIR LIKE A... LIKE A CRIPPLE.
AND THE WHOLE TIME I'M THINKING, I USED TO FUCK THIS PERSON?
WHAT DID HE DO? WHAT DID YOU SEE...?
TELL ME BECAUSE I DON'T UNDERSTAND.

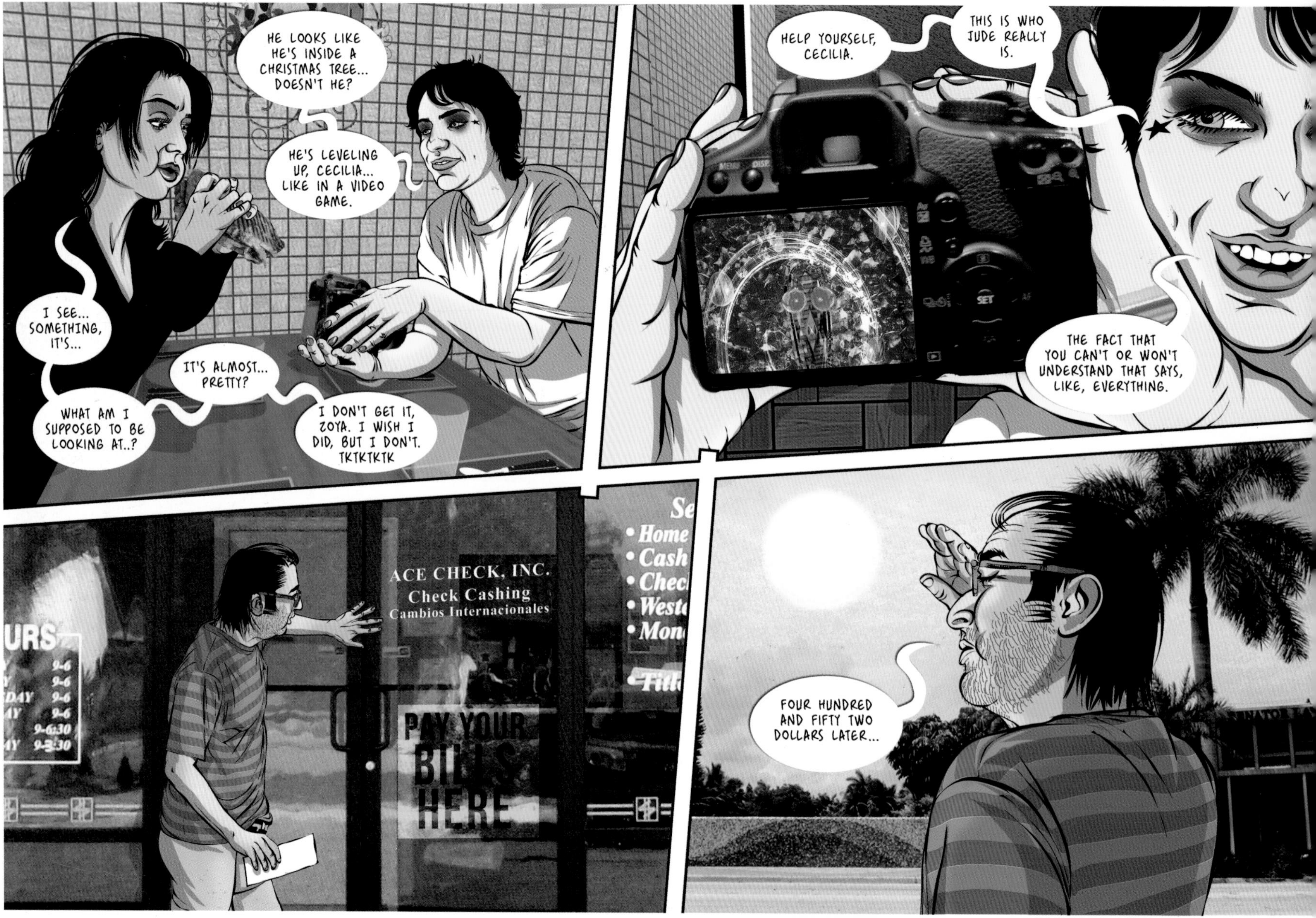
HE LOOKS LIKE HE'S INSIDE A CHRISTMAS TREE... DOESN'T HE?
HE'S LEVELING UP, CECILIA... LIKE IN A VIDEO GAME.
I SEE... SOMETHING, IT'S...
WHAT AM I SUPPOSED TO BE LOOKING AT..?
IT'S ALMOST... PRETTY?
I DON'T GET IT, ZOYA. I WISH I DID, BUT I DON'T. TKTKTKTK
HELP YOURSELF, CECILIA.
THIS IS WHO JUDE REALLY IS.
THE FACT THAT YOU CAN'T OR WON'T UNDERSTAND THAT SAYS, LIKE, EVERYTHING.
ACE CHECK, INC.
Check Cashing
Cambios Internacionales
Home
PAY YOUR BILLS HERE
FOUR HUNDRED AND FIFTY TWO DOLLARS LATER...

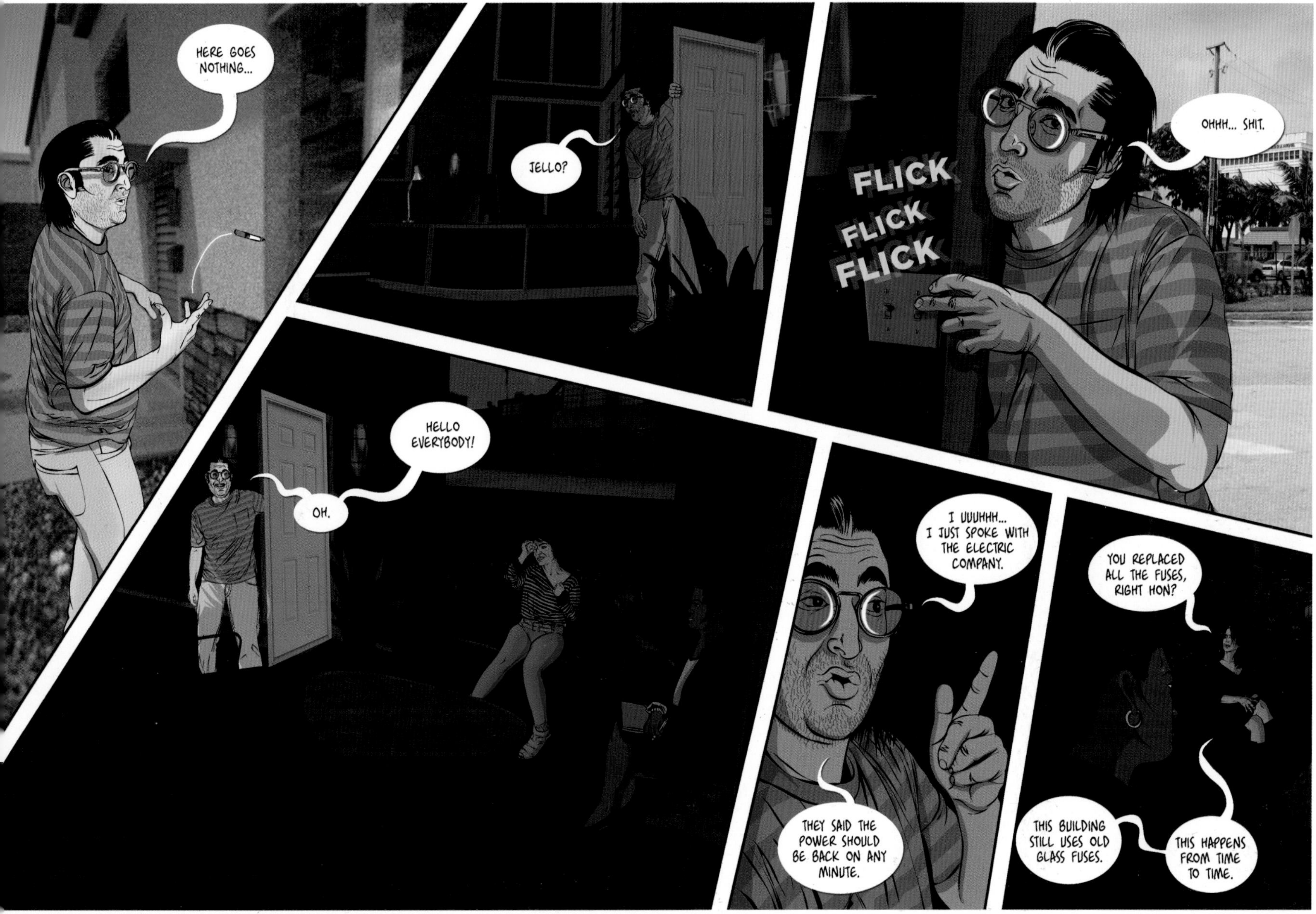
HERE GOES NOTHING...
JELLO?
FLICK
FLICK
FLICK
OHHH... SHIT.
HELLO EVERYBODY!
OH.
I UUUHHH... I JUST SPOKE WITH THE ELECTRIC COMPANY.
THEY SAID THE POWER SHOULD BE BACK ON ANY MINUTE.
YOU REPLACED ALL THE FUSES, RIGHT HON?
THIS BUILDING STILL USES OLD GLASS FUSES.
THIS HAPPENS FROM TIME TO TIME.

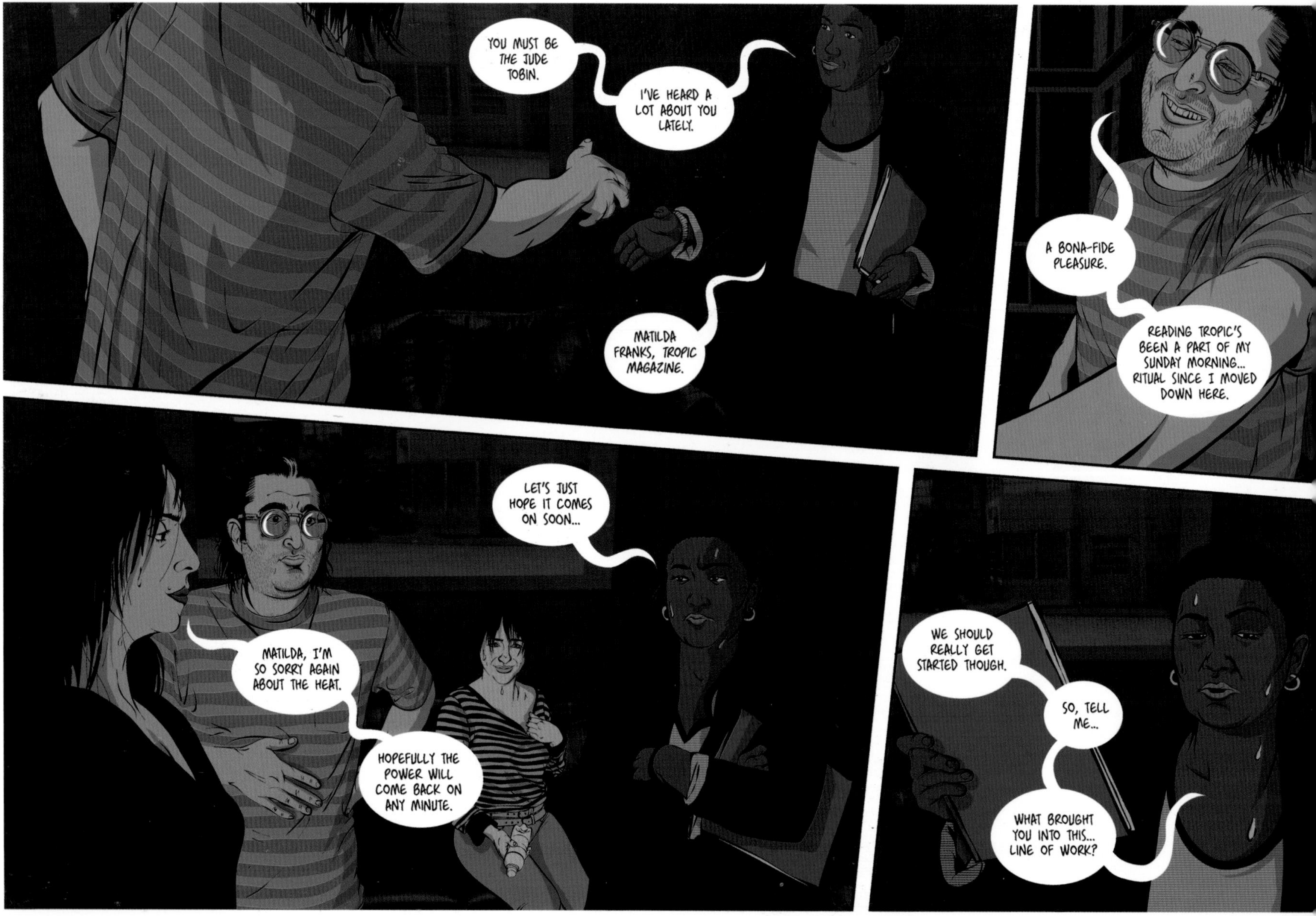
YOU MUST BE THE JUDE TOBIN.
I'VE HEARD A LOT ABOUT YOU LATELY.
MATILDA FRANKS, TROPIC MAGAZINE.
A BONA-FIDE PLEASURE.
READING TROPIC'S BEEN A PART OF MY SUNDAY MORNING... RITUAL SINCE I MOVED DOWN HERE.
MATILDA, I'M SO SORRY AGAIN ABOUT THE HEAT.
HOPEFULLY THE POWER WILL COME BACK ON ANY MINUTE.
LET'S JUST HOPE IT COMES ON SOON...
WE SHOULD REALLY GET STARTED THOUGH.
SO, TELL ME...
WHAT BROUGHT YOU INTO THIS... LINE OF WORK?

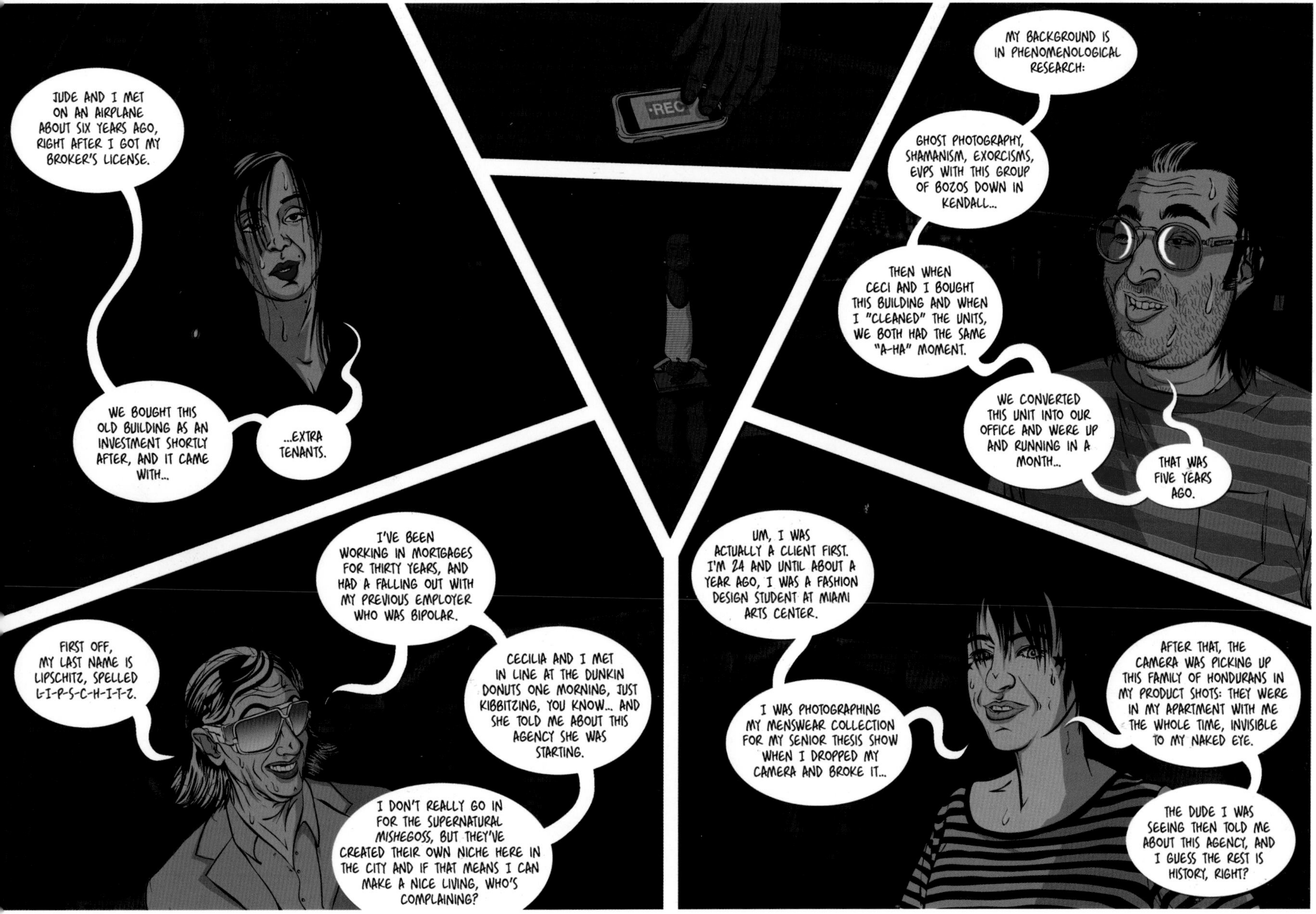
JUDE AND I MET ON AN AIRPLANE ABOUT SIX YEARS AGO, RIGHT AFTER I GOT MY BROKER'S LICENSE.
WE BOUGHT THIS OLD BUILDING AS AN INVESTMENT SHORTLY AFTER, AND IT CAME WITH...
...EXTRA TENANTS.
·REC
MY BACKGROUND IS IN PHENOMENOLOGICAL RESEARCH:
GHOST PHOTOGRAPHY, SHAMANISM, EXORCISMS, EVPS WITH THIS GROUP OF BOZOS DOWN IN KENDALL...
THEN WHEN CECI AND I BOUGHT THIS BUILDING AND WHEN I "CLEANED" THE UNITS, WE BOTH HAD THE SAME "A-HA" MOMENT.
WE CONVERTED THIS UNIT INTO OUR OFFICE AND WERE UP AND RUNNING IN A MONTH...
THAT WAS FIVE YEARS AGO.
FIRST OFF, MY LAST NAME IS LIPSCHITZ, SPELLED L-I-P-S-C-H-I-T-Z.
I'VE BEEN WORKING IN MORTGAGES FOR THIRTY YEARS, AND HAD A FALLING OUT WITH MY PREVIOUS EMPLOYER WHO WAS BIPOLAR.
CECILIA AND I MET IN LINE AT THE DUNKIN DONUTS ONE MORNING, JUST KIBBITZING, YOU KNOW... AND SHE TOLD ME ABOUT THIS AGENCY SHE WAS STARTING.
I DON'T REALLY GO IN FOR THE SUPERNATURAL MISHEGOSS, BUT THEY'VE CREATED THEIR OWN NICHE HERE IN THE CITY AND IF THAT MEANS I CAN MAKE A NICE LIVING, WHO'S COMPLAINING?
UM, I WAS ACTUALLY A CLIENT FIRST. I'M 24 AND UNTIL ABOUT A YEAR AGO, I WAS A FASHION DESIGN STUDENT AT MIAMI ARTS CENTER.
I WAS PHOTOGRAPHING MY MENSWEAR COLLECTION FOR MY SENIOR THESIS SHOW WHEN I DROPPED MY CAMERA AND BROKE IT...
AFTER THAT, THE CAMERA WAS PICKING UP THIS FAMILY OF HONDURANS IN MY PRODUCT SHOTS: THEY WERE IN MY APARTMENT WITH ME THE WHOLE TIME, INVISIBLE TO MY NAKED EYE.
THE DUDE I WAS SEEING THEN TOLD ME ABOUT THIS AGENCY, AND I GUESS THE REST IS HISTORY, RIGHT?

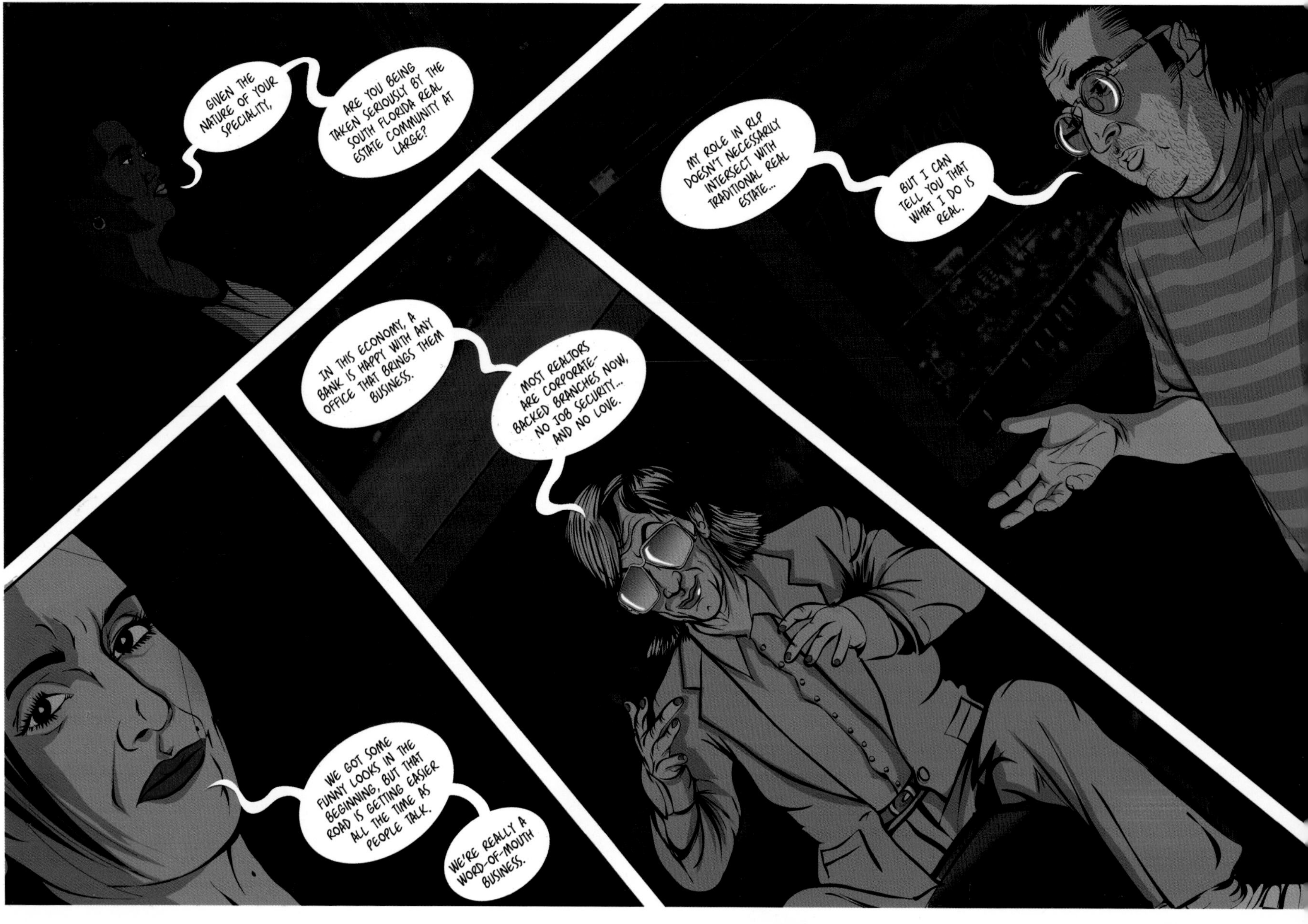
GIVEN THE NATURE OF YOUR SPECIALITY,
ARE YOU BEING TAKEN SERIOUSLY BY THE SOUTH FLORIDA REAL ESTATE COMMUNITY AT LARGE?
MY ROLE IN RLP DOESN'T NECESSARILY INTERSECT WITH TRADITIONAL REAL ESTATE...
BUT I CAN TELL YOU THAT WHAT I DO IS REAL.
IN THIS ECONOMY, A BANK IS HAPPY WITH ANY OFFICE THAT BRINGS THEM BUSINESS.
MOST REALTORS ARE CORPORATE-BACKED BRANCHES NOW, NO JOB SECURITY... AND NO LOVE.
WE GOT SOME FUNNY LOOKS IN THE BEGINNING, BUT THAT ROAD IS GETTING EASIER ALL THE TIME AS PEOPLE TALK.
WE'RE REALLY A WORD-OF-MOUTH BUSINESS.

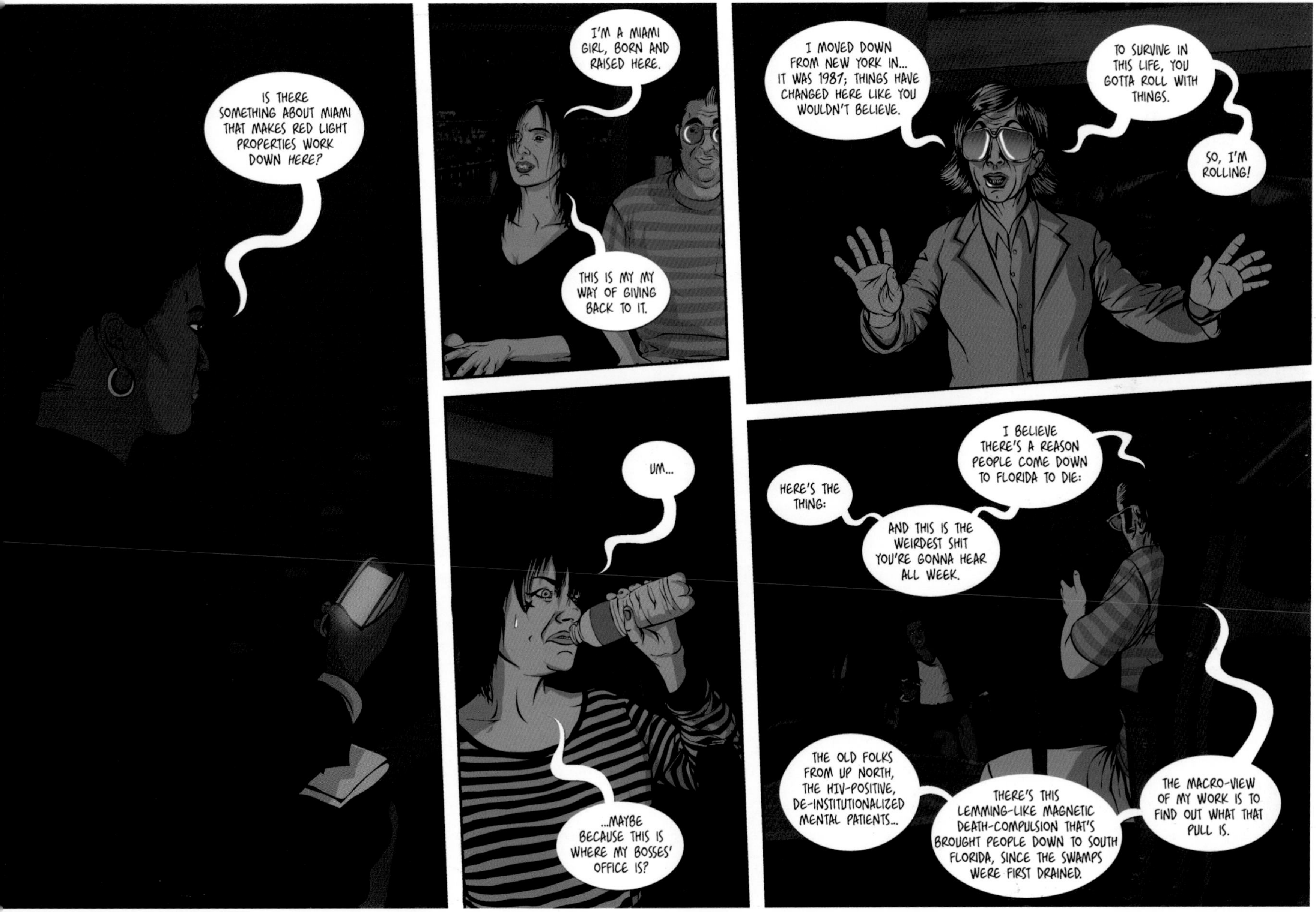
IS THERE SOMETHING ABOUT MIAMI THAT MAKES RED LIGHT PROPERTIES WORK DOWN HERE?
I'M A MIAMI GIRL, BORN AND RAISED HERE.
THIS IS MY MY WAY OF GIVING BACK TO IT.
UM...
...MAYBE BECAUSE THIS IS WHERE MY BOSSES' OFFICE IS?
I MOVED DOWN FROM NEW YORK IN... IT WAS 1987; THINGS HAVE CHANGED HERE LIKE YOU WOULDN'T BELIEVE.
TO SURVIVE IN THIS LIFE, YOU GOTTA ROLL WITH THINGS.
SO, I'M ROLLING!
HERE'S THE THING:
AND THIS IS THE WEIRDEST SHIT YOU'RE GONNA HEAR ALL WEEK.
I BELIEVE THERE'S A REASON PEOPLE COME DOWN TO FLORIDA TO DIE:
THE OLD FOLKS FROM UP NORTH, THE HIV-POSITIVE, DE-INSTITUTIONALIZED MENTAL PATIENTS...
THERE'S THIS LEMMING-LIKE MAGNETIC DEATH-COMPULSION THAT'S BROUGHT PEOPLE DOWN TO SOUTH FLORIDA, SINCE THE SWAMPS WERE FIRST DRAINED.
THE MACRO-VIEW OF MY WORK IS TO FIND OUT WHAT THAT PULL IS.

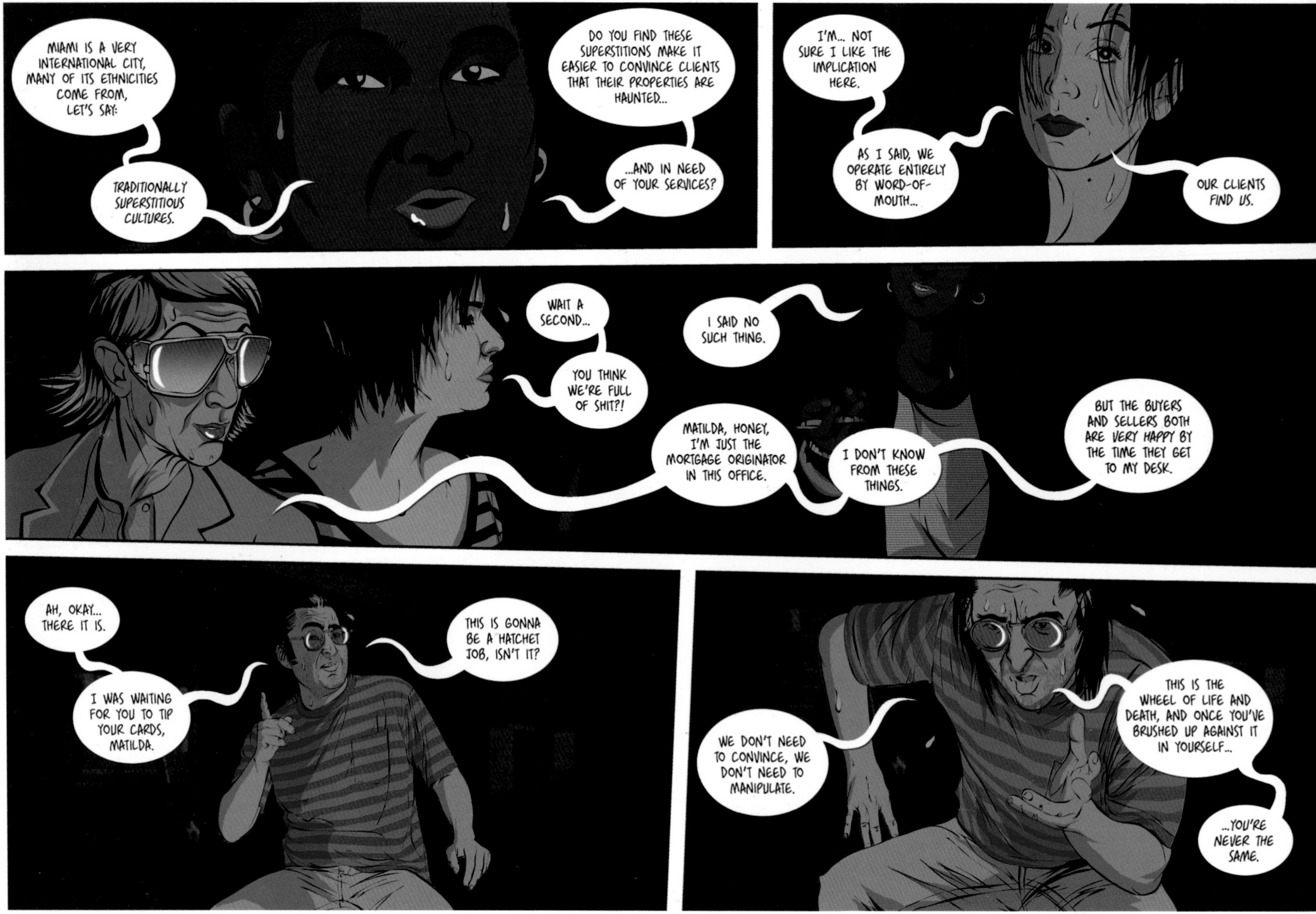

MIAMI IS A VERY INTERNATIONAL CITY, MANY OF ITS ETHNICITIES COME FROM, LET'S SAY:
TRADITIONALLY SUPERSTITIOUS CULTURES.
DO YOU FIND THESE SUPERSTITIONS MAKE IT EASIER TO CONVINCE CLIENTS THAT THEIR PROPERTIES ARE HAUNTED...
...AND IN NEED OF YOUR SERVICES?
I'M... NOT SURE I LIKE THE IMPLICATION HERE.
AS I SAID, WE OPERATE ENTIRELY BY WORD-OF-MOUTH...
OUR CLIENTS FIND US.
WAIT A SECOND...
YOU THINK WE'RE FULL OF SHIT?!
I SAID NO SUCH THING.
MATILDA, HONEY, I'M JUST THE MORTGAGE ORIGINATOR IN THIS OFFICE.
I DON'T KNOW FROM THESE THINGS.
BUT THE BUYERS AND SELLERS BOTH ARE VERY HAPPY BY THE TIME THEY GET TO MY DESK.
AH, OKAY... THERE IT IS.
I WAS WAITING FOR YOU TO TIP YOUR CARDS, MATILDA.
THIS IS GONNA BE A HATCHET JOB, ISN'T IT?
WE DON'T NEED TO CONVINCE, WE DON'T NEED TO MANIPULATE.
THIS IS THE WHEEL OF LIFE AND DEATH, AND ONCE YOU'VE BRUSHED UP AGAINST IT IN YOURSELF...
...YOU'RE NEVER THE SAME.

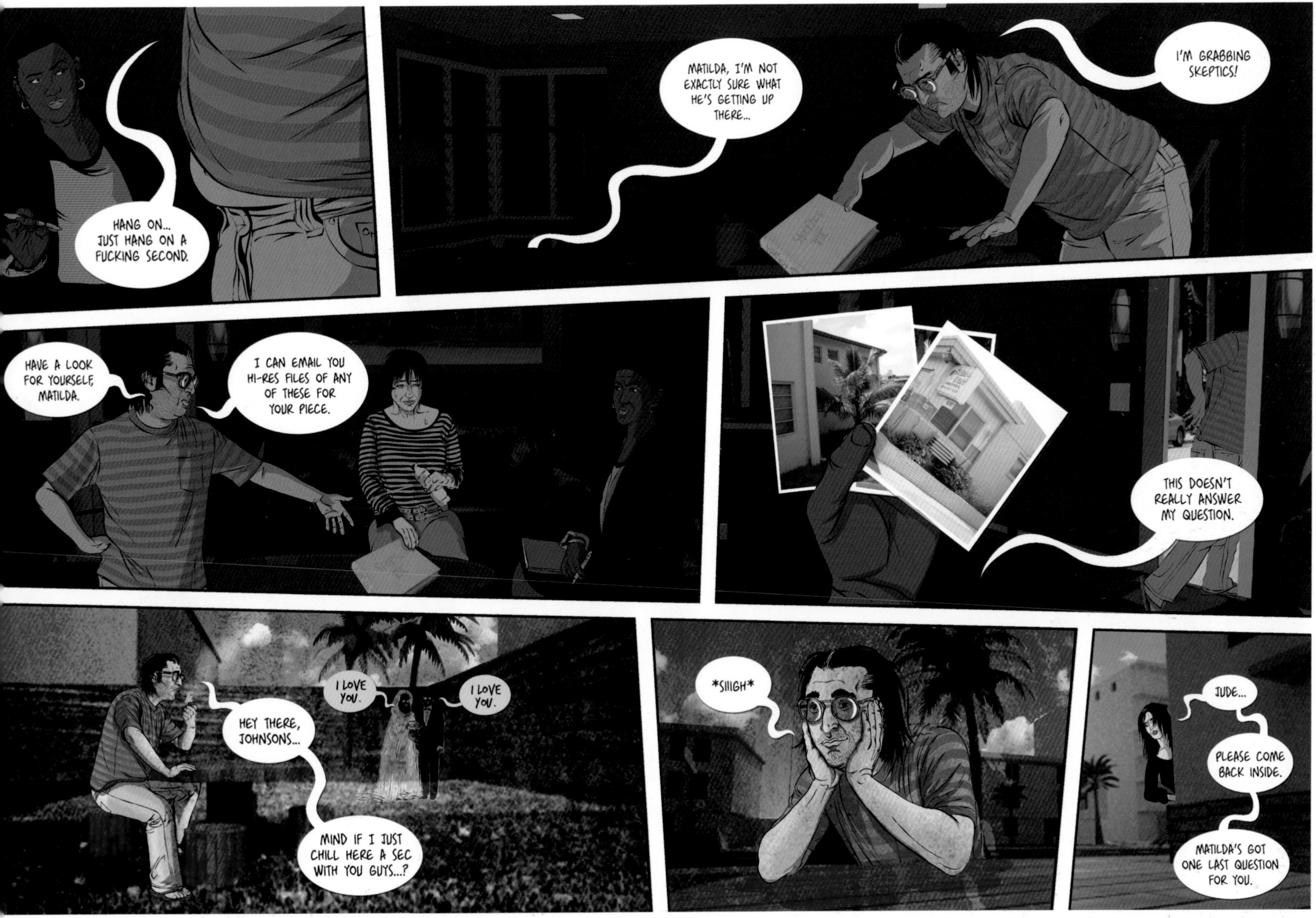
HANG ON...
JUST HANG ON A FUCKING SECOND.
MATILDA, I'M NOT EXACTLY SURE WHAT HE'S GETTING UP THERE...
I'M GRABBING SKEPTICS!
HAVE A LOOK FOR YOURSELF, MATILDA.
I CAN EMAIL YOU HI-RES FILES OF ANY OF THESE FOR YOUR PIECE.
THIS DOESN'T REALLY ANSWER MY QUESTION.
HEY THERE, JOHNSONS...
I LOVE YOU.
I LOVE YOU.
MIND IF I JUST CHILL HERE A SEC WITH YOU GUYS...?
SIIIGH
JUDE...
PLEASE COME BACK INSIDE.
MATILDA'S GOT ONE LAST QUESTION FOR YOU.

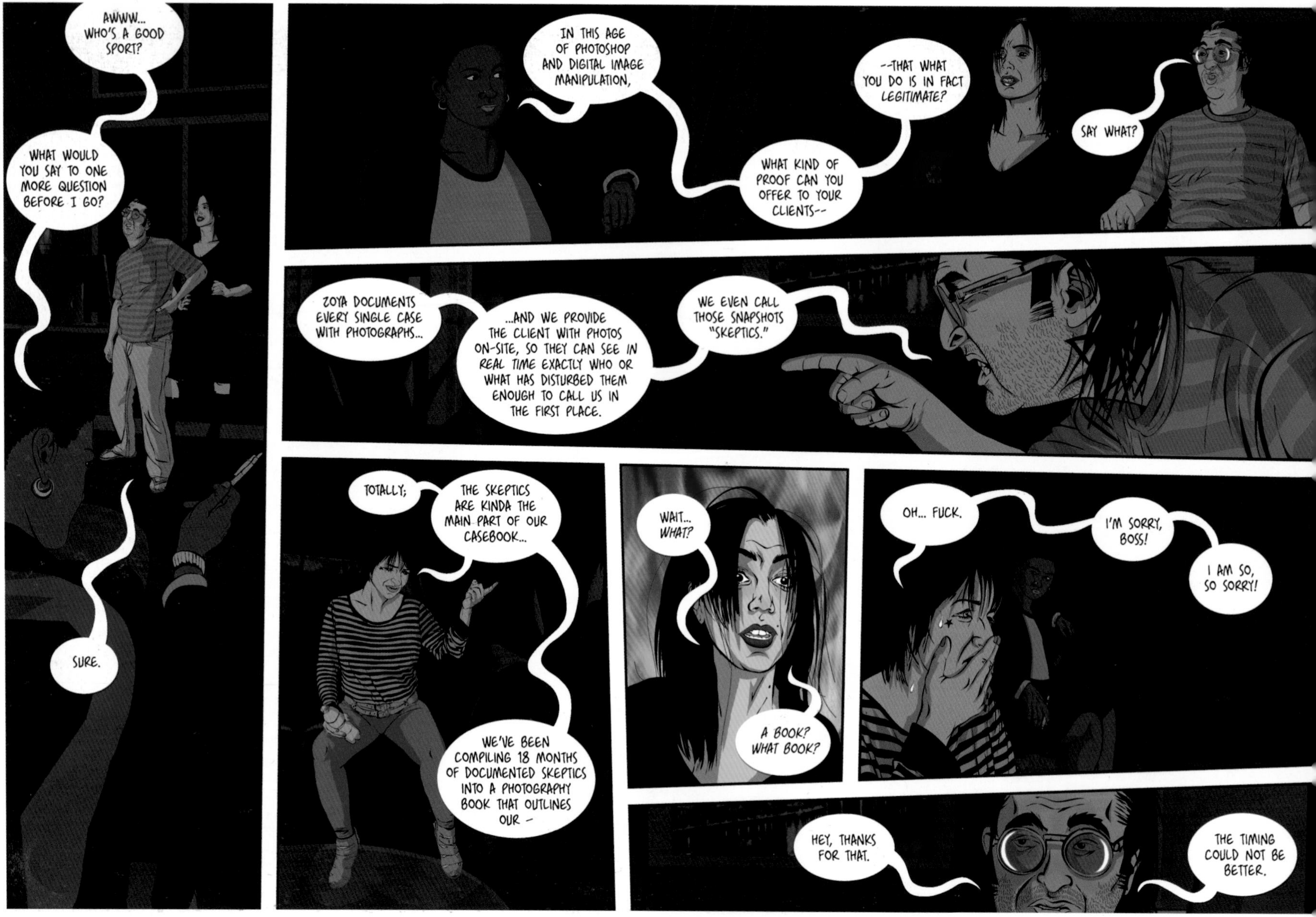
AWWW... WHO'S A GOOD SPORT?
WHAT WOULD YOU SAY TO ONE MORE QUESTION BEFORE I GO?
SURE.
IN THIS AGE OF PHOTOSHOP AND DIGITAL IMAGE MANIPULATION,
WHAT KIND OF PROOF CAN YOU OFFER TO YOUR CLIENTS--
--THAT WHAT YOU DO IS IN FACT LEGITIMATE?
SAY WHAT?
ZOYA DOCUMENTS EVERY SINGLE CASE WITH PHOTOGRAPHS...
...AND WE PROVIDE THE CLIENT WITH PHOTOS ON-SITE, SO THEY CAN SEE IN REAL TIME EXACTLY WHO OR WHAT HAS DISTURBED THEM ENOUGH TO CALL US IN THE FIRST PLACE.
WE EVEN CALL THOSE SNAPSHOTS "SKEPTICS."
TOTALLY;
THE SKEPTICS ARE KINDA THE MAIN PART OF OUR CASEBOOK...
WE'VE BEEN COMPILING 18 MONTHS OF DOCUMENTED SKEPTICS INTO A PHOTOGRAPHY BOOK THAT OUTLINES OUR -
WAIT... WHAT?
A BOOK? WHAT BOOK?
OH... FUCK.
I'M SORRY, BOSS!
I AM SO, SO SORRY!
HEY, THANKS FOR THAT.
THE TIMING COULD NOT BE BETTER.

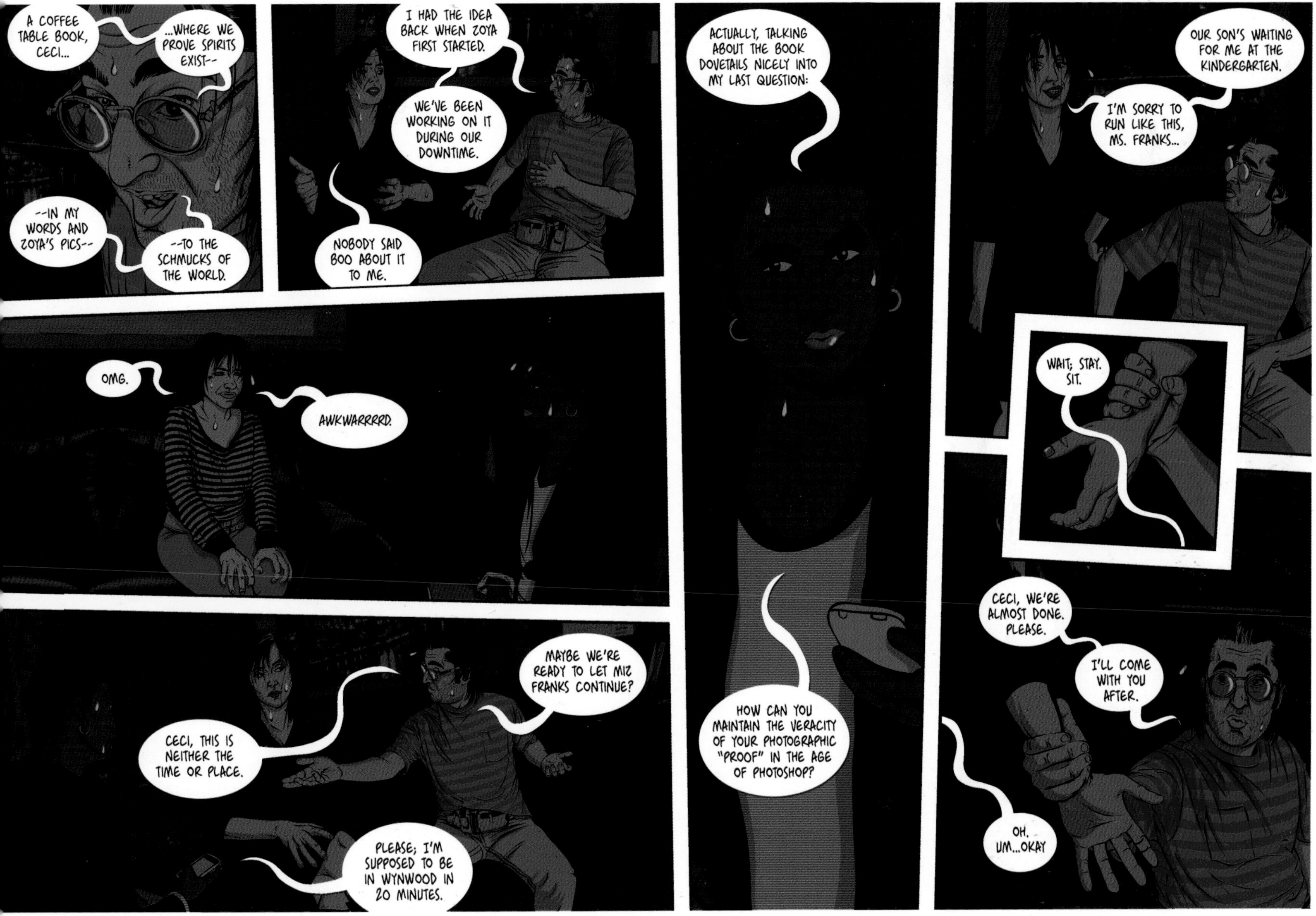
A COFFEE TABLE BOOK, CECI...
...WHERE WE PROVE SPIRITS EXIST--
--IN MY WORDS AND ZOYA'S PICS--
--TO THE SCHMUCKS OF THE WORLD.
I HAD THE IDEA BACK WHEN ZOYA FIRST STARTED.
WE'VE BEEN WORKING ON IT DURING OUR DOWNTIME.
NOBODY SAID BOO ABOUT IT TO ME.
OMG.
AWKWARRRRD.
MAYBE WE'RE READY TO LET MIZ FRANKS CONTINUE?
CECI, THIS IS NEITHER THE TIME OR PLACE.
PLEASE; I'M SUPPOSED TO BE IN WYNWOOD IN 20 MINUTES.
ACTUALLY, TALKING ABOUT THE BOOK DOVETAILS NICELY INTO MY LAST QUESTION:
HOW CAN YOU MAINTAIN THE VERACITY OF YOUR PHOTOGRAPHIC "PROOF" IN THE AGE OF PHOTOSHOP?
OUR SON'S WAITING FOR ME AT THE KINDERGARTEN.
I'M SORRY TO RUN LIKE THIS, MS. FRANKS...
WAIT; STAY. SIT.
CECI, WE'RE ALMOST DONE. PLEASE.
I'LL COME WITH YOU AFTER.
OH. UM...OKAY

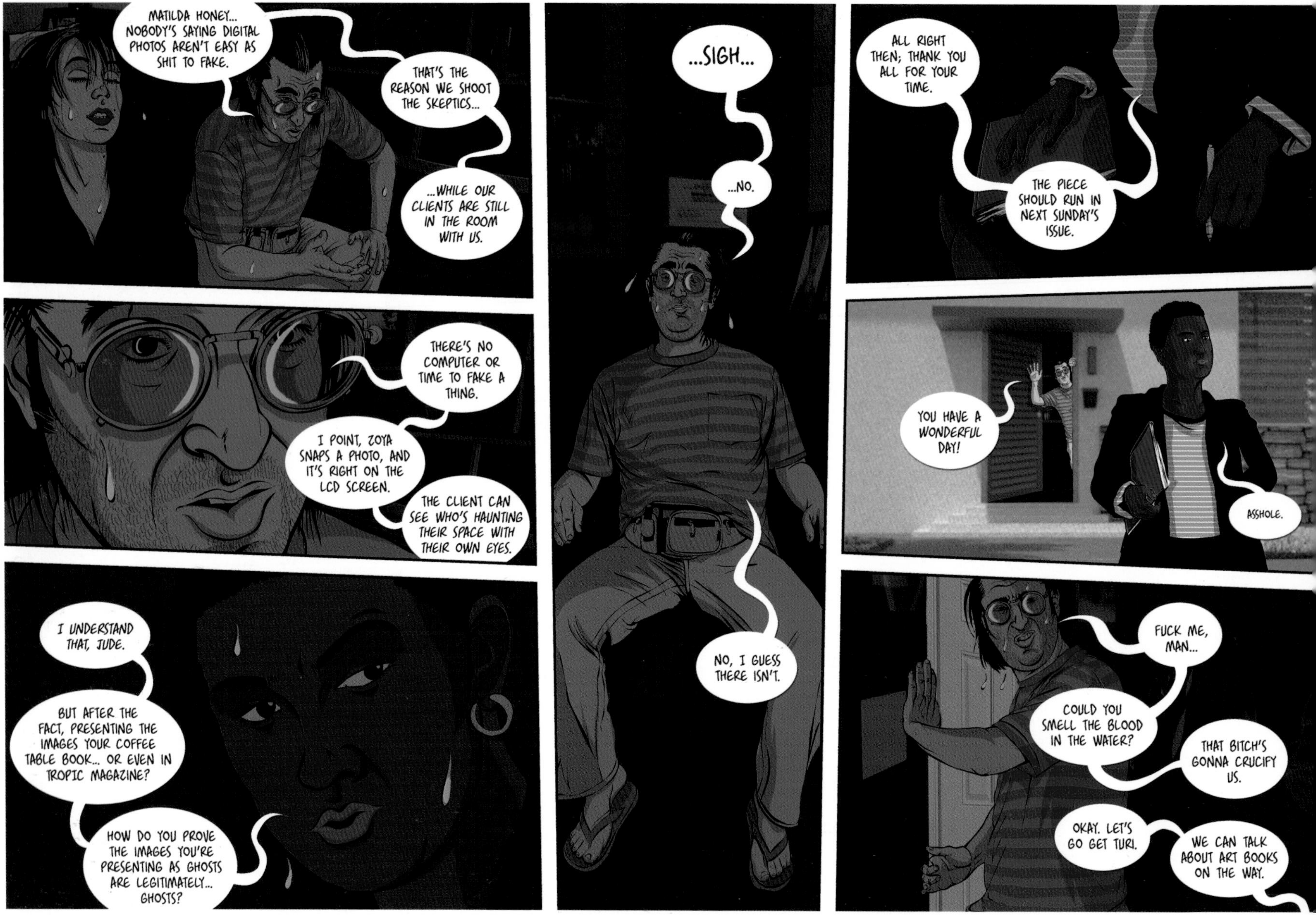
MATILDA HONEY... NOBODY'S SAYING DIGITAL PHOTOS AREN'T EASY AS SHIT TO FAKE.
THAT'S THE REASON WE SHOOT THE SKEPTICS...
...WHILE OUR CLIENTS ARE STILL IN THE ROOM WITH US.
THERE'S NO COMPUTER OR TIME TO FAKE A THING.
I POINT, ZOYA SNAPS A PHOTO, AND IT'S RIGHT ON THE LCD SCREEN.
THE CLIENT CAN SEE WHO'S HAUNTING THEIR SPACE WITH THEIR OWN EYES.
I UNDERSTAND THAT, JUDE.
BUT AFTER THE FACT, PRESENTING THE IMAGES YOUR COFFEE TABLE BOOK... OR EVEN IN TROPIC MAGAZINE?
HOW DO YOU PROVE THE IMAGES YOU'RE PRESENTING AS GHOSTS ARE LEGITIMATELY... GHOSTS?
...SIGH...
...NO.
NO, I GUESS THERE ISN'T.
ALL RIGHT THEN; THANK YOU ALL FOR YOUR TIME.
THE PIECE SHOULD RUN IN NEXT SUNDAY'S ISSUE.
YOU HAVE A WONDERFUL DAY!
ASSHOLE.
FUCK ME, MAN...
COULD YOU SMELL THE BLOOD IN THE WATER?
THAT BITCH'S GONNA CRUCIFY US.
OKAY. LET'S GO GET TURI.
WE CAN TALK ABOUT ART BOOKS ON THE WAY.

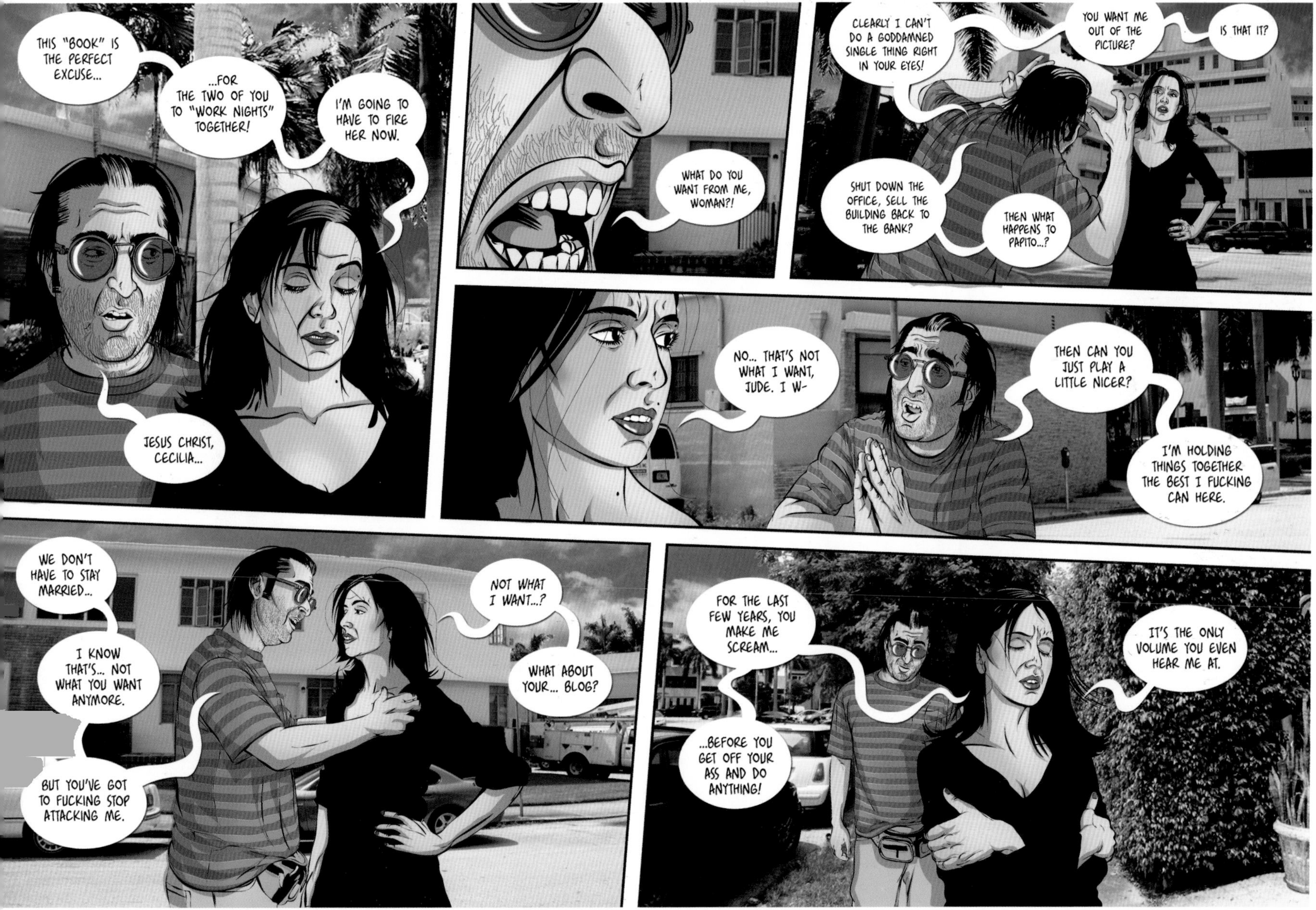
THIS "BOOK" IS THE PERFECT EXCUSE...
...FOR THE TWO OF YOU TO "WORK NIGHTS" TOGETHER!
I'M GOING TO HAVE TO FIRE HER NOW.
JESUS CHRIST, CECILIA...
WHAT DO YOU WANT FROM ME, WOMAN?!
CLEARLY I CAN'T DO A GODDAMNED SINGLE THING RIGHT IN YOUR EYES!
YOU WANT ME OUT OF THE PICTURE?
IS THAT IT?
SHUT DOWN THE OFFICE, SELL THE BUILDING BACK TO THE BANK?
THEN WHAT HAPPENS TO PAPITO...?
NO... THAT'S NOT WHAT I WANT, JUDE. I W-
THEN CAN YOU JUST PLAY A LITTLE NICER?
I'M HOLDING THINGS TOGETHER THE BEST I FUCKING CAN HERE.
WE DON'T HAVE TO STAY MARRIED...
I KNOW THAT'S... NOT WHAT YOU WANT ANYMORE.
BUT YOU'VE GOT TO FUCKING STOP ATTACKING ME.
NOT WHAT I WANT...?
WHAT ABOUT YOUR... BLOG?
FOR THE LAST FEW YEARS, YOU MAKE ME SCREAM...
...BEFORE YOU GET OFF YOUR ASS AND DO ANYTHING!
IT'S THE ONLY VOLUME YOU EVEN HEAR ME AT.

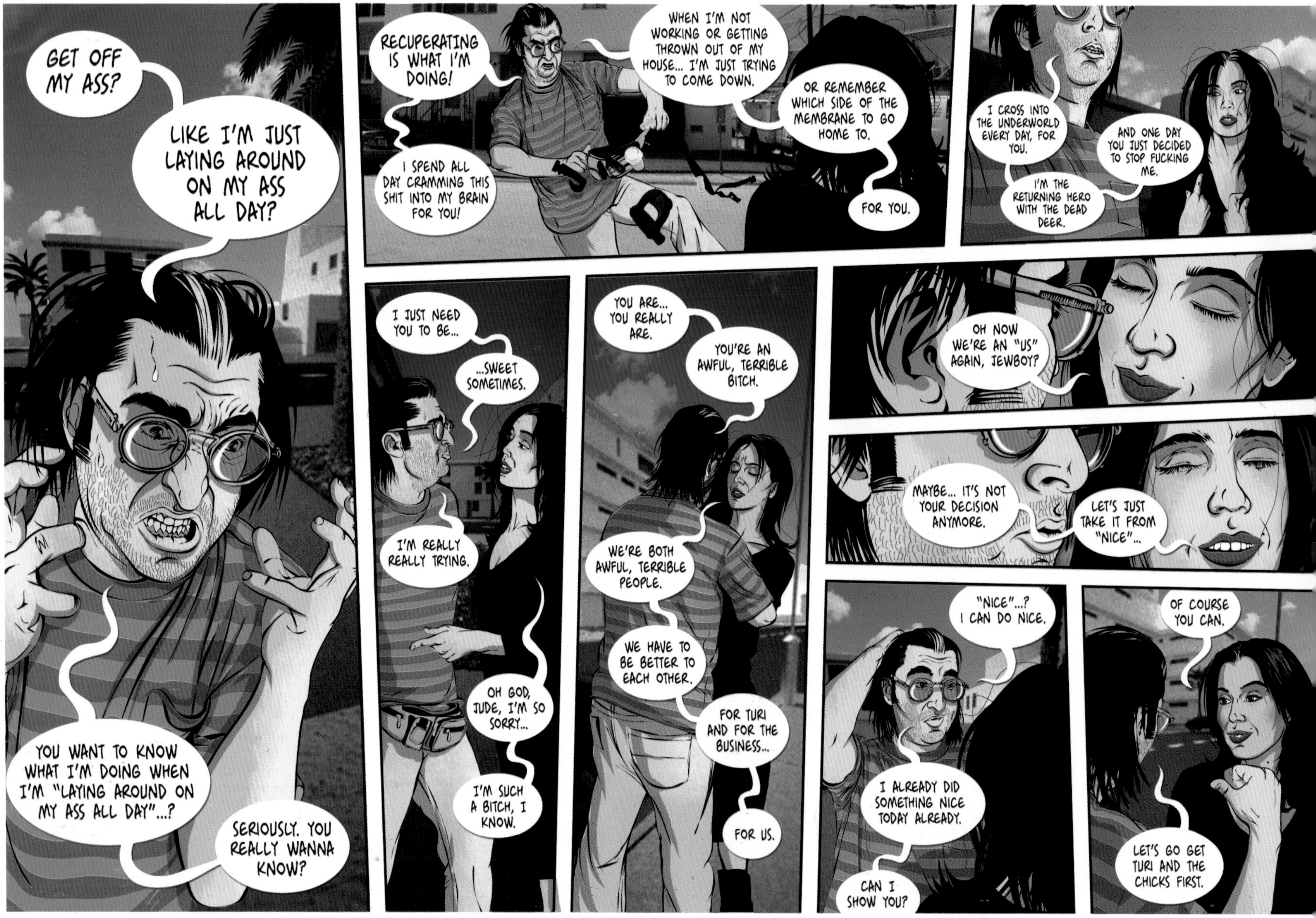
GET OFF MY ASS?
LIKE I'M JUST LAYING AROUND ON MY ASS ALL DAY?
YOU WANT TO KNOW WHAT I'M DOING WHEN I'M "LAYING AROUND ON MY ASS ALL DAY"...?
SERIOUSLY. YOU REALLY WANNA KNOW?
RECUPERATING IS WHAT I'M DOING!
I SPEND ALL DAY CRAMMING THIS SHIT INTO MY BRAIN FOR YOU!
WHEN I'M NOT WORKING OR GETTING THROWN OUT OF MY HOUSE... I'M JUST TRYING TO COME DOWN.
OR REMEMBER WHICH SIDE OF THE MEMBRANE TO GO HOME TO.
FOR YOU.
I CROSS INTO THE UNDERWORLD EVERY DAY, FOR YOU.
I'M THE RETURNING HERO WITH THE DEAD DEER.
AND ONE DAY YOU JUST DECIDED TO STOP FUCKING ME.
I JUST NEED YOU TO BE...
...SWEET SOMETIMES.
I'M REALLY REALLY TRYING.
OH GOD, JUDE, I'M SO SORRY...
I'M SUCH A BITCH, I KNOW.
YOU ARE... YOU REALLY ARE.
YOU'RE AN AWFUL, TERRIBLE BITCH.
WE'RE BOTH AWFUL, TERRIBLE PEOPLE.
WE HAVE TO BE BETTER TO EACH OTHER.
FOR TURI AND FOR THE BUSINESS...
FOR US.
OH NOW WE'RE AN "US" AGAIN, JEWBOY?
MAYBE... IT'S NOT YOUR DECISION ANYMORE.
LET'S JUST TAKE IT FROM "NICE"...
"NICE"...? I CAN DO NICE.
I ALREADY DID SOMETHING NICE TODAY ALREADY.
CAN I SHOW YOU?
OF COURSE YOU CAN.
LET'S GO GET TURI AND THE CHICKS FIRST.

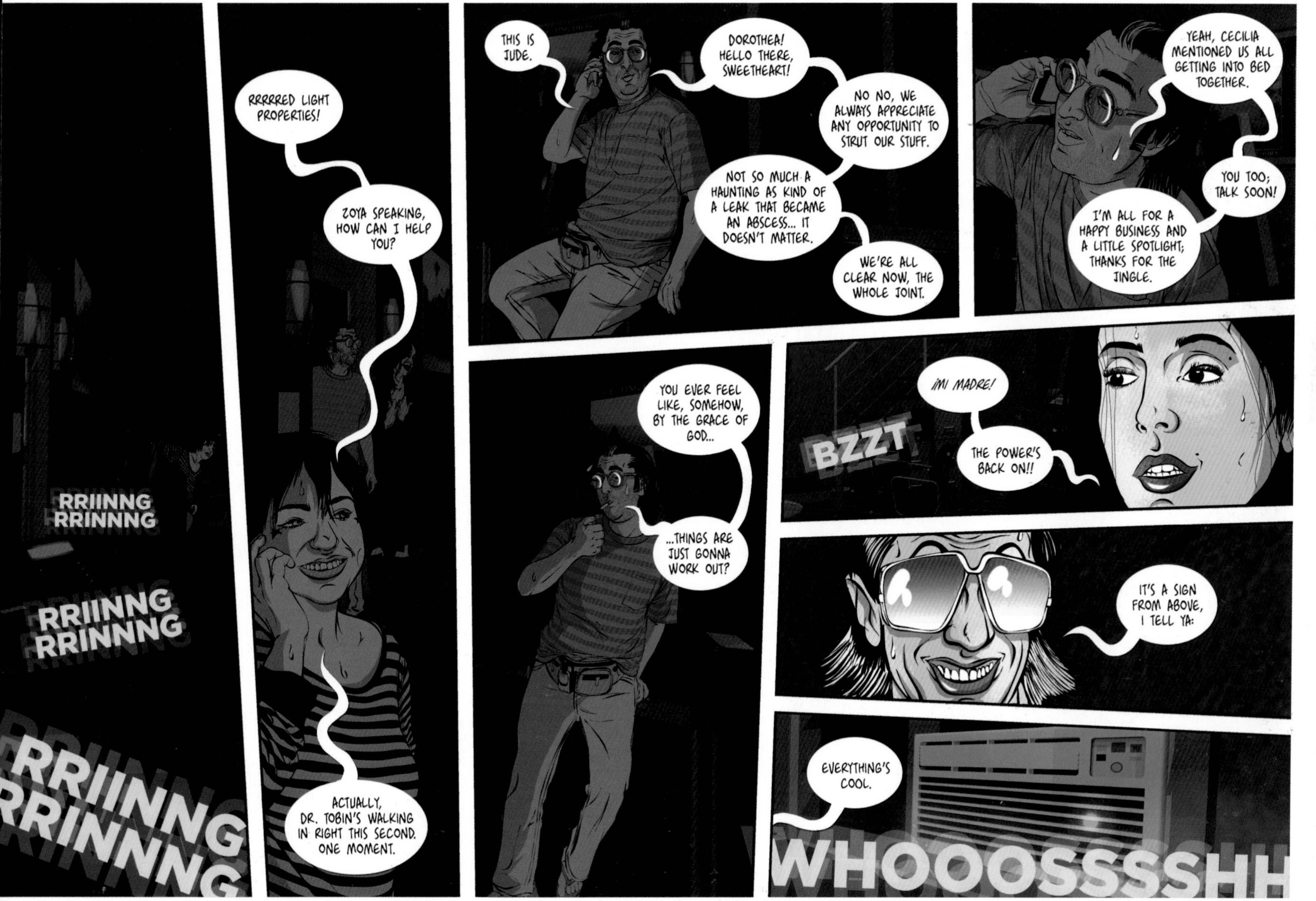
RRIINNG RRINNNG
RRIINNG RRINNNG
RRIINNG RRINNNG
RRRRRED LIGHT PROPERTIES!
ZOYA SPEAKING, HOW CAN I HELP YOU?
ACTUALLY, DR. TOBIN'S WALKING IN RIGHT THIS SECOND. ONE MOMENT.
THIS IS JUDE.
DOROTHEA! HELLO THERE, SWEETHEART!
NO NO, WE ALWAYS APPRECIATE ANY OPPORTUNITY TO STRUT OUR STUFF.
NOT SO MUCH A HAUNTING AS KIND OF A LEAK THAT BECAME AN ABSCESS... IT DOESN'T MATTER.
WE'RE ALL CLEAR NOW, THE WHOLE JOINT.
YEAH, CECILIA MENTIONED US ALL GETTING INTO BED TOGETHER.
I'M ALL FOR A HAPPY BUSINESS AND A LITTLE SPOTLIGHT; THANKS FOR THE JINGLE.
YOU TOO; TALK SOON!
YOU EVER FEEL LIKE, SOMEHOW, BY THE GRACE OF GOD...
...THINGS ARE JUST GONNA WORK OUT?
BZZT
¡MI MADRE!
THE POWER'S BACK ON!!
IT'S A SIGN FROM ABOVE, I TELL YA:
EVERYTHING'S COOL.
WHOOOSSSSHH

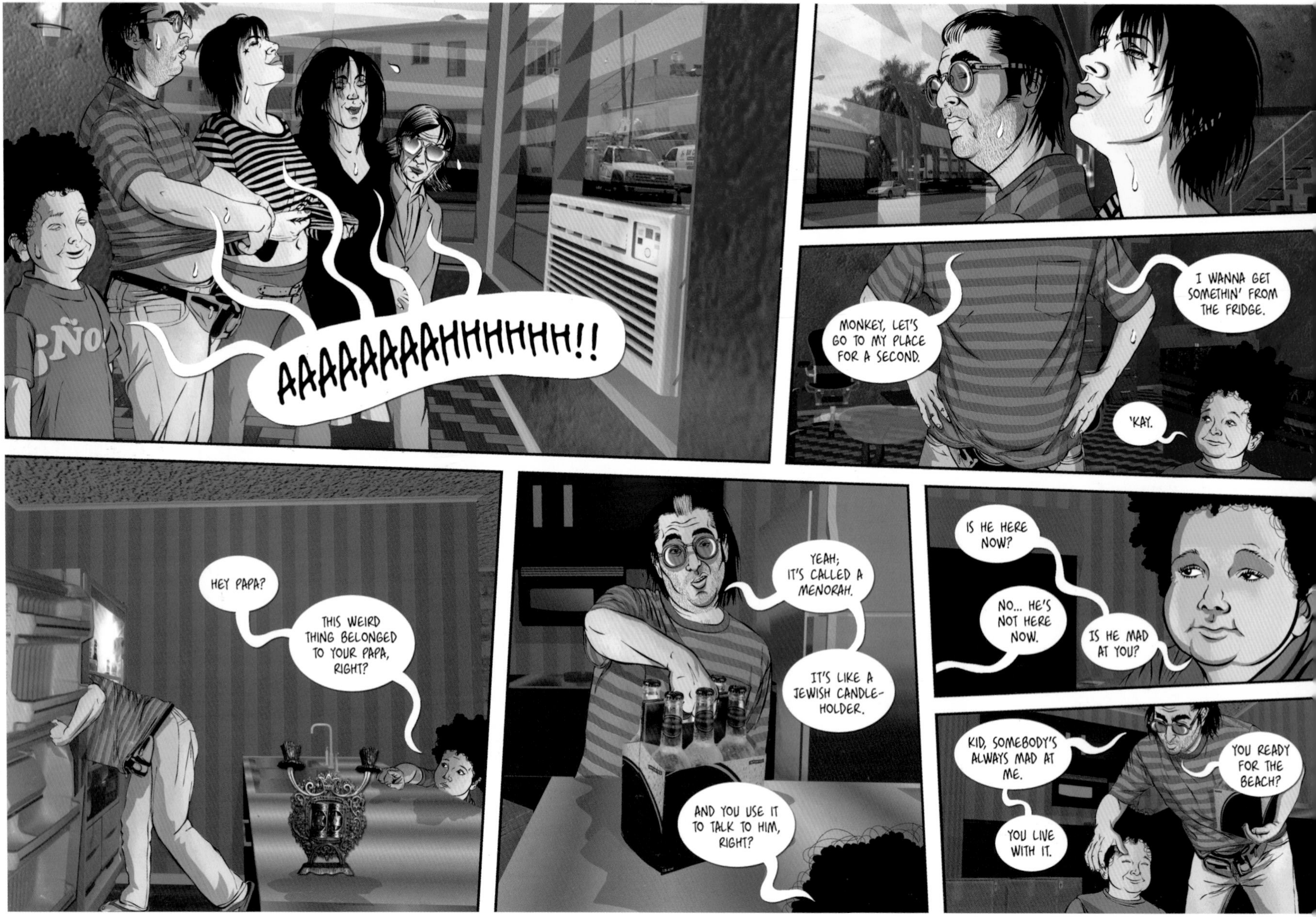
¡Ño!
AAAAAAAHHHHHH!!
MONKEY, LET'S GO TO MY PLACE FOR A SECOND.
I WANNA GET SOMETHIN' FROM THE FRIDGE.
'KAY.
HEY PAPA?
THIS WEIRD THING BELONGED TO YOUR PAPA, RIGHT?
YEAH; IT'S CALLED A MENORAH.
IT'S LIKE A JEWISH CANDLE-HOLDER.
AND YOU USE IT TO TALK TO HIM, RIGHT?
IS HE HERE NOW?
NO... HE'S NOT HERE NOW.
IS HE MAD AT YOU?
KID, SOMEBODY'S ALWAYS MAD AT ME.
YOU LIVE WITH IT.
YOU READY FOR THE BEACH?

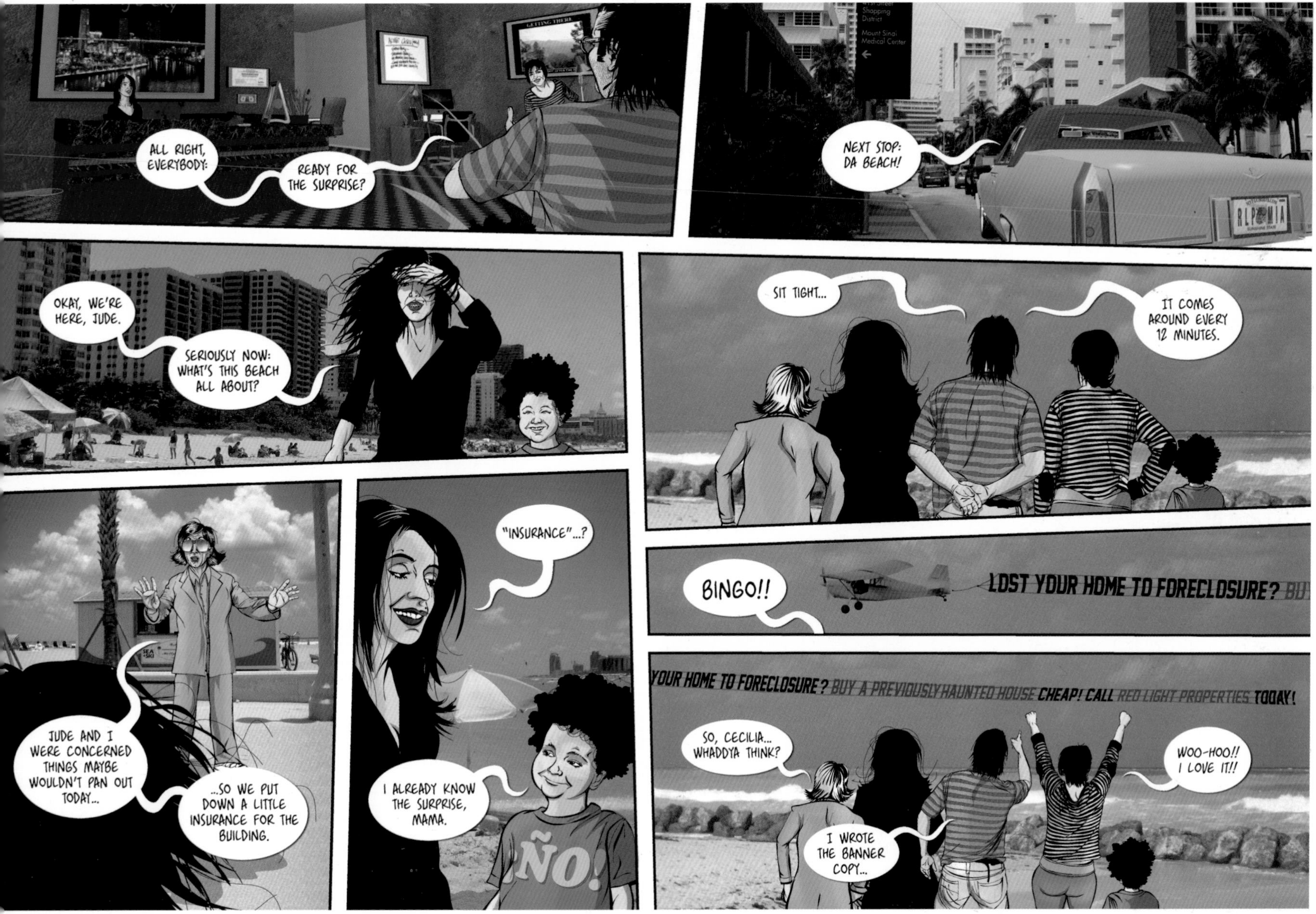
ALL RIGHT, EVERYBODY:
READY FOR THE SURPRISE?
Shopping District
Mount Sinai Medical Center
NEXT STOP: DA BEACH!
OKAY, WE'RE HERE, JUDE.
SERIOUSLY NOW: WHAT'S THIS BEACH ALL ABOUT?
SIT TIGHT...
IT COMES AROUND EVERY 12 MINUTES.
JUDE AND I WERE CONCERNED THINGS MAYBE WOULDN'T PAN OUT TODAY...
...SO WE PUT DOWN A LITTLE INSURANCE FOR THE BUILDING.
"INSURANCE"...?
I ALREADY KNOW THE SURPRISE, MAMA.
ÑO!
BINGO!!
LOST YOUR HOME TO FORECLOSURE?
YOUR HOME TO FORECLOSURE? BUY A PREVIOUSLY HAUNTED HOUSE CHEAP! CALL RED LIGHT PROPERTIES TODAY!
SO, CECILIA... WHADDYA THINK?
WOO-HOO!! I LOVE IT!!
I WROTE THE BANNER COPY...

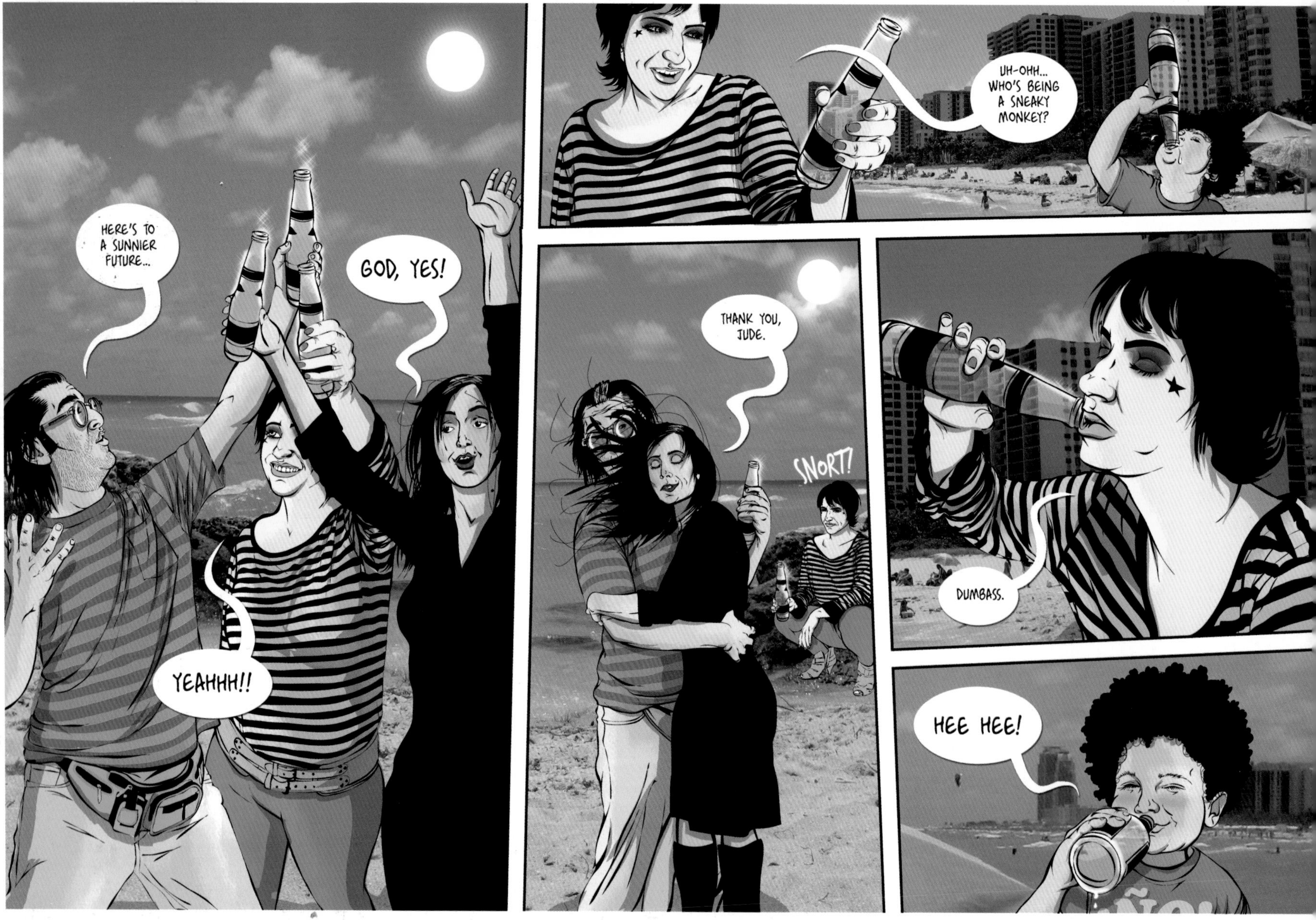
HERE'S TO A SUNNIER FUTURE...
GOD, YES!
YEAHHH!!
UH-OHH... WHO'S BEING A SNEAKY MONKEY?
THANK YOU, JUDE.
SNORT!
DUMBASS.
HEE HEE!

THERE'S MORE WHERE THIS CAME FROM

REDLIGHTPROPERTIES.COM

@RedLightProps

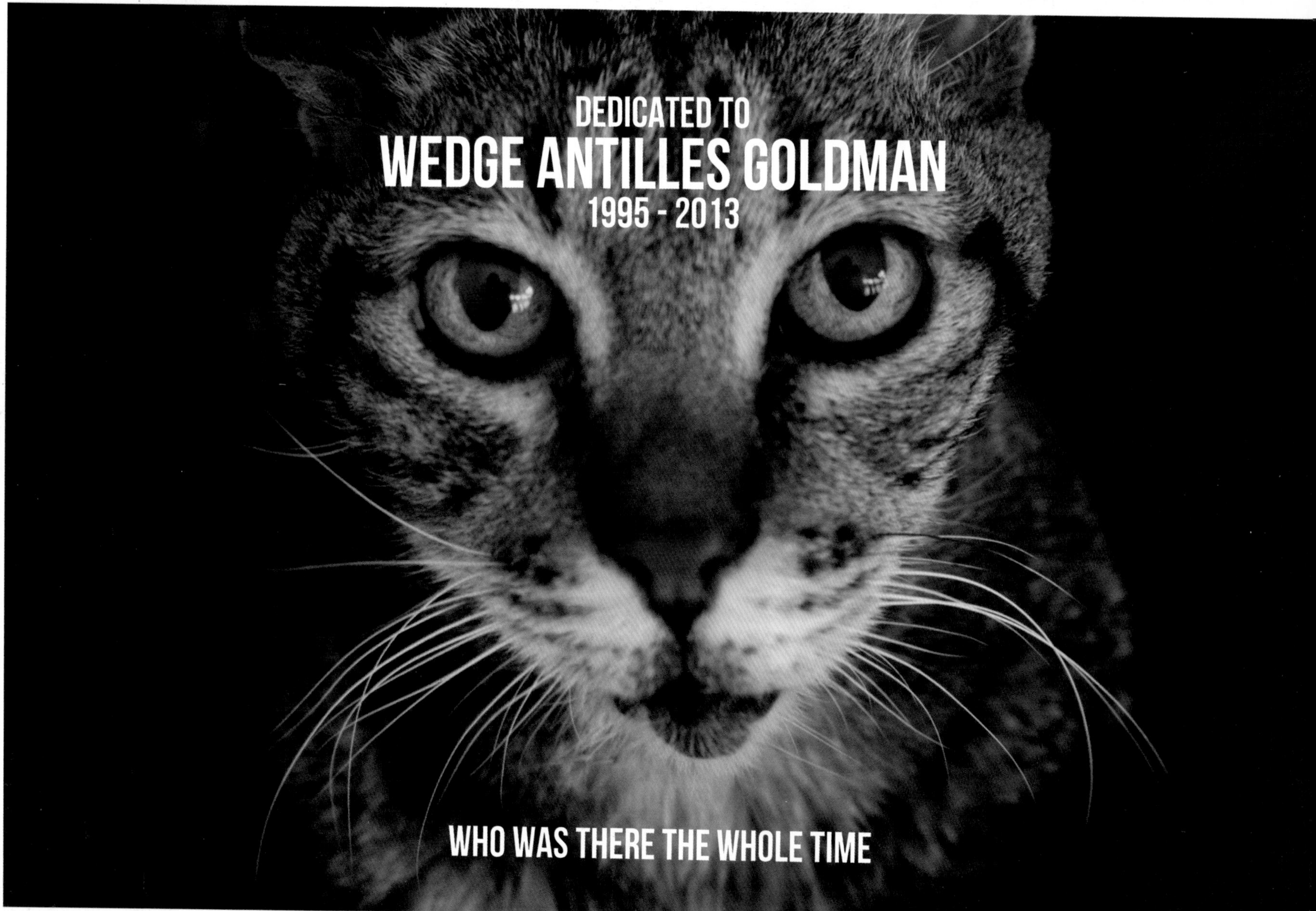
DEDICATED TO
WEDGE ANTILLES GOLDMAN
1995 - 2013
WHO WAS THERE THE WHOLE TIME

ABOUT DAN

DAN GOLDMAN writes for comics, videogames and screen, and has illustrated long-form graphic novels for Random House and Hachette Books USA, including his Eisner-nominated *Shooting War* and the real-time docu-comic *08: A Graphic Diary of the Campaign Trail*.

A champion of digital art, publishing and distribution, he has lectured about the new digital possibilities for comics in today's media landscape at events ranging from SXSW Interactive Festival, New York Comic-Con, Pixel Show São Paulo to M.I.T.'s annual Futures of Entertainment.

His illustration work was recently featured in Taschen Books' *Illustration Now!* series. He has created artwork (and comics) for clients ranging from *Vanity Fair, Wired, TIME Magazine,* AMC Television, *GQ Magazine, Foreign Policy, Bloomberg Business Week, New York Magazine* and *Entertainment Weekly*.

He lives and works in New York City with his lady.

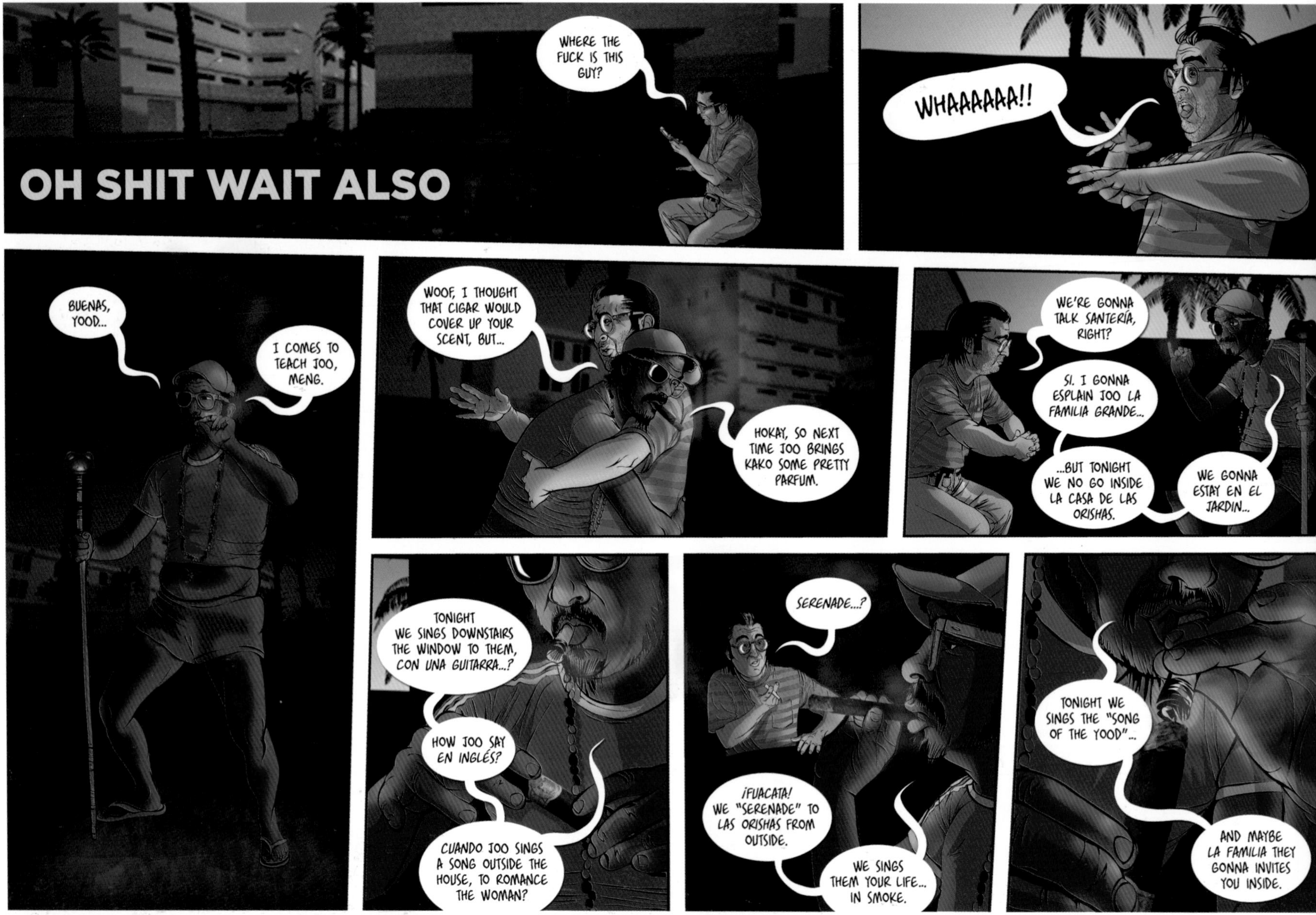

OH SHIT WAIT ALSO
WHERE THE FUCK IS THIS GUY?
WHAAAAAA!!
BUENAS, YOOD...
I COMES TO TEACH JOO, MENG.
WOOF, I THOUGHT THAT CIGAR WOULD COVER UP YOUR SCENT, BUT...
HOKAY, SO NEXT TIME JOO BRINGS KAKO SOME PRETTY PARFUM.
WE'RE GONNA TALK SANTERÍA, RIGHT?
SI. I GONNA ESPLAIN JOO LA FAMILIA GRANDE...
...BUT TONIGHT WE NO GO INSIDE LA CASA DE LAS ORISHAS.
WE GONNA ESTAY EN EL JARDIN...
TONIGHT WE SINGS DOWNSTAIRS THE WINDOW TO THEM, CON UNA GUITARRA...?
HOW JOO SAY EN INGLÉS?
CUANDO JOO SINGS A SONG OUTSIDE THE HOUSE, TO ROMANCE THE WOMAN?
SERENADE...?
¡FUACATA! WE "SERENADE" TO LAS ORISHAS FROM OUTSIDE.
WE SINGS THEM YOUR LIFE... IN SMOKE.
TONIGHT WE SINGS THE "SONG OF THE YOOD"...
AND MAYBE LA FAMILIA THEY GONNA INVITES YOU INSIDE.

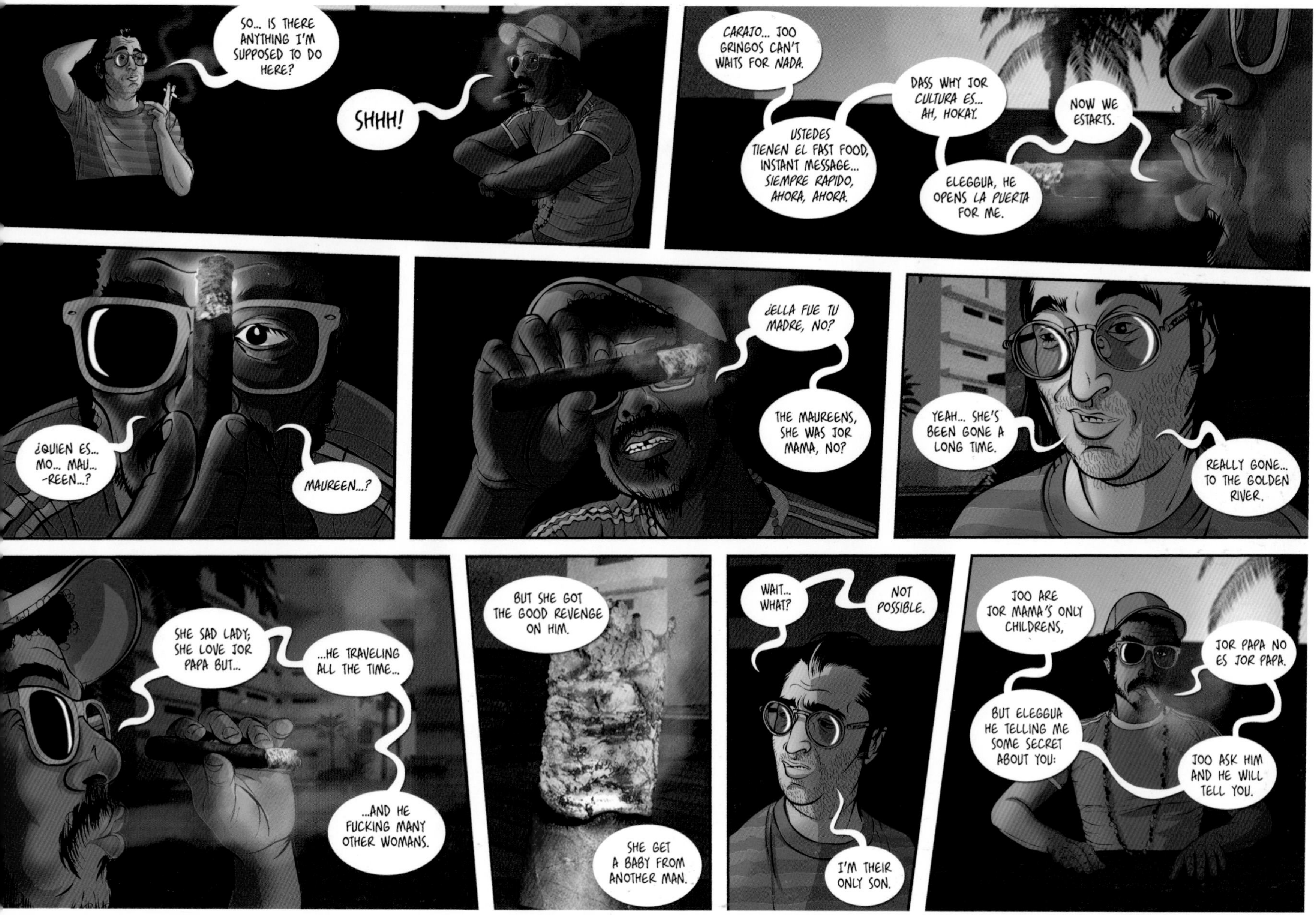

SO... IS THERE ANYTHING I'M SUPPOSED TO DO HERE?
SHHH!
CARAJO... JOO GRINGOS CAN'T WAITS FOR NADA.
USTEDES TIENEN EL FAST FOOD, INSTANT MESSAGE... SIEMPRE RAPIDO, AHORA, AHORA.
DASS WHY JOR CULTURA ES... AH, HOKAY.
ELEGGUA, HE OPENS LA PUERTA FOR ME.
NOW WE ESTARTS.
¿QUIEN ES... MO... MAU... -REEN...?
MAUREEN...?
¿ELLA FUE TU MADRE, NO?
THE MAUREENS, SHE WAS JOR MAMA, NO?
YEAH... SHE'S BEEN GONE A LONG TIME.
REALLY GONE... TO THE GOLDEN RIVER.
SHE SAD LADY; SHE LOVE JOR PAPA BUT...
...HE TRAVELING ALL THE TIME...
...AND HE FUCKING MANY OTHER WOMANS.
BUT SHE GOT THE GOOD REVENGE ON HIM.
SHE GET A BABY FROM ANOTHER MAN.
WAIT... WHAT?
NOT POSSIBLE.
I'M THEIR ONLY SON.
JOO ARE JOR MAMA'S ONLY CHILDRENS,
BUT ELEGGUA HE TELLING ME SOME SECRET ABOUT YOU:
JOR PAPA NO ES JOR PAPA.
JOO ASK HIM AND HE WILL TELL YOU.

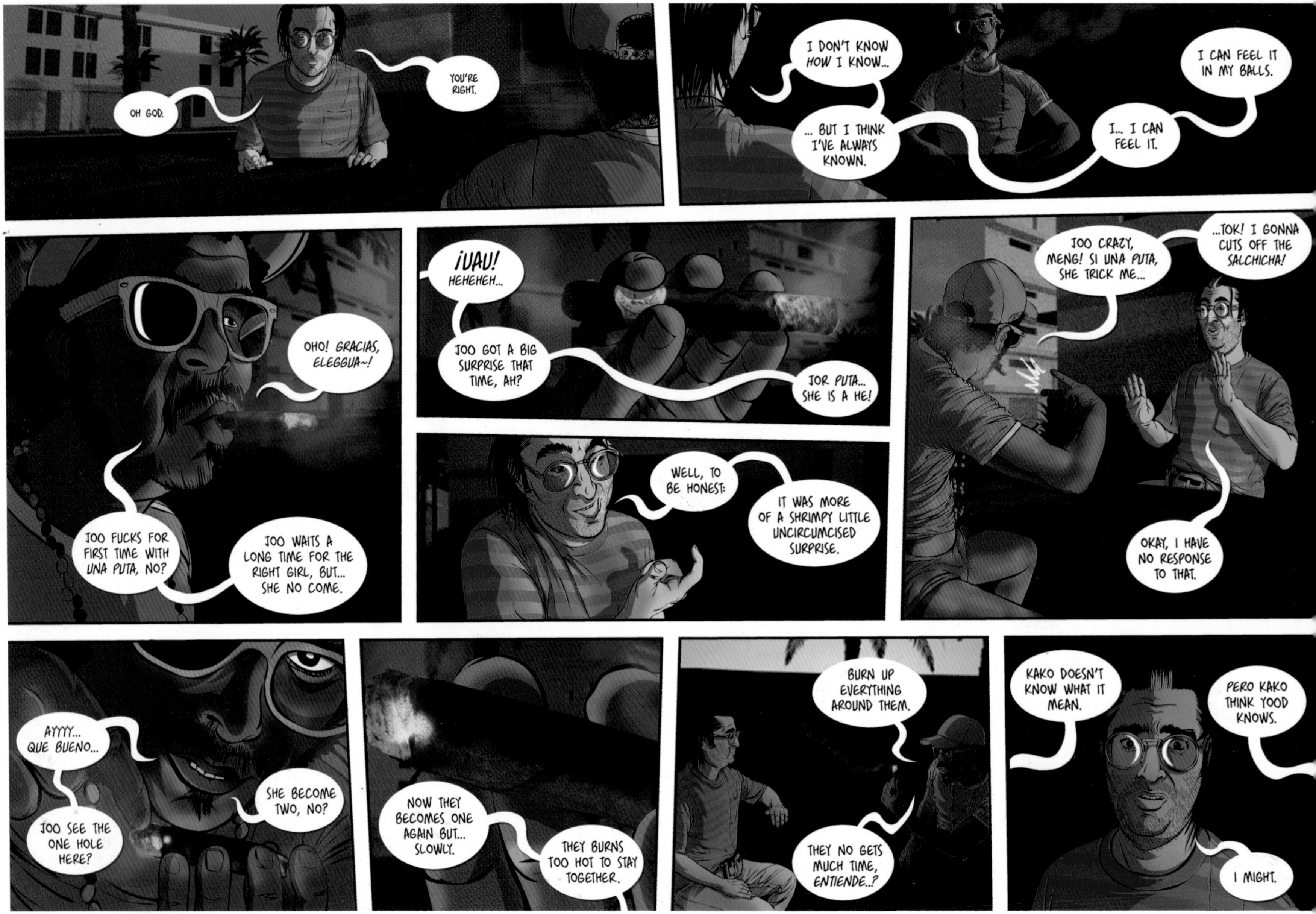

OH GOD.
YOU'RE RIGHT.
I DON'T KNOW HOW I KNOW...
... BUT I THINK I'VE ALWAYS KNOWN.
I... I CAN FEEL IT.
I CAN FEEL IT IN MY BALLS.
OHO! GRACIAS, ELEGGUA~!
JOO FUCKS FOR FIRST TIME WITH UNA PUTA, NO?
JOO WAITS A LONG TIME FOR THE RIGHT GIRL, BUT... SHE NO COME.
¡UAU! HEHEHEH...
JOO GOT A BIG SURPRISE THAT TIME, AH?
JOR PUTA... SHE IS A HE!
WELL, TO BE HONEST:
IT WAS MORE OF A SHRIMPY LITTLE UNCIRCUMCISED SURPRISE.
JOO CRAZY, MENG! SI UNA PUTA, SHE TRICK ME...
...TOK! I GONNA CUTS OFF THE SALCHICHA!
OKAY, I HAVE NO RESPONSE TO THAT.
AYYYY... QUE BUENO...
JOO SEE THE ONE HOLE HERE?
SHE BECOME TWO, NO?
NOW THEY BECOMES ONE AGAIN BUT... SLOWLY.
THEY BURNS TOO HOT TO STAY TOGETHER.
BURN UP EVERYTHING AROUND THEM.
THEY NO GETS MUCH TIME, ENTIENDE..?
KAKO DOESN'T KNOW WHAT IT MEAN.
PERO KAKO THINK YOOD KNOWS.
I MIGHT.

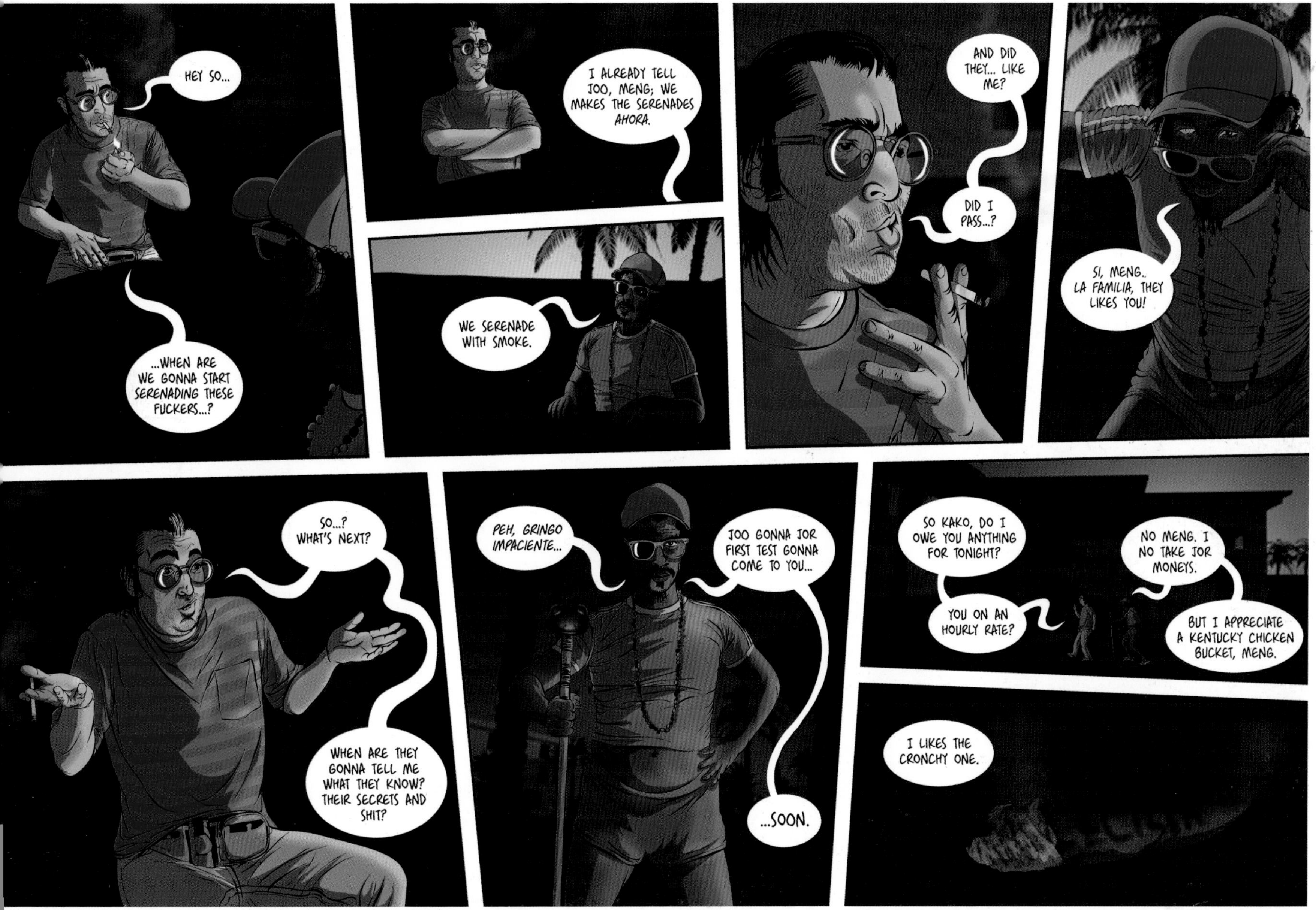
HEY SO...
...WHEN ARE WE GONNA START SERENADING THESE FUCKERS...?
I ALREADY TELL JOO, MENG; WE MAKES THE SERENADES AHORA.
WE SERENADE WITH SMOKE.
AND DID THEY... LIKE ME?
DID I PASS...?
SI, MENG.. LA FAMILIA, THEY LIKES YOU!
SO...? WHAT'S NEXT?
WHEN ARE THEY GONNA TELL ME WHAT THEY KNOW? THEIR SECRETS AND SHIT?
PEH, GRINGO IMPACIENTE...
JOO GONNA JOR FIRST TEST GONNA COME TO YOU...
...SOON.
SO KAKO, DO I OWE YOU ANYTHING FOR TONIGHT?
YOU ON AN HOURLY RATE?
NO MENG. I NO TAKE JOR MONEYS.
BUT I APPRECIATE A KENTUCKY CHICKEN BUCKET, MENG.
I LIKES THE CRONCHY ONE.

RED LIGHT PROPERTIES

WILL RETURN SUMMER 2014 IN

UNDERWATER